AWS All-in-One Security Guide

Design, Build, Monitor, and Manage a Fortified Application Ecosystem on AWS

Adrin Mukherjee

www.bpbonline.com

FIRST EDITION 2022

ISBN: 978-93-55510-327

LIMITS OF LIABILITY AND DISCLAIMER OF WARRANTY

To View Complete
BPB Publications Catalogue
Scan the QR Code:

www.bpbonline.com

In loving memory of

Anindya Kanti Roy

- a maverick philosopher, mentor, and techie.

About the Author

Adrin Mukherjee is an experienced solutions architect who has taken up several challenging roles throughout his career, building distributed applications and high-performance systems. He enjoys helping customers in their digital transformation journeys, especially migrating applications to the cloud and creating highly scalable, secure, and resilient cloud-native platforms.

He is a certified AWS and Google Cloud solutions architect and security engineer. His interests include serverless computing, containerization, cloud security, and machine learning.

When not dabbling at the keyboard, he loves to trek, listens to hard rock, and enjoys spending time with his family.

LinkedIn: **https://www.linkedin.com/in/adrinmukherjee**

Blog: **https://adrin-mukherjee.medium.com**

About the Reviewer

Javid Ur Rahman is a distinguished database product manager and enterprise solution architect and has been actively involved in productizing and promoting cross-ecosystem collaboration in the Cloud Infrastructure, Edge & Analytics Platform space for over half a decade. He's focused on research and development of blockchain-based database algorithm designs and cloud-native-run engine development.

In his current role, he's taken the Enterprise Architect role in Fourth Square Inc, US Based Product, and Consulting Firm to new geographies.

LinkedIn: **https://www.linkedin.com/in/jrahaman7/**

Acknowledgement

First and foremost, thanks to my better half, Sakuntala, for giving me the initial nudge to take up this project and putting up with me while I was engrossed in writing this book over many weekends- I could not have finished this without her continuous support.

I am eternally grateful to my mother, who has been a pillar of strength and the one I have always turned for comfort during difficult times.

To my son Arik, who happens to be the source of my laughter and immense joy- I can't imagine a life without his childish pranks and exhibitions of newly acquired antics.

To Choco, my best friend and canine companion, who was equally enthusiastic and ignorant of my work- Thanks for keeping me company during the writing of this book, even in the ungodly hours.

My heartfelt gratitude towards my colleagues and friends who believed in me and have shown interest in my work. Special thanks to Binson Paul, Ratnadeep Bardhan Roy, Angshuman Mukherjee, Arijit Mazumdar and Animesh Das.

Finally, sincere thanks to the team at BPB Publications for providing me with this exciting opportunity of writing my first book for them.

Preface

With enterprises moving their workloads and assets to public clouds, securing application ecosystems and resources on multi-tenanted public cloud providers like Amazon Web Services (AWS) is a primary concern. In AWS, security is considered "job-zero" as such, the customers can leverage AWS's highly secure global infrastructure and various infrastructure and abstract services. However, in the public cloud, the customers also have their share of responsibility towards securing applications and workloads.

The goal of this book is to provide in-depth information on various security-focused AWS services and features that can be leveraged to design and implement a fortified application ecosystem on AWS. The book takes a layered approach to security which introduces multiple security controls across the cloud environment. Each layer has to be secured independently with a chosen set of security controls and guardrails. This ensures that a gap or flaw in one layer can be countered by controls and measures in another layer. This book dedicates individual chapters to each such layer and introduces specific security measures and AWS services that can help to establish the necessary security fences.

In the course of seven chapters, the readers will learn the following:

Chapter 1 introduces the shared responsibility model of security on AWS and various service offerings that can help secure applications and workloads on AWS.

Chapter 2 discusses the fundamental service in AWS- Identity and Access Management (IAM). The chapter shows how to create IAM policies to secure AWS resources with the help of multiple examples. It also introduces the commonly used access management strategies like delegation and federation. Finally, the chapter explains various AWS tools available for easy creation, management, and governance of access policies.

Chapter 3 moves through the various AWS features, services, and strategies available to secure cloud infrastructure. These include security of Virtual Private Cloud, patch management for EC2 instances, privileged session management, etc. The chapter also covers Distributed Denial of Service (DDoS) attacks, mitigation steps and introduces AWS Shield- a managed service that can help fight such attacks.

Chapter 4 is related to the security of data in the AWS cloud. The chapter introduces AWS Key Management Service (KMS) and AWS CloudHSM, which are at the core of data protection on AWS. It also visits the data security features of popular services like S3, EBS, DynamoDB, and RDS. Lastly, it introduces Amazon Macie, a fully managed service for data loss prevention.

Chapter 5 focuses on how AWS can help in securing the application layer. The chapter takes a deeper look into securing APIs deployed on AWS API Gateway, leveraging Amazon Cognito to design authentication and authorization schemes, securing web applications hosted on Amazon S3 and Amazon CloudFront, etc. The chapter emphasizes using AWS Secrets Manager and AWS Systems Manager-Parameter Store services to externalize various application-level secrets and configuration parameters. It also takes a closer look at using AWS Web Application Firewall (WAF) to safeguard applications from Layer-7 attacks and how appropriate use of Elastic Load Balancers (ELBs) can go a long way in securing applications deployed on AWS.

Chapter 6 focuses on essential logging, monitoring, and auditing services like Amazon CloudWatch, AWS CloudTrail, AWS Config, etc. The chapter briefly introduces advanced monitoring services like Amazon GuardDuty, AWS Security Hub, Amazon Detective, etc.

Chapter 7 is all about security best practices recommended to be followed in the AWS cloud to improve the security posture of the application ecosystem. The best practices have been grouped into the following layers- IAM, infrastructure, data, application, logging, and monitoring.

Code Bundle and Coloured Images

Please follow the link to download the
Code Bundle and the ***Coloured Images*** of the book:

https://rebrand.ly/db7792

The code bundle for the book is also hosted on GitHub at **https://github.com/bpbpublications/AWS-All-in-One-Security-Guide**. In case there's an update to the code, it will be updated on the existing GitHub repository.

We have code bundles from our rich catalogue of books and videos available at **https://github.com/bpbpublications**. Check them out!

Errata

We take immense pride in our work at BPB Publications and follow best practices to ensure the accuracy of our content to provide with an indulging reading experience to our subscribers. Our readers are our mirrors, and we use their inputs to reflect and improve upon human errors, if any, that may have occurred during the publishing processes involved. To let us maintain the quality and help us reach out to any readers who might be having difficulties due to any unforeseen errors, please write to us at :

errata@bpbonline.com

Your support, suggestions and feedbacks are highly appreciated by the BPB Publications' Family.

Piracy

If you come across any illegal copies of our works in any form on the internet, we would be grateful if you would provide us with the location address or website name. Please contact us at **business@bpbonline.com** with a link to the material.

If you are interested in becoming an author

If there is a topic that you have expertise in, and you are interested in either writing or contributing to a book, please visit **www.bpbonline.com**. We have worked with thousands of developers and tech professionals, just like you, to help them share their insights with the global tech community. You can make a general application, apply for a specific hot topic that we are recruiting an author for, or submit your own idea.

Reviews

Please leave a review. Once you have read and used this book, why not leave a review on the site that you purchased it from? Potential readers can then see and use your unbiased opinion to make purchase decisions. We at BPB can understand what you think about our products, and our authors can see your feedback on their book. Thank you!

For more information about BPB, please visit **www.bpbonline.com**.

Table of Contents

CHAPTER 1
Introduction to Security in AWS

Introduction

As the enterprises and businesses move their workloads into the public cloud, security has become the most talked about subject in cloud migration and cloud adoption journeys. Design for security is pervasive throughout the Amazon's infrastructure and is built into every service offered by **Amazon Web Services** (**AWS**). However, security on the public cloud is different in many respects from security on-premises, and thus, it must be seen from different angles. As such, there is a shared responsibility model of security on the AWS cloud. While AWS is responsible for the "Security of the cloud", the customers are responsible for the "*Security in the cloud.*"

Structure

In this chapter, we will cover the following topics:

- Shared responsibility model
- Important AWS security service offerings
- Security guidance offered by AWS
- Quick note on AWS Management Console

Objectives

In this chapter, we will gather the basic understanding of the security in the AWS cloud, which primarily revolves around the concept of the shared responsibility model. We will also identify some of the critical AWS security service offerings. We will cover some security guidance tools, documentation, and other resources that are provided by AWS and **AWS Partner Network** (**APN**) partners. These can help us create highly secure and resilient workloads and applications hosted on the AWS cloud.

Shared responsibility model

Security of the workloads and applications on the AWS cloud is a shared responsibility. This responsibility is shared between AWS and the customer. AWS is responsible for securing the global infrastructure and hardware that supports the cloud. The customer, on the other hand, is responsible for anything that they put on the cloud. This model can essentially improve the security posture of the customer and increase operational efficiency. The key goal is to create highly secure and resilient applications and workloads on the AWS cloud. *Figure 1.1* explains the responsibilities shared by AWS and customers as follows:

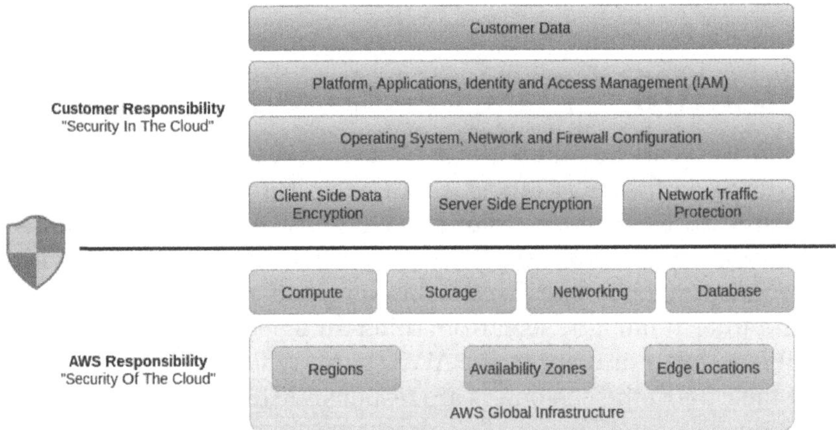

Figure 1.1: *Shared responsibility in AWS cloud*

In the subsequent sections, we will dive deeper into understanding the responsibilities pertaining to each player.

Security of the cloud – AWS responsibility

AWS is responsible for protecting the global infrastructure that runs all the services offered in the AWS Cloud. This infrastructure is composed of hardware, software, networking, and facilities/data centers that run the AWS Cloud services. Securing this infrastructure is AWS's utmost priority, and as such, the infrastructure undergoes regular audits to meet the required security and compliance standards. These audit reports are made available to the AWS customers digitally. AWS is also responsible for the security of the basic essential infrastructure services like compute, storage, networking, and database (managed database services like Amazon RDS or Amazon DynamoDB, etc.).

The *figure 1.2* provides an overview of AWS's slice pertaining to the shared responsibility model as follows:

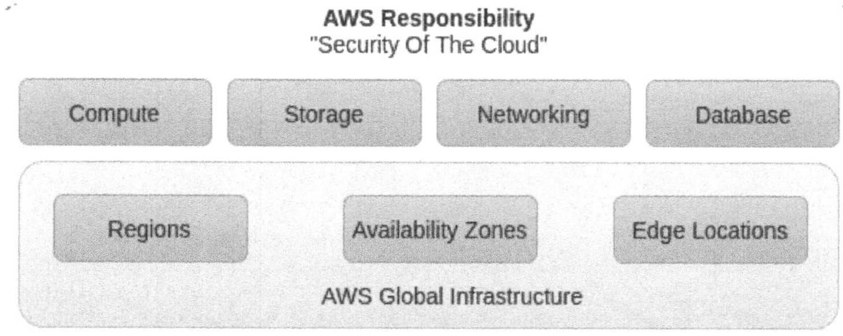

Figure 1.2: *Security of the cloud*

For pure infrastructure services like Amazon EC2, Amazon EBS, Amazon VPC, etc., AWS is responsible for the security of the underlying global infrastructure and the other infrastructure-related services, including the hypervisor layer (wherever applicable).

For the managed or abstracted services like Amazon RDS, Amazon DynamoDB, Amazon S3, in addition to the security of the infrastructure and related infrastructure services, AWS also handles the fundamental security tasks like guest OS patching, database patching, firewall configurations, and disaster recovery.

Security in the cloud – customer responsibility

Customer responsibility is determined by the AWS Cloud services that a customer uses. The AWS services that fall clearly into the category of **Infrastructure-as-a-Service (IaaS)** – such as Amazon EC2, Amazon VPC, etc. – are entirely under the customer's control, and the customers are expected to perform all of the necessary security configuration and management tasks. For example, for Amazon EC2 instances, the customer is responsible for the guest OS updates and patches, any application software or utilities installed on these instances, and the configuration of AWS firewall (called **security groups**) on each instance.

In the case of managed or abstracted services like Amazon S3, Amazon DynamoDB, or Amazon RDS, the customer is relieved of the burden of launching and maintaining the underlying instances, patching the guest OS or database, etc. AWS handles the infrastructure layer, operating system, and the platforms on behalf of the customer.

However, the customer still needs to access the service endpoints to store and retrieve the data, setup necessary permissions, and access control policies, etc. The customer also needs to decide on the classification of the data and security of the data at rest and in motion and apply the appropriate encryption options. Auditing and tracking of the API/user activity need to be performed by the customer.

The *figure 1.3* gives the basic set of responsibilities that needs to be managed by the customers who have deployed their applications and workloads on the AWS cloud as follows:

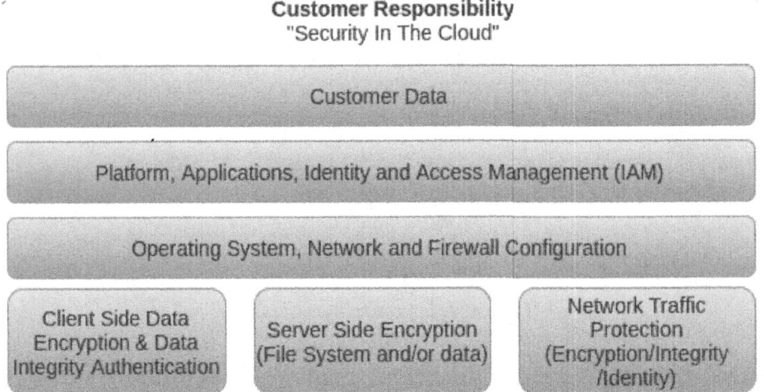

***Figure 1.3:** Security in the cloud*

Controls in shared responsibility model

In this section, we will look into "who is responsible for what" in the context of Shared Responsibility Model and IT controls in the AWS cloud. The IT controls can be differentiated into the following three categories:

Inherited controls

These controls are inherited by the customers from AWS. Some examples are as follows:

- **Physical and environmental controls**: This includes the physical access to the AWS facilities and involves various strict and controlled access to the facilities, professional security staff at ingress points, video surveillance, intrusion detection systems, multi-factor authentication, decommissioning physical storage devices, etc. The environmental controls like fire detection and suppression, power, climate, and temperature controls also fall under this category.
- **Controls For Business Continuity Management**: The AWS data centers are always built in clusters in various geographical regions to offer greater availability. The core applications are load-balanced and deployed in the N+1

configurations, so that the architecture can handle the data center failures. **Availability Zones (AZs)** are engineered to be physically separated within a metropolitan region and are located in the lower-risk flood plains. To reduce the single point of failure, in addition to the **uninterruptable power supply (UPS)** and the on-site backup generation facilities, AZs are also fed via different power grids from the independent sources.

- **Network Security Controls**: AWS has state-of-the-art, high bandwidth, fault-tolerant network infrastructure that is strictly monitored and managed. The boundary devices and other network devices manage the rulesets and traffic flow policies that are approved by Amazon Information Security. AWS has a limited number of access points to the cloud placed strategically that offer comprehensive ingress and egress traffic monitoring. These are called API endpoints, and they allow the HTTPS traffic only.

Shared controls

These controls apply to both the infrastructure and the customer layers. Here, AWS provides the requirements specific to the infrastructure, and the customers provide their own implementation of the controls within the context of their use of the AWS services. Some common examples are as follows:

- **Patch management**: AWS is responsible for patching and fixing the issues within the infrastructure, including network, hypervisor, host OS, etc. The customers are responsible for patching their guest OS and applications hosted on top of the infrastructure. AWS does provide services like AWS Systems Manager-Patch Manager that can be used by the customers to facilitate the patching process.
- **Configuration management**: AWS maintains and manages the configuration of its infrastructure devices, and the customers are responsible for configuring their own guest OS, databases, and applications.
- **Awareness and training**: While AWS train the AWS employees with the knowledge about the security controls in place, the customers are responsible for training and educating the internal cloud employees.

Fully controlled by the customer

These controls are solely the responsibility of the customers, based on the nature of the workload or the application deployed within the AWS services. Here's an example:

- **Service and communications protection/zone security:** The customers may require routing or zoning the data within the specific security environments.

Important AWS security service offerings

AWS has a plethora of related security services which can help the customer to create a highly secured platform or application on the AWS cloud. The following section provides with the introductory notes on some of the essential and vital services that can be leveraged.

AWS Identity and Access Management (IAM)

AWS Identity and Access Management (**IAM**) enables the customers to control and manage the access to the AWS services and resources securely. AWS IAM can be leveraged to create the human identities and/or machine identities and provide the fine-grained permission and access control to these identities. It supports the complex conditions to control the access, like originating IP address, whether SSL is used, or whether the user has been authenticated with Multi-Factor Authentication (MFA) device, etc. AWS IAM also helps to integrate the users with the existing corporate identity providers, like Microsoft Active Directory, or with the web identity providers, like Google, Facebook, etc., through Identity Federation.

Amazon Virtual Private Cloud (VPC)

Amazon Virtual Private Cloud, or VPC for short, is a foundational regional service that allows us to launch or instantiate the AWS resources in a logically isolated virtual network that we define. A VPC is a **software-defined network** (**SDN**) optimized for moving massive amounts of network packets from the source to the destination. It gives us complete control over the virtual networking environment which includes, selection of the IP ranges (or classless inter-domain routing/CIDR ranges), creation of the subnets, configuration of the route tables, network gateways (like Internet Gateways), etc. Support for both the IPv4 and the IPv6 is available for most resources in the VPC. Amazon VPC supports multiple layers of security that includes security groups and **Network Access Control Lists** (**NACLs**). In essence, VPC is our own chunk of AWS cloud that creates a network fabric, abstracting the inherent complexities of the routers, switches, and other networking devices.

VPC Flow Logs

VPC Flow Logs is a feature that enables us to capture information about the IP traffic going to and from the network interfaces in the VPC. Flow log data can be published to the Amazon CloudWatch Logs or Amazon S3. VPC Flow Logs can be enabled at the VPC level, subnet level, or network interface level.

Amazon CloudWatch

Amazon CloudWatch is the primary logging and monitoring service available in the AWS service arsenal. CloudWatch collects the monitoring and operational data from the AWS resources, applications, and services in the form of logs, metrics, and events, thereby providing a unified view with actionable insights.

AWS CloudTrail

AWS CloudTrail helps with the governance, compliance, and operational/risk auditing of the AWS accounts. Actions taken by a user, role, or an AWS service are recorded as events in CloudTrail. The events include actions taken in the AWS Management Console, AWS Command Line Interface, and AWS SDKs and APIs. This event history helps in the compliance auditing, operational analysis, security analysis, resource change tracking, and other troubleshooting.

AWS Config

AWS Config is a regional service that helps us to continuously keep track of the configuration changes made to the AWS resources. We can evaluate and audit the recorded configurations against the desired state of the resources, thereby simplifying the compliance auditing, security/forensic analysis, change management, operational troubleshooting, and enterprise-wide compliance monitoring. As part of the tracking, AWS Config sends the updated configuration details to a specified Amazon S3 bucket. For each resource type that AWS Config records, it sends a configuration history file (in JSON format) every six hours. Each configuration history file contains the details about the resources that changed in that period of six hours. AWS Config can also deliver the configuration snapshots to an Amazon S3 bucket, on demand. AWS Config can also be configured to send the configuration change notifications to a specified Amazon Simple Notification Service (SNS) topic. AWS Config supports several resource types.

Amazon Inspector

Amazon Inspector is an automated security assessment service. It can perform the assessments based on the pre-defined templates and produce a detailed list of security findings that are prioritized by severity. Amazon Inspector primarily supports two types of assessments – host assessment and network assessment. For the host assessment, an agent, also known as inspector agent, is required to be installed in the EC2 instances (also known as **assessment targets**). However, for the network assessment, an inspector agent is optional. The following pre-defined assessment templates are supported:

- Common Vulnerabilities and Exposures (CVE)

- CIS Operating System Security Configuration Benchmarks
- Network Reachability
- Security Best Practices

Amazon GuardDuty

Amazon GuardDuty is an intelligent threat detection service that can continuously monitor for malicious activity and unauthorized behavior to protect the AWS accounts and workloads. The service uses machine learning, anomaly detection, and integrated threat intelligence to identify the potential threats. GuardDuty can detect activities like crypto-currency mining, credential compromise behavior, unauthorized and unusual data access, API calls from known malicious IPs, etc. GuardDuty actively monitors the following three types of resources and can generate comprehensive findings along with severities:

- CloudTrail events
- VPC Flow Logs
- Route53 DNS Logs

AWS Shield

AWS Shield is a managed service for protection against the **Open Systems Interconnection** (**OSI**) layers 3 & 4 and **Distributed Denial of Service** (**DDoS**) attacks. AWS Shield provides the always-on detection and automatic inline mitigation that essentially minimize the application downtime and latency due to the DDoS attacks. There are two tiers of AWS Shield service, which are as follows:

- The **standard tier** provides protection against the most common network and transport layer DDoS attacks.
- The **advanced tier** protects against the large and sophisticated DDoS attacks with near real-time visibility. It also provides 24x7 access to AWS **DDoS Response Team** (**DRT**) and cost protection. The cost protection is provided by AWS in terms of credits to services like Amazon Route53, **Elastic Load Balancer** (**ELB**), Amazon CloudFront, etc.

AWS WAF

AWS WAF is a web application firewall that helps protect the web applications and/or APIs against the common OSI layer-7 attacks like SQL injection, **Cross-Site Scripting** (**XSS**), etc., by filtering out the malicious traffic patterns using managed rules. These managed rules can be used to address well-known issues like **Open Web Application Security Project** (**OWASP**) Top 10 security risks. AWS WAF can be deployed on the following AWS services:

- Amazon CloudFront
- Application Load Balancer
- Amazon API Gateway (to protect RESTful APIs)
- AWS AppSync (to protect GraphQL APIs)

Amazon Macie

Amazon Macie is a fully managed, Machine Learning powered, sensitive data discovery and classification service that helps to implement the Data Loss Prevention (DLP) solutions. It can continuously evaluate the Amazon S3 environment, which includes buckets, bucket contents, and relevant access controls, and can automatically discover and classify sensitive data like **personally identifiable information** (**PII**). It can additionally generate findings that could be sent to CloudWatch Events for further action and remediation.

AWS Security Hub

AWS Security Hub is a regional service that provides a comprehensive and aggregated view of the high-priority security alerts and compliance status across multiple AWS accounts, thus, providing a single source of truth for the security audits. AWS Security Hub can aggregate, organize, and prioritize the security findings from multiple AWS Services. The following services are supported out-of-the-box:

- Amazon GuardDuty
- Amazon Macie
- Amazon Inspector
- AWS Systems Manager
- AWS Firewall Manager
- AWS IAM Access Analyzer

AWS Security Hub also provides integrations with other third-party security solution providers like AlertLogic, Twistlock, Symantec, Barracuda, etc. AWS Security Hub can significantly improve the security posture with aggregated findings and automated checks.

AWS Key Management Service (KMS)

AWS Key Management Service (**KMS**) is a fully managed service that helps to create and manage the cryptographic keys. AWS KMS is highly secure and resilient, and leverages **hardware security modules** (**HSM**) to protect the keys. It provides centralized key management and helps to define the consistent policies around the ownership and access of the keys.

AWS Secrets Manager

AWS Secrets Manager is a fully managed service that can securely store and manage the lifecycle of the secrets like database credentials, API-keys, security tokens, etc. AWS Secrets Manager supports the versioning of these sensitive pieces of information and could be used for rotating these secrets as well. Essentially, AWS Secrets Manager can help the application developers to eliminate the need to hardcode sensitive information in the code or configuration files.

AWS Systems Manager

AWS Systems Manager is a suite of services that gives better visibility and control over our infrastructure on AWS. It supports the grouping of resources like Amazon EC2 instances, Amazon S3 buckets, Amazon RDS instances, etc., by application. Some of the crucial services under AWS Systems Manager are as follows:

- **Parameter Store** is a centralized store to manage the application configuration data. It can also act as a cost-effective alternative to AWS Secrets Manager for storing the secrets in the form of **`SecureString`**, provided automatic rotation requirements are not being considered for such secrets.
- **Sessions Manager** helps to start a session on the EC2 instance with an SSM agent installed and get access into the instance from the browser-based shell (and execute shell commands) or through AWS CLI without having to explicitly open any inbound SSH port (22) or setup any VPN.
- **Patch Manager** automates the process of patching managed instances. It can be used to scan for missing patches using the Patch baseline service.

AWS Artifact

AWS Artifact is the central resource for compliance-related information on AWS. It gives on-demand access to AWS security and compliance audit reports like **Payment Card Industry** (**PCI**) reports, **Service Organization Control** (**SOC**) reports, etc.

Security Guidance

AWS provides the customers with guidance and expertise through online tools, resources, support, and professional services provided by AWS and its partners. This guidance helps the customer to create and deploy the applications and manage the workloads following the AWS security best practices. Here is a list of some of the commonly used security guidance tools and resources.

AWS Trusted Advisor

AWS Trusted Advisor is an online tool that provides real-time guidance and helps us in provisioning the AWS resources following the AWS best practices. AWS Trusted Advisor analyzes the AWS environment and provides recommendations that fall under the following five distinct categories:

- Security
- Cost optimization
- Performance
- Fault tolerance
- Service limits

Under `AWS Basic Support and Developer Support`, we can get access to security checks like S3 bucket permissions that are open/insecure, improper IAM usage, **Multi-Factor Authentication** (**MFA**) on root account, public **Amazon Elastic Block Storage** (**EBS**), and **Amazon Relational Database Service** (**RDS**) snapshots. With AWS Business Support and AWS Enterprise Support, a lot more security checks can be accessed.

AWS Account Teams

Account Teams provide the first point of contact. This team can guide the customers through their deployments and implementations and point them to the right resources to resolve the security issues that they may encounter.

AWS Enterprise Support

AWS Enterprise Support provides a 15-minute response time and is available 24×7 over the phone, chat, or email, along with a dedicated Technical Account Manager. This is a concierge service that ensures that the customers' issues are addressed as quickly as possible.

AWS Partner Network

AWS Partner Network offers hundreds of industry-leading products that are equivalent, identical to, or integrated with the existing controls in your on-premises environments. These products complement the existing AWS services to enable you to deploy a comprehensive security architecture and a more seamless experience across your cloud and on-premises environments, as well as hundreds of certified AWS Consulting Partners worldwide to help with your security and compliance needs.

AWS Professional Services

AWS professional services has a security, risk, and compliance specialty practice to help the customers develop confidence and technical capability when migrating the sensitive workloads to the AWS Cloud. AWS Professional Services helps the customers develop security policies and practices based on the well-proven designs and helps ensure that the customers' security design meets the internal and external compliance requirements.

AWS Marketplace

AWS marketplace is a digital marketplace with thousands of software listings from the independent software vendors that make it easier to find, test, buy, and deploy the software that runs on AWS. AWS Marketplace Security products complement the existing AWS services to enable the customers to deploy a comprehensive security architecture and a more seamless experience across the cloud and on-premises environments.

AWS Security Bulletins

AWS security bulletins provide security bulletins around current vulnerabilities and threats and enables the customers to work with the AWS security experts to address various concerns like reporting abuse, vulnerabilities, and penetration testing.

AWS Security Documentation

AWS security documentation shows how to configure the AWS services to meet the security and compliance objectives. The AWS customers benefit from a data center and network architecture that are built to meet the requirements of the security-sensitive organizations. AWS provides a security blog with posts covering a wide range of security topics that include, but are not limited to, security best practices, advanced security patterns, threat modeling, data masking, etc.

Click on the following link to access the security blogs from AWS: https://aws.amazon.com/blogs/security/

AWS Well-Architected Framework

AWS Well-Architected Framework helps the cloud architects to build secure, high-performing, resilient, and efficient infrastructure for their applications. The framework includes a security pillar that focuses on protecting the information and systems. The customers can use the AWS Well-Architected Tool from the AWS Management Console or engage the services of one of the **AWS Partner Network (APN)** partners to assist them in conducting an automated review of the security posture of their AWS hosted applications and workloads.

AWS Well-architected Tool

AWS well-architected tool helps the customers to review the state of their workloads and compares them to the latest AWS architectural best practices. This is a free tool and is available in the AWS Management Console. The customers are required to answer a set of questions regarding the operational excellence, security, reliability, performance efficiency, and cost optimization. The AWS well-architected tool then provides a plan on how to architect for the cloud using the established best practices.

Quick Note on AWS Management Console

There are quite a few ways to interact with the AWS services and resources. AWS Management Console, AWS **Command Line Interface** (**CLI**), and AWS **Software Development Kit** (**SDK**) are the commonly used options. Throughout this book, we will use AWS Management Console and AWS CLI interchangeably to work with the AWS services and their features.

AWS Management Console is a friendly web-based portal to search and configure the AWS services, build new cloud-based applications, manage AWS account, and much more. Once an AWS account has been created and we have successfully logged in, the easiest way to explore all the available AWS services is to click on the `Services` menu on the top-left corner of the landing page, as shown in *figure 1.4* as follows:

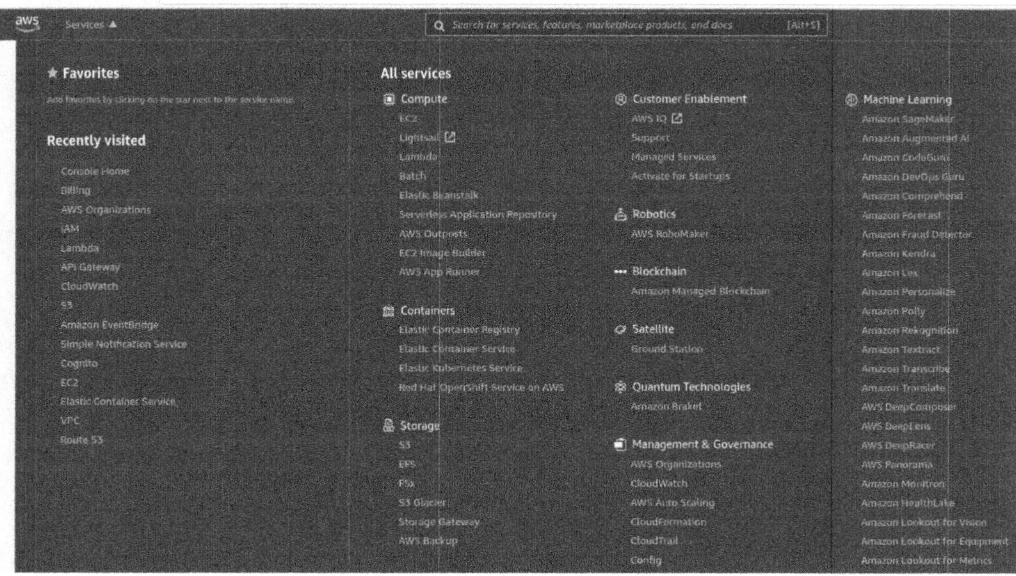

Figure 1.4: *Exploring AWS services from AWS Management Console*

For quick access to the Management Console pertaining to a specific AWS service, we can simply type the name of the service in the **`Search`** bar at the top of the AWS Management Console's landing page, as shown in *figure 1.5* as follows:

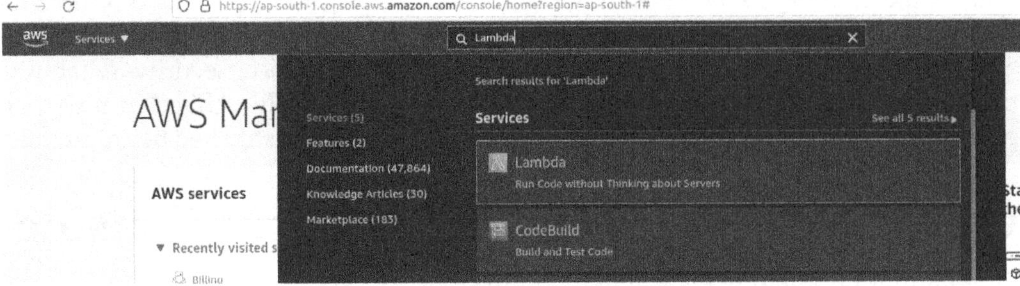

Figure 1.5: *Quick search for AWS services from AWS Management Console*

The recently visited services are also listed on the **`Recently visited services`** section under **`AWS Services`** on the landing page, as shown in *figure 1.6* as follows:

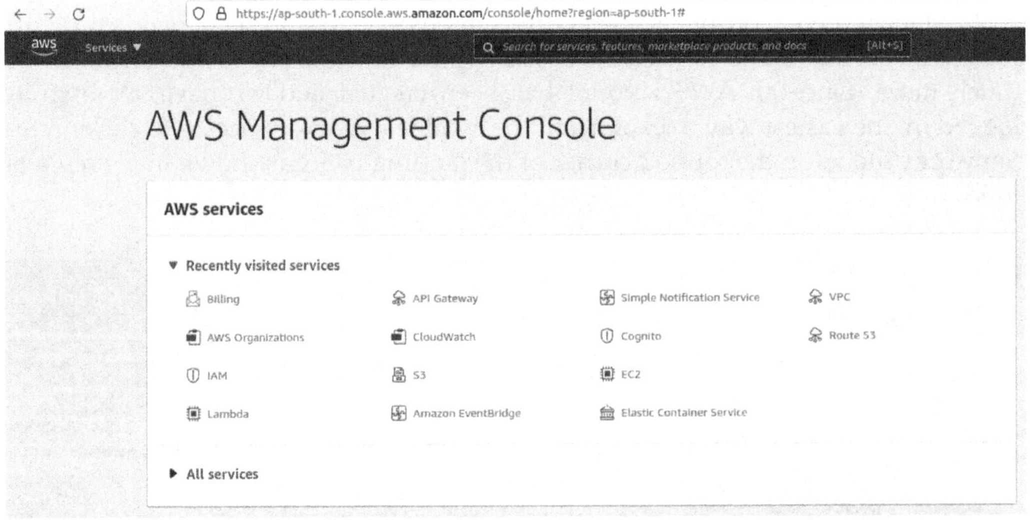

Figure 1.6: *Recently visited services section in AWS Management Console*

As mentioned earlier, we will also use AWS CLI extensively to interact with the AWS services and resources. We will take a detailed look at AWS CLI in *Chapter 2: Identity and Access Management.*

Conclusion

Security on the AWS public cloud is a shared responsibility. Both AWS and the customers who run their applications and workloads on top of AWS are partly responsible. While this chapter introduces some of the significant and widely used security service offerings by AWS, it is in no way an exhaustive list. AWS continuously introduces new services and announces new features pertaining to the existing services.

In the subsequent chapters, we will dive deeper into the layered approach to security, map the important AWS service offerings in each layer (IAM controls, network, and infrastructure security, data security, logging, monitoring, and tracking), and learn how to leverage these services to create highly secure and reliable applications on the AWS cloud. The next chapter is dedicated to the introduction and working of the AWS IAM service.

CHAPTER 2
Identity and Access Management

Introduction

One of the fundamental pillars of security is **Identity and Access Management (IAM)**. IAM, in general, governs 'WHO' can perform 'WHAT' actions on 'WHICH' resources. IAM is all about protecting, controlling, and governing the access to the resources. AWS IAM is a web service that helps in the identity management, and establishes the guard rails, security controls, and policies to protect the AWS services and resources.

Structure

In this chapter, we will cover the following topics:

- Fundamentals of IAM
- Identity
- Access Management
- AWS Tools for IAM

Objectives

The objective of this chapter is to introduce AWS Identity and Access Management (IAM) service. We will learn how to create the various types of identities supported by AWS IAM and manage them. We will understand how to leverage the various access management strategies like delegation and federation and create the policies and other controls to safeguard the AWS services and resources. We will also take a quick look at the various tools provided by AWS to help us create the policies and govern them.

Fundamentals of IAM

As the name suggests, Identity and Access Management has two parts – *identity* and *access* management. Identities are essential principals that must be provided with regulated access to the systems and resources. Identities are mapped to some credential that is used to authenticate the identity in a system. Access management defines the policies and control mechanisms that are placed to protect the resources from an unauthorized access. Thus, access management serves to authorize the identities in a system and defines what they can do in the system. *Figure 2.1* provides a schematic of the significant elements in AWS IAM as follows:

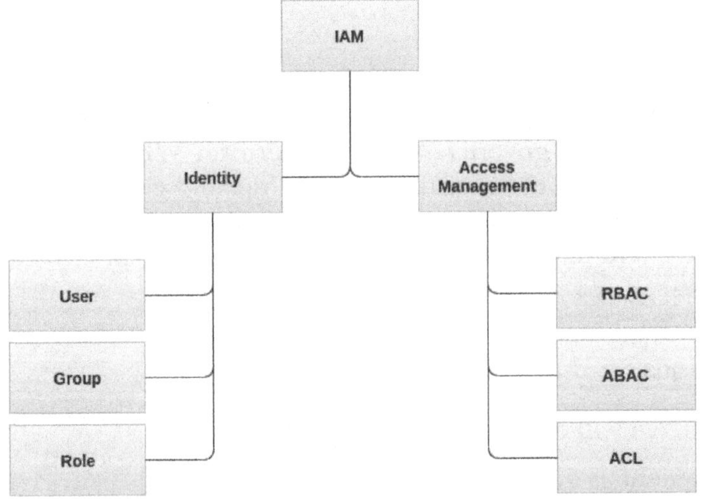

Figure 2.1: *Elements of Identity and Access Management in AWS*

In AWS, identities are represented by the IAM users, IAM groups, and IAM roles. Access management for these identities can be performed with **Role Based Access Control** (**RBAC**), **Attribute Based Access Control** (**ABAC**), or **Access Control List** (**ACL**). Both RBAC and ABAC are the IAM policy-based strategies and are generally recommended by AWS to be used with the fine-grained as well as the coarse-grained permissions. The following are the description of these access control strategies.

- **Role Based Access Control**: RBAC essentially defines the permissions based on the user's job function; for example, administrator, database administrator, DevOps engineer, security auditor, etc. Here, 'role' is a general term that points to the part played by a user and not to be confused with IAM Role which is an identity within AWS. AWS IAM includes the managed policies that aligns to the regular job functions. We can also create the customer managed policies to tailor the permissions associated with the job functions. These policies are then attached to identities like IAM user, IAM group, and IAM role.
- **Attribute Based Access Control**: ABAC is an access control strategy that defines the permissions based on additional contextual attributes. Within AWS, these attributes are called 'tags'. The tags can be attached to the AWS resources including the IAM resources, like users or roles. Unlike RBAC, where with the addition of new resources, the permission policy must be updated, ABAC is a scalable strategy and solely relies on the tags to automatically apply the permissions. We must have strict control over the addition/deletion of the tags to/from the resources, in order to implement this strategy.
- **Access Control List**: ACLs are a legacy access control mechanism and predates IAM. ACLs are used with the Amazon Simple Storage Service (S3) buckets and objects. They are attached to a bucket or object as a sub-resource and are evaluated when a request to access the bucket or object is made.

Identity

In AWS IAM, there are primarily three types of identities – users, groups, and roles. Let's look at each one of them in detail.

IAM user

An IAM user is an identity that is created in AWS to either represent a person or an application, that interacts with the AWS resources. An IAM user is identified by a friendly name, an **Amazon Resource Name** (**ARN**) and an internal unique identifier. Each user has associated credentials for the purpose of authentication. These long-term credentials can take the form of console passwords, access key, etc. A user is granted the authorization permissions to access the services or resources by associating the user with a permission policy that defines what the user can do in AWS.

AWS account root user

The "*Root*" user is a special "*all-powerful*" IAM user that gets created along with the AWS account. It is considered a best practice to avoid using this user for the everyday operations and delete all the access keys associated with the user and enable **multi factor authentication (MFA)**. The root user can be used initially to create the administrators who could then take up the responsibility of creating or delegating the rights to create new users, groups, and roles, and other actions.

The security of the root user is of utmost importance, and as such, the IAM console dashboard offers some security recommendations in association with the root user. *Figure 2.2* shows a snapshot of the IAM console dashboard with security recommendations; the green check against each recommendation ensures that the root user has been secured:

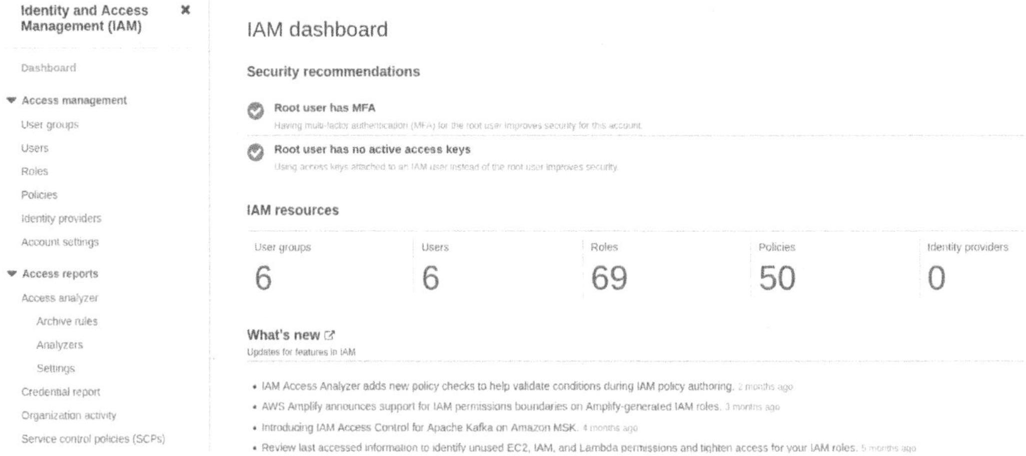

Figure 2.2: IAM dashboard with security recommendations

User creation and credential management

The users can be created by selecting the **`Access Management | Users`** link from the left navigation panel in the IAM console and then clicking on the **`Add users`** button in the **`Users`** page. Each IAM user can have a set of credentials to perform the activities within the AWS account; these credentials are used to authenticate the user. There are primarily two types of credentials that can be associated with an IAM user. The first type is long term credential that comes in the form of programmatic access and AWS Console access password. The second type is short-term credential that is powered by AWS Security Token Service (STS). There is another type of credential in the form of SSH key, that can be associated with a user to authenticate the user to the AWS CodeCommit repository, but we will not cover AWS CodeCommit in this book. *Figure 2.3* shows how to assign long-term credentials during the creation of a user from the IAM console as follows:

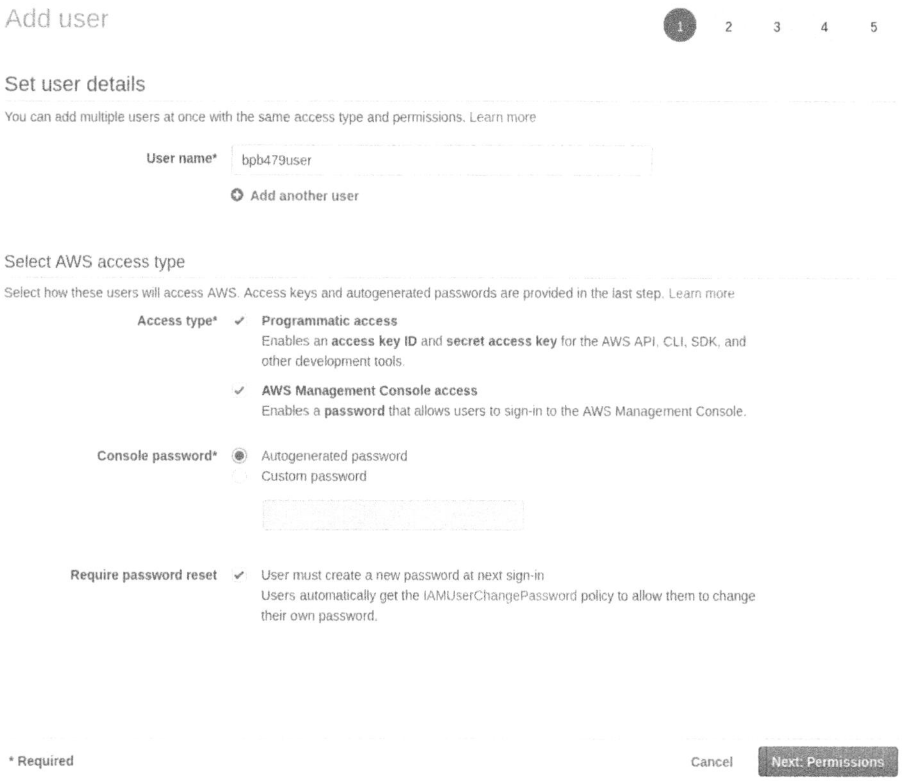

Add user

1 2 3 4 5

Set user details

You can add multiple users at once with the same access type and permissions. Learn more

User name* bpb479user

Add another user

Select AWS access type

Select how these users will access AWS. Access keys and autogenerated passwords are provided in the last step. Learn more

Access type* ✓ **Programmatic access**
Enables an **access key ID** and **secret access key** for the AWS API, CLI, SDK, and other development tools.

✓ **AWS Management Console access**
Enables a **password** that allows users to sign-in to the AWS Management Console.

Console password* Autogenerated password
Custom password

Require password reset ✓ User must create a new password at next sign-in
Users automatically get the IAMUserChangePassword policy to allow them to change their own password.

* Required

Cancel Next: Permissions

Figure 2.3: *Associating the credentials to a user from the IAM console*

Note that, with only the programmatic access, a user will not be able to access the AWS Management Console. However, the usage of AWS **Command Line Interface (CLI)** and / or AWS **Software Development Kit (SDK)** is still allowed for such a user.

The permission policies will also have to be associated with a user which will essentially authorize the user to take the actions in the AWS account. The users could be added to a group and inherit the permission from that group or the inline policies could be attached directly to the user. We will look at the IAM groups in the next section and the policies in a subsequent section. If no permission policy is attached to the user, then the user will not be able to perform anything in the AWS account.

If the console access is enabled for an IAM user, the user can access the AWS console through the following URL:

https://<account-id>.signin.aws.amazon.com/console

Here, "account-id" refers to AWS account ID, which is a unique identifier for an account.

Password policy

The AWS Management Console passwords are governed by a password policy. A strong password policy helps to keep our AWS account safe. The existing password policy could be accessed and edited by clicking the "**`Access management | Account settings`** link in the left navigation panel in the IAM console. To edit the policy, we have to click on the **`Change`** button under the **`Password Policy`** section on the **`Account Settings`** page. *Figure 2.4* shows the page to modify the password policy as follows:

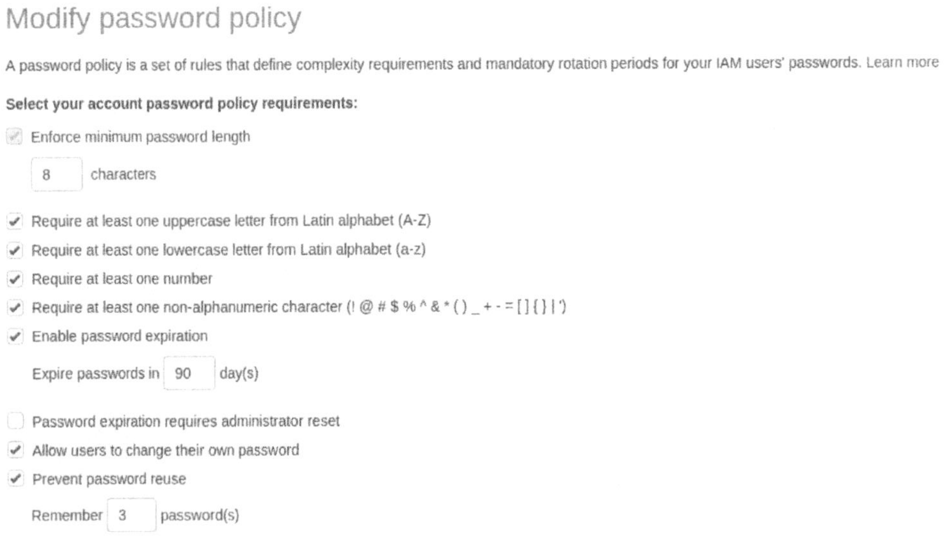

Modify password policy

A password policy is a set of rules that define complexity requirements and mandatory rotation periods for your IAM users' passwords. Learn more

Select your account password policy requirements:

- [x] Enforce minimum password length

8 characters

- [x] Require at least one uppercase letter from Latin alphabet (A-Z)
- [x] Require at least one lowercase letter from Latin alphabet (a-z)
- [x] Require at least one number
- [x] Require at least one non-alphanumeric character (! @ # $ % ^ & * ( ) _ + - = [ ] { } | ')
- [x] Enable password expiration

Expire passwords in 90 day(s)

- [ ] Password expiration requires administrator reset
- [x] Allow users to change their own password
- [x] Prevent password reuse

Remember 3 password(s)

Figure 2.4: *Password policy modification page in IAM console*

IAM group

The IAM group is essentially a collection of logically grouped IAM users. Permission management becomes a lot easier with the IAM groups. An IAM group could be granted permissions by associating it with a permissions policy. A user, when added to the group, automatically gets the permissions assigned to the group. Similarly, if a user is moved out of the group, that user will automatically have to give up the permissions associated with that group. Note that, a group, in itself, is not mapped with any credentials. The members of a group carry their individual credentials. The relationship between the IAM user and the IAM group is many-to-many. An IAM user can belong to more than one group and a group can contain more than one IAM user. In AWS, the groups cannot be nested, which means an IAM group can contain only IAM users and no other groups. *Figure 2.5* shows the relation between the users and the groups. In the diagram, User1 is part of the Administrator group, User2 is part of both the Administrator as well as the DevOpsEngineer group, while User3 is part of the DevOpsEngineer group only. Take a look at *Figure 2.5* as follows:

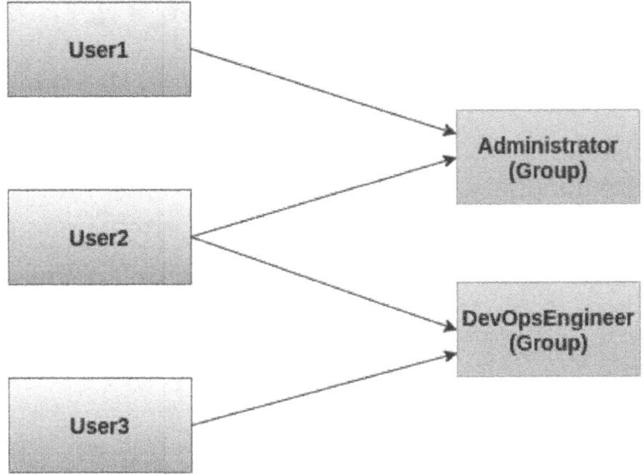

***Figure 2.5:** Relation between IAM users and IAM groups*

The creation of a group is very straightforward and could be easily done from the IAM console by selecting the **`Access Management | User groups`** link in the left navigation panel in the IAM console.

IAM role

The IAM role is a special type of identity that can be assumed by a trusted entity. Once the role is assumed, the short-term credentials are provided leveraging the AWS **Security Token Service** (**STS**) for that role session. The IAM roles are unique in terms of the policies that are attached to them. There are two types of policies that are attached to an IAM role, which are as follows:

- **Trust Policy**: Trust policy is a JSON document that is used to define the trusted principals or entities that can assume the role. An IAM role can be assumed by the following types of trusted entities:
    - IAM users in the same AWS account or a different AWS account
    - AWS services like EC2, Lambda, etc.
    - Federated users authenticated by an external identity provider (IdP) that is SAML2.0 or OpenID Connect (OIDC) compliant

  We will take a closer look at the various trusted entities in the subsequent sections.
- **Permissions Policy**: Permissions policy is a JSON document that defines the actions that the role can perform and the resources on which such actions can be performed. We will learn about the permission policy in greater detail in a subsequent section.

The details of these policies will be discussed in a subsequent section.

A quick introduction to AWS-CLI

Before we proceed any further, let's take a quick look at AWS CLI and how to install, configure, and use it. AWS CLI is a unified tool to access and manage the AWS services. Throughout this book, we will use AWS CLI, and this section will provide the details around the installation and configuration of the same. The following is the link that explains the installation steps for AWS CLI on the major operating systems:

https://docs.aws.amazon.com/cli/latest/userguide/cli-chap-install.html

We can easily check for a successful installation by using the following command:

```
$ aws --version
```

With the installation steps out of the way, let's turn our attention to configuration. AWS CLI works with the credentials which are placed in the file called **`credentials`** that is located in the user's home directory inside a folder named **`.aws`** (In Linux, the full path is: **`~/.aws/credentials`**). We can start configuring AWS CLI by typing the following command:

```
$ aws configure
```

This will configure the "*default*" profile for AWS CLI. The configuration option interactively asks for the following – "*AWS Access Key ID*", "*AWS Secret Access Key*", "*Default region name*" and "*Default output format*". The access key ID and secret access key generally corresponds to the long-term credentials associated with a user. However, the short-term credentials powered by Amazon STS could also be used.

> **TIP: Instead of placing the credentials in a file, we could also use the environment variables to setup the credentials: `AWS_ACCESS_KEY_ID`, `AWS_SECRET_ACCESS_KEY`**

We could also create a custom profile and set up the credentials associated to that profile (instead of default). In fact, we could create multiple profiles to suit our needs. The following is the command to configure a custom profile:

```
$ aws configure --profile s3admin
```

The name of a profile is generally guided by the permissions granted to the corresponding user.

While using AWS CLI to access the various AWS services, we will have to specify the profile name explicitly in the command line with the **`--profile`** option, unless we want to use the default profile, in which case the **`--profile`** option could be omitted. This option (**`--profile`**) offers an easy way to switch between the profiles when executing the AWS CLI commands. The following is an example that uses the Amazon **Simple Storage Service** (S3) CLI command with a custom profile:

```
$ aws s3 ls --profile s3admin
```

For simplicity, we will use the default profile with the **AdministratorAccess** policy permission throughout this book, unless there is a specific need to use a custom profile. However, note that the **AdminstratorAccess** policy is very powerful and broad; hence it might not always be the best fit considering the principle of least privilege.

Now that we know how to work with AWS CLI, let's use this tool to perform some user and group management operations. First, we will create a user and assign the credentials. The following are the set of commands to carry this out:

```
$ aws iam create-user --user-name bpb479user2
$ aws iam create-login-profile --user-name bpb479user2 \
  --password xxxxxxxx --password-reset-required
$ aws iam create-access-key --user-name bpb479user2
```

At this point, the user has been created and has been given both the AWS Management Console access as well as the programmatic access. The **create-access-key** command produces **AccessKeyId** and **SecretAccessKey** combination for the user and outputs the same. The following is a sample output of the command:

```
{
    "AccessKey": {
        "UserName": "bpb479user2",
        "AccessKeyId": "AKIASACILIXPL67WXTHK",
        "Status": "Active",
        "SecretAccessKey": "e58PlT7dnyxxxxxxxxxxxxxxxxxxxxxxxx",
        "CreateDate": "2021-09-01T23:50:15Z"
    }
}
```

At this point, we will have to take note of the **AccessKeyId** and **SecretAccessKey** (or create a new profile with these credentials), since there is no way to get back the **SecretAccessKey** after this, not even from the AWS Management Console.

The next set of commands will create a new group, add the user to that group, and then attach the policy to the group. In this case, we have used an AWS managed policy named "**ReadOnlyAccess**" identified by the policy ARN. This ARN could be retrieved from the IAM console by visiting the **Access Management | Policies** page, then searching for the specific policy, clicking on it, and finally copying the policy ARN from the policy **Summary** page. The policy ARN could also be retrieved by using the **list-policies** command with AWS CLI (**aws iam list-policies**).

```
$ aws iam create-group --group-name bpb479group
$ aws iam add-user-to-group --user-name bpb479user2 \
  --group-name bpb479group
```

```
$ aws iam attach-group-policy --group-name bpb479group \
  --policy-arn arn:aws:iam::aws:policy/ReadOnlyAccess
```

TIP: Use the following link to check the documentation on the AWS CLI commands: https://awscli.amazonaws.com/v2/documentation/api/latest/index.html

Access Management

Access management is all about creating policies and controls (and governing them), so that only the authorized identities are granted rights to use a service or access a resource, while preventing such usage rights and access for the unauthorized identities.

IAM Policy

IAM policy is at the core of access management in AWS. Authorization strategies like **Role Based Access Control** (**RBAC**) and **Attribute Based Access Control** (**ABAC**) are based on the IAM policies. AWS IAM primarily uses policies which are defined in the JSON format to allow or deny access protected resources. An IAM policy essentially encapsulates the granular level permissions that can be associated with an identity or resource. The permissions typically establish the actions that can be performed or 'not' performed on a set of resources. The IAM policy can either be AWS managed or customer managed or inline (directly attached to the identity). Let us delve into the details of the structure of a policy to understand this better.

Structure of a policy

The important elements in a JSON format IAM policy document are as follows:

- **Version**: Represents the supported versions of a policy document. There are two versions – "2012-10-17" and "2008-10-17". The version "2008-10-17", is the default version when Version element is not explicitly defined. However, "2012-10-17" is the recommended and latest version, and features like policy variables are supported in this version.
- **Statement**: Statement is a mandatory element and can be either of type object or array. Statement consists of four sub elements – "*Effect*", "*Action*", "*Resource*", and "*Condition*" (optional), which are defined as follows:
    - **Statement/Effect**: Effect can have two values – "Allow" or "Deny" – and it specifies the outcome of the statement in terms of granting or denying access. Note that, explicit "Deny" always has a higher precedence over "Allow" on a given set of resources.

- **Statement/Action**: Action represents an array of actions for which we are either granting or denying access. Each item in this array is a "*key:value*" pair, where the key represents a service and the value represents an action on that service (for example: *s3:ListBucket*, *sqs:SendMessage*, *ec2:StartInstances*, etc.).
- **Statement/Resource**: Resource defines the AWS resources or objects that the statement covers. Resources are specified using **Amazon Resource Names** (**ARNs**) and wildcards (*) to indicate the statement applied to all the resources.
- **Statement/Condition**: Condition element is optional and is typically used to control when the policy is in effect. The condition element is used to build the expressions that take the following form:

  `"Condition" : { "<condition-operator>" : { "<condition-key>" : "<condition-value>" }}`

There are several condition operators available which can be used to create very powerful IAM policies; these are as follows:

- **String condition operators**: **`StringEquals`**, **`StringNotEquals`**, **`StringLike`**, **`StringNotLike`**, **`StringEqualsIgnoreCase`**, **`StringNotEqualsIgnoreCase`**
- **Numeric condition operators**: **`NumericEquals`**, **`NumericNotEquals`**, **`NumericLessThan`**, **`NumericLessThanEquals`**, **`NumericGreaterThan`**, **`NumericGreaterThanEquals`**
- **Date condition operators**: **`DateEquals`**, **`DateNotEquals`**, **`DateLessThan`**
- **Boolean condition operator**: **`Bool`**
- **IP address condition operators**: **`IpAddress`**, **`NotIpAddress`**
- **ARN condition operators**: **`ArnEquals`**, **`ArnNotEquals`**

The condition keys can be global or service specific. The global condition keys have a **`aws:`** prefix, whereas the service specific condition keys have the prefix of the service name like **`secretsmanager:SecretId`**. Some of the significant global condition keys are **`aws:userid`**, **`aws:username`**, **`aws:SourceIp`**, **`aws:SourceVpce`**, **`aws:MultiFactorAuthPresent`**, **`aws:PrincipalAccount`**, **`aws:PrincipalArn`**, **`aws.PrincipalType`**, **`aws:PrincipalTag`**, **`aws:RequestTag`**, **`aws:SecureTransport`**, **`aws:SourceAccount`**, **`aws:SourceArn`**, etc.

Some examples of the service level condition keys are **`secretsManager:SecretId`**, **`secretsManager:VersionId`**, **`secertsManager:VersionStage`**,

s3:TlsVersion, **s3:authType**, **s3:signatureAge**, **s3:prefix**, **s3:x-amz-acl**.

- **Policy variables**: The policy variables are basically placeholders when the exact value of a resource or condition key is not known during the creation of the IAM policy. The values of the condition keys in the policies can be used as the policy variables. A policy variable is marked by a "$" followed by a pair of curly braces in the policy document. The variable name is placed inside the curly braces; for example, **${aws:username}**.

IAM policy examples

A good understanding of the IAM policies is necessary for implementing appropriate access control. The following are some interesting examples that leverage the policy structure elements that we just discussed:

- **Administrator Access:** This is an extremely powerful, AWS managed policy and provides full access to all the AWS services and resources. It goes by the name **AdministratorAccess**. The statement reads that "**all**" actions on "**all**" resources are allowed. This policy should be used with caution as it provides unlimited access to the identity (user, group, or role) with which it is attached. Note that, this is an example of how **Role Based Access Control** (**RBAC**) is implemented with the IAM policy. The following is an example of Administrator Access policy:

```
{
    "Version": "2012-10-17",
    "Statement": [
        {
            "Effect": "Allow",
            "Action": "*",
            "Resource": "*"
        }
    ]
}
```

- **Describe EC2 images and instances**: The following is an example of a customer managed policy that essentially provides two permissions (describe EC2 images and describe EC2 instances) on all the images and EC2 instances.

```
{
    "Version": "2012-10-17",
    "Statement": [
        {
```

```
            "Sid": "EC2Describe",
            "Effect": "Allow",
            "Action": [
                "ec2:DescribeImages",
                "ec2:DescribeInstances"
            ],
            "Resource": "*"
        }
    ]
}
```

- **Controlling access to S3**: This policy leverages the policy variable (`aws:username`) to control the access to the bucket named "`bpb479-bucket`". When the policy is evaluated, `${aws:username}` is replaced by the name of the current user. Moreover, the policy also uses the condition operator "`StringLike`" and the condition key "`s3:prefix`". Basically, the statement allows the read/write/list permissions on the bucket named "`bpb479-bucket`" to a user only if the prefix contains the user's name. Note that, a prefix is the complete path in front of the S3 object name. Thus, this policy assumes that every user will have their own directory in the bucket. Look at the following example:

```
{
    "Version": "2012-10-17",
    "Statement": [
        {
            "Action": [
                "s3:ListBucket",
            "s3:GetObject",
            "s3:PutObject"
        ],
            "Effect": "Allow",
            "Resource": ["arn:aws:s3:::bpb479-bucket"],
            "Condition": {
                "StringLike": {"s3:prefix":
            ["${aws:username}/*"]
            }
          }
        }
```

```
    ]
    }
```

- **Date based access to DynamoDB**: This policy allows all actions on DynamoDB only if the user is authenticated for using multi-factor authentication (MFA). Additionally, these actions are only allowed between specific dates. The policy leverages Boolean condition key – **`aws:MultiFactorAuthPresent`** and date-based conditions with **`aws:CurrentTime`** key. Look at the following example:

```
{
        "Version": "2012-10-17",
        "Statement": {
            "Effect": "Allow",
            "Action": [
              "dynamodb:*"
           ],
           "Resource": "*",
           "Condition": {
              "Bool": {"aws:MultiFactorAuthPresent": true},
              "DateGreaterThan": {"aws:CurrentTime":
"2021-08-30T00:00:00Z"},
              "DateLessThan": {"aws:CurrentTime":
"2021-09-03T23:59:59Z"}
           }
        }
    }
```

- **Attribute Based Access Control (ABAC):** This policy is an example of how the ABAC authorization strategy could be implemented using the IAM policy. The policy leverages the "Condition" element with specific condition keys – **`iam:ResourceTag`** and **`aws:PrincipalTag`**. Essentially, this policy allows the users to assume any role only when the `project` tag associated with the identity and the role matches. This means when the role is created, it has to be assigned the `project` tag with a specific value. Also, when the IAM user is created, it must also be assigned the `project` tag along with the same value. Look at the following example:

```
{
    "Version": "2012-10-17",
    "Statement": [
    {
```

```
        "Sid": "AssumeRoleWithMatchingTags",
        "Effect": "Allow",
        "Action": "sts:AssumeRole",
        "Resource": "*",
        "Condition": {
           "StringEquals": {
             "iam:ResourceTag/project": "${aws:PrincipalTag/
project}"
           }
        }
    }]
}
```

TIP: Refer to the following link to study some interesting IAM policy examples: https://docs.aws.amazon.com/IAM/latest/UserGuide/access_policies_examples.html

AWS Organizations

In practice, the enterprises tend to use multiple AWS accounts to isolate the departments, deployment environments, workstreams, etc. While this multi-account strategy provides the required isolation, it however introduces complexity in terms of creation and maintenance of accounts, billing, policies, IAM, etc. The AWS Organizations can help to centrally manage, govern, and consolidate the entire AWS ecosystem of an enterprise that is spread across multiple AWS accounts. AWS Organizations introduce the concept of a master account and multiple child accounts created or invited (to join the AWS Organization) by the master account.

AWS Organizations come in two flavors based on the feature sets, which are as follows:

- **Consolidated billing features**: Consolidated billing allows us to access the account wise billing directly in the master account, which includes both the master as well as the child accounts. Moreover, a single payment method could be used across all the accounts under an AWS Organization. Note that, the consolidated billing does provide the cost benefits (or volume discounts) which is a major driver for the enterprises to adopt AWS Organizations, which as a service is free.
- **All features (default)**: When using the 'All features' flavor, in addition to the consolidated billing, we can create new accounts and/or invite the existing accounts to join the organization. It also helps to group the accounts into **Organizational Units** (**OU**) by use-case, project, business units, etc.

Furthermore, we can apply **Service Control Policies** (**SCP**) and associate them with OUs or individual accounts, create organization-wide backup policies, create tag policies to standardize tags across an organization, etc.

We must note that while we can migrate from 'Consolidated billing features' to 'All features', this migration is one-way. Once migrated, we cannot migrate back to 'Consolidated billing features'.

The Figure 2.6 shows a sample hierarchy that can be created with AWS Organizations. The figure shows the master management account being part of the root OU. Root OU is the parent of all the other OUs and accounts in the organization. There are two child OUs ("*Production*" and "*Non-Prod*") under Root OU. Each of these have multiple accounts under them. Note that, OUs can be nested, and the policies (like SCP) are inherited from the parent OU or master account into a nested OU or child account. Look at *Figure 2.6* as follows:

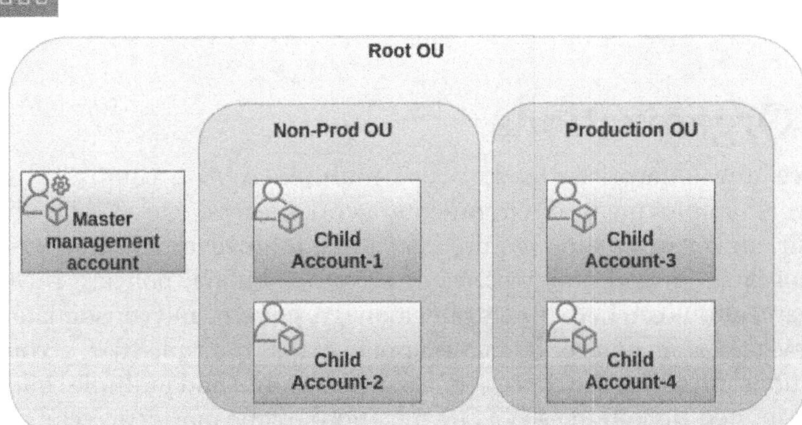

Figure 2.6: *Hierarchy of root OU, child OUs and accounts*

Service control policy

Service control policy (**SCP**) is a very powerful feature to centrally manage and control the AWS child accounts and OUs from the master account in an AWS Organization. The policies set in the master account cannot be bypassed by the roots and administrators of the child accounts.

Once AWS Organizations is enabled in the master account, to enable SCP, we need to select **`Policies`** from the left navigation panel in the AWS Organizations service page and then select **`Service control policies`** from the **`Policies`** page on the right. Finally, on the **`Service control policies`** page, click on **`Enable service control policies`** as shown in the following *figure 2.7*

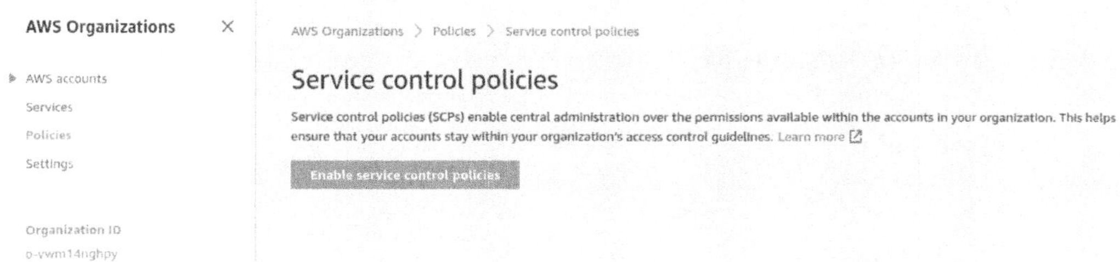

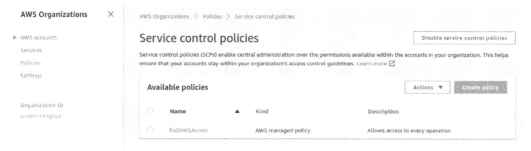

Figure 2.7: *Enabling Service control policies for AWS Organizations*

As mentioned earlier, SCPs are inherited from the parent OUs or master account. However, an explicit 'deny' (appearing anywhere in the hierarchy) always takes precedence.

Once enabled, **`FullAWSAccess`** is an AWS managed policy that is available to be attached to the Root OU or master account or any child OUs. We can also create custom policies, by clicking on the **`Create policy`** button on the **`Service control policies`** page and then subsequently attaching the policy to a target OU or account. *Figure 2.8* shows the relevant page from where we can create the new policies and attach them (from **`Actions`** drop-down) to targets, as follows:

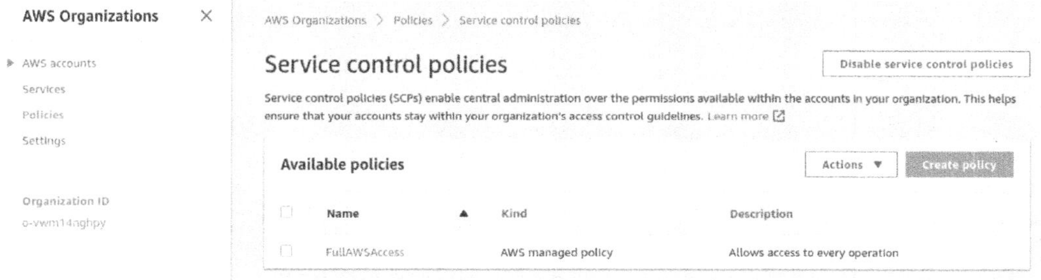

Figure 2.8: *Create a custom service control policy*

SCP can help to whitelist or blacklist the IAM actions that can be applied to the OU or accounts. However, the master account is outside the scope of SCP. When blacklisting, we can specify certain AWS services to be explicitly denied in the policy and then attach it to a target OU or account; whereas, with whitelisting, we can specify the AWS services that are allowed. The following is an example of an SCP that when attached to an OU or account can prevent the users (in the child accounts or target account) from deleting the Amazon VPC flow logs:

```
{
  "Version": "2012-10-17",
  "Statement": [
    {
      "Effect": "Deny",
```

```
      "Action": [
        "ec2:DeleteFlowLogs"
      ],
      "Resource": "*"
    }
  ]
}
```

TIP: The following link could be used to study some Service control policy examples: https://docs.aws.amazon.com/organizations/latest/userguide/orgs_manage_policies_scps_examples.html

Identity-based policy

The identity-based policies are attached to an identity like IAM user, group, or role. Such a policy is used to define what an identity can do on a set of AWS resources. *Figure 2.9* shows how an identity-based policy is attached to the identities to access a representative AWS resource (like S3 bucket), as follows:

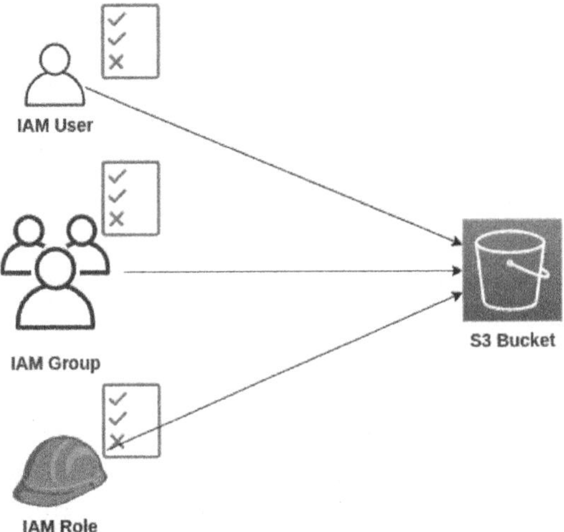

Figure 2.9: *Identity based policy*

All the examples, which we have seen in the *IAM policy examples* section, are identity-based policies.

The identity-based policies can be categorized as either managed policies or inline policies. Managed policies can be managed either by AWS or by the customer, and they can be attached to multiple identities. In other words, the managed policies are reusable. Inline policies, on the other hand, are directly attached to the identities and form a strict one-to-one relationship.

Let's looks at the AWS CLI commands that could be used to create a customer managed policy and associate it with an identity. We assume that the file **policy.json** has the required permissions defined in the JSON format. Then, we go ahead to create a policy named **CustomReviewerPolicy** and use it's ARN to attach the policy directly to a user named **bpb479reviewer** and to a group named **Reviewers**. The following are the AWS CLI commands:

```
$ aws iam create-policy --policy-name CustomReviewerPolicy \
  --policy-document file://./policy.json

$ aws iam attach-user-policy --user-name bpb479reviewer \
  --policy-arn arn:aws:iam::<account-id>:policy/CustomReviewerPolicy

$ aws iam attach-group-policy --group-name Reviewers \
  --policy-arn arn:aws:iam::<account-id>:policy/CustomReviewerPolicy
```

Note that, for the AWS managed policies, we can simply get the policy ARN and use the same to attach the policy to an identity. However, for a customer managed policy, we will have to create the policy first and then attach the same with an identity.

Permission boundaries

A permission boundary is used to set the maximum permissions that can be granted to an IAM entity (users and roles) by an identity-based policy. Thus, if the permission boundary is set, the effective permissions granted to the identity is the intersection between the permissions granted to the identity, by the identity-based policies and the permission boundary. So essentially, a permission boundary is used to set the permission limits for an identity. It does not grant any permissions on its own. It helps to limit the scope of the IAM users and roles and prevent privilege escalation.

Let's try to understand this with an example. We consider a user named "**bpb479user**". Now, we'd like to set the permission boundary for this user, so that the user can perform anything with S3 and EC2, but nothing more. So, we create an IAM policy (named **PermissionBoudaryForS3AndEC2Policy**) that looks like the following:

```
{
    "Version": "2012-10-17",
    "Statement": [
        {
            "Effect": "Allow",
            "Action": [
                "s3:*",
                "ec2:*"
            ],
```

```
            "Resource": "*"
        }
    ]
}
```

Now we can associate this policy as a permission boundary for the **bpb479user** user with the following AWS CLI command:

```
$ aws iam put-user-permissions-boundary \
    --permissions-boundary arn:aws:iam::<account-id>:policy/
PermissionBoudaryForS3AndEC2Policy \
    --user-name bpb479user
```

Of course, we could have used an AWS managed policy as well to define the permissions boundary for the user.

> **To create a permission boundary for an IAM role (instead of an IAM user), use the following AWS CLI command:**
> ```
> $ aws iam put-role-permissions-boundary
>   --permissions-boundary <policy-arn>
>   --role-name <role-name>
> ```

At this point, if the "**bpb479user**" is granted the DynamoDB related permissions (for example, "**dynamodb:GetItem**", "**dynamodb:Scan**", "**dynamodb:Query**", etc.) by virtue of an identity based policy that is attached to the user, the user still cannot perform any actions outside the permission boundary. This means, any DynamoDB operation by the user will fail.

Resource-based policy

The resource-based policies are attached to the AWS resources (like Lambda functions, S3 buckets, SQS queue, SNS topics, KMS keys, Secrets Manager secrets, etc.) instead of the identities. Such a policy specifies which principals or entities have access to that specific resource and what actions they can perform on it. *Figure 2.10* shows how a resource-based policy is attached to the representative AWS resource (like S3 bucket), as follows:

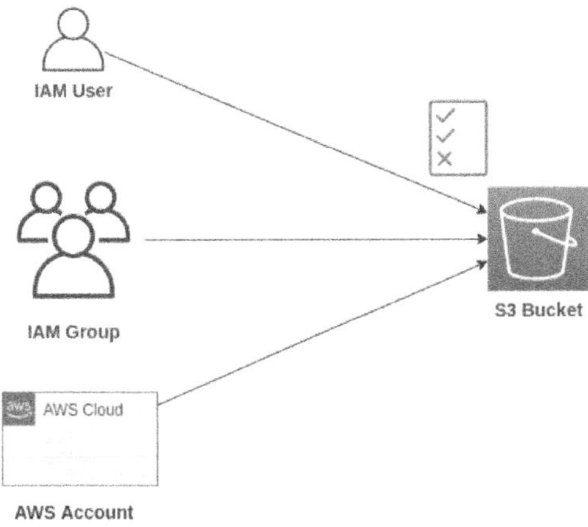

Figure 2.10: Resource based policy

Essentially, a resource-based access policy has an embedded trust policy signified by the **`Principal`** element in the JSON. The following is an example of a simple resource-based access policy that could be attached to a Lambda function named **`BPB479Lambda`**. The policy grants permission to a particular API's method (identified by ARN which also includes API Id: **`9f2eds6pii`**) to invoke the Lambda function, as follows:

```
{
  "Version": "2012-10-17",
  "Statement": [
    {
      "Effect": "Allow",
      "Principal": {
        "Service": "apigateway.amazonaws.com"
      },
      "Action": "lambda:InvokeFunction",
      "Resource": "arn:aws:lambda:<region>:<account-
id>:function:BPB479Lambda",
      "Condition": {
        "ArnLike": {
          "AWS:SourceArn": "arn:aws:execute-api:<region>:<account-
id>:9f2eds6pii/*/GET/companies"
        }
      }
    }]
}
```

S3 Bucket Policy

Amazon S3 bucket policy is basically an implementation of `the` resource-based policy. Such a policy is directly attached to `the` S3 bucket and introduces a granular level of permission for the bucket and its contents. The bucket policies are very effective in certain scenarios which are mentioned as follows:

- Make objects within the bucket public.
- Make objects in a bucket accessible only from a specific Classless Inter-Domain Routing (CIDR) range.
- Allow cross account access to S3 bucket.

The following is an example of a simple bucket policy:

```
// File: policy.json
{
   "Version": "2012-10-17",
   "Statement": [{
      "Effect": "Allow",
      "Principal": {
         "AWS": ["arn:aws:iam::<account-id>:root"]
  },
      "Action": "s3:*",
  "Resource": [
     "arn:aws:s3:::bpb479-bucket",
         "arn:aws:s3:::bpb479-bucket/*"
      ]
   }]
}
```

The scope of access could be reduced by specifying a user instead of "root" in the Principal element; for example, `arn:aws:iam::<account-id>:user/<user-name>`.

The preceding policy grants all the S3 based actions to the AWS account (specified by **`<account-id>`**) on the bucket named **`bpb479-bucket`** and its contents. This policy also signifies that **`bpb479-bucket`** trusts the AWS account (specified by **`<account-id>`**) to take such actions on it. The important point to note here is that the suffix **`root`** in the **`Principal`** element basically points to the authenticated and authorized principals in the account and not the special omnipotent root user created along with the creation of an AWS account.

Here is the following is the AWS CLI command to apply the bucket policy (in **policy.json** file) described earlier, to a bucket named **bpb479-bucket**:

```
$ aws s3api put-bucket-policy --bucket bpb479-bucket \
  --policy file://policy.json
```

Trust policy

We already know that the IAM roles must be associated with a trust policy that signifies which principals can assume that role. A trust policy is a required resource-based policy attached to a role. The following is an example of a trust policy:

```
// File: trustpolicy.json
{
  "Version": "2012-10-17",
  "Statement": [
    {
      "Effect": "Allow",
      "Principal": {
        "Service": "lambda.amazonaws.com"
      },
      "Action": "sts:AssumeRole"
    }
  ]
}
```

If this trust policy is attached with an IAM role, then based on the trust, only AWS Lambda can assume that role by virtue of the allowed **sts:AssumeRole** action. Here, we have considered the AWS Lambda service as the principal; however, any other AWS service or account could have acted as the trusted principal.

Let us quickly review how everything ties together – trust policy, permissions policy, and IAM role. We will use AWS CLI to better understand how these associations work. The first command is meant to create a role named **BPB479LambdaRole** with a trust policy that was introduced recently. The trust policy essentially signifies that only the Lambda service can assume this role, as follows:

```
$ aws iam create-role --role-name BPB479LambdaRole \
 --assume-role-policy-document file://./trustpolicy.json
```

The next command creates a permission policy for the IAM role named **BPB479LambdaPermissionsPolicy**. This policy file is an identity-based policy JSON that describes all the permissions that needs to be granted to the Lambda function in order to enable it to carry out its responsibilities, as follows:

```
$ aws iam create-policy --policy-name BPB479LambdaPermissionsPolicy \
 --policy-document file://./policy.json
```

Here'The following are the contents of the sample **policy.json** file. As we can easily see, it's an identity based policy that grants **s3:GetObject** action on **bpb479-bucket**. In addition, it also grants the permission to create a specific log group (named **BPB479Lambda**) and create the log streams within that log group, as follows:

```
// File: policy.json
{
    "Version": "2012-10-17",
    "Statement": [
        {
            "Effect": "Allow",
            "Action": [
                "s3:GetObject"
            ],
            "Resource": [
                "arn:aws:s3:::bpb479-bucket/*"
            ]
        },
        {
            "Effect": "Allow",
            "Action": [
                "logs:CreateLogStream",
                "logs:CreateLogGroup",
                "logs:PutLogEvents"
            ],
            "Resource": [
                "arn:aws:logs:*:<account-id>:log-group:/aws/lambda/
BPB479Lambda:log-stream:*",
                "arn:aws:logs:*:<account-id>:log-group:/aws/lambda/
BPB479Lambda"
            ]
        }
    ]
}
```

Finally, we associate the IAM role with the permissions policy ARN as follows:

```
$ aws iam attach-role-policy --role-name BPB479LambdaRole \
 --policy-arn arn:aws:iam::<account-id>:policy/
BPB479LambdaPermissionsPolicy
```

Resource based policy versus IAM role

The distinction between the resource-based policy and the IAM role becomes very clear when we consider them with respect to the cross-account access. Cross account access could be managed in two ways – use IAM role as a proxy or attach the resource-based policy to the resource. Here, we assume that the resource in question, supports the resource-based policy (for example, S3 bucket).

When using an IAM role as a proxy, the user in the trusted account will have to assume the cross-account role to access the S3 bucket. However, in doing so, the user gives up all the original permissions and takes up the permissions assigned to the role. However, when using a resource-based policy, the principal does not give up any existing permissions.

Session policy

The session policies are passed as a parameter when creating a temporary session for a role or federated user. When a role is assumed by calling **AssumeRole**, **AssumeRoleWithSAML**, or **AssumeRoleWithWebIdentity**, Amazon STS APIs (we will discuss these APIs in detail in an upcoming section - "*Federation*"), a unique session is created and the session policies, in the form of JSON policy documents, could be passed. The resulting session permissions are the intersection of the session policies and identity-based policies and the intersection of session policies and the resource-based policies.

Evaluation of policies

Now that we have looked into the various types of policies that can be used to enforce access control, let's take a deeper look at how these policies are evaluated. The first and foremost point to realize is that "*deny*" always takes precedence over "*allow*". AWS starts the evaluation of the policies with an implicit deny. Implicit deny is a situation where there is neither an explicit deny nor an explicit allow. In contrast, an explicit deny is characterized by an explicit deny statement. Let's consider some specific cases to understand how the policies are evaluated by AWS.

Identity based policies and resource-based policies

When an IAM entity requests access to a resource within the same account, AWS evaluates all the permissions granted by both the identity-based as well as the resource-based policies attached to the IAM entity and the resource respectively.

The outcome is the *union* of permissions in both the policies. This means, if an action is allowed in any one of the policies or both, then AWS allows the action. However, an explicit deny in any one of the policies results in a deny.

Identity based policies and permission boundary

Evaluation of the permissions in the identity-based policies and permission boundary results in a permission set that represents the *intersection* of the two policies. Essentially, a permission boundary, if applied, can reduce the scope of an identity-based policy. Once again, an explicit deny in any one of the policies results in a deny.

Identity based policies and service control policies (SCP)

If the user belongs to an AWS account that is part of an AWS Organization, then the service control policies or SCPs will affect the policy evaluation. The resulting permissions are the intersection of the two policies. Effectively, this means that an action will have to be allowed in both the policies to be finally allowed by AWS. Explicit deny in the policies will result in a deny.

The following link provides a flowchart based view of the IAM policy evaluation for both the intra account and the cross account scenarios: https://docs.aws.amazon.com/IAM/latest/UserGuide/reference_policies_evaluation-logic.html

Delegation

Delegation refers to granting of permissions to some other account to allow access to the resources that we control. Thus, delegation involves setting up of trust between the two accounts. Delegation of authority involves delegating roles that the identities from the trusted account can assume temporarily, without any overall privilege escalation. Delegation plays an important role in simplifying the identity and access management when multiple AWS accounts are involved. The delegation model allows us to maintain the identities and policies in a single place and use the cross-account roles to delegate authority, based on the trust construct of an IAM role.

Cross account role

A cross-account role establishes trust between two accounts and allows one account to access the resources in the other. Let's consider the scenario where an organization has multiple AWS accounts and one of them is an "identity or landing account". The identity account is basically a central account for the identities and users/groups should not have access to services or create resources in this account. In this setup, all other accounts must trust the identity account. Any user will first log into the identity account and then jump onto other accounts based on the assigned permissions. The following are the steps to achieve this trust:

1. Create a cross account role in the non-identity account with the following details:

    - The role has a trust policy that trusts the identity account to assume this role. The trust-policy would look like the following:

    ```
    {
    "Version": "2012-10-17",
    "Statement": [
      {
        "Effect": "Allow",
        "Principal": {
          "AWS": "arn:aws:iam::<identity-account-id>:root"
        },
        "Action": "sts:AssumeRole"
      }
    ]
    }
    ```

    Note that, this trust policy could leverage the IAM policy **`Condition`** to enforce MFA to be used by the identities of the trusted account.

    - The role is attached to a permission policy that grants access to a specific set of resources in the non-identity account, to the identity account based on requirements (for example, access to the S3 buckets or EC2 instances).

2. Take note of the cross-account role ARN that got created in the non-identity account. The ARN would look like the following:

    `arn:aws:iam::`**`<non-identity-account-id>`**`:role/`**`<cross-account-role-name>`**

3. Create an IAM policy in the identity account that allows the **`sts:AssumeRole`** action against the resource identified by the role ARN in step-2. The permission policy would look like the following:

    ```
    {
     "Version": "2012-10-17",
     "Statement": [
    ```

```
        {
          "Effect": "Allow",
          "Action": "sts:AssumeRole",
    "Resources": "arn:aws:iam::<non-identity-account-id>:role/<cross-
    account-role-name>"
        }
      ]
    }
```

4. Attach the IAM policy in step-3 with specific identities in the identity account.

At this point, the authenticated and authorized users in the identity account that have been granted permission to assume the cross-account role (created by the non-identity account), can access specific resources in the non-identity account based on the permission policy attached to the cross-account role. The cross-account role leverages AWS STS to provide short-term credentials to identities in the trusted account (identity account), which could in turn, be used to access the resources.

Cross account role with third-party accounts

When a cross account role has to be shared with an external account that belongs to a third-party, extra security measures needs to be taken. This is so because, the cross-account role construct can be subjected to a privilege escalation attack, also known as the **confused deputy problem**. Let's look at *Figure 2.11* and see how this attack works, as follows:

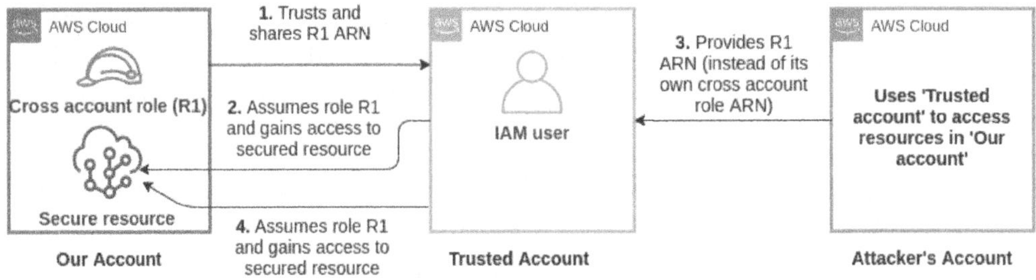

***Figure 2.11:** Confused deputy problem*

In *Figure 2.11*, we assume that the blue account on left is ours and we trust the green account (trusted account) in the middle. We have also created a cross account role (R1) with appropriate permissions to access the resources in our account and then shared the ARN of the cross-account role with the trusted account. Thus, the trust setup enables the green account to assume the R1 role and access the resource in our account. So far, so good.

Now, assume that the trusted account works with multiple AWS accounts, and a malicious red account on the right somehow gets to know or guesses R1's ARN, and instead of sharing its own cross account role ARN, it shares R1's ARN with the green account. The green account doesn't verify the owner of the shared role. At this point, the red account could trick the green account, which is trusted by our account, to gain unauthorized access to our 'blue' secure resources. The trusted green account is the confused deputy here, that can unwittingly give access to the resources in our account to an untrusted and malicious red account.

To avoid such a situation, **external Id** is used. In essence, the external Id is a shared secret between our account and the trusted account. Unless the correct external Id is supplied while assuming the role, the operation fails. The following is a two-step modification to the standard cross account role situation:

- Add a condition to the trust policy of the blue account's cross account role that uses the **sts:ExternalId** condition key and assign it a value equal to the shared secret as follows:

```
{
  "Version": "2012-10-17",
  "Statement": [
    {
      "Effect": "Allow",
      "Principal": {
        "AWS": "arn:aws:iam::<green-account-id>:root"
      },
      "Action": "sts:AssumeRole",
      "Condition": {
         "StringEquals": {"sts:ExternalId": "<shared-secret>"}
      }
    }
  ]
}
```

- The trusted green account will have to pass the correct shared secret as **external Id** in order to assume the role. In the following AWS CLI command, if the external Id is not supplied, then the operation fails:

```
$ aws sts assume-role \
 --role-arn arn:aws:iam:<blue-account-id>:role/<cross-account-
role-name> \
 --role-session-name-temp session1 \
 --external-id <shared-secret>
```

With the "**external Id**" setup, even if the red account shares the ARN of our cross-account role (R1), it will not know the secret external Id, and hence the attempt to assume role R1 by the green account fails due to condition mismatch. Typically, the external Id is a non-guessable, long string of arbitrary characters.

Federation

In identity federation, the service provider trusts an external identity provider (IdP) to authenticate the users and then lets the authenticated users to assume temporary roles for accessing the resources. In essence, the user management remains outside the scope of the service provider.

AWS supports several flavors of federation where AWS acts as the service provider and trusts the external IdPs to authenticate the users. The authenticated users are given temporary credentials to either access the AWS resources or the AWS Management console.

SAML2.0 based federation

This type of federation plays a vital role when there exists a SAML2.0 compliant directory or identity store (like Microsoft Active Directory, ADFS, etc.), possibly on-premise, which needs to be integrated with AWS. The integration essentially links the on-premise directory or identity store with the role based AWS access.

SAML based federation rests on the trust between AWS and the on-premise identity provider (IdP). To establish this trust, SAML metadata files need to be exchanged between the IdP and AWS. The SAML metadata files describe the corresponding identity provider and service provider (that is, AWS). The SAML metadata file from IdP is uploaded to create an SAML identity provider in AWS. *Figure 2.12* shows how to configure an SAML provider (named **BPB479SAMLProvider**) from the IAM Management console page, as follows:

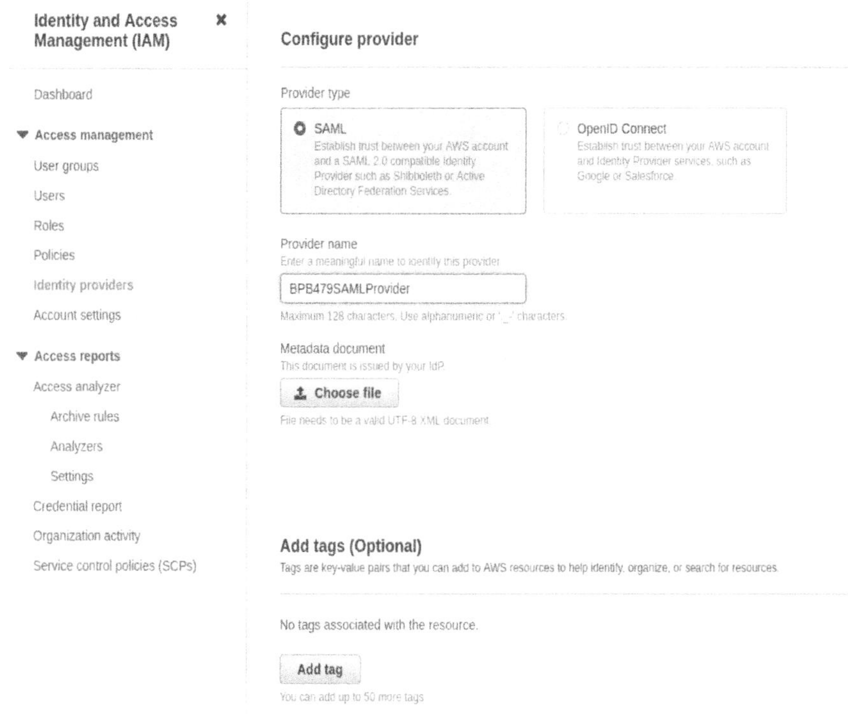

Figure 2.12: Configuration of a SAML identity provider

The SAML metadata XML from AWS side is available at the following link: https://signin.aws.amazon.com/static/saml-metadata.xml

Once the identity provider is configured, the IAM role needs to be created which the application will attempt to assume. The trust policy associated with this role must specify the recently created SAML identity provider (in AWS) as **`Principal`** and the action as **`sts:AssumeRoleWithSAML`**. The trust policy looks somewhat like the following:

```
{
  "Version": "2012-10-17",
  "Statement": [{
    "Effect": "Allow",
    "Principal": {
        "Federated": "arn:aws:iam::<account-id>:saml-provider/
BPB479SAMLProvider"
    },
    "Action": "sts:AssumeRoleWithSAML"
  }]
}
```

This trust policy could specify additional conditions to allow the federated users that match certain SAML attributes to access the IAM role (for example, **`saml:aud`**, **`saml:iss`**, etc.).

Figure 2.13 shows how the users of a client application are authenticated in real time by the IdP against an on-premise SAML2.0 based identity store, and in return, gets necessary SAML assertions. These assertions, along with role ARN (to be assumed), are then sent to Amazon STS by calling **`AssumeRoleWithSAML`** API. Upon success, the API returns the credentials which can then be used to access the AWS resources (like S3 buckets or DynamoDB, etc.), as shown in *Figure 2.13* as follows:

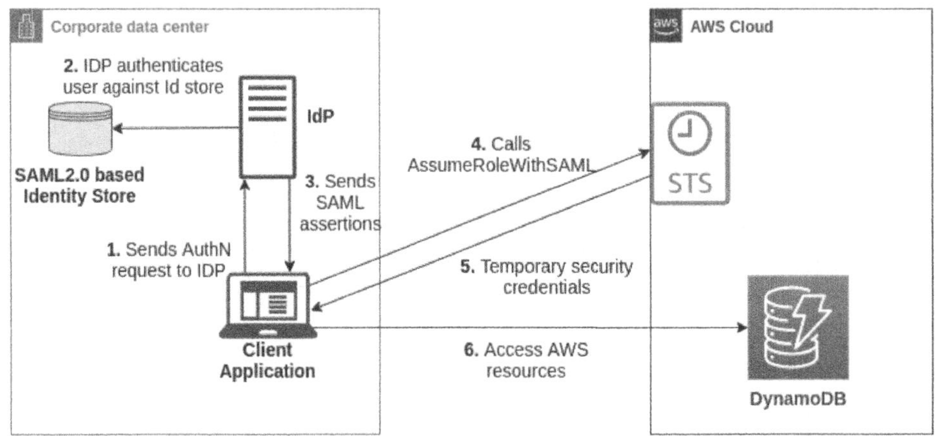

Figure 2.13: *Interaction for SAML2.0 based federation*

AssumeRoleWithSAML

The Amazon STS **`AssumeRoleWithSAML`** API call is at the heart of this integration. The application requesting access to the AWS resource, calls the **`AssumeRoleWithSAML`** API and passes the following:

- **RoleArn**: ARN of the IAM role that the application wishes to assume.
- **PrincipalArn**: ARN of the SAML identity provider in IAM that describes the on-premise IdP.
- **SAMLAssertion**: SAML authentication response (base64 encoded) provided by the IdP.
- Optionally, the session duration and session policy could also be passed.

In response, along with the other parameters, Amazon STS returns the AWS scoped credentials (combination of **`AccessKeyId`**, **`SecretAccessKey`**, and **`SessionToken`**), which then could be used by the application to access the resources in the AWS account as defined by the assumed role's permission policy.

Note that, SAML2.0 based federation could also be used to access the AWS Management console.

Web Identity Federation

With the Web Identity Federation, the users of mobile or web applications can authenticate themselves with the well-known web identity providers like Google, Facebook, Amazon, or any other OpenID Connect (OIDC) compatible IdP. With an existing trust in place between AWS and these OpenID Connect providers, the users can then exchange provider-specific tokens for the AWS scoped temporary credentials (from Amazon STS) that is mapped to an IAM role with the required permissions. Subsequently, these credentials could be used to access the AWS resources (as allowed by the permissions policy associated with the assumed IAM role).

With well-known web identity providers like Amazon, Cognito, Google, and Facebook, AWS has a pre-configured trust relationship with these providers. This means, we do not have to create the identity provider entities from them in the IAM console. However, for any other OIDC complaint provider, we have to first establish the trust by creating an identity provider, as shown in *Figure 2.14* as follows:

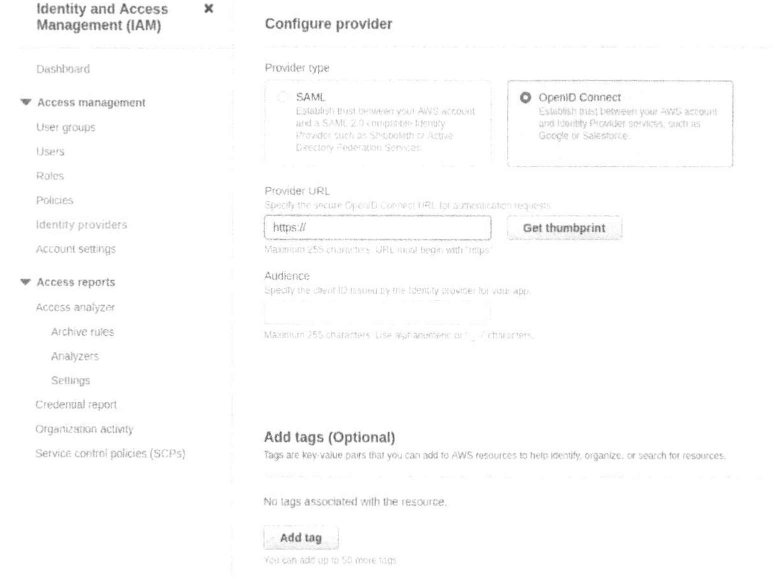

Figure 2.14: *Configuration of custom OIDC identity provider in IAM console*

The next step is to create the IAM role with a trust policy that declares the OIDC provider as the **`Principal`**. The following is how the trust policy looks like for the Google provider:

```
{
    "Version": "2012-10-17",
    "Statement": [{
        "Effect": "Allow",
```

```
            "Principal": {
            "Federated": "accounts.google.com"
            },
            "Action": "sts:AssumeRoleWithWebIdentity",
            "Condition": {
            "StringEquals": {
        "accounts.google.com:aud": "<app-id>"
            }
            }
      }]
}
```

The trust policy specifies a **`Condition`** to restrict the permissions only to the specific application by using the pre-defined key, **`accounts.google.com:aud`**. The value corresponding to this key is the application Id received from the Google developer portal while registering our application.

Table 2.1 shows the designated **`Principal`** for the common OIDC providers along with the **`Condition`** keys that could be used to create a trust policy, as follows:

Web Identity Provider	Principal	Condition Key
Amazon	"Principal":{"Federated":"www.amazon.com"}	"Condition": {"StringEquals": {"www.amazon.com:app_id": "<app-id>"}}
Facebook	"Principal":{"Federated":"graph.facebook.com"}	"Condition": {"StringEquals": {"graph.facebook.com:app_id": "<app-id>"}}
Google	"Principal":{"Federated":"accounts.google.com"}	"Condition": {"StringEquals": {"accounts.google.com:aud": "<app-id>"}}
Cognito	"Principal":{"Federated":"cognito-identity.amazonaws.com"}	"Condition": {"StringEquals": {"cognito-identity.amazonaws.com:aud": "<app-id>"}}
Custom OIDC provider	"Principal":{"Federated":"arn:aws:iam::<account-id>:oidc-provider/<provider-url>"}	"Condition": {"StringEquals": {"<provider-url>:aud": "<app-id>"}}

Table 2.1: *Common OIDC principals and condition keys for creating trust policy*

The IAM role permissions policy could also be tailored to restrict access to the federated identities with policy variables. The available policy variables for the well-known web identity providers are given as follows:

- **Amazon**: "www.amazon.com:user_id"
- **Facebook**: "graph.facebook.com:id"
- **Google**: "accounts.google.com:sub"
- **Cognito**: "cognito-identity.amazonaws.com:sub"

Let's look at an example around how to use these policy variables in the permissions policy of the IAM role. We assume that the access needs to be provided to a Google federated user to list the contents of a folder in a S3 bucket that belongs to the user. The policy might look like the following:

```
{
      "Version": "2012-10-17",
      "Statement": [{
          "Effect": "Allow",
          "Action": "s3:ListBucket",
          "Resource": ["arn:aws:s3:::bpb479-bucket"]
          "Condition": {
          "StringLike": {
           "s3:prefix": ["contents/${accounts.google.com:sub}/*"]
      }
          }
      }]
}
```

Now that we have setup the trust between the AWS and OIDC provider and have looked at the creation of the IAM role that will be assumed by the federated identities, let's turn our attention to the interaction between the application, identity provider, and AWS service provider. *Figure 2.15* shows how the application authenticates the user against a web identity provider (Amazon in the diagram) and gets an OAuth2.0 access token or OIDC Id token in return. Subsequently, this token, along with the IAM role ARN and other parameters are passed in the Amazon STS **`AssumeRoleWithWebIdentity`** API call. STS validates the request and sends the short-term AWS credentials to the application. The application can now use these credentials to access the AWS resources (S3 bucket in the diagram). Look at *Figure 2.15* as follows:

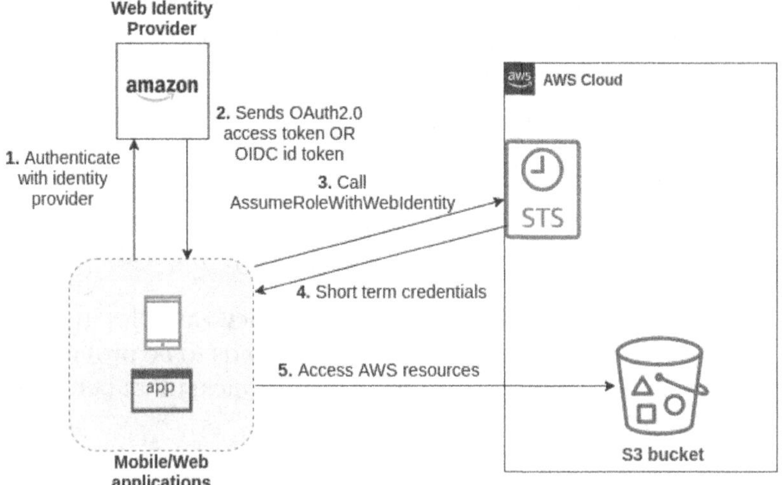

Figure 2.15: Interaction for web identity federation

AssumeRoleWithWebIdentity

The applications will have to call Amazon STS *AssumeRoleWithWebIdentity* API on behalf of the federated identities to get the AWS scoped short-term credentials, in order to access the AWS resources. The following needs to be passed to this API call:

- **RoleArn:** ARN of the IAM role that the application wishes to assume.
- **RoleSessionName:** Identifier for the assumed role session. The temporary credentials received in the response will be associated with this identifier.
- **WebIdentityToken:** OAuth2.0 access token or OIDC Id token that is received from the web identity provider once the user is authenticated.
- **ProviderId:** Fully qualified host component of the identity provider's domain name like www.amazon.com or graph.facebook.com.
- Optionally, the session duration and session policy could also be passed.

In response, along with the other parameters, Amazon STS returns AWS scoped credentials (combination of **`AccessKeyId`**, **`SecretAccessKey`**, and "**`SessionToken`**"), which then could be used by the application to access the resources in the AWS account as defined by the assumed role's permission policy.

Web Identity Federation with Cognito

AWS recommends using Cognito for the web identity federation instead of using the **`AssumeRoleWithWebIdentity`** API call. This is so because, Cognito supports anonymous users, data synchronization, and MFA, and has an optimized flow. We will study this detailed enhanced flow in *Chapter 5: Application Security* under the section *AuthN/AuthZ with Amazon Cognito / Identity Pool/ Authentication.*

Essentially, the mobile or web application can integrate with a web identity provider to authenticate the user and then call Cognito API to exchange the ID token received from the identity provider for the Cognito token. The application then calls another Cognito API and passes the Cognito token to fetch the AWS scoped credentials (note that, the application does not integrate with Amazon STS directly). Once the AWS credentials are received, the application can then access the AWS resources.

In this interaction, Cognito does a lot of undifferentiated heavy lifting which includes the verification of the ID token with the identity provider, calling Amazon STS API to fetch the short-term AWS credentials, etc.

AWS Directory Service

Active Directory is a popular directory service developed by Microsoft and is widely used across enterprises. The servers running Microsoft Active Directory (AD) are called domain controllers and these servers can authenticate and authorize the associated users, machines, and other objects. The objects in AD are organized as *trees* and a group of trees is called a *forest*.

AWS Directory Service is a managed service that can alleviate the challenges of managing an AD installation with respect to the infrastructure management, replication, patching, etc. AWS Directory Service supports the following directory types for the AWS services, AD-aware, or LDAP-aware workloads running on AWS to integrate with Active Directory.

- **AWS Directory Service for Microsoft AD:** This is a managed service offering from AWS that is powered by the actual Microsoft Windows Server Active Directory. It helps to migrate a wide range of AD-aware applications to the AWS cloud. It supports the integration with numerous AD-aware applications, including the AWS managed services like Amazon WorkSpaces, Amazon QuickSight, Amazon Relational Database Service (RDS) for MS SQL Server, etc. AWS Directory Service for Microsoft AD can be used in the standalone mode or could be joined to the on-premise AD via a *forest trust* over an AWS Direct Connect or VPN connection. Note that, in a forest trust, the users are not replicated; there exists a trust relationship (one-way or two-way) between the on-premise AD and the AWS Directory Service for MS AD on AWS.

TIP: The direction of the forest trust and that of the resource access, works in opposite directions. For example, if domain X trusts domain Y, then Y can access the resources registered with domain X (not the other way round).

- **AD Connector:** Directory gateway or proxy essentially provides easy integration of the cloud-based application to the on-premise AD. The users are managed in the on-premise AD. Thus, the AD-aware workloads and services (like AWS Workspaces, AWS QuickSight, Amazon EC2 instances with Windows Server) can take advantage of connecting to the existing on-premise AD for the authentication and authorization needs. AD Connector also allows the users to access AWS Management Console and could be used to enable MFA by connecting to the existing RADIUS based MFA infrastructure. AD Connector is not compatible with Amazon RDS SQL Server.

- **Simple AD:** Simple AD is a standalone, AD-compatible (powered by Samba 4) managed directory service on AWS. Simple AD does not support trust relationships, MFA, and other advanced AD features. However, this is a simple and cost-effective AD solution on AWS, for smaller organizations that need basic AD features.

AWS Single Sign On (SSO)

The AWS Single Sign On or SSO service provides a centralized solution for creating or connecting the workforce identities from Microsoft AD or a standard identity provider. It helps to centrally manage the permissions across multiple accounts in an AWS Organization (optionally) and third-party business applications that support SAML 2.0. We need to understand that the identities could be created solely in AWS SSO, or could be federated to an on-premise AD (leveraging AD Connector), or Standalone AWS Directory Service for MS AD or AWS Directory Service for MS AD with a two-way forest trust setup with the on-premise AD. With AWS SSO, the users could have access to several AWS services as well as the many business applications. The following *figure 2.16* shows the interaction between the application, AWS SSO and AWS resources as follows:

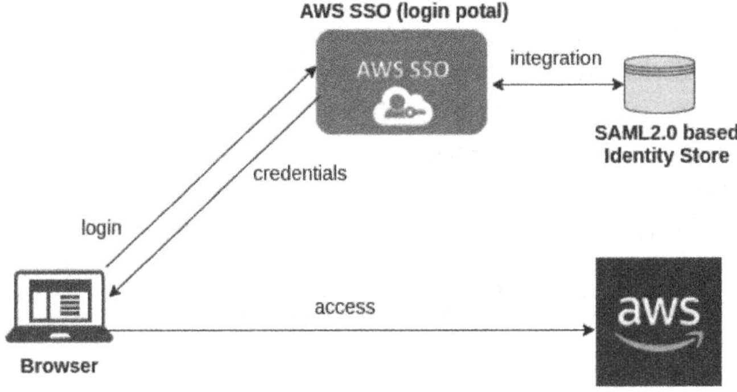

Figure 2.16: *Interaction with AWS SSO*

Amazon S3 ACL

AWS recommends the use of the IAM policies and bucket policies to control access to the S3 buckets and objects. Amazon S3 ACL happens to be a legacy access control mechanism. ACL is a sub-resource attached to every bucket or object. Essentially, an ACL defines which AWS accounts or groups are granted access and the type of access they have (**READ**, **WRITE**, **FULL_CONTROL**, etc.).

Amazon S3 Canned ACLs

Canned ACLs are a set of predefined grants. Each canned ACL has a predefined set of grantees and permissions associated with it. When a bucket or an object gets created, Amazon S3, by default, grants the resource owner a full control over these resources. The situation becomes a little tricky when the cross-account role is used to create an object in a bucket. In such a scenario, the object owner is the account that created the object. This means, the bucket owner will not have access to the particular object inside the bucket, by default.

The following are some of the significant canned ACLs:

- **private**: Owner gets **FULL_CONTROL**. No one else has access rights. This is the default ACL. Applies to both bucket and object.
- **public-read**: Owner gets **FULL_CONTROL** and **AllUsers** (predefined S3 group) group gets **READ** access. Applies to both bucket and object.
- **authenticated-read**: Owner gets **FULL_CONTROL** and **AuthenticatedUsers** (predefined S3 group) group gets **READ** access. Applies to both bucket and object.
- **bucket-owner-read**: Object owner gets **FULL_CONTROL**. Bucket owner gets **READ** access. Applies only to object.
- **bucket-owner-full-control**: Both, the object owner as well as the bucket owner gets **FULL_CONTROL** over the object. Applies only to object.

Canned ACLs can be specified when copying an object to a bucket. The following is the AWS CLI command to assign canned ACL (**bucket-owner-full**) to an object being copied to the S3 bucket named "**bpb479-bucket**":

```
$ aws s3 cp ./contents.txt s3://bpb479-bucket/ --acl bucket-own-
er-full-control
```

AWS tools for IAM

AWS provides targeted tools to simplify role creation, policy governance, and continuous adherence to the principle of least privilege.

Visual editor for policies

When starting out with the IAM policies, it's easier to use the visual editor to create the custom policies. The editor is available under the **Create policy** page in the IAM console. The editor helps to select the services, actions, resources, and conditions easily, and then one can also take a look at the generated JSON policy. *Figure 2.17* shows how the editor can simplify the creation of a policy, as follows:

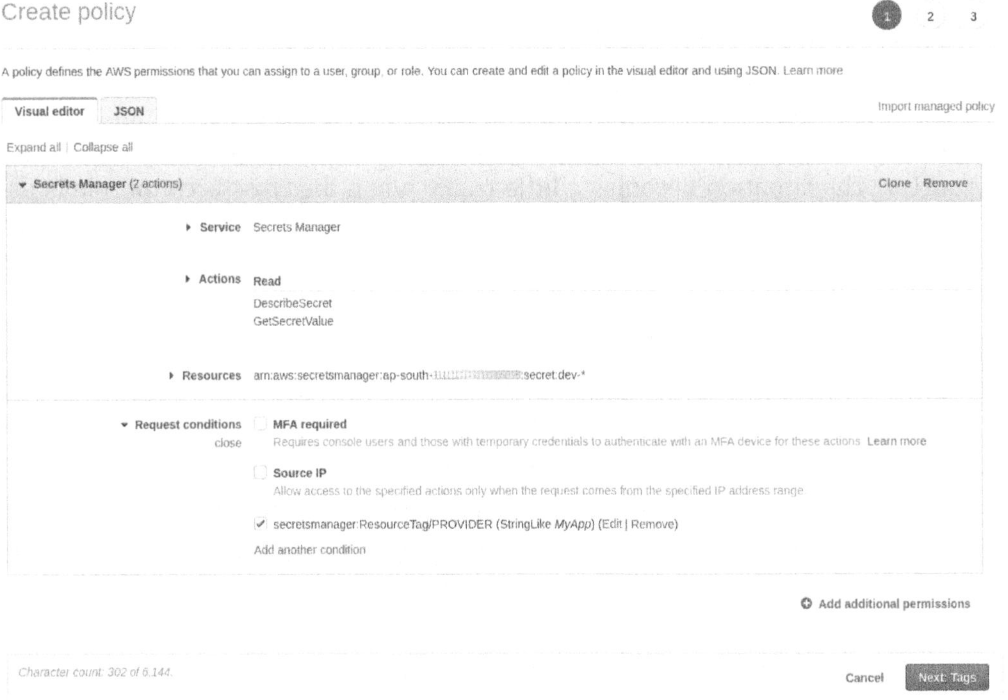

Figure 2.17: Policy visual editor

Access advisor

The AWS IAM access advisor can be used as a governance tool to determine the services that have not been accessed by the identities based on the `Last Accessed` information and the permissions granted to them. This may help setup the permission guardrails using **Service Control Policies** (**SCP**) which can then restrict the access to such services at an AWS Organization or **Organizational Unit** (**OU**) level. Note that, access advisor could also be used outside the scope of an AWS Organization and can help to refine the permissions assigned to the identities and better adhere to the principle of least privilege. The tracking period for the service information in the IAM console is the last 400 days. The following permissions will be required to be granted in order to check the IAM's last accessed information:

- `iam:GenerateServiceLastAccessedDetails`
- `iam:Get*`
- `iam:List*`

To see access advisor at work, we need to visit the IAM console, and for any particular user, group, or role, we have to click on the **`Access Advisor`** tab in the **`Summary`** page. *Figure 2.18* shows the **`Access Advisor`** related findings for a user named **`admin1`**, as follows:

Figure 2.18: *Access Advisor related findings for a user from IAM Console*

The **`Last accessed`** column provides a good idea around which services were accessed by the user within the tracking period. The **`Policies granting permissions`** column shows the name of the policy through which the access to the service was granted.

Access analyzer

AWS IAM Access Analyzer acts as a guide towards the continuous process of implementing the principle of least privilege and can be accessed from the IAM console. It helps to generate the fine-grained policies based on the access activity captured in the logs. It also implements the policy validation checks. These validations can help in identifying the resources in our accounts and organization that are shared with the external parties. Policy checks can produce findings that includes security warnings, errors, general warnings, and other suggestions for the policies. Access Analyzer can also help in removing the unused IAM entities based on the "*last-used*" timestamp for the roles and access keys, which may otherwise pose a security threat. At the time of writing this chapter, Access Analyzer could analyze the following resource types:

- Amazon S3 buckets
- AWS IAM roles
- AWS Key Management Service key
- AWS Lambda functions

- Amazon Simple Queue Service queues
- AWS Secrets Manager secrets

Conclusion

AWS Identity and Access Management is a fundamental security service. A good understanding of this service and its features, and leveraging it properly helps keep the AWS account and resources within it, safe. AWS IAM will be utilized time and again in the upcoming chapters, and thus, a working knowledge of AWS IAM will surely help in grasping the advanced service level concepts.

In the next chapter, we will delve into the depths of infrastructure security, which will establish the foundation of creating a secure AWS application ecosystem.

CHAPTER 3
Infrastructure Security

Introduction

The importance of infrastructure security is paramount in public cloud. As part of the shared responsibility model, AWS manages the security of AWS Global Infrastructure, which provides the necessary backbone for hosting the highly scalable, reliable, and resilient AWS services. This backbone and AWS services provide several controls to fine-tune the security of the infrastructure components and cloud resources that we provision in AWS. This chapter will cover some of the available AWS services and their security features, which can help us improve the infrastructure security posture.

Structure

In this chapter, we will cover the following topics:

- AWS global infrastructure
- Securing networks with Virtual Private Cloud
- Patch management
- Secure SSH and RDP session management
- IP filtering

- Vulnerability assessment
- Distributed Denial of Service and AWS Shield

Objectives

The objective of this chapter is to introduce the techniques and strategies for securing the customer's infrastructure components on AWS Cloud. We will learn how to secure the Virtual Private Clouds and how to configure the associated network components with security in mind. The chapter will also help in understanding how to safely perform patching and session management for privileged access. We will learn about the various strategies to apply IP filtering and perform vulnerability assessment of the EC2 instances and container images. Finally, we will take a closer look at safeguarding the infrastructure elements and services deployed on AWS, from the Distributed Denial of Service (DDoS) attacks.

AWS Global Infrastructure

AWS Global Infrastructure is an extensive, secure, and reliable network of AWS data centers, hardware, appliances, operational software, and IT networks. It has a global footprint and is comprised of the following entities:

- **Region:** A region is defined as a geographical area with a cluster of data centers featuring latency optimizations and cost minimizations. Regions are completely isolated from each other, and the region-to-region communication happens over the web.
- **Availability zone:** An **availability zone** (**AZ**) is one or more discrete data centers in a specific region. AZs are engineered to be isolated by a fast low latency, high throughput, and highly redundant networking. They also have redundant power sources. Multiple AZs are used in a highly available, fault tolerant design to gracefully handle a disaster amounting to an AZ failure.
- **Edge network:** Edge networks offer low latency and high throughput network connectivity. On one hand, they are peered with the telecom providers globally, and on the other hand, they are connected to the nearest AWS region through the AWS network backbone. The global edge network is a collection of **points of presence** (**PoP**) that includes edge locations and regional edge caches to deliver fast and low latency contents to the end users. Amazon CloudFront (a content delivery network operated by AWS) leverages the global edge network to serve static and dynamic contents. The requests for content are automatically routed to the nearest edge location.

As per *shared responsibility model*, the security of the AWS global infrastructure lies with AWS. AWS employs state-of-the-art physical and environmental security controls and processes to safeguard its globally distributed infrastructure. This includes restricted perimeter access and building ingress point access to the AWS facilities and data centers, professional physical security staff, video surveillance, intrusion detection systems, multi-factor authentication for authorized personnel, etc. In addition, fire detection and suppression systems, fully redundant power supply, temperature, and other climate control features are installed in the AWS data centers to minimize the risk of outages. AWS also takes care of instance isolation at the hypervisor level, memory isolation by allocating pre-scrubbed memory to instances, and disk isolation by scrubbing the disks right before they are reused. All these and more helps AWS to provide highly available, secure, and fault tolerant cloud services to the customers around the globe.

Now, let's take a closer look into securing our AWS accounts and resources there-in. As we will see in this chapter, AWS provides several services that can help us secure our AWS cloud-based networks, instances, and services.

Securing networks with Virtual Private Cloud

Amazon Virtual Private Cloud web service allows us to provision our own logically isolated section of the AWS cloud for our resources. VPCs are based on **software defined networking** (**SDN**). The configuration of a VPC depends upon several factors like which users or systems will access the resources within the VPC, from where they will access the resources, etc.

We will not get into the details of each of the fundamental network elements, and for this book, we will assume that the readers have a working knowledge of these elements, so that we can focus on the security aspects of Amazon VPC. Let us take a quick look at the components involved in the creation of a functional VPC as follows:

- **Virtual Private Cloud (VPC)**: A dedicated regional virtual network for our AWS account. A VPC is associated with a range of IP addresses, designated by one or more **Classless Inter-Domain Routing** (**CIDR**) blocks.
- **Subnet**: A range of IP address associated with the VPC and tied to an AZ. If a subnet has a route to the Internet gateway, it's called a **public subnet**. On the other hand, if a subnet does not have a route to the Internet gateway, it's called a **private subnet**. A special case of a private subnet is a *VPN-only subnet* in which there is no route to the Internet gateway; however, traffic is routed to a virtual private gateway for site-to-site **virtual private connection** (**VPN**).
- **Route table**: A set of routing rules to define how a network traffic is routed to a destination. The route tables are attached with one or more subnets.
- **Internet gateway**: A gateway that, when attached to a subnet of a VPC, enables the communication between the resources in the subnet and the public Internet.

- **NAT device**: A NAT device allows the instances in the private subnets to connect to the Internet. We will cover the NAT devices in detail, in a subsequent section.

Hybrid networks

Often, there are requirements to connect the VPC with remote networks in a fault tolerant and secure manner. AWS provides various VPN connectivity options and AWS Direct Connect to achieve this type of hybrid networking.

VPN connectivity

A VPN connection can help establish network connectivity between VPCs and other remote networks (like on-premises or co-location networks). The VPN connections are established over the public Internet; however, the connections can still leverage private IP addresses. AWS offers various VPN connectivity options, which are mentioned as follows:

- **AWS Site-to-Site VPN**: With this option, we can create a site-to-site IPSec (Internet Protocol Security) VPN connection between a remote network and our VPC. Site-to-Site VPN connection offers two VPN tunnels for failover support, between a VPN concentrator known as *Virtual Private Gateway* or a *transit gateway* on the AWS side and a *customer gateway* (representing a VPN device) on the remote side. The necessary changes will have to be made to the route table associated with the private subnet to route the traffic to the virtual private gateway. *Figure 3.1* shows the schematics of a site-to-site VPN with a virtual private gateway attached to the VPC, as follows:

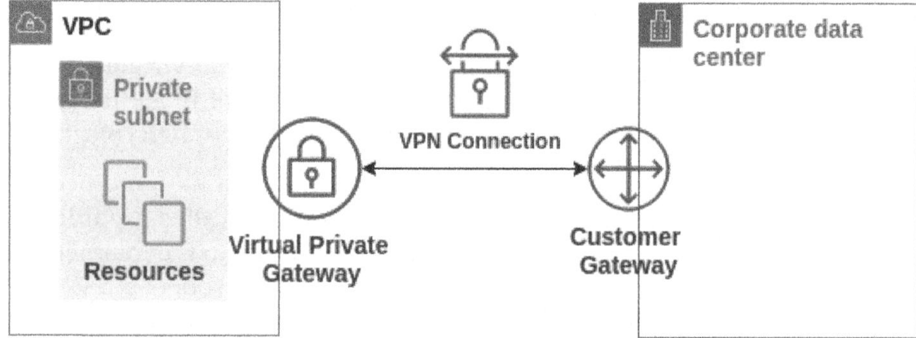

Figure 3.1: *Site-to-Site VPN Connection with virtual private gateway*

Figure 3.2 shows another way to achieve site-to-site VPN, where the VPN connection is specified as an attachment on the transit gateway. We will learn more about transit gateways in a subsequent section. Refer to *Figure 3.2* as follows:

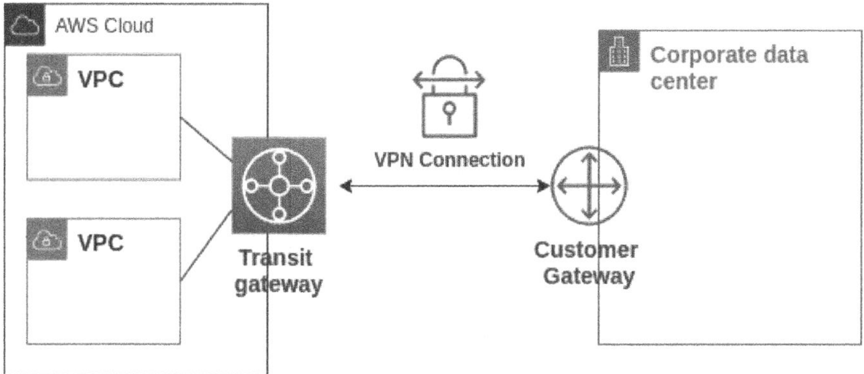

Figure 3.2: *Site-to-Site VPN Connection with transit gateway*

With IPSec VPN tunnels, data in transit can be encrypted with AES128 or AES256 ciphers and the redundancy created by the two tunnels makes the connection resilient.

- **AWS Client VPN**: AWS Client VPN enables us to establish a client-to-site VPN connection. AWS Client VPN can help us configure an endpoint to which OpenVPN-based VPN clients can connect from any location over a secure TLS VPN session. Once the client has established a VPN session, it can access the resources in the VPC in which the associated subnet exists. In addition, the client can also access the other AWS resources, like resources in a peered VPC, a VPN connection to a remote network, or the Internet via an Internet gateway, as shown in *Figure 3.3*. Appropriate routes and authorization rules have to be in place for such access. Refer to *Figure 3.3* as follows:

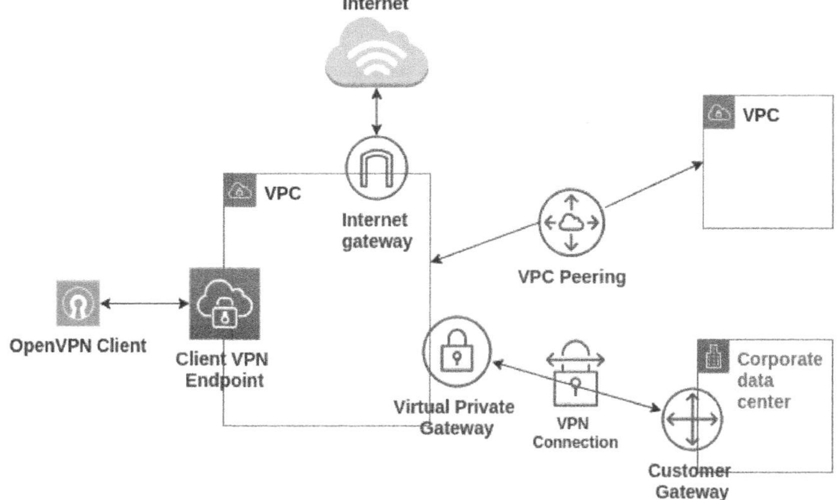

Figure 3.3: *Client-to-site VPN connectivity with AWS Client VPN*

VPN Clients can be authenticated with *certificate based mutual authentication* or *user-based authentication* (based on Active Directory or SAML based federation). We can also use a combination of mutual authentication plus AD authentication or mutual authentication plus federated authentication. Client VPN supports two types of authorization with *security groups* and *network-based authorization*. Security groups can be associated with the Client VPN endpoint to authorize the traffic and the network-based authorization is implemented with the authorization rules. Each network can be configured with the AD group or SAML-based IdP group to authorize access. In the absence of AD or SAML based federated authentication, we can specify the ingress rules that grants access to the VPN clients.

- **AWS VPN CloudHub**: We can use AWS as a VPN connection hub in scenarios where we have to connect multiple remote sites securely via the VPN connection. We have to establish the AWS site-to-site VPN connectivity with each remote network. This enables the remote networks to connect as well as our VPC. The VPN CloudHub architecture is shown in *Figure 3.4* where the green lines represent VPN traffic between the remote sites over the site-to-site VPN connections, as follows:

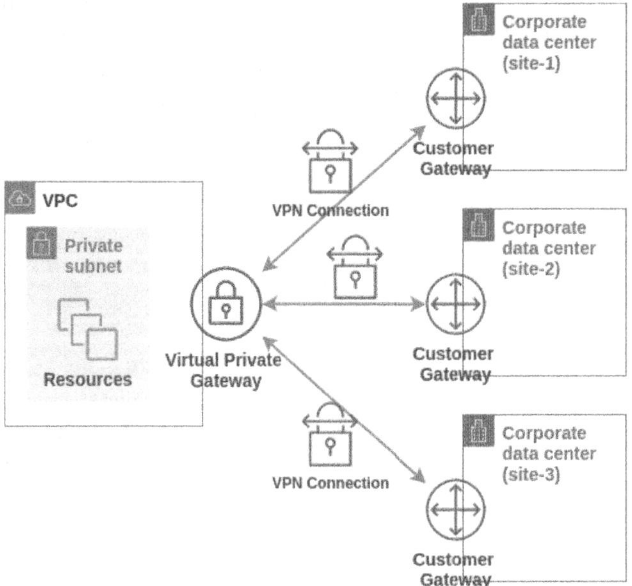

***Figure 3.4:** AWS VPN CloudHub architecture*

- **VPN appliance**: A third party software VPN appliance could be installed on the EC2 instance which can then provide private connectivity to the remote networks over the public Internet. This option is not provided or maintained by AWS, and we will have to be responsible for the high availability and fault tolerance of this setup.

AWS Direct Connect

AWS Direct Connect helps to create a dedicated private connection over the standard Ethernet fiber-optic cable, between the remote networks and AWS. AWS Direct Connect features stable, high bandwidth (ranging from 50Mbps to 100Gbps) and low latency connections. One end of the cable is connected to the on-premises router and the other to the nearest AWS Direct Connect router in the AWS Direct Connect location. With AWS Direct Connect, we can create *public virtual interfaces* to connect directly with the public AWS services (like Amazon S3) and *private virtual interfaces* to connect with resources in our VPCs from the on-premises network.

With AWS Direct Connect, there are two options to protect the data in transit, which are as follows:

- AWS Direct Connect can be combined with AWS Site-to-Site VPN to create an IPSec encrypted connection with any AWS Direct Connect line.
- For the 10 Gbps and 100 Gbps connections, AWS Direct Connect offers MACsec (Layer-2 protocol that relies on AES-GCM-128-bit cipher) point-to-point encryption at selected AWS Direct Connect locations.

With the understanding of the basic networking constructs in place, let us now dive deeper and look at the various AWS services and AWS recommended strategies available to secure our VPCs and the resources in it.

A quick note on VPC based AWS CLI commands

Most of the VPC related activities can be done by setting up a user that has an AWS managed permission policy called **`NetworkAdministrator`** or a custom permission policy, attached to it. Subsequently, we can create an AWS CLI profile with this user's credentials and fire away the AWS CLI commands. Needless to say, we can also use the more powerful **`AdministratorAccess`** policy; however that setup might not follow the principle of least privilege.

We must also note that the VPC related features are grouped inside the EC2 command in AWS CLI. For example, if we want to create a VPC with CIDR block **`10.0.0.0/16`** in **`ap-south-1`** region leveraging AWS CLI, we can use the following command:

```
$ aws ec2 create-vpc --cidr-block 10.0.0.0/16 --region ap-south-1
```

As another example, if we want to create an Internet Gateway and attach the same with our VPC (identified by **`vpc-id`**), we can use the commands mentioned here. The first command creates an Internet Gateway and publishes the ID of the new created Internet Gateway as the output. This must be extracted and used in the second command that attaches this newly created Internet Gateway with an existing VPC. Look at the following command:

```
$ aws ec2 create-internet-gateway
```

The create-internet-gateway command will generate an output that looks like the following:

```
{
    "InternetGateway": {
        "Attachments": [],
        "InternetGatewayId": "igw-06115e77bf9833364",
        "OwnerId": "679359112763",
        "Tags": []
    }
}
```

As mentioned earlier, we have to extract the Internet Gateway ID from this output and execute the **attach-internet-gateway** command to attach this gateway to the VPC. Here's the command that attaches the Internet Gateway to the VPC:

```
$ aws ec2 attach-internet-gateway --internet-gateway-id <igw-id> \
  --vpc-id <vpc-id>
```

Inter VPC private communication

There can be situations where inter VPC communication needs to be kept private for security reasons. A private communication between VPCs is possible via VPC Peering and transit gateway. These enable the VPCs to communicate with each other over RFC 1918 address space or private IPs. Transit gateway takes this one step further and provides a transit hub that supports the private connections between VPCs and the on-premise networks.

VPC peering

A VPC peering connection is a private networking connection between two VPCs using internal AWS network. Instances in VPC can communicate as if they were in the same network by using their private IPs (RFC 1918 address space). A VPC peering connection can be set up with another VPC in the same AWS Region that belongs to the same AWS account, a different AWS account, or a VPC in a different AWS Region (cross region VPC peering). AWS VPC peering connection has no bandwidth bottleneck and no single point of failure. *Figure 3.5* shows how a VPC peering works, as follows:

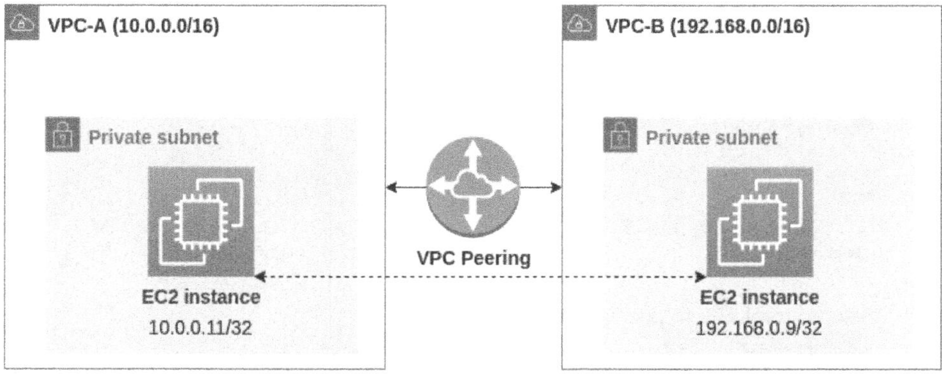

Figure 3.5: *Schematic diagram of a VPC peering*

VPC-A and VPC-B must have non-overlapping CIDR ranges. With a peering setup between these two, an EC2 instance in a private subnet of VPC-A can communicate with another EC2 instance in a private subnet of VPC-B, over private IP addresses.

Certain considerations need to be taken into account before setting out to create a VPC peering connection, as follows:

- The peered VPCs must not have overlapping CIDR blocks.
- VPC peering connection is not transitive, which means, each pair of VPCs will have to be peered separately.
- VPC peering does not support edge-to-edge routing, which means, instances in one VPC cannot leverage the existing Internet gateway, VPN, or Direct Connect connection, NAT gateway and Gateway VPC endpoint (described in a subsequent section), in a peered VPC.
- It requires route tables in each VPC's subnet to be updated for the instances to communicate.
- Security groups can be referenced from a peered VPC.
- VPC peering uses the longest prefix match to select the most specific route.
- With a VPC peering, all instances in the two peered VPCs can essentially communicate with each other, and in certain scenarios, this might not be the optimal solution considering the network security.

To create a VPC peering connection from VPC Console, we have to select **`Peering Connections`** under **`VIRTUAL PRIVATE CLOUD`** in the left navigation panel, and in the **`Peering Connections`** page, click on the **`Create peering connection`** button. In the **`Create peering connection`** page (shown in *Figure 3.6*), we have to select the local VPC (or requester) and select the other VPC (accepter) and click on the **`Create peering connection`** button. As already stated, the accepter VPC could be in the same AWS account or in a different AWS account in the same AWS Region as the requester or in a different AWS Region. Refer *Figure 3.6* as follows:

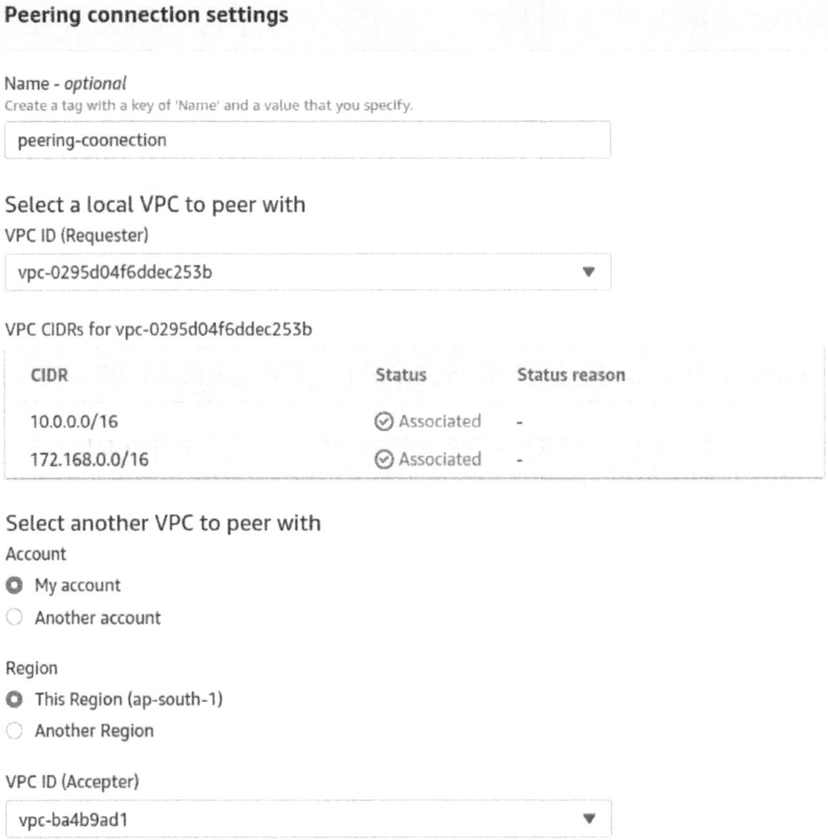

Peering connection settings

Name - *optional*
Create a tag with a key of 'Name' and a value that you specify.

peering-coonection

Select a local VPC to peer with
VPC ID (Requester)

vpc-0295d04f6ddec253b

VPC CIDRs for vpc-0295d04f6ddec253b

CIDR	Status	Status reason
10.0.0.0/16	Associated	-
172.168.0.0/16	Associated	-

Select another VPC to peer with
Account

My account
Another account

Region

This Region (ap-south-1)
Another Region

VPC ID (Accepter)

vpc-ba4b9ad1

Figure 3.6: *Setting up a peering connection from VPC Console*

Transit gateway

Managing the VPC peering connections can become very complex as the network grows primarily due to the peering mesh that gets created. In such complex networking scenarios, *transit gateway* can prove beneficial. A transit gateway is a regional network transit hub that can be used to interconnect the VPCs and the on-premises networks. Moreover, the transit gateway can be shared across multiple accounts using AWS **Resource Access Manager** (**RAM**) and can support cross region peering. Transit gateway supports a hub-spoke connection model, as shown in *Figure 3.7*, as follows:

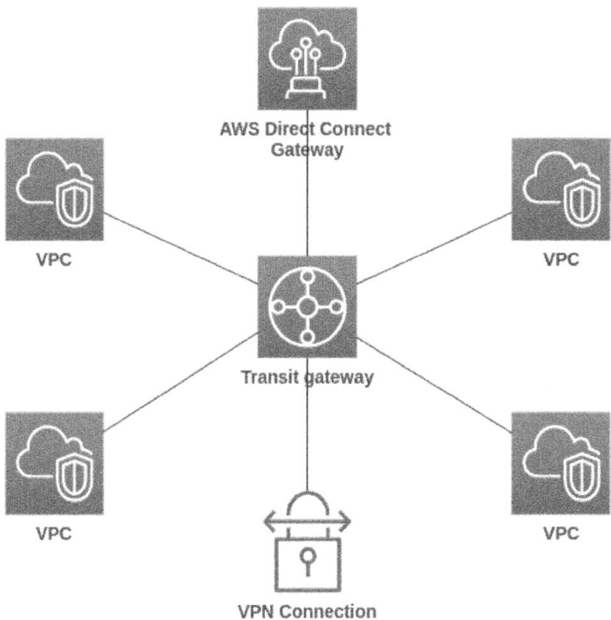

***Figure 3.7:** Hub-and-spoke connection model of a transit gateway*

Figure 3.7 shows the various types of *attachments* that can be attached with a transit gateway. These include one or more VPCs, an AWS Direct Connect gateway, a peering connection with another transit gateway, a VPN connection to a transit gateway, etc. Each attachment can be associated with exactly one route table. A route table, however, can be associated with zero or many attachments. Transit gateway has a default route table and supports additional route tables as well. A route table can include both, the dynamic as well as the static routes, and a route table entry can have any transit gateway attachment as the target.

Transit gateway enables us to design complex network architectures like central NAT gateway or central Internet gateway, where there is an egress VPC which is connected to a transit gateway and the traffic from the other VPCs must pass through the transit gateway into the egress VPC and then communicate with the Internet. However, these network architectures are outside the scope of this book.

Private communication with AWS services

While VPCs can communicate privately with each other via a VPC peering or transit gateway, there are often security requirements to connect privately with the AWS services from within a VPC. A VPC endpoint enables us to privately connect our VPC with the supported AWS services and *VPC endpoint services* (powered by AWS PrivateLink, described in a subsequent section), without requiring the traffic to leave the Amazon network. That is, there is no need for the public IP addresses, Internet gateway, NAT device, VPN connection or AWS Direct Connect. Essentially, the VPC endpoints are virtual devices that are horizontally scalable and highly available and comes primarily in two forms – *gateway type endpoints* and *interface type endpoints.* There is another type of VPC endpoint known as *Gateway Load Balancer endpoints* that are similar to the interface endpoints and serves as an entry point to intercept the traffic and route it to a service that has been configured using a Gateway Load Balancer. We will, however, focus our attention on the first two types.

Gateway endpoints

Gateway endpoints are available for Amazon S3 and Amazon DynamoDB only. A gateway endpoint is defined as a route table target for any traffic destined for the supported AWS services. Such traffic is routed through Amazon's private network. Gateway endpoints do not impose any additional costs. However, they do have certain limitations that should be considered. Some of the important limitations are as follows:

- Gateway endpoints are only supported within the same region. This means, the endpoint and the service must be in the same region.
- Gateway endpoints only support IPv4.
- Gateway endpoint connections cannot extend out of a VPC. This means, resources on the other end of a VPN or AWS Direct Connect connection, VPC peering, or Transit gateway cannot use the endpoint to integrate with the endpoint service.
- DNS resolution must be turned on in the VPC, so that the DNS requests to the supported AWS services are resolved correctly.

An extra layer of protection for a gateway endpoint is to attach a *custom endpoint policy* with the endpoint to control the access from the endpoint to the endpoint service. An endpoint policy is a resource-based IAM policy (refer to *Chapter 2: Identity and Access Management*) and does not override the identity policies or the service-specific policies. The default endpoint policy provides *full access* and looks like the following:

```
{
    "Statement": [
        {
            "Action": "*",
            "Effect": "Allow",
            "Resource": "*",
            "Principal": "*"
        }
    ]
}
```

To create a gateway endpoint for Amazon S3, we can use the following AWS CLI v2 command. The command attempts to create a **Gateway** endpoint in the **ap-south-1** region, for a given VPC ID and route table ID. To attach a custom endpoint policy document stored in a file named **policy.json**, we can use the **policy-document** option which can then point to that policy file (for example, **--policy-document file://policy.json**). Look at the following command:

```
$ aws ec2 create-vpc-endpoint --vpc-id <vpc-id>  \
  --vpc-endpoint-type Gateway --service-name com.amazonaws.ap-south-1.
s3 \
  --route-table-ids <route-table-id> \
```

Note that, to create a gateway endpoint for DynamoDB gateway endpoint service, only the service name will have to be changed to **com.amazonaws.ap-south-1.dynamodb**.

Amazon VPC Management Console provides a very intuitive interface for creating the endpoints and could prove to be very helpful when starting out with the VPC endpoints. To create a VPC endpoint from Management Console, go to VPC Console and select **Endpoints** under **VIRTUAL PRIVATE CLOUD**, from the left navigation panel. In the endpoints summary page, click on the **Create Endpoint** button. This opens the **Create Endpoint** page, as shown in *Figure 3.8* (partially), as follows:

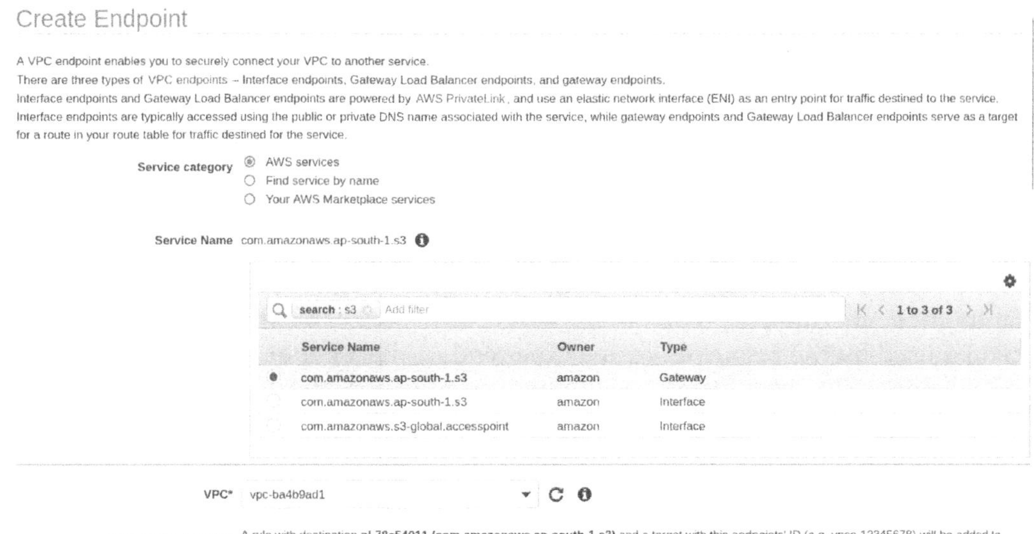

Figure 3.8: *Create a VPC endpoint from VPC Console*

As we can see, when **Service Category** is chosen as **AWS services**, the **Service Name** table shows both the Gateway as well as the Interface endpoint services. In *Figure 3.8*, we have filtered the table for S3 and have selected the S3 Gateway endpoint service. This graphical interface allows us to select the route table, as well as the endpoint policy document to be attached to the endpoint.

When a gateway endpoint is created, it essentially creates an AWS managed *prefix list* (a set of IPv4 or IPv6 address ranges) that corresponds to the gateway endpoint service in that region. The corresponding prefix list identifier takes the format **pl-xxxxxxx**. This prefix list ID is then added to the route table as a destination, with a target pointing to the VPC endpoint. Refer to *Figure 3.9* for a representative route table entry, as follows:

Destination	Target	Status
172.31.0.0/16	local	Active
[illegible]	[illegible]	Active
pl-78a54011	vpce-082d9d49699e01821	Active

Figure 3.9: *A route table entry with a prefix list ID as the destination and VPC endpoint as target*

Interface endpoints

An interface endpoint is an **elastic network interface** (**ENI**) with a private IP address, and it allows us to connect with the services powered by AWS PrivateLink. The private IP address belongs to the range of an IP address of a selected subnet and serves as an entry point for the traffic that are destined for the supported AWS services, service hosted by other AWS customer and partners in their VPCs, and supported AWS Marketplace Partner services. AWS Services like Amazon S3, AWS Lambda, Amazon API Gateway, Amazon EC2, Amazon ECR, Amazon ECS, Amazon RDS, AWS Secrets Manager etc., supports this type of VPC endpoint for private connectivity.

Interface endpoints are different from the gateway endpoints, in that they are billed and powered by AWS PrivateLink and leverages ENI. Additionally, an interface endpoint connection can extend out of a VPC. This means, the interface endpoint can be used by the resources on the other end of the VPN or AWS Direct Connect connections, VPC peering or transit gateway to communicate with the supported AWS services. Some of the limitations associated with interface endpoint are mentioned as follows:

- Only one subnet per AZ could be selected for each interface endpoint.
- Each interface endpoint, by default, supports a bandwidth of up to 10 Gbps per AZ and can burst up to 40 Gbps.
- Interface endpoints are supported within the same region only. This means, the endpoint and the service must be in the same region.
- Interface endpoints support IPv4 traffic only and they support TCP based traffic.

The security of an interface endpoint can be improved in the following two ways:

1. Attach a *custom endpoint policy* with the endpoint to control the access from the endpoint to the interface endpoint service (similar to a gateway endpoint).
2. Create and associate a *security group* with the ENI corresponding to the interface endpoint, to selectively allow the traffic through the ENI.

The following AWS CLI **v2** command can be used to create an interface endpoint for a representative AWS Service like Secrets Manager. The command enables us to connect with the Secrets Manager from our VPC, directly through a private endpoint. Note that, the private DNS is enabled by default for an interface endpoint; however, the flag (**private-dns-enabled**) has been explicitly used for clarity. Here's the AWS CLI **v2** command to create an Interface endpoint:

```
$ aws ec2 create-vpc-endpoint --vpc-id <vpc-id> \
 --vpc-endpoint-type Interface \
 --service-name com.amazonaws.ap-south-1.secretsmanager \
 --subnet-ids <subnet-id-1> <subnet-id-2> \
 --security-group-id <security-group-id>
 --private-dns-enabled
```

The output of the preceding command includes the DNS names that we can use to connect to the new interface endpoint. A portion of the sample output is given as follows:


```
{
  "VpcEndpoint": {
  ...
     "DnsEntries": [
     {
         "DnsName": "vpce-053972fdb75d5e757-28pg7i60.secretsmanager.ap-
south-1.vpce.amazonaws.com",
         "HostedZoneId": "Z2KVTB3ZLFM7JR"
     },
     {
         "DnsName": "vpce-053972fdb75d5e757-28pg7i60-ap-south-1b.
secretsmanager.ap-south-1.vpce.amazonaws.com",
         "HostedZoneId": "Z2KVTB3ZLFM7JR"
     },
     {
         "DnsName": "vpce-053972fdb85d5e757-28pg7i59-ap-south-1a.
```

```
secretsmanager.ap-south-1.vpce.amazonaws.com",
            "HostedZoneId": "Z2KVTB3ZLFM7JR"
        },
        {
            "DnsName": "secretsmanager.ap-south-1.amazonaws.com",
            "HostedZoneId": "ZONEIDPENDING"
        }
        ...
        }
```

By default, when a VPC private endpoint is created, a private hosted zone is automatically associated with the VPC that contains a record set, enabling us to privately invoke a supported AWS service, while still making requests to the service's default public endpoint DNS name. To use this feature, we must remember to enable the **DNS resolution** and **DNS hostnames** attributes in the VPC. With these settings in place, we can use the standard Secrets Manager endpoint DNS name for the region (like **secretsmanager.ap-south-1.amazonaws.com**). It will automatically resolve to the correct endpoint within the region VPC by leveraging the private DNS.

In cases where we don't enable the private DNS names, we can still access the Secrets Manager endpoint privately by using the fully qualified DNS name (like **vpce-053972fdb75d5e757-28pg7i60.secretsmanager.ap-south-1.vpce.amazonaws.com as shown in the DNS entries output of create-vpc-endpoint command**).

A note on AWS PrivateLink

AWS PrivateLink is a highly available and scalable technology that helps establish a private connectivity between VPC and the supported AWS services, VPC endpoint services hosted by other AWS accounts, and supported AWS Marketplace partner services. The PrivateLink traffic is never exposed to the Internet and is thus a comparatively secure way to access the AWS services and other VPC endpoint services. To leverage AWS PrivateLink, we must create a VPC endpoint for a chosen service. This essentially creates an ENI with a private IP address that acts as the entry point for the traffic that is destined for the service.

TIP: The following link provides the list of AWS services that integrate with AWS PrivateLink:

https://docs.aws.amazon.com/vpc/latest/privatelink/integrated-services-vpce-list.html

Figure 3.10 shows a simplified view of how the applications in a private subnet can access the representative AWS service (Amazon S3) leveraging the VPC interface endpoint, which is powered by AWS PrivateLink, as follows:

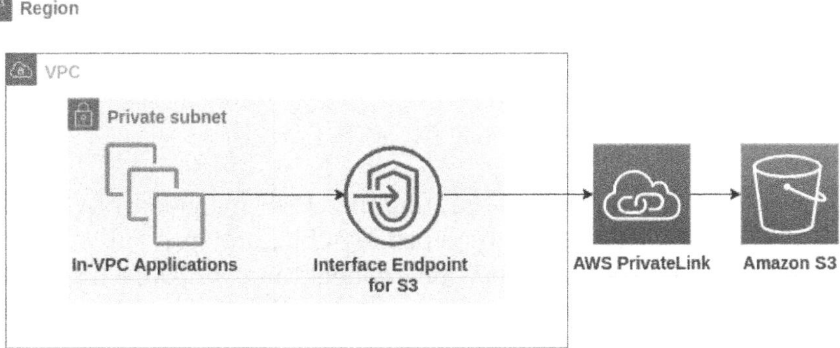

Figure 3.10: Schematic of how VPC interface endpoint works with AWS PrivateLink to achieve private connectivity

In case of custom endpoint services like a SaaS application provider deployed on AWS (endpoint service provider), the endpoint service will have to expose a network load balancer which will be on the other side of AWS PrivateLink and will distribute the traffic coming from multiple consumer VPC interface endpoints to the provider application nodes, as shown in *Figure 3.11*, as follows:

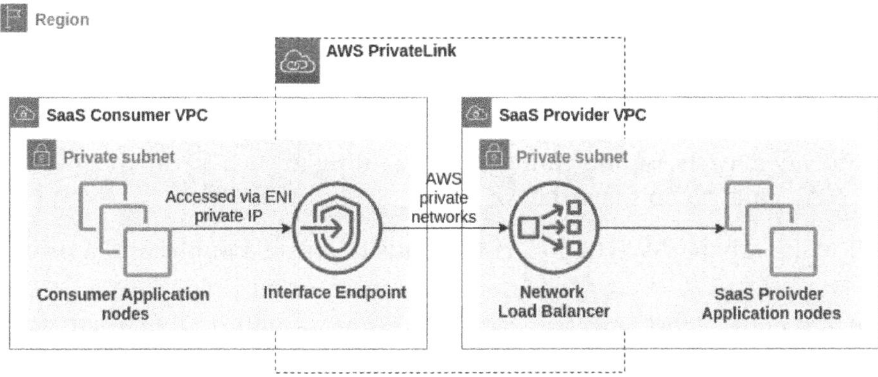

Figure 3.11: Schematic of how a VPC Endpoint Service (here a SaaS provider) works

NAT devices and egress-only Internet gateways

A **Network Address Translation** (**NAT**) device allows the instances in the private subnets to connect to the Internet, other VPCs, or the on-premises network, without the risk of receiving unsolicited inbound connection requests. Essentially, the source IPv4 address of the instances is replaced with the address of the NAT device during an outbound connection. When the response traffic is sent to the respective instances, the NAT device translates the addresses back to the original source IPv4 addresses. When it comes to using the NAT devices, we have two choices – use a managed NAT device (NAT gateway) or use our own NAT device on an EC2 instance. The NAT gateways are an obvious better choice owing to their better scalability, bandwidth, and less operational headache. However, we must note that the NAT devices are not supported for the IPv6 traffic, and we can use *egress-only Internet gateways* for this purpose.

NAT gateways

NAT gateway is a highly scalable, redundant, AWS managed NAT device. NAT gateways come in two connectivity types – public and private. With the public connectivity, the instances in the private subnets can connect to the Internet via a public NAT gateway (but cannot receive unsolicited VPC bound connections from the Internet). A public NAT gateway is created in a public subnet and is associated with an **elastic IP address (EIP)**. The traffic from the instances in the private subnets is routed to the Internet gateway for the VPC. With the public NAT gateways, the source IP addresses of the instances is replaced with the EIP of the NAT gateway.

On the other hand, a private NAT gateway is created in a private subnet and cannot be associated with an EIP or route traffic to the Internet gateway. It can, however, be used to connect the instances in the private subnets to the other VPCs or the on-premises network through a transit gateway or virtual private gateway and still get the benefits of NAT. A private NAT gateway replaces the private source IP addresses of the instances with the private IP address of the NAT gateway.

A NAT gateway is created in a specific AZ and is implemented with redundancy in that AZ. To create a NAT solution that can withstand an AZ failure, we can create a NAT gateway in each AZ and configure the routing in such a way that the resources use the NAT gateway in the same AZ.

The following are the AWS CLI v2 commands to create a public and a private NAT gateway:

```
# Create a public NAT gateway and specify the public subnet ID and
# allocation ID of the EIP to associate with the NAT gateway
$ aws ec2 create-nat-gateway --subnet-id <public-subnet-id> \
  --allocation-id <eip-alloc-id>

# Create a private NAT gateway and supply the private subnet ID
$ aws ec2 create-nat-gateway --subnet-id <private-subnet-id>
```

Note that, the NAT gateway ID can be used as targets to create the entries in the route table in order to route the traffic to the NAT gateway, as shown in *Figure 3.12*, as follows:

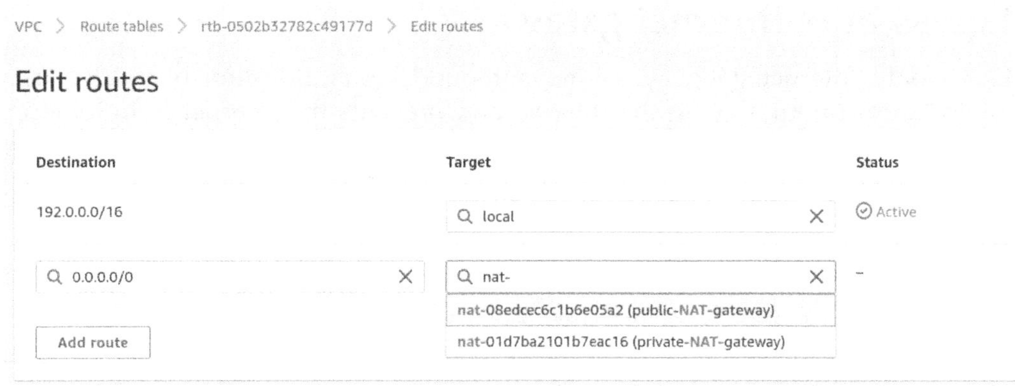

Figure 3.12: *Edit routes in a route table to route traffic to the NAT gateways*

NAT instance

NAT instance is basically an EC2 instance in a public subnet which has been configured to act as a NAT instance. The easiest way to get started with a NAT instance is to select a community AMI (by searching for **NAT**) and start an EC2 instance based on that AMI in a public subnet. The NAT instance will have its own public IP address or an EIP will have to be associated with the instance. For security reasons, the instance will have to be placed behind an appropriate security group which will generally allow HTTP/HTTPS traffic. Additionally, *source/destination check* will have to be disabled for the NAT instance. By default, each EC2 instance performs a source/destination check, whereby the instance must be the source or destination for each traffic that it sends or receives. However, a NAT instance should be able to send or receive traffic when it is not the source or destination itself. The following AWS CLI command can be used to disable the source/destination check:

```
$ aws ec2 modify-instance-attribute --instance-id=<instance-id> \
  --no-source-dest-check
```

To route the traffic from the private subnets to the NAT instance, we will have to make changes to the route table associated with the private subnets to target the NAT instance (identified by the NAT instance ID).

We must note that the NAT AMI is built on the last version of Amazon Linux (2018.03) and has reached its end of life on 2020-12-31 and as such, will not receive any regular updates except critical security patches. While we can create our own AMIs to run NAT, the recommended strategy is to use the NAT gateways instead. Also, from a design perspective, the challenge with the NAT instance is that it introduces a single point of failure, unless we explicitly take appropriate measures to create the redundancy on our own.

Egress-only Internet gateways

Egress-only Internet gateways allow outbound communication over IPv6 from the instances in our VPC to the Internet and prevents the Internet from initiating unsolicited IPv6 connections to our instances. Egress-only Internet gateways are horizontally scaled, redundant, and are highly available VPC components.

Firewalls

Amazon VPC supports several types of firewalls, that can be deployed on the perimeter, associated with subnets and even with the instances. We could also install the host-based firewalls in the EC2 instances; however, that is outside the scope of this book.

Security groups

A security group is essentially a virtual firewall for the EC2 instances (they are however, used with the other AWS resources as well, like Elastic Load Balancers) that can control both the inbound and the outbound traffic to/from the instances. The security groups are associated with the network interfaces. In case of the EC2 instances, they are attached with the primary network interface (**`eth0`**), by default.

Let's summarize the important characteristics of security groups, as follows:

- Security groups are associated with the EC2 instances or network interfaces (including elastic network interface or ENI).
- Security groups are *stateful*, which means, if an inbound traffic is allowed by the inbound rules, then the response to that traffic will be automatically allowed regardless of the outbound rules. Similarly, if an outbound traffic is allowed by the outbound rules, then the response to that traffic will be allowed, regardless of the inbound rules.
- Security groups support only "allow" rules and cannot be used to explicitly "deny" a traffic. As a corollary, if a traffic is not explicitly allowed, then it will be denied by default, with an implicit deny rule.
- Traffic filtering in the security groups is based on protocols, port numbers, and source/destination as follows:
    - Commonly used protocols are TCP, UDP, ICMP, or All (to signify all protocols).
    - Port numbers can be represented as a single number (value between 0 to 65535) or a port range (like 0-65535).
    - Source and destination can be represented by a single IPv4 or IPv6 address, or a range of IPv4 or IPv6 address in the CIDR block notation, or an ID of the prefix list (described in the VPC gateway endpoints section), or another security group identified by its ID.

- When a security group is created, it has no inbound rules by default. However, it has an outbound rule that allows all the outbound traffic. Ideally, this must be deleted, and a new restrictive outbound rule should be created.
- In case of an inbound traffic, all the inbound rules are evaluated before deciding whether to allow the traffic. Similarly, for an outbound traffic, all the outbound rules are evaluated before deciding whether to allow the traffic.

The default VPC in each AWS Region is assigned a default security group named "default." If any instance or network interface is not assigned a security group explicitly, the default security group of the VPC is assigned to it. If we look into the inbound and outbound rules of this default security group, we will notice that it allows all the inbound traffic from the network interfaces and instances that are assigned to the same security group (identified by the security group ID), as shown in *Figure 3.13*, as follows:

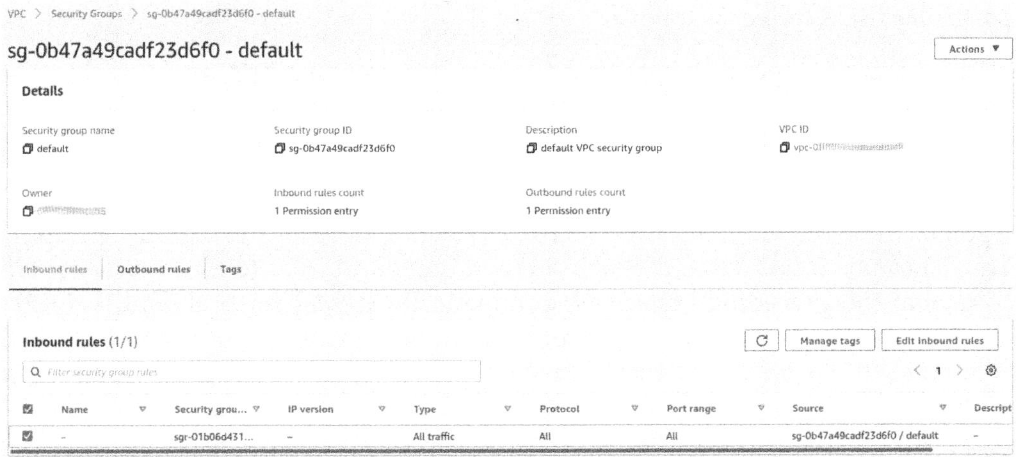

Figure 3.13: *Default security group's inbound rules*

However, the outbound rule is more lenient and allows all the outbound traffic, as shown in *Figure 3.14*, as follows:

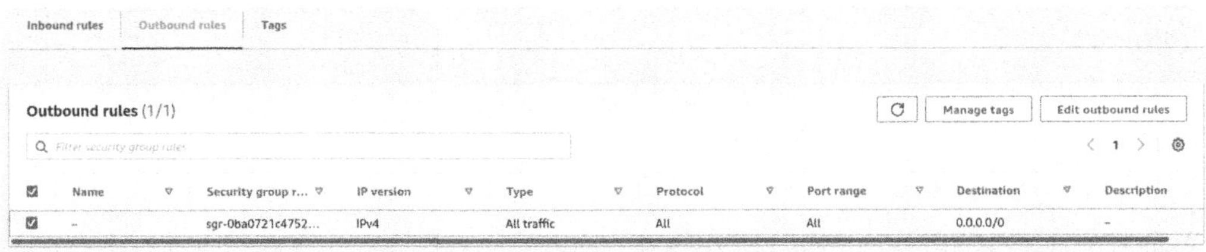

Figure 3.14: *Default security group's outbound rules*

While the default security group is a good starting point, we should seriously consider creating custom security groups which can be fine-tuned for our specific purposes.

It is simple to create a security group and manage the inbound and outbound rules by selecting **Security Groups** under the **SECURITY** option on the left navigation panel of the VPC Console (or from the EC2 Console under **Network & Security | Security Groups** on the left navigation panel). The readers are encouraged to perform these actions from the VPC Console on their own.

> **We can reference other security groups (by their ID) as Source in the inbound rules and Destination in the outbound rules of a security group. This is a very powerful feature and is highly recommended.**

Now, let's create a custom security group with AWS CLI. We will assume that this security group allows the inbound HTTPS traffic on port **443** from an ELB security group (identified by the security group ID) and SSH traffic on port **22** from a particular CIDR range, as follows:

```
# Create a new security group named sg_webservers for an existing VPC
$ aws ec2 create-security-group --group-name "sg_webservers" \
  --description "Web Servers" --vpc-id <vpc-id>
```

Upon success, this command produces an output that gives the security group ID. This ID can be used to add the inbound and outbound rules to the security group. Note that the preceding command automatically creates an outbound rule that allows all the traffic to any destination (identified by the CIDR range 0.0.0.0/0). A representative output of the **create-security-group** command is shown as follows:

```
{
    "GroupId": "sg-0407d3a7564d4efc4"
}
```

Now, let's add the inbound and outbound rules to the newly created security group, identified by **GroupId** in the output of the **create-security-group** command as follows:

```
# Add inbound rule that allows HTTPS (TCP) traffic on port 443 from an
# existing security group associated with an elastic load balancer
# identified by elb-sg-id
$ aws ec2 authorize-security-group-ingress \
    --group-id sg-0407d3a7564d4efc4 \
    --protocol tcp \
```

```
    --port 443 \
    --source-group <elb-sg-id>
# Add another inbound rule that allows SSH (TCP) traffic on port 22 from a
# representative CIDR range
$ aws ec2 authorize-security-group-ingress \
    --group-id sg-0407d3a7564d4efc4 \
    --protocol tcp \
    --port 22 \
    --cidr 220.221.222.0/24
```

Similarly, we can create the outbound rules for the security group with the **authorize-security-group-egress** subcommand. Moreover, in order to remove an inbound or outbound rule from a security group, we can use the corresponding **revoke-security-group-ingress**" and "**revoke-security-group-egress** subcommands.

Finally, to apply the security group to an EC2 instance (identified by instance ID), we can use the following command. However, since this involves working primarily with an EC2 instance, we must use a profile (say **ec2.admin**) that corresponds to a user with **AmazonEC2FullAccess** or similar permissions, as follows:

```
$ aws ec2 modify-instance-attribute \
  --instance-id <instance-id> \
  --groups sg-03d3c28779404d166 --profile ec2.admin
```

Network Access Control Lists

Network Access Control List, or NACL in short, is yet another fundamental firewall construct within an Amazon VPC. When used properly, they can filter the unwanted and malicious traffic at the subnet level very effectively.

NACLs differ from the security groups in many important respects. Let's summarize the characteristics of a NACL, as follows:

- NACLs are associated with subnets in a VPC. Each subnet in a VPC must be associated with a single NACL. If not explicitly associated with an NACL, the subnet gets automatically associated with the default NACL. An NACL however, can be associated with more than one subnet.
- NACLs are *stateless*, that is, if an inbound traffic is allowed by the inbound rules, then the response to that particular traffic will have to be explicitly allowed in the outbound rules. Similarly, if an outbound traffic is allowed by the outbound rules, then the response to that traffic will have to be explicitly allowed in the inbound rules.

- NACLs support both the "allow" and the "deny" rules and as such can be used to explicitly "deny" a traffic.
- A NACL filters the traffic based on the protocols, port numbers, and source/ destination, as follows:
  - Commonly used protocols are TCP, UDP, ICMP, SMTP, telnet, etc.
  - Port numbers can be represented as a single number (value between 0 to 65535) or a port range (like 0-65535).
  - The source for the inbound rules and destination for the outbound rules can be represented by the CIDR ranges.
- When a custom NACL is created, by default, it denies all the inbound as well as the outbound traffic, unless the rules are explicitly added to allow traffic.
- A NACL contains a numbered list of rules which are evaluated in order, starting with the lowest numbered rule (which has the highest priority) to determine whether the traffic is allowed in or out of the associated subnets.

Every VPC has a default NACL that allows all the inbound and outbound traffic. Subnets in a VPC are associated with this default NACL, unless explicitly associated with a custom NACL. *Figure 3.15* shows the inbound rules of the default NACL in a VPC. NACLs can be accessed from the **Network ACLs** option under **SECURITY** from the left navigation panel in the VPC Console. Notice that each rule has a corresponding rule number and that the "allow" rule has a rule number 100 and precedes the default "deny" rule with * as the rule number which has an underlying value of 32767 with the lowest priority. As such, the overall effect is that of "allow" for all traffic on all ports. Refer to *Figure 3.15*, as follows:

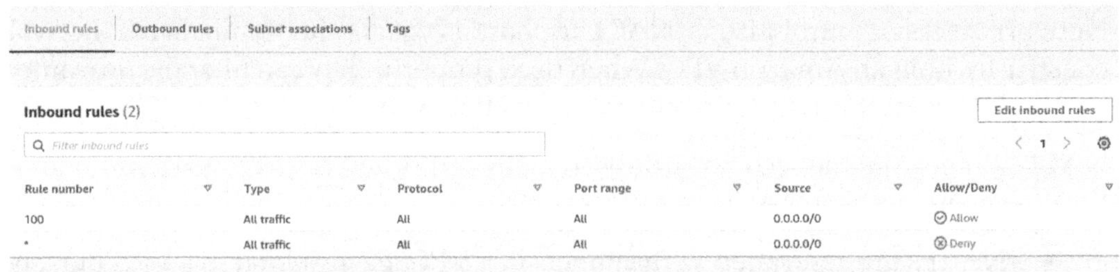

Figure 3.15: *Inbound rules of default NACL*

Similarly, each rule in the outbound rules (shown in *Figure 3.16*) of the default NACL has a rule number. The "allow" rule with rule number 100 takes precedence when compared with the default "deny" rule and effectively all the outbound traffic is allowed on all the ports. Refer to *Figure 3.16* as follows:

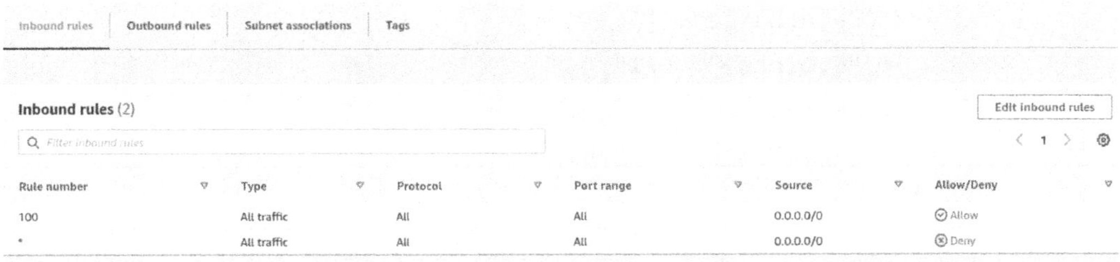

Inbound rules | Outbound rules | Subnet associations | Tags

Inbound rules (2) Edit inbound rules

Filter inbound rules

Rule number	Type	Protocol	Port range	Source	Allow/Deny
100	All traffic	All	All	0.0.0.0/0	Allow
*	All traffic	All	All	0.0.0.0/0	Deny

Figure 3.16: *Outbound rules of default NACL*

For all practical purposes, the default NACL can be used as-is. However, the "allow-all" strategy is too open and we might have to create custom NACLs with the inbound/outbound rules. As with the security groups, its fairly simple to create and manage NACLs from the VPC Console, and in fact, in many ways, it is similar to the security groups.

Let's use AWS CLI to create a custom NACL and associate it with a VPC (identified by **`vpc-id`**). When a custom NACL is created, a default inbound and outbound deny rule gets associated with it. In essence, all the inbound and outbound traffic is denied when a custom NACL is created. We must explicitly add/update the rules to ensure that it meets our requirements. Here's the CLI command to create a NACL:

```
$ aws ec2 create-network-acl --vpc-id <vpc-id>
```

The preceding command will produce a representative output as follows: .

```
{
    "NetworkAcl": {
        "Associations": [],
        "Entries": [
            {
                "CidrBlock": "0.0.0.0/0",
                "Egress": true,
                "IcmpTypeCode": {},
                "PortRange": {},
                "Protocol": "-1",
                "RuleAction": "deny",
                "RuleNumber": 32767
            },
            {
                "CidrBlock": "0.0.0.0/0",
                "Egress": false,
                "IcmpTypeCode": {},
```

```
                "PortRange": {},
                "Protocol": "-1",
                "RuleAction": "deny",
                "RuleNumber": 32767
            }
        ],
        "IsDefault": false,
        "NetworkAclId": "acl-0e91d5a4ec013caf8",
        "Tags": [],
        "VpcId": "vpc-029XXXXXXXXXXXXXXX",
        "OwnerId": "123456789111"
    }
}
```

As evident, the output provides details about the default inbound and outbound deny rules that get created automatically. Each receives the highest rule number 32767 (with the lowest priority). With the custom NACL created (with default inbound and outbound rules), let's add an inbound rule to the newly created NACL that allows the SSH traffic on port **22** from a specific representative CIDR block. Also, NACL being stateless, we will have to ensure that the response traffic is explicitly allowed in the outbound rule. To allow this response, we will essentially allow the outbound TCP traffic on the port range 1024-65535 (TCP high ports). Note that the protocol number **6** represents TCP. Similarly, UDP is **17** and ICMP is **1** and value **-1** is used to represent **All** protocols. Here are the commands to add ingress and egress rules to the NACL:

```
$ aws ec2 create-network-acl-entry --network-acl-id acl-
0e91d5a4ec013caf8 \
--ingress --rule-number 100 --protocol 6 \
--port-range From=22,To=22 --cidr-block 220.221.222.0/24 \
--rule-action allow

$ aws ec2 create-network-acl-entry --network-acl-id acl-
0e91d5a4ec013caf8 \
--egress --rule-number 100 --protocol 6 \
--port-range From=1024,To=65535 --cidr-block 220.221.222.0/24 \
--rule-action allow
```

With these rules in place, all the EC2 instances in the associated subnets of this NACL will receive the inbound SSH traffic on port **22** from a specific CIDR range. However, the security groups for each of these instances might decide to disallow such traffic. Since the subnets are, by default, associated with the default NACL, we can use the **replace-network-acl-association** subcommand to replace the existing association of a subnet (identified by the **acl** association id), with a new association pertaining to the newly created NACL (identified by **acl-id**), as follows:

```
$ aws ec2 replace-network-acl-association \
--association-id <aclassoc-id> \
--network-acl-id <acl-id>
```

The existing association IDs can be retrieved from the output of the **describe-network-acls** subcommand, shown as follows:

```
$ aws ec2 describe-network-acls --network-acl-ids <acl-id>
```

DNS Firewall

Route 53 Resolver DNS Firewall is an AWS managed firewall that enables us to define the rule groups with the domain name filtering rules. Essentially, DNS Firewall provides granular level control over the DNS querying by resources within Amazon VPC. As such, DNS Firewall can be used to block the DNS queries made for the malicious domains and allow the queries for the trusted ones. We can create both *blocklists* and *allowlists* (stricter option) for the domains with DNS Firewall.

The first step is to create a domain list. A domain list, as the name suggests, is a reusable set of domain specifications that can be used in a DNS Firewall rule. A DNS Firewall rule then becomes part of a DNS Firewall rule group. To create a domain list, we will have to select the **Domain Lists** option under **DNS FIREWALL** from the left navigation panel in the VPC Console. Then, on the **Domain lists** page, we will have to click on the **Add domain list** button. This opens the **Add domain list** page, as shown in *Figure 3.17*. We must provide a name for the domain list and specify the set of domain names for the domain list. Finally, we will click on the

Add domain list button which creates a custom domain list. Refer to *Figure 3.17* as follows:

Figure 3.17: Create a custom domain list from VPC Console > DNS Firewall

AWS managed domain lists like **AWSManagedDomainsMalwareDomainList** and **AWSManagedDomainsBotnetCommandandControl** are also made available for getting started with the DNS Firewall (from the **Domain lists** page).

Once we have the domain list (custom or AWS managed), we can then create a rule group and add one or more rules that utilize the domain lists. To create a rule group, we must select the **Rule Groups** option under **DNS FIREWALL** on the left navigation panel of the VPC Console. This opens the **Rule groups** summary page. We can then click on the "Add rule group" button to open the **Add rule group** wizard. Next, we must specify the name and description of the rule group and click on the **Next** button. On the next page, we must add one or more rules to the rule group from the **Add rules** page, as shown in *Figure 3.18* (partial snapshot). It is here, that we must select the domain list (custom or AWS managed) and specify an action if the rule matches. The actions can be **ALLOW**, **BLOCK**, or **ALERT**. If **BLOCK** is selected as an action, we can also specify the type of DNS query response to send. Refer to *Figure 3.18* as follows:

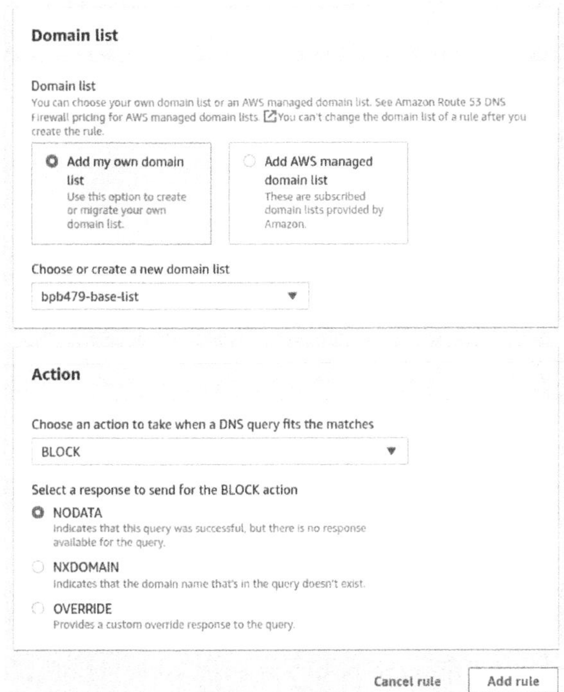

Figure 3.18: *Create a custom domain list from VPC Console > DNS Firewall*

In the subsequent pages, we must select the rule priority (in case there are multiple rules in the rule group), add tags optionally, and finally review the configurations made so far and create the rule group.

Once the rule group is created, the final step is to associate them with one or more VPCs. To do so, we must click on the rule group (in the **Rule groups** summary page) and in the **Associate VPCs** tab, as shown in *Figure 3.19*, click on the **Associate VPC** button to associate the rule group with one or more VPCs, as follows:

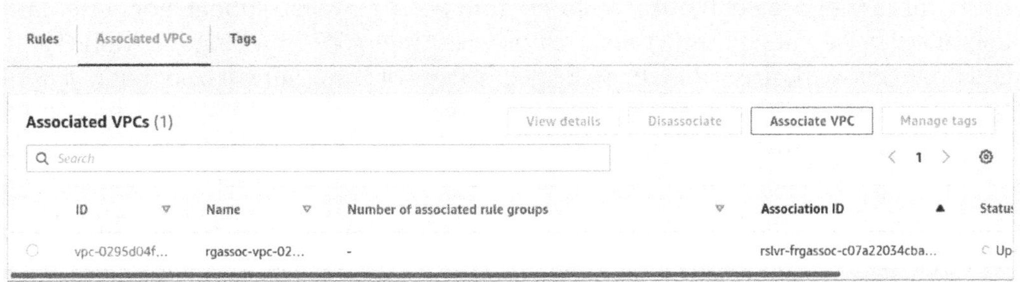

Figure 3.19: *Associate VPCs with a DNS Firewall rule group*

The rule groups can be shared across multiple accounts with the help of AWS Resource Access Manager (RAM). This helps create a consistent DNS query behavior across the organization. Moreover, the rule groups can be managed in AWS Firewall Manager and used across AWS Organizations.

AWS Network Firewall

We already know that NACL works at the subnet level and the security groups work at the instance level. With AWS Network Firewall, we can filter the traffic at the VPC perimeter, which means, we can use this managed firewall service to filter the traffic going to or coming out of an Internet gateway, NAT gateway, VPN connection, or AWS Direct Connect connection. It can serve as a useful intrusion detection and prevention service (IDS/IPS).

The following are the components of a network firewall:

- **Rule Group**: Rule group is a reusable collection of stateless or stateful rules that defines the inspection and traffic filtering criteria and actions to take (like allow or drop packets) when the criteria match. In addition to the common stateful rules like 5-tuple (protocol, source/destination IP, and source/destination port), domain list, etc., the rule groups also support *Suricata compatible IPS rules* (Suricata is an open-sourced threat detection engine).
- **Firewall Policy**: A firewall policy is a reusable set of rule groups along with the policy behavior configuration.
- **Firewall**: An instance of a firewall associates the single firewall policy to the VPC that we want to protect.

AWS Network Firewall uses *capacity units* to control the resources required to process the rule groups and firewall policy. As such, each rule group has a capacity setting reserved for it in the firewall policy in which it gets added.

We must note that installing and using a network firewall requires that we create subnets (in our VPC) in each AZ where we want to have the firewall endpoint. Such subnets are reserved exclusively for AWS Network Firewall, since a firewall endpoint cannot protect the applications running in the same subnet. For better fault tolerance, these subnets must span across multiple AZs in a single region. While creating a network firewall, we must specify each of these subnets, so that a *network endpoint* gets created in each. These endpoints in turn, can monitor and protect the resources in the other subnets whose traffic is routed through the firewall subnet.

Additionally, to route the traffic from/to the perimeter components like Internet gateway or NAT gateway into/from the other subnets through the firewall subnet, we must make the necessary changes to the corresponding routing tables. Essentially, the routing table configurations should insert the firewall between the subnets that we want to protect and the perimeter components. *Figure 3.20* shows a simplified diagram to visualize this interaction, as follows:

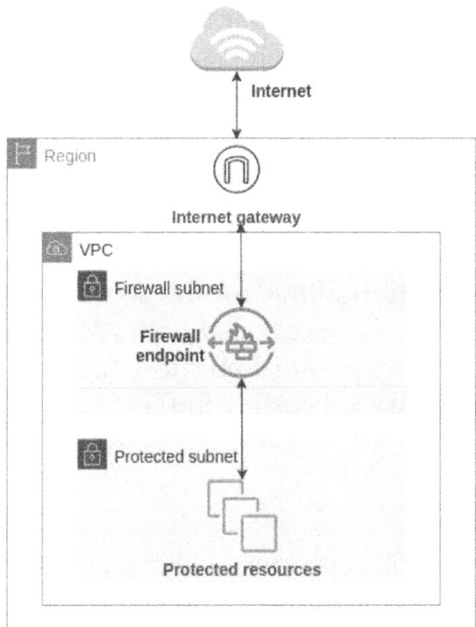

Figure 3.20: *Sample deployment of AWS Network Firewall*

The virtual firewall instance created by AWS Network Firewall, leverages the stateless and stateful rule engines to inspect the network packets. The firewall policy defines the packet inspection rules. First, the *stateless rule engine* inspects the packet against the configured stateless rules. Depending on the inspection criteria and firewall policy settings, the stateless rule engine can either drop the packet, pass it to the destination, or forward it to the stateful rule engine. The *stateful rule engine*, in turn, inspects the packet and either drops it or passes it to the destination, depending on the configured stateful rules.

AWS Network Firewall has integrations with AWS Firewall Manager (discussed in a subsequent section), and thus, Firewall Manager could be used to centrally manage and configure Network Firewall across multiple accounts and applications within AWS Organization.

In AWS Management Console, the AWS Network Firewall related options are available under **`NETWORK FIREWALL`** on the left navigation panel of the VPC Console. AWS CLI V2 also provides the necessary CLI commands grouped under the **`network-firewall`** command. The readers are encouraged to try the AWS Network Firewall features on their own.

A note on AWS Firewall Manager

AWS Firewall Manager is a one-stop service for the administration and maintenance of several types of protection like AWS WAF, AWS Shield (Advanced), VPC security groups, AWS Network Firewall, DNS Firewall, etc. AWS Firewall Manager allows us to setup these types of protection from the Firewall Manager Console, and then applies them across all the accounts and resources. Firewall Manager also takes the responsibility of applying these types of protection when new resources are added. As such, AWS Firewall Manager helps keep tighter security control and compliance across multiple accounts or throughout an organization.

We can use AWS Firewall Manager to view the compliance status for all the accounts and resources of an organization in scope of a Firewall Manager policy. Firewall Manager also creates relevant findings for the accounts/resources that are out-of-compliance. Firewall Manager is integrated with AWS Security Hub and can send the findings directly to Security Hub (refer to *Chapter 6: Logging, Monitoring and Auditing* for details around AWS Security Hub).

Traffic mirroring

Amazon VPC supports traffic mirroring which can be used to copy the network traffic (both inbound and outbound) from ENI attached to the Amazon EC2 instances and send them to a *target*, which is often a security and/or monitoring appliance. Traffic mirroring can thus help with the root cause analysis of a network performance issue, reverse engineering sophisticated network attacks, packet inspection, threat monitoring, etc. We can apply mirror *filters* (a set of inbound and outbound traffic rules) to define the mirrored traffic. Filtering could be done based on the traffic direction (inbound/outbound), action (accept/reject), protocol, source/destination port range, source/destination CIDR block. Traffic mirroring establishes a *session* from the source ENI to the target and applies relevant filters on the mirroring process.

The following are some of the essential considerations for implementing traffic mirroring:

- The source and the target could be in the same VPC or in a different VPC (even belonging to a different AWS Account), connected via intra-region VPC peering or transit gateway.
- Traffic mirror target could be network interfaces or **Network Load Balancers** (**NLB**) with a UDP listener on port `4789`. NLB can help to send mirrored traffic across zones.
- Mirrored traffic is encapsulated in the VXLAN header. As such, if targets receive mirrored traffic directly, they must be able to parse the VXLAN encapsulated packets.
- Security group corresponding to the source ENI and security group attached to the target must allow the UDP traffic on port `4789`.

Traffic mirroring is available under `TRAFFIC MIRRORING` on the left navigation panel of the VPC Console. From here, we can easily create and manage `Mirror Targets`, `Mirror Filters`, and `Mirror Sessions`.

Patch management

Appropriate patch management is crucial in improving the security posture of the applications deployed on AWS. AWS Systems Manager's Patch Manager capability centralizes the patch management and automates the process of patching *managed instances*. Patch Manager can be used to apply patches to both the operating systems as well as the applications. We can use default *patch baselines* or create custom ones. Patching operation may be scheduled to run as a Systems Manager maintenance window or on-demand. The instances can be logically grouped into *patch groups* by leveraging the EC2 instance tags. Patch Manager can scan the instances, report any non-compliance, and push these reports to AWS Security Hub (if enabled).

A patch baseline defines which patches are approved or rejected for our environment. There are several pre-defined patch baselines for the different operating systems which can be used. However, custom patch baselines offer more control over the patches and one can also create custom patch baselines and mark them as default for a patch group. *Figure 3.21* shows some of the existing patch baselines available from AWS Systems Manager – **`Patch Manager | Patch baselines`** (tab), as follows:

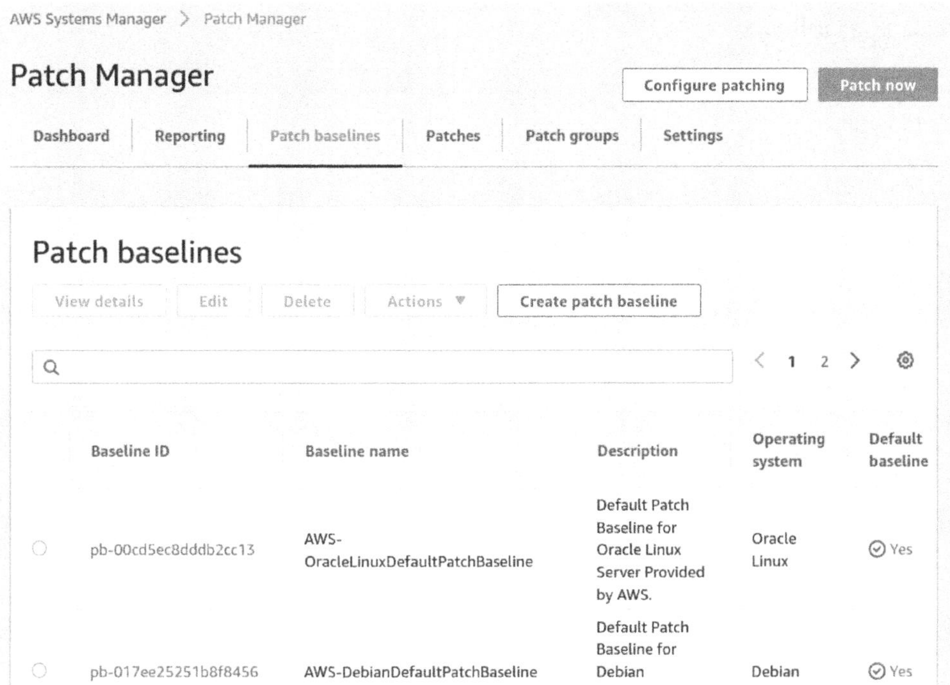

Figure 3.21: *Existing patch baselines*

The easiest way to create a patch group is to create a tag for the identified EC2 instances or AWS Systems Manager managed instances, with a key named **`Patch Group`** and a value representing the patch group, say **`Development`**. Note that a managed instance is a machine configured for AWS Systems Manager like the EC2 instances or the on-premise instances. Let us assume, we have two **Amazon Linux 2** based EC2 instances that meets the following criteria:

- Carries a tag with key=*Patch Group* and value=*Development.*
- IAM role is attached to the instances, which in turn, is associated with the permission policy named **AmazonSSMManagedInstanceCore**.
- Instances have Amazon SSM agent installed and running in them.

Amazon Linux 2 ships with the pre-installed Amazon SSM Agent, hence there is no need to install the agent separately.

> **TIP: The following link provides the details on Amazon SSM agent including the process of manual installation:**
>
> **https://docs.aws.amazon.com/systems-manager/latest/userguide/ssm-agent.html**

Figure 3.22 shows the two EC2 (managed) instances on the **Fleet Manager** page under **Node Management** from the left navigation panel of AWS System Manager Console, as follows:

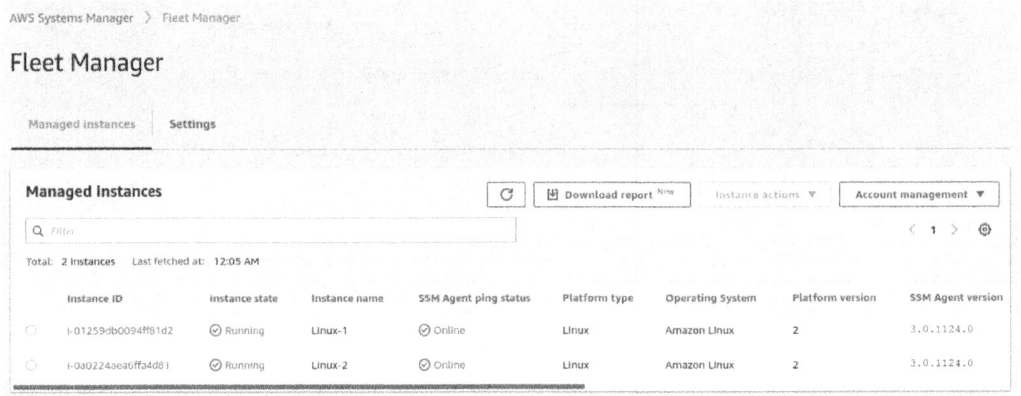

Figure 3.22: *Managed instances on the Fleet Manager page*

The next step is to modify the patch group of a patch baseline. For that purpose, we select the patch baseline corresponding to Amazon Linux 2 from the **Patch baselines** tab on the Patch Manager page. Once we are in the baseline page, we must click on the **Actions** button and select **Modify patch groups**. This will open the **Modify patch groups** page, as shown in *Figure 3.23*. We add the new patch group named **Development** and click on **Close** on this page, as follows:

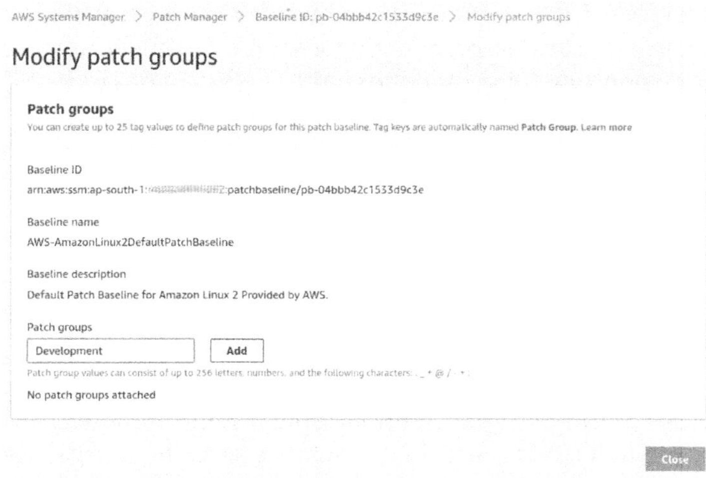

***Figure 3.23:** Modify the patch group of a patch baseline*

Next, to configure patching, we must click on the **`Configure patching`** button on the **`Patch Manager`** page. *Figure 3.24* shows the portion of the **`Configure patching`** page, where we can select the **`Select a patch group`** option and specify the patch group name (**`Development`**), as follows:

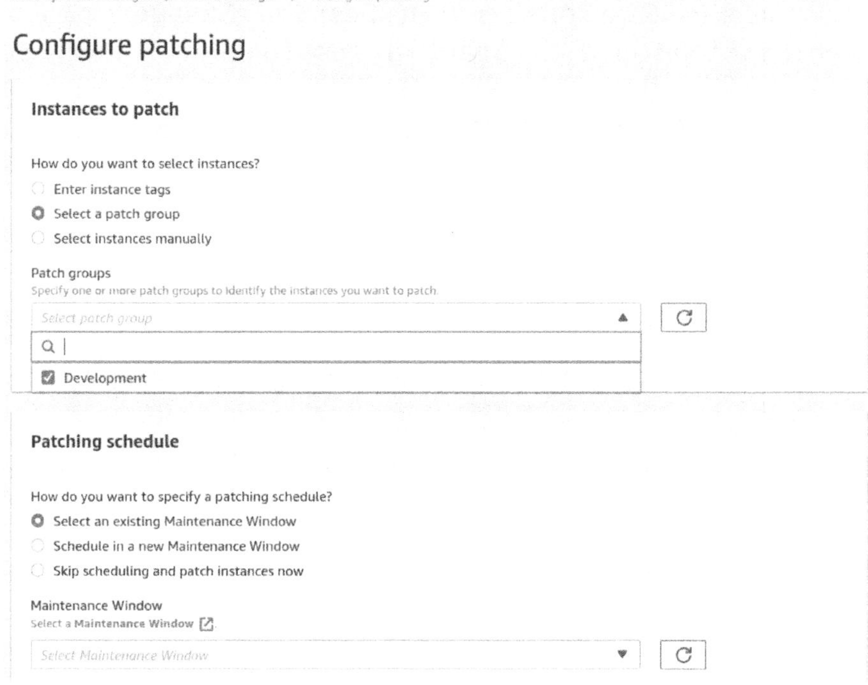

***Figure 3.24:** Configure patching*

By doing so, we select the instances in the patch group for patching. We can also schedule the patch or run the patching operation on-demand and select the patch operation (the options are **`Scan and install`** and **`Scan only`**).

The instance patching summary can be seen from the **`Reporting`** tab in AWS Systems Manager – Patch Manager Console. The details are also accessible from this page and can be exported to Amazon S3.

Secure SSH and RDP session management

AWS Systems Manager's Session Manager capability can improve the instance security by limiting the surface area of attacks. Session Manager enables us to get the RDP/SSH access to the instances without opening the **Remote Desktop Protocol (RDP)** or **Secure Shell (SSH)** ports in the instance security groups. Session Manager also provides secured and auditable sessions. Essentially, there is no need to maintain bastion hosts, manage SSH keys, etc.

Assuming that we are using a Session Manager supported operating system with the SSM agent installed in the instance and having started the instance with an IAM role that has permissions to start the SSM sessions (for example AWS managed IAM policy like **`AmazonSSMManagedInstanceCore`**), we should be able to start the sessions from AWS Systems Manager – Session Manager Console, as shown in *Figure 3.25*. Under the **`Sessions`** tab on the **`Session Manager`** page, click on the **`Start Session`** button. The **`Start a session`** page shows the managed instances to establish a browser-based session. We can select the instances and click on the **`Start session`** button, as shown in *Figure 3.25* as follows:

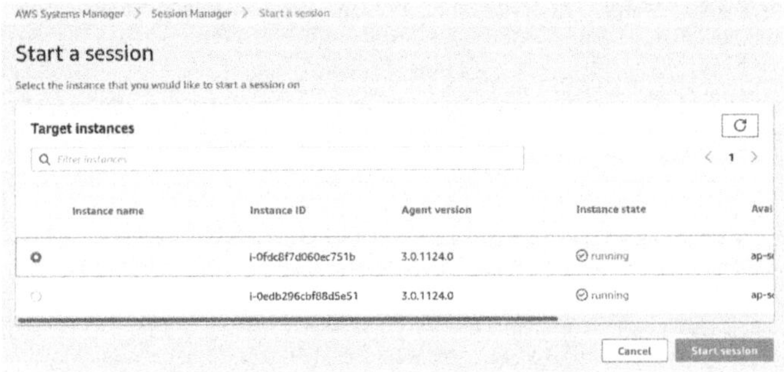

Figure 3.25: *Start a session with a managed instance*

The vital aspect of this session management is that the access control mechanism is solely based on IAM. We can control the access to the instances via the IAM policies and users; no need to distribute the SSH keys, etc. Access could be limited to a pre-defined maintenance window by using the date-based condition operator in an IAM policy. The users can start the sessions from Session Manager Console, EC2 Console, AWS CLI, or any combination of the three.

TIP: The following link provides the sample IAM policies that can be created to allow the users or groups to access Session Manager:

https://docs.aws.amazon.com/systems-manager/latest/userguide/getting-started-restrict-access-quickstart.html

To start the SSM sessionsvia AWS CLI, we must install the Session Manager plugin for AWS CLI. This plugin can be installed (in Ubuntu) using the following commands:

```
# Download Session Manager plugin for AWS CLI
$ curl "https://s3.amazonaws.com/session-manager-downloads/plugin/
latest/ubuntu_64bit/session-manager-plugin.deb" -o "session-manager-
plugin.deb"

# Install the plugin
$ sudo dpkg -i session-manager-plugin.deb

# Verify the installation- If installed correctly, this command should show
# a message like- The Session Manager plugin was installed successfully.
$ session-manager-plugin
```

TIP: The following link provides the details on how to install the Session Manager plugin for AWS CLI, in the different operating systems:

https://docs.aws.amazon.com/systems-manager/latest/userguide/session-manager-working-with-install-plugin.html

Now, with the Session Manager plugin installed, we can start a session by using the following AWS CLI command:

$ aws ssm start-session **--target <ec2-instance-id> --profile session-user**

Note that, we must specify the target which is an EC2 instance ID and ensure to use a profile (here **`session-user`**) that corresponds to a user that has the relevant **`ssm:StartSession`** permission on that instance.

IP filtering

Filtering or blocking the IP addresses is a commonly used technique to reject the traffic from the IP addresses that are known to have a low/bad IP reputation or have been previously flagged as malicious or harmful actors. In AWS, IP blocking could be carried out in several ways.

AWS WAF Rule based on IP set

AWS **Web Application Firewall (WAF)** has been discussed in *Chapter 5: Application Security*; however, in this section, we will see how AWS WAF can be leveraged to create a web ACL (Access Control List) that can block a set of IP addresses. The advantage of using a web ACL to block the IP addresses is that the same web ACL could be reused with the regional resources like Application Load Balancers and APIs published on Amazon API Gateway. The following steps explain how to create an IP blocking rule in AWS WAF:

1. In AWS WAF & Shield Console, we select **`AWS WAF | IP sets`** from the left navigation panel, and on the **`IP sets`** page, we must click on the **`Create IP set`** button.
2. On the **`Create IP set`** page, we must provide the name and description of the IP set, select the appropriate region where this IP set will get created, select the IP version for the IP set, and paste the IP addresses – one IP address per line in the CIDR format. *Figure 3.26* shows a snapshot of how to create an IP set, as follows:

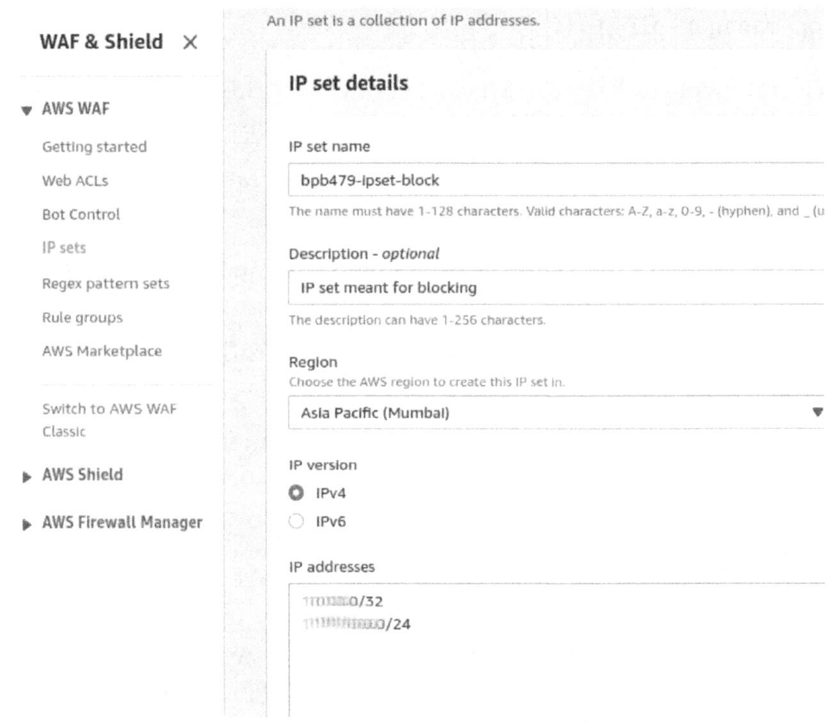

Figure 3.26: Creation of IP set from AWS WAF & Shield Console

3. Next, we click on the **`Create IP set`** button. This will create the new IP set in the selected AWS region and will appear in the **`AWS WAF | IP sets`** page.

4. Once the IP set has been created, the next step is to create the Web ACL. To do so, we will select **`AWS WAF | Web ACLs`** from the left navigation panel in AWS WAF & Shield Console, and on the following **`Web ACLs`** page, click on the **`Create Web ACL`** button.

5. On the **`Create web ACL`** page, we will provide the name, description, and CloudWatch metric name, and select the global or regional resources with which this web ACL will be associated, and then click on **`Next`**. *Figure 3.27* shows how an API published on Amazon API Gateway (named **`echo`**) is associated with the web ACL, shown as follows in *Figure 3.27*.

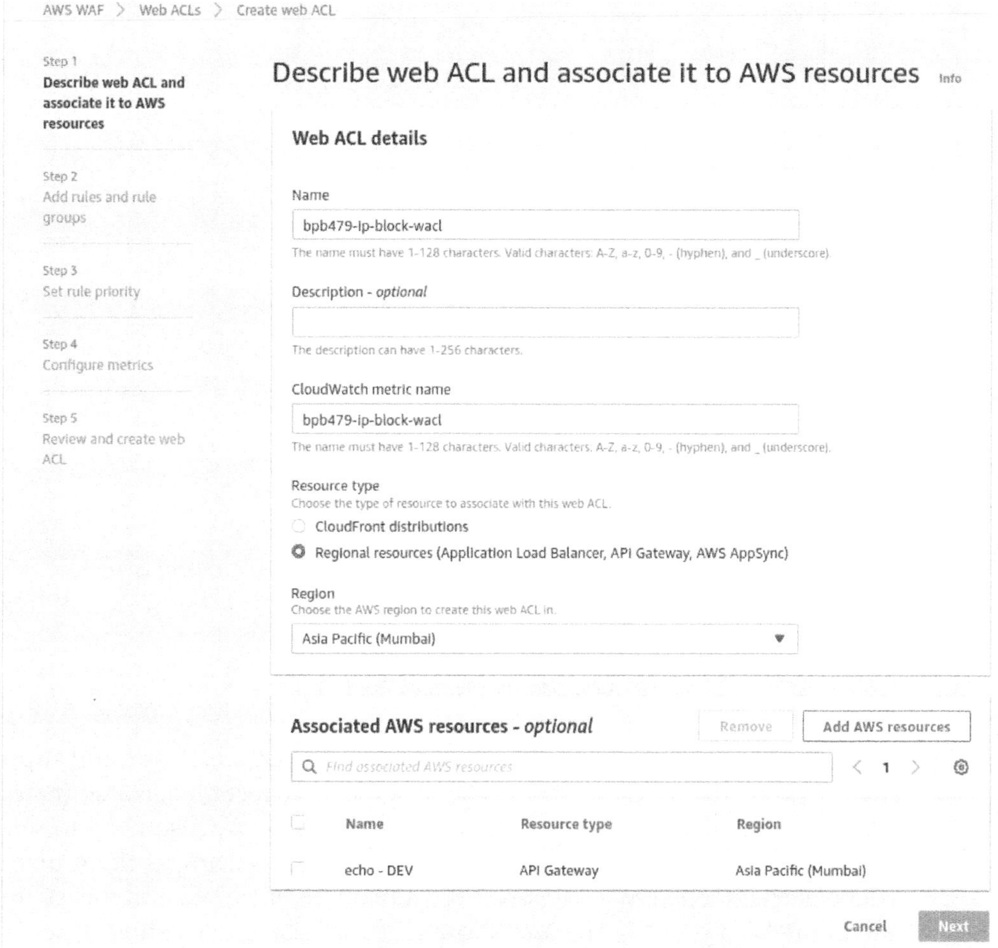

Figure 3.27: *Associate AWS resources like APIs, ALBs, etc. with Web ACL*

6. On the **`Add rules and rule groups`** page, in the **`Rules`** section, we will select **`Add my own rules and rule groups`** from the **`Add rules`** dropdown

and click on the **Next** button. *Figure 3.28* shows how to add a custom rule to Web ACL, as follows:

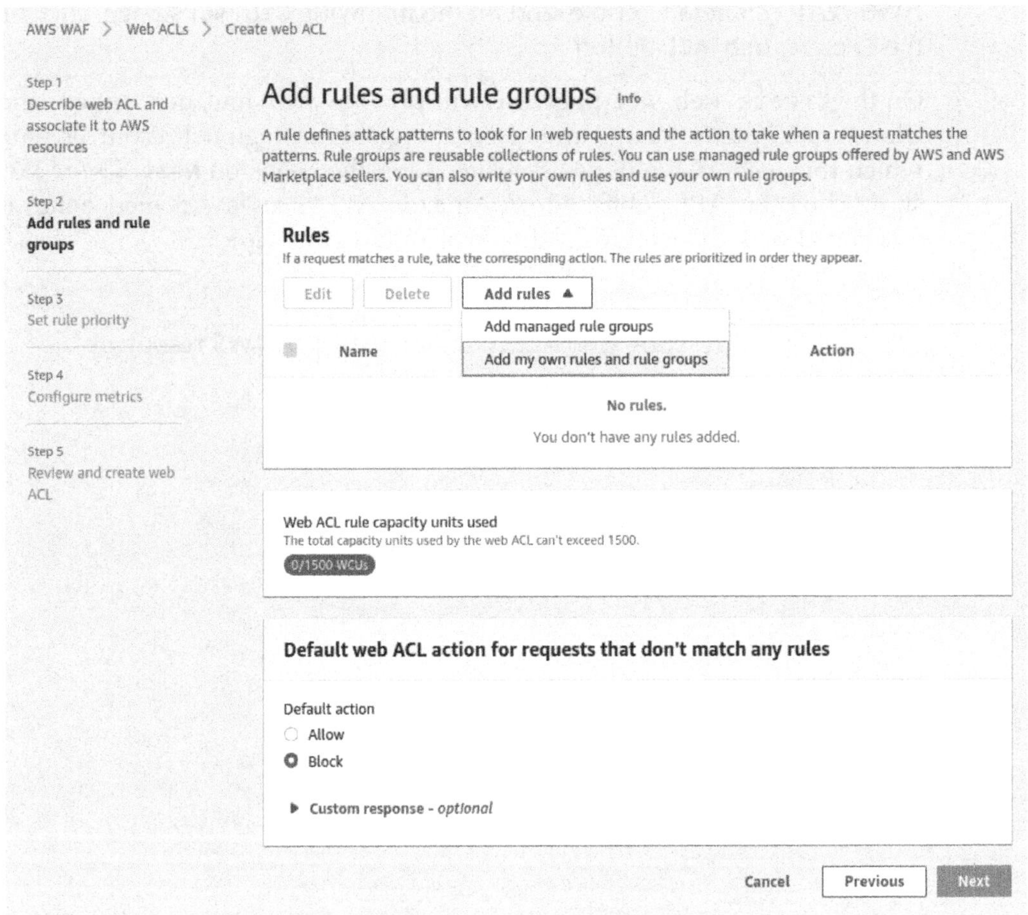

Figure 3.28: Add custom rule to Web ACL

7. On the **Rule type** page, we will select the **Rule type** as **IP set** and supply a name for the rule and then select the IP set that we recently created (named **bpb479-Ipset-block**) from the **IP set** dropdown. We also need to select the options where any IP address from the IP set appearing as the source IP will be blocked. Next, we will select the **Add rule** button to add this custom rule to the Web ACL. *Figure 3.29* shows how to select an existing IP set and associate it with Web ACL and ensure that the traffic from this IP set will be blocked by the Web ACL, as follows:

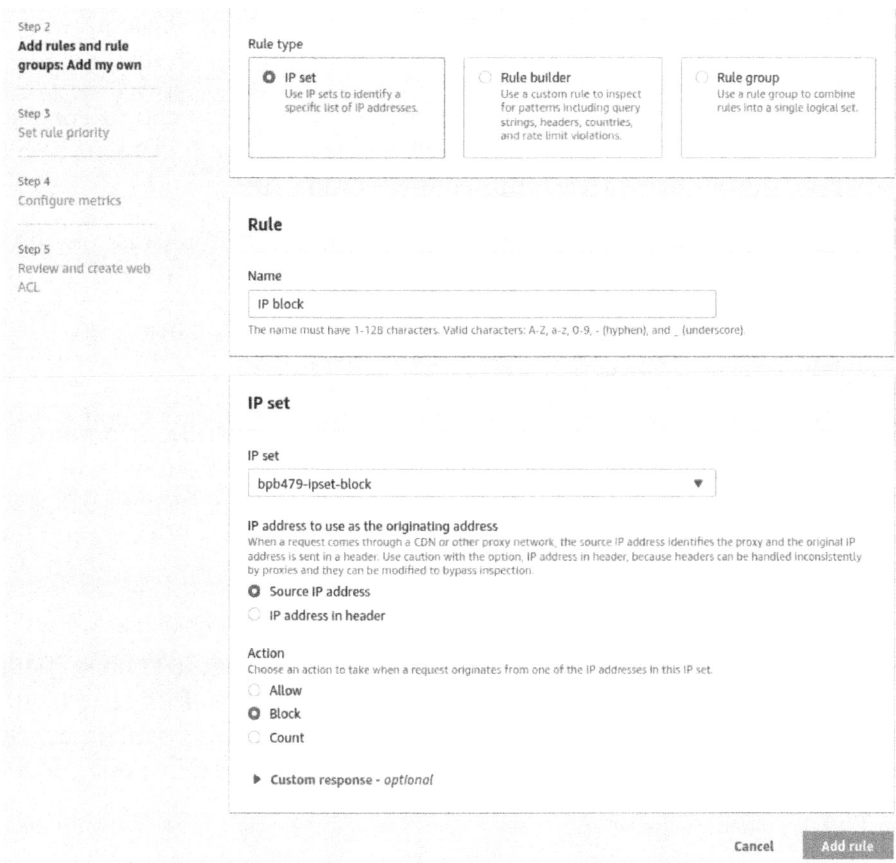

Figure 3.29: *Apply IP set rule to Web ACL*

8. Once back to the **`Add rules and rule groups`** page, we must remember to ensure that the **`Default action`** is **`Allow`**, for the requests that don't match any rules in the web ACL (as shown in *Figure 3.30*). Otherwise, the requests from the valid IPs will also get blocked. Refer to *Figure 3.30* as follows:

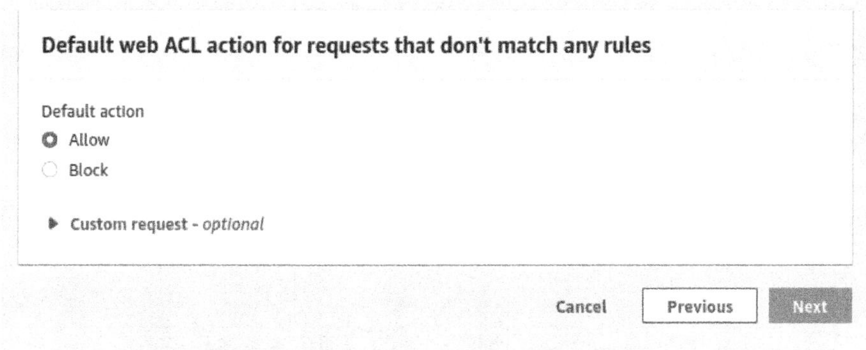

Figure 3.30: *Allow if requests do not match the IP set rule*

9. In the following steps, select a high priority for the IP blocking rule, create some CloudWatch metrics, review the configurations, and create the web ACL.

Note that, now with the web ACL created and associated with **echo** API on Amazon API Gateway, any API requests from the IPs included in the IP set will be blocked and HTTP 403 Forbidden will be returned by the API Gateway.

Amazon CloudFront has integrations with AWS WAF, which means, we can easily have the IP filtering done at the edge by enabling the IP set-based web ACL on the CloudFront distribution.

Blacklisting with resource policy

The IAM resource-based policies could be used to blacklist the IP ranges for the services that support the resource based policies. In this section, we will primarily learn how to block the API traffic from a list of IP ranges. With Amazon API Gateway, we can actually create a resource policy associated with an API that can block the specific IP addresses or CIDR ranges.

To set a resource policy for an API in Amazon API Gateway Console, we will select the API and click on **API | Resource Policy** from the left navigation panel. On the **Resource Policy** page, we can select the **IP Range Denylist** button at the bottom which generates a sample resource policy. This policy will be amended to match our requirements. *Figure 3.31* shows the generated resource policy, as follows:

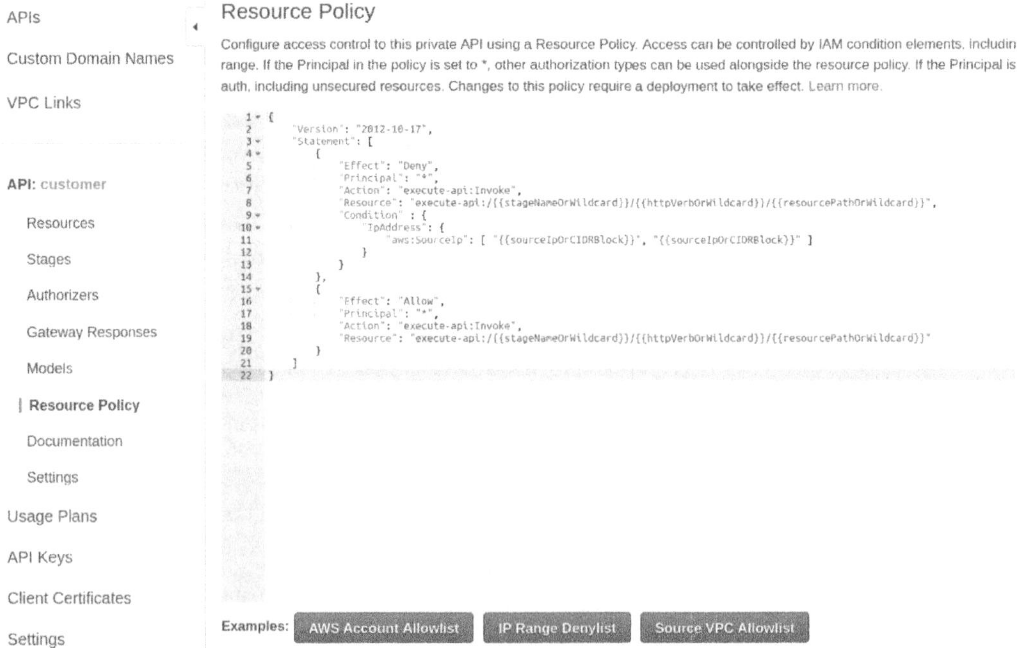

Figure 3.31: *Configure API resource policy to block IPs in Amazon API Gateway Console*

The following sample resource policy, utilizes the **IpAddress** condition operator with the **aws:SourceIp** condition key to deny access to the API when the source IP of the request falls within the blacklisted IP address ranges mentioned in the resource policy. The blacklisted IP ranges designated by CIDR-n in the JSON, will have to be replaced by actual CIDR based IP ranges (for example: 1.2.3.4/32), as follows:

```
{
    "Version": "2012-10-17",
    "Statement": [
       {
            "Effect": "Deny",
            "Principal": "*",
            "Action": "execute-api:Invoke",
            "Resource": [
               "execute-api:/PROD/*"
            ],
            "Condition" : {
                "IpAddress": {
                    "aws:SourceIp": ["<CIDR-1>", "<CIDR-2>" ]
                }
            }
        }
        {
            "Effect": "Allow",
            "Principal": "*",
            "Action": "execute-api:Invoke",
            "Resource": [
                "execute-api:/PROD/*"
            ]
        }
    ]
}
```

Note that, the **Allow** statement is required, without which, the requests coming from the other legitimate source IP will be blocked, owing to the implicit deny rule of the IAM policies.

Blacklisting with NACL

We have already covered NACL in this chapter. However, in this section, we will specifically focus on how the IP addresses can be blacklisted at the subnet level using NACL. Unlike the security groups, NACL supports the **DENY** action, which means that the traffic from a specific set of source IP address or IP ranges could be denied entry to the associated subnets. *Figure 3.32* shows how to edit an existing network ACL to deny the subnet level traffic from a representative blacklisted IP address (1.2.3.4/32). Note that the **DENY** rule must have a higher priority (lower rule number). Refer to *Figure 3.32* as follows:

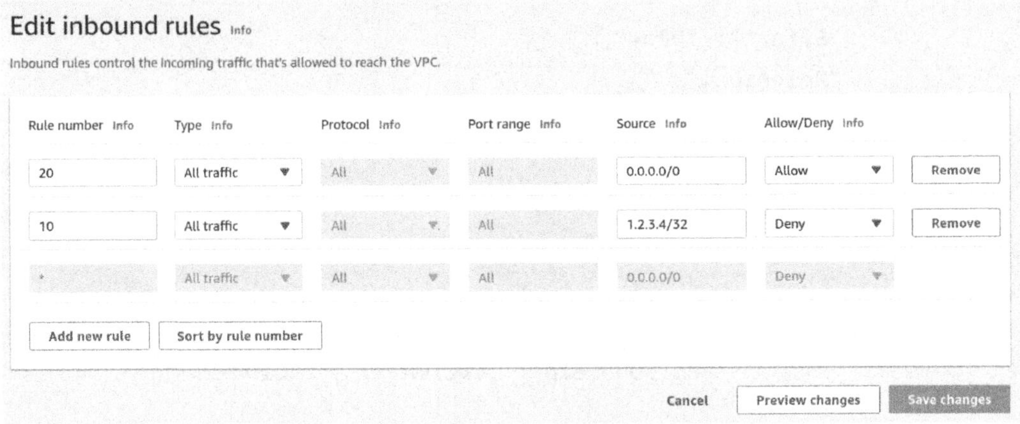

Figure 3.32: Configure a network ACL with DENY action

Whitelisting with security groups

The security groups can be used to whitelist a set of IP addresses. This is applicable when we know the specific set of IP addresses (or CIDR ranges) allowed access to the instance or network interface safeguarded by the security group. The security groups have an implicit deny policy on the inbound traffic, as such, whitelisting will allow the traffic only from the specific IP ranges. Blacklisting cannot be done with the security groups, as unlike NACLs, they do not allow explicit deny rules.

Vulnerability assessment

Vulnerability Assessment is the process of identifying the risks and vulnerabilities in a system along with their classification and rating. In this section, we will look at Amazon Inspector which is a tool for vulnerability assessment of the Amazon EC2 instances and Amazon Elastic Container Registry (ECR) image scanning feature, primarily meant for vulnerability assessment of the container images.

Amazon Inspector

Amazon Inspector is an automated security and vulnerability assessment service that can improve security and enforce compliance of the applications deployed primarily on Amazon EC2. Amazon Inspector can perform automated assessments and generate findings based on selected rules packages.

A *rules package* is essentially a collection of rules that corresponds to a security goal. The security goal can be specified by selecting an appropriate combination of supported rules packages in an assessment template. The following rules packages are supported by Amazon Inspector:

- **Network assessment**
  - o Network Reachability-1.1
- **Host assessment**
  - o Common Vulnerabilities and Exposures-1.1
  - o CIS Operating System Security Configuration Benchmarks-1.0
  - o Security Best Practices-1.0

Amazon Inspector performs an agent-assisted assessment. In most cases, Amazon Inspector agent must be running in the EC2 instances that are part of the assessment target. Note that, *Network Reachability-1.1* rules package does not require the Amazon Inspector agent to be installed in the targets.

The following link provides the details on how to install Amazon Inspector agent: **https://docs.aws.amazon.com/inspector/latest/userguide/inspector_installing-uninstalling-agents.html**

To avoid manual installation of Amazon Inspector agent, we may want to use *Amazon Linux 2 AMI with Amazon Inspector Agent* AMI in which the agent comes pre-installed and is available in the AWS marketplace, as shown in *Figure 3.33*, as follows:

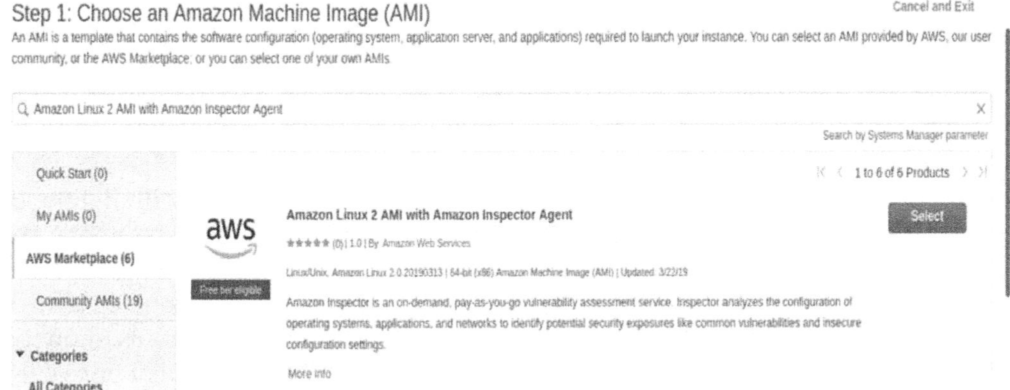

Figure 3.33: *Amazon Linux 2 AMI with pre-installed Amazon Inspector Agent*

Let's see how to create an assessment template and run an assessment using AWS Management Console. We assume that we already have the EC2 instances with the installed Amazon Inspector agent. Refer to the following steps:

1. First, we will create the assessment targets. For this, we will click on the **Assessment targets** on the left navigation panel of Amazon Inspector Console. On the **Assessment targets** page, we will click on the **Create** button.
2. The assessment targets could include all the EC2 instances, or we could also identify the targets by **tags**. In this case, we assume that each of our EC2 targets carry a tag named **PROJECT** with a value **bpb479**, as shown in *Figure 3.34*. (A tag can be easily added to an EC2 instance during the creation process). With these changes, we can click on the **Save** button. This should create a new assessment target, as shown in *Figure 3.34* as follows:

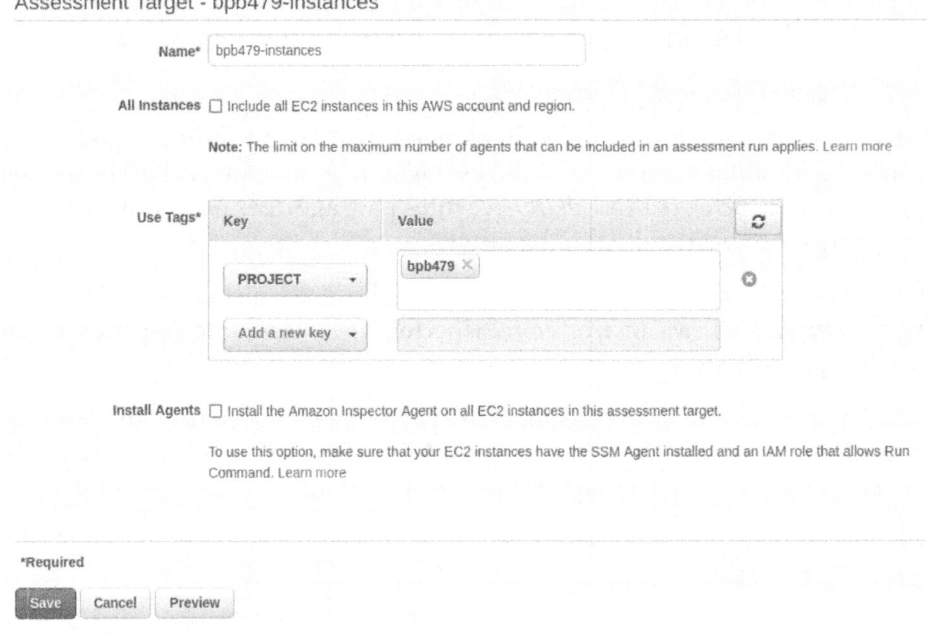

Figure 3.34: Creation of assessment targets from Amazon Inspector Console

3. Next, we need to create the assessment template that will define the assessment targets, rules packages to use, duration of assessment run, assessment schedule, etc. For this, we will click on **Assessment templates** from the left navigation panel in the Amazon Inspector Console. On the **Assessment templates** page, we will specify our choices, as shown in *Figure 3.35*. Note that, we could schedule a recurring assessment once every day, week, month, etc. Finally, we will click on the **Create and run** button, which will run the assessment. Refer to *Figure 3.35* as follows:

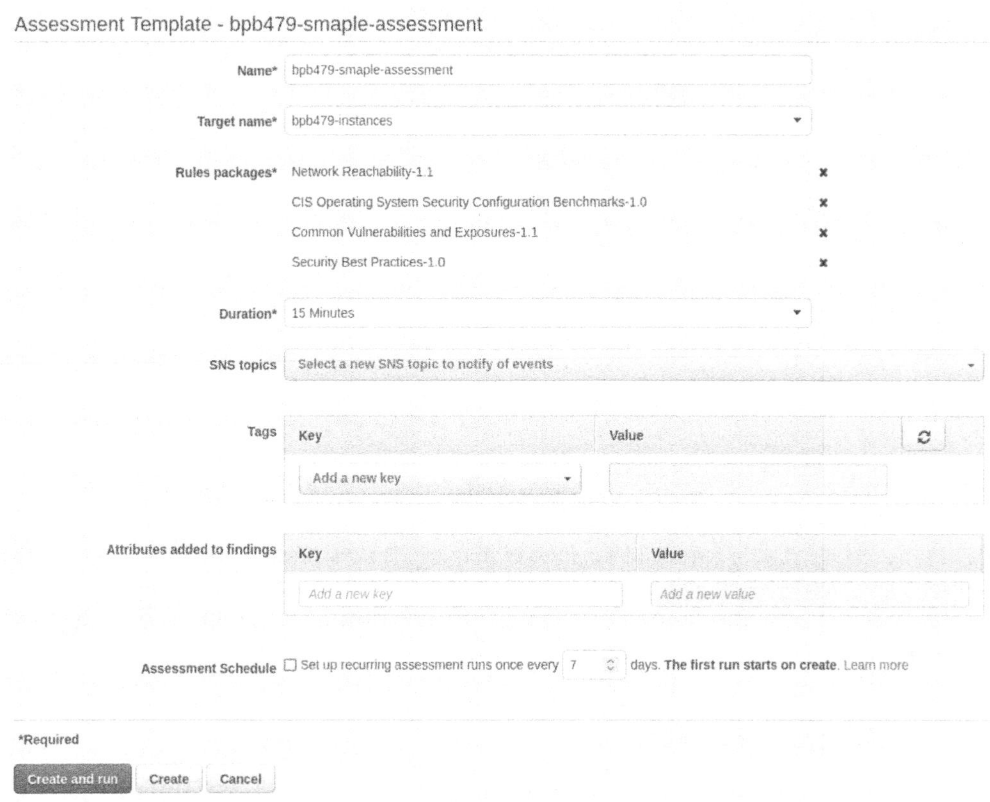

Figure 3.35: Creation of assessment template from Amazon Inspector Console

4. Once the assessment run is started, it can be seen from the **`Assessment runs`** page (selected from the left navigation panel). Initially, the status of the run would show **`Collecting data`**. Once the run completes, the status would change to **`Analysis complete`** and the report is made available in the HTML or PDF format via a download link, as shown in *Figure 3.36*, as follows:

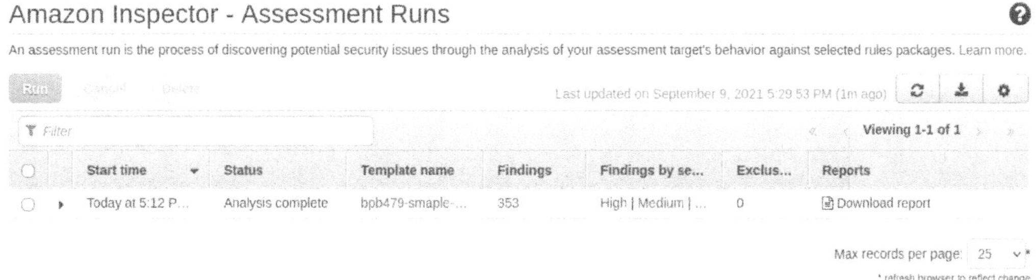

Figure 3.36: Assessment run completion in Amazon Inspector Console

5. The findings could be seen from the **Findings** page (selected from the left navigation panel) which could be filtered based on severity, as shown in *Figure 3.37* as follows:

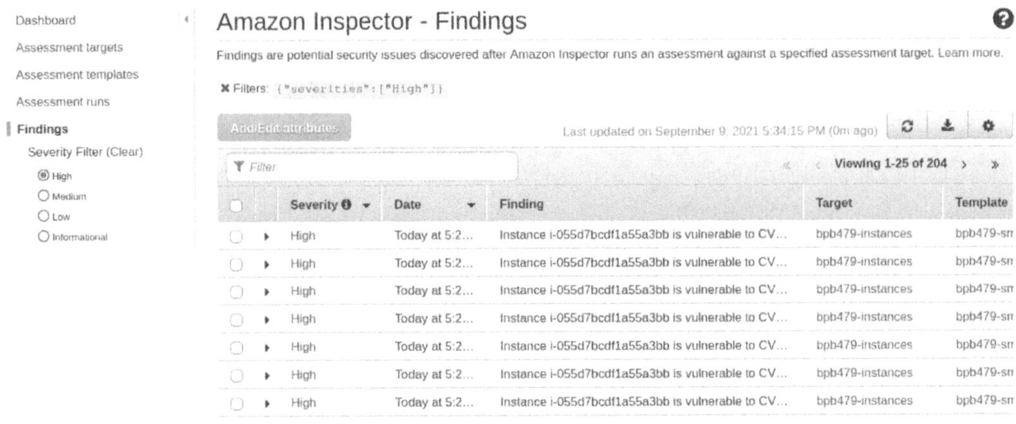

Figure 3.37: *Findings in Amazon Inspector Console*

Each finding shows the details along with the recommendations on how to fix the vulnerability.

ECR image scans

Amazon **Elastic Container Registry** (**ECR**) is a fully managed container registry that supports image scanning of the container images that are pushed to ECR. Image scanning is an automated vulnerability assessment feature available in ECR. This feature is useful in improving the security of the container images by scanning the images against the **Common Vulnerabilities and Exposures** (**CVEs**) database which represents a broad set of common vulnerabilities.

Figure 3.38 shows how to enable **Scan on push** (under the **Image scan settings** section), when creating a new repository from the **Amazon ECR | Repositories** page in the **Amazon Container Services** Console.

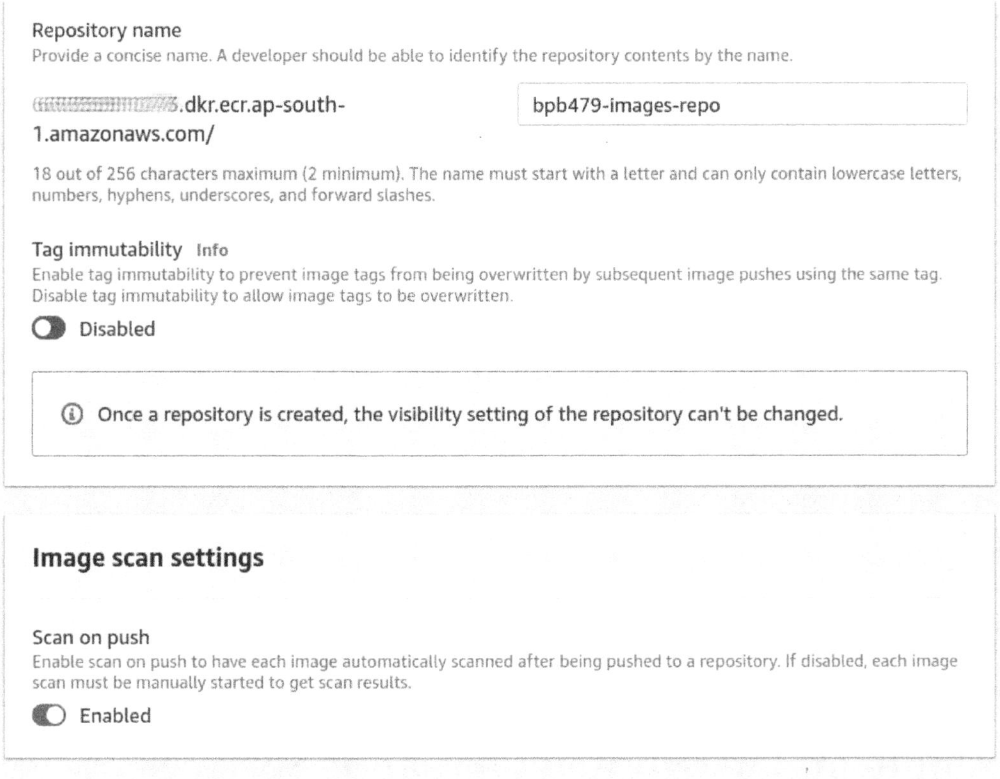

Repository name

Provide a concise name. A developer should be able to identify the repository contents by the name.

.dkr.ecr.ap-south-1.amazonaws.com/ bpb479-images-repo

18 out of 256 characters maximum (2 minimum). The name must start with a letter and can only contain lowercase letters, numbers, hyphens, underscores, and forward slashes.

Tag immutability Info

Enable tag immutability to prevent image tags from being overwritten by subsequent image pushes using the same tag. Disable tag immutability to allow image tags to be overwritten.

Disabled

Once a repository is created, the visibility setting of the repository can't be changed.

Image scan settings

Scan on push

Enable scan on push to have each image automatically scanned after being pushed to a repository. If disabled, each image scan must be manually started to get scan results.

Enabled

Figure 3.38: *Enable "scan on push" flag for an ECR repository*

Note that the existing repositories can also be updated with this flag.

Let's look into the following AWS CLI commands to create an ECR repository (named **`bpb479-images-repo`**) with the **`scan-on-push`** flag enabled, and update the flag for an existing repository (named **`bpb479-images-repo-2`**):

```
# Set scanOnPush = true while creating an ECR repository
$ aws ecr create-repository --repository-name bpb479-images-repo \
  --image-scanning-configuration scanOnPush=true --region ap-south-1

# Set scanOnPush = true for an existing ECR repository
$ aws ecr put-image-scanning-configuration \
  --repository-name bpb479-images-repo-2 \
  --image-scanning-configuration scanOnPush=true --region ap-south-1
```

Image scanning could be scheduled manually on an image at any point either via ECR Console or AWS CLI. The following is the AWS CLI command to initiate a manual image scanning for an image with the tag equal to "bpb479-base" in the ECR repository named "bpb479-images-repo":

```
$ aws ecr start-image-scan --repository-name bpb479-images-repo \
  --image-id imageTag=bpb479-base --region ap-south-1
```

The scan findings are made available in the ECR Console under **Amazon Container Services | Amazon ECR | Repositories | Select Repository | Images** page | **Vulnerabilities** column. To retrieve the scan findings, we must select **Details** for the image. Otherwise, we could fetch the findings for an image with the tag equal to **bpb479-base**, using AWS CLI, as follows:

```
$ aws ecr describe-image-scan-findings \
  --repository-name bpb479-images-repo \
  --image-id imageTag=bpb479-base --region ap-south-1
```

Distributed Denial of Service and AWS Shield

AWS Shield is a managed DDoS protection service. It provides two levels of protection – AWS Shield Standard and AWS Shield Advanced. Before getting into the details of this service, let's first try to understand what a DDoS attack looks like and the general guidelines around how to mitigate such an attack.

A note on Distributed Denial of Service

A **Distributed Denial of Service** (**DDoS**) attack is a malicious attempt to temporarily disrupt or suspend the online services of a site or hosting server. A DDoS attack is triggered from numerous globally distributed network of compromised devices (or bots). This distributed network is known as a botnet. Essentially, a DDoS attack can be classified into the following types:

- **Volume based attacks**: A volume-based attack like the UDP flood or ICMP flood, saturates the victim's bandwidth. The magnitude of such an attack is measured in terms of bits per second (bps).
- **Protocol attacks**: Protocol attacks like SYN flood, **Ping of Death (PoD)**, Smurf DDoS, etc., consumes the resources of the victim or the intermediate communication devices like load balancers and firewalls. The magnitude of such an attack is measured in packets per second (pps).
- **Application layer attacks**: Application layer (layer-7) attacks like GET/POST flood, are low-and-slow attacks that target the application directly by sending seemingly legitimate requests with the goal to crash the victim's web server. The magnitude of such an attack is measured in requests per second (rps).

Figure 3.39 shows the schematics of a UDP flood attack in which the attacker leverages the globally distributed infected devices to launch a volume based UDP attack on the victim (site).

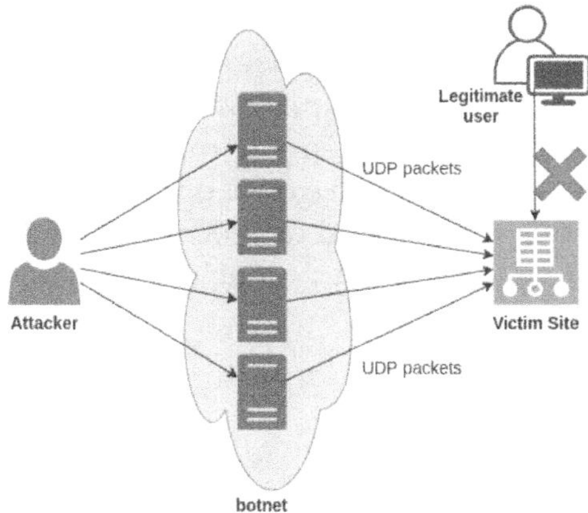

Figure 3.39: *Simplified schematic of a UDP Flood DDoS attack*

Essentially, this results in the choking of the available bandwidth for the legitimate users of the site.

DDoS Mitigation

While AWS Shield can provide active monitoring and protection from the common DDoS attacks, there are quite a few steps that we can take while planning our infrastructure and designing our applications, which can help to mitigate the impact of a large-scale DDoS attack. The steps are as follows:

- **Reduce attack surface area**: It is always a good idea to limit the number of publicly accessible endpoints, safeguard publicly exposed resources, and isolate the internal traffic from the external world. The use of VPC, private load balancers for internal traffic distribution (instead of public load balancers), bastion hosts for SSH/RDP access (we have already checked a better alternative to using bastion hosts – AWS Systems Manager Session Manager), NAT gateways, etc., can reduce the surface area of an attack and make it relatively easier to control the attack. Setting up of appropriate firewall rules using the security groups (or otherwise) and opening the ports that are essential to the working of an application can also prove helpful to reduce the scope of an attack.
- **Leverage resource quota and rate limiting**: AWS assigns regional service usage quotas on the services, which can be very useful during a DDoS attack to keep a tighter leash on the mounting resource usage costs in the event of an attack. The rate limiting features in services like Amazon API Gateway can also help throttle the onslaught of the incoming API requests.

- **Provision to scale**: In the event of a DDoS attack, the application infrastructure must have the ability to scale to absorb the attack. The AWS services like Route 53, **Elastic Load Balancers (ELB)**, Autoscaling, CloudFront, S3 and many more, could be leveraged to operate at a high scalability factor.
- **Learn normal behavior**: The knowledge of normal behavior in terms of the traffic pattern and load of an application, can greatly help in responding quickly to a DDoS event. A sudden abnormal spike in the traffic during the off-peak business hours or a massive onslaught of requests or requests pouring in from certain parts of the world where the presence of the application users is limited, can point to an ongoing attack.

AWS Shield

As stated earlier, AWS Shield provides two levels of DDoS protection – Standard and Advanced. Standard is automatically enabled and provides an always-on protection. However, AWS Shield Advanced requires explicit enabling and offers additional protection against the DDoS attacks. Note that AWS Shield Advanced costs 3000 USD per month.

AWS Shield Standard

AWS Shield Standard is available to the customers at no additional cost and offers automatic protection against the common transport layer attacks. We can reap the benefits of AWS Shield Standard if we use CloudFront or Route 53, since these services get availability protection by leveraging the global edge network, against the known infrastructure attacks in layer 3 and 4.

AWS Shield Advanced

AWS Shield Advanced offers higher levels of protection against the DDoS attacks and needs to be explicitly subscribed from AWS WAF & Shield Console. The service allows us to add specific resources that needs protection. These resources can also be logically grouped together as `Protection groups`. The following AWS resource types can be protected by AWS Shield Advanced:

- **Amazon CloudFront** distributions
- **Amazon Route 53** hosted zones
- **AWS Global Accelerator** accelerators
- Amazon EC2 **Elastic IP addresses**
- **Application Load Balancers** and other ELBs

Note that, Network Load Balancers, or NLBs, could be protected by associating them with the elastic IP and then adding this elastic IP to the AWS Shield Advanced protection list.

AWS Shield Advanced has several other features that can prove useful, which are as follows:

- In addition to protection from the common layer 3 and 4 attacks, AWS Shield Advanced also provides monitoring and mitigation of layer 7 (application layer) attacks.
- AWS WAF is offered free of cost, along with AWS Shield Advanced. While Web Application Firewall is not primarily used to stop DDoS attacks, it can still be used to filter the traffic based on rules like request size constraint conditions, geo-match conditions, rate-based rules, etc.
- AWS Shield Advanced provides real-time metrics and extensive visibility into the details of layer 3, 4, and 7 attacks.
- It offers cost protection against spikes in the AWS bill due to a DDoS attack on the protected resources.
- AWS Shield Response Team (SRT) is available 24x7 for assistance during a DDoS attack. This feature is subject to subscription to either Business Support Plan or Enterprise Support Plan.

Global threat dashboard

AWS Shield provides an informational global threat dashboard which covers the statistics relevant to the most recent attacks (ranging from 1 day to 2 weeks) that AWS is presently monitoring and mitigating. The services covered are Amazon EC2, Amazon CloudFront, Elastic Load Balancing, and Amazon Route 53. This dashboard is accessible under **`AWS Shield | Global threat dashboard`** from the **`AWS WAF & Shield`** Console. The dashboard also provides information around the most common vector of attack, total number of attacks, largest packet per second, bit per second, and requests per second. *Figure 3.40* shows a portion of the threat dashboard, as follows:

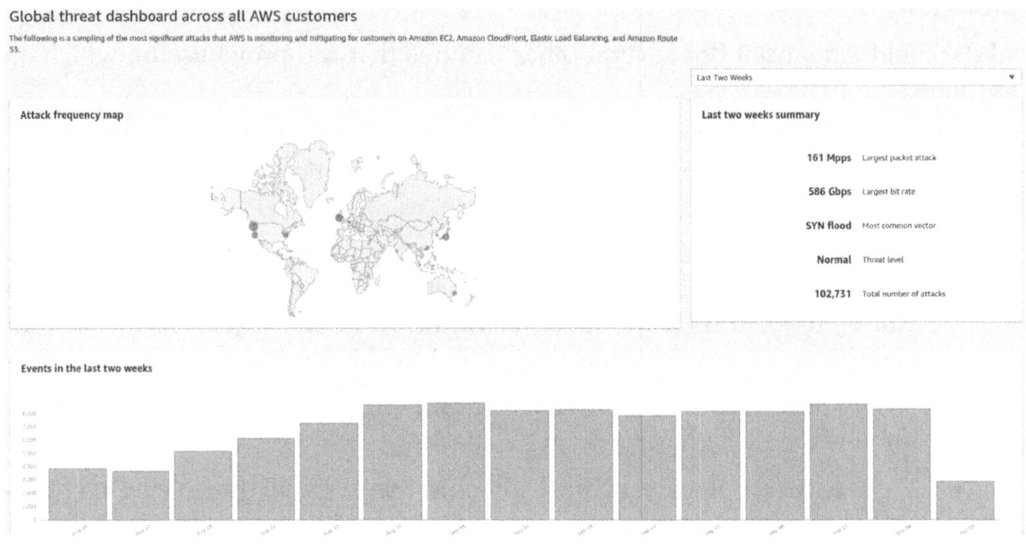

Figure 3.40: *Global threat dashboard*

Conclusion

In addition to the range of security services and features provided by AWS, we can also employ third party solutions available on AWS Marketplace or otherwise to boost our infrastructure security. The modern network security solutions (like Barracuda CloudGen Firewall, etc.) can perform behavioral and heuristic analysis in addition to the standard network protection. There are popular intrusion detection and prevention solutions in the market which could be applied for better security of the resources in AWS. While the security of the infrastructure is important, the security of the data stored within this infrastructure is equally important.

In the next chapter, we will take a look at the various data security features and services provided by AWS.

CHAPTER 4
Data Security

Introduction

The importance of data security is paramount in the public cloud. Therefore, **Amazon Web Services** (**AWS**) has introduced several services and controls to ensure the security and safety of the customers' data. These services go a long way to bolster the confidence of the enterprises and businesses to move and persist their data in AWS as part of their cloud transformation journey.

Structure

In this chapter, we will cover the following topics:

- Fundamental concepts of securing data
- AWS Key Management Service (KMS)
- AWS CloudHSM
- Amazon S3
- Amazon EBS
- Amazon DynamoDB
- Amazon RDS
- Amazon Macie for data loss prevention

Objectives

In this chapter, we will learn the fundamental concepts of cryptography, digital signature, and security of data at rest and in motion. These concepts play a vital role in the understanding of data security in AWS. We will learn about the fundamental AWS data security service – **Key Management Service** (**KMS**). We will take a quick introductory view of AWS CloudHSM (Hardware Security Module). Furthermore, we will understand how services like Amazon S3, Amazon RDS, and Amazon DynamoDB leverage AWS KMS and various other controls to help secure the data persisted by them. Finally, we will understand how Amazon Macie can help us create scheduled jobs or one-time jobs to discover and classify sensitive data.

Fundamental concepts of securing data

In this chapter, we will understand some concepts to better grasp how data security works. These include the process of encryption and decryption which uses symmetric and/or asymmetric ciphers, digital signature, and security of data at rest and in motion. All these are methods and techniques that can help us protect sensitive data.

Fundamentals of cryptography

Cryptography is the art and science of keeping messages or data secure. A *cipher* or cryptographic algorithm is a mathematical function used for encryption and decryption. Thus, a cipher is a combination of two related mathematical functions – one serving the purpose of encryption and the other of decryption. The primary goal is to ensure that the message itself is safeguarded from the prying eyes of any eavesdropper who might get access to the encrypted message, which is also known as *confidentiality*. Here's a more formal definition of the encryption and decryption processes:

- Encryption or enciphering is the process of disguising a message, or **cleartext**, into an unintelligible form, also known as **ciphertext**.
- Decryption or deciphering is just the reverse process, where a **ciphertext** is transformed into the original **cleartext**.

Now, one could think of keeping this cipher a secret and using this secret cipher for encryption and decryption of messages. However, such algorithms (also known as **restricted algorithms**) are simply inadequate for high security applications. This is so because this strategy will not scale to a large group of users, plus there is always a risk of the secret algorithm being revealed to unintended parties. Additionally, there is always a question of quality of the cipher and its standardization.

This problem is essentially solved with a *key*. This key is an individual value from a range of possible values known as the **keyspace**. Both the encryption and decryption operations are dependent on this key. The security of such a *key based algorithm* is not based on the secrecy of the implementation but on the strength of the key. This means, the cipher itself could be published and analyzed.

Figure 4.1 illustrates how a cleartext message (M) can be encrypted into a ciphertext (C) using a key (K). Furthermore, the ciphertext (C) can then be decrypted into the original cleartext message (M) with the help of the key (K). Some ciphers use different encryption and decryption keys (also termed as key-pair). Refer to *figure 4.1* as follows:

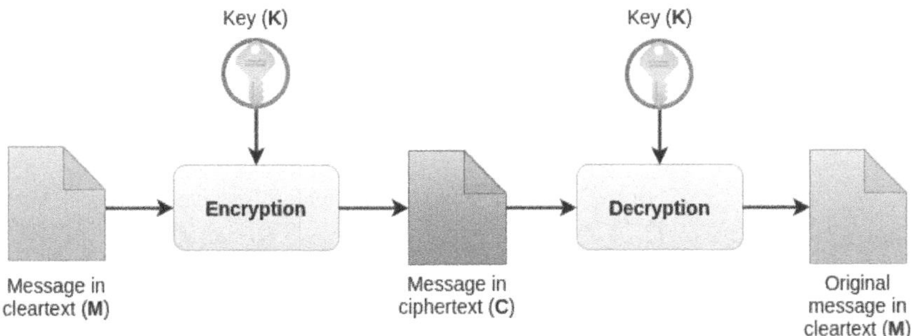

Figure 4.1: *Process of encryption and decryption with symmetric key*

Symmetric and asymmetric algorithms

Key based algorithms are generally grouped into two categories – symmetric and public-key (asymmetric) algorithms. *Symmetric algorithms* are the ones where the encryption and decryption keys are the same (refer to *figure 4.1*). Thus, if a cleartext message is encrypted using a key (K) and this ciphertext is sent to the intended recipients, then the intended recipients need to have the same key (K) to decrypt the message. This type of algorithm basically comes with the complexity of the secure key exchange protocols since anyone in possession of the key will decrypt the ciphertext. Note that, there are symmetric key algorithms which use encryption keys that can be calculated from the decryption keys and vice versa. However, for explaining the concept of symmetric algorithms, we will assume the use of the same key for both the encryption and the decryption, and in fact, most symmetric algorithms use this strategy. **Advanced Encryption Standard** (**AES**) and **Data Encryption Standard** (**DES**) are some of the commonly used symmetric algorithms.

Asymmetric or *public key algorithms* use different encryption and decryption keys. Additionally, the encryption key cannot be used to calculate the decryption key and vice versa, in a reasonable amount of time. The essence of public-key algorithms is that the encryption key (or public key) can be made public. This means, anyone can use the public key to encrypt a message. However, only the intended recipient, who owns the decryption key (or private key), can decrypt the message. This process is illustrated in *figure 4.2*, where a cleartext message (M) is encrypted using the public key (PK) and the resulting ciphertext (C) is decrypted using the private key (K), as follows:

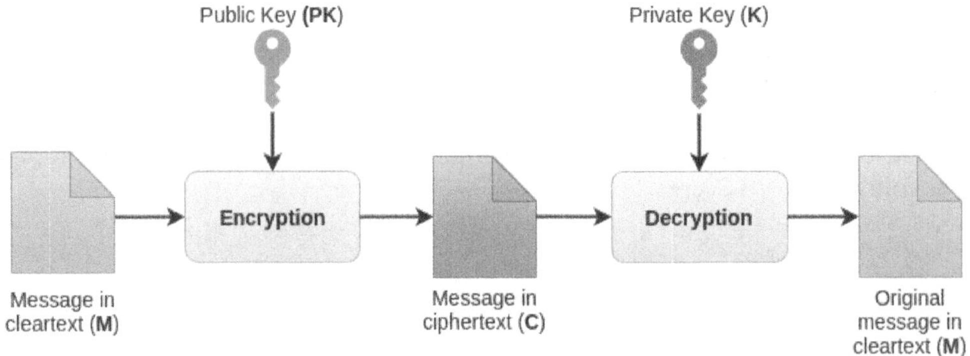

Figure 4.2: *Process of encryption and decryption with asymmetric key*

The most common public key algorithms in use today are **Rivest-Shamir-Adleman** (**RSA**), **Elliptic Curve Digital Signature Algorithm** (**ECDSA**), **Digital Signature Algorithm** (**DSA**), etc.

Digital signature and message security

While *cryptographic algorithms* or ciphers can be used primarily for confidentiality, they are often used for other purposes as well, like – *authentication, integrity,* and *nonrepudiation*. These are explained as follows:

- **Authentication**: The message receiver should be able to authenticate the source or origin of the message. An intruder should not be able to pose or masquerade as the message sender.
- **Integrity**: The message receiver should be able to verify that the message has not been altered or updated during transit.
- **Nonrepudiation**: The message sender should not be able to deny being the sender of the message falsely.

A *digital signature* can provide the message recipient with a firm reason to believe that an authenticated (known) sender created the message, that the message was not tampered with during transmission, and that the signer cannot successfully claim that they did not sign the message. *figure 4.3* illustrates how digital signature works, as follows:

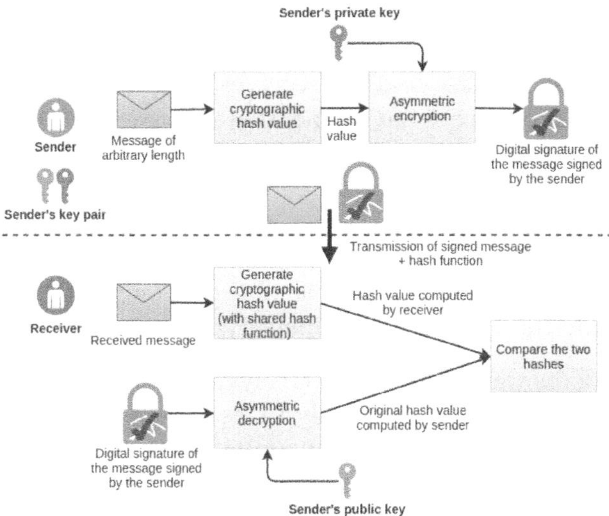

Figure 4.3: Digital signature

Let's consider a message sender who intends to send a digitally signed message (not encrypted) to a receiver. We assume that the sender has generated a key-pair comprising of a public and a private key. Furthermore, the sender has shared the public key with the receiver. With this setup, the sender can create any message of an arbitrary length and leverage a *cryptographic hash function* to generate a fixed-length hash value representing the original message. This hash value is then encrypted using the sender's private key and this encrypted value happens to be the digital signature of the message signed by the sender.

TIP: A cryptographic hash function is a mathematical function that can take the data of any arbitrary length as the input and produce a fixed length encrypted text called a hash value (also referred to as message digest, digital fingerprint, or digest). Click on the following link for a quick introduction: https://www.synopsys.com/blogs/software-security/cryptographic-hash-functions/

At some point, the message and digital signature and details of the cryptographic hash function are transmitted to the receiver. The receiver generates the cryptographic hash value of the received message using the knowledge of the cryptographic hash function details sent by the sender. Then, the receiver attempts asymmetric decryption of the message's digital signature using the sender's public key. This decryption will yield the original hash value of the message computed by the sender. As the final step, the receiver can compare the original hash value (computed by the sender) with the hash value computed from the message (computed by the receiver). If the two hashes match, the receiver can ensure that the message has not been altered in transit. Also, since the sender's public key was used to decrypt the digital signature successfully, the receiver can be sure that it was indeed the authentic sender who had sent the message.

So far, we have been explaining how to create a digital signature and how to verify the same. Now, let's put *confidentiality* in the mix (refer to *figure 4.4*). We assume a setup where both the sender and the receiver have their own key pairs. That is, both the communicating parties have generated their own sets of public and private keys. Moreover, they have exchanged their public keys. In this setup, the receiver, in addition to generating a digital message signature, can also encrypt the message using a symmetric algorithm and a randomly generated key. This symmetric (random) key is then asymmetrically encrypted using the public key of the receiver. Finally, the encrypted message, digital signature (along with cryptographic hash function details) and the encrypted symmetric key are transmitted to the receiver.

On the other side of the transmission, the receiver uses its own private key to decrypt the encrypted random key asymmetrically. Once the random key is decrypted, it can be used to decrypt the message symmetrically. Now, to verify the signatory and integrity, the digital signature verification can be used. Refer to *figure 4.4* as follows:

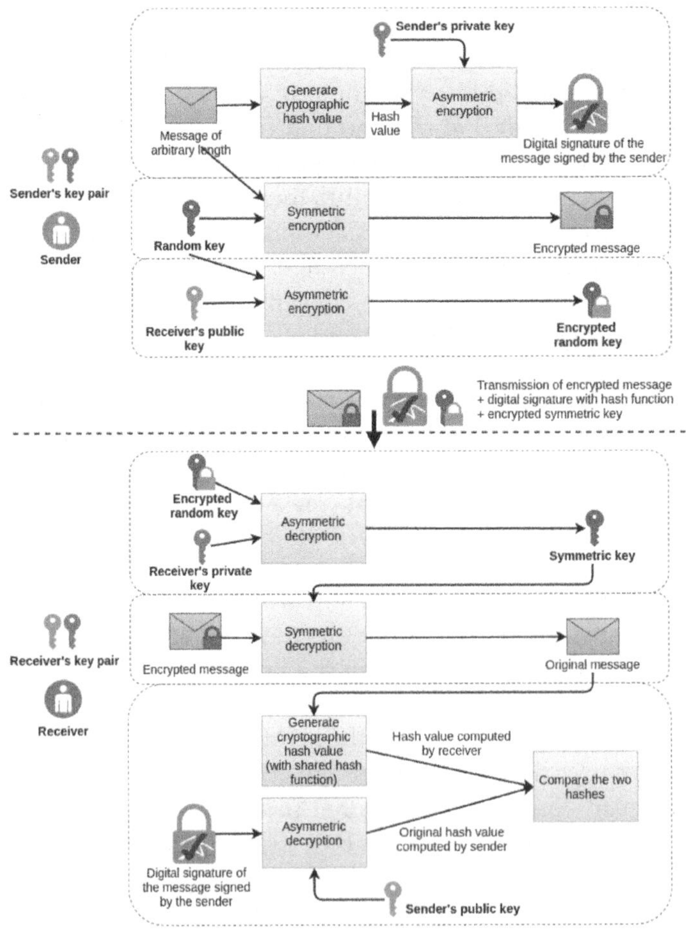

Figure 4.4: Digital signature with message security

Security of data in motion and at rest

When the data is being moved from one system to another or from one storage to another, across the Internet or through a private network, it is considered in *motion*. Adequate security measures for the data-in-transit are of utmost importance, as the data is often considered at a higher risk of breach while in transit. On the other hand, the data is considered in a state of *rest* when it is not being actively moved between the devices and networks and is stored inside the boundaries of an application or service in some form of the data storage device or network. Undoubtedly, sensitive data should be protected both *in motion* and *at rest*.

Cryptography plays a major role in protecting the data. While storing the data in a device, robust encryption algorithms are used to either encrypt the data itself prior to storing them and/or encrypt the storage device. Strong cipher suites and secure protocols (like HTTPS, SSL/TLS, SFTP, etc.) are nowadays commonly used for securing the data in motion.

AWS Key Management Service (KMS)

As the name suggests, AWS KMS is the cryptographic key management service which is integrated with several other AWS services like Amazon EBS, Amazon S3, Amazon RDS, Amazon DynamoDB, etc., and it manages the encryption for these services. Internally, AWS KMS uses highly secure and tamper proof **hardware security modules** (**HSMs**) to store and manage the keys. Let's dive in and get acquainted with some concepts prevalent with this service.

Customer Master Key (CMK)

Customer master keys (**CMKs**) are essentially a logical abstraction of the encryption keys used to encrypt the data. In addition to the key material that is used for the purpose of encryption and decryption, CMKs also contain metadata like the key identifier, key alias, creation date, description, and key state. These metadata help in managing the lifecycle of the key. Support for both the symmetric (AES 256-bit key) and the asymmetric CMKs (RSA keypair or Elliptic curve keypair) are available in AWS KMS.

CMKs can be used to encrypt the data no larger than 4 KB (4096 bytes), and as such, they are not used for the full-fledged encryption/decryption of the application data. In fact, they are primarily used to encrypt the data keys.

There are three types of CMKs supported by AWS KMS, which are as follows:

- **AWS Owned CMKs:** These types of CMKs are owned and managed by AWS for use in multiple AWS accounts. These CMKs are not part of the customer's account, and therefore, the customer cannot create, view, use, or track these

CMKs. AWS services, however, can use their AWS owned CMKs to protect the resources in a customer's account. The key rotation strategy for this type of CMK is defined by the AWS service that creates and manages the CMKs.

- **AWS Managed CMKs:** AWS managed CMKs are created, managed, and used on behalf of the customer, by an AWS service that is integrated with AWS KMS (like S3, RDS, etc.). These CMKs appear under the **`AWS managed keys`** page in the AWS KMS Console and cannot be managed or rotated by the customer. These CMKs are automatically rotated every three years. The easiest way to identify an AWS Managed CMK is to check the '*key alias*' (refer to *figure 4.5*), which has the following format – **`aws/<service-name>`** (for example: **`aws/s3`** or **`aws/sns`**, etc.). Refer to *figure 4.5* as follows:

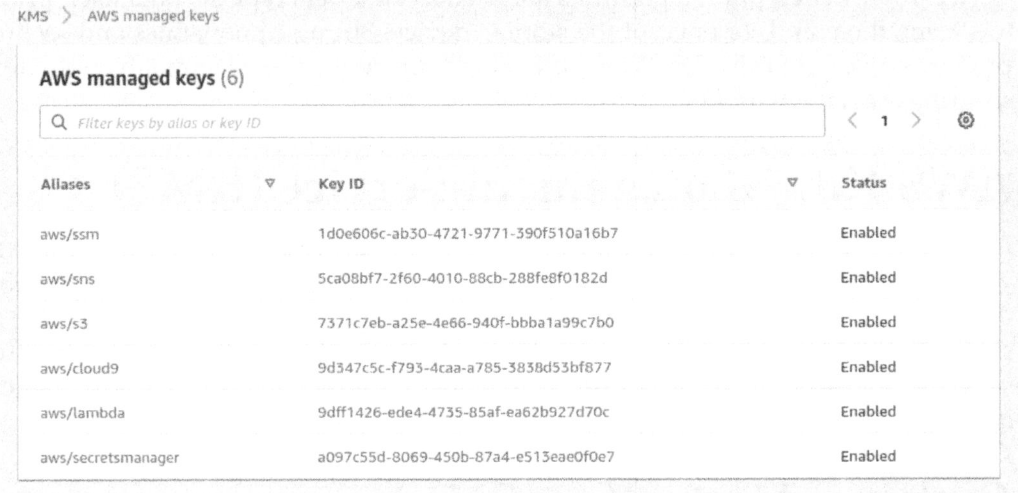

Aliases	Key ID	Status
aws/ssm	1d0e606c-ab30-4721-9771-390f510a16b7	Enabled
aws/sns	5ca08bf7-2f60-4010-88cb-288fe8f0182d	Enabled
aws/s3	7371c7eb-a25e-4e66-940f-bbba1a99c7b0	Enabled
aws/cloud9	9d347c5c-f793-4caa-a785-3838d53bf877	Enabled
aws/lambda	9dff1426-ede4-4735-85af-ea62b927d70c	Enabled
aws/secretsmanager	a097c55d-8069-450b-87a4-e513eae0f0e7	Enabled

Figure 4.5: *AWS managed CMKs in KMS Console*

- **Customer Managed CMKs**: These are the CMKs that are fully controlled by the customer, and as such, these are created, owned, and managed by them. These keys appear under the **`Customer managed keys`** page in the AWS KMS Console and could be optionally rotated once every year automatically. We can create two types of Customer managed CMKs – *Symmetric* and *Asymmetric*. There are, in turn, two types of asymmetric customer managed CMKs that can be created based on the key usage – *encrypt/decrypt* and *sign/verify*.

Key material origin

Symmetric CMKs have a special property called the key material origin. This property identifies the source of the key material in the CMK. When creating a symmetric CMK (from AWS Management Console), we are given three options (refer to *figure 4.6*), which are as follows:

- **KMS**: This is the default option and points to the fact that AWS KMS creates and manages the CMK key material in its own key store. This is the recommended option in most cases.
- **External**: With this option, we can create a CMK with the key material imported from an external source known as the *backing key*. In this case, when the CMK is created, it has no key material. The key material is imported later into the CMK. This option is commonly known as **Bring Your Own Key (BYOK)**. The security and management of the external key material is outside the scope of AWS KMS.
- **Custom key store (CloudHSM)**: Once we create a custom key store using AWS CloudHSM service (AWS CloudHSM has been explained in a separate section in this chapter), we can then create the symmetric CMKs in that key store, with the key material generated by AWS KMS.

Figure 4.6 shows the three key material options in AWS Management Console as follows:

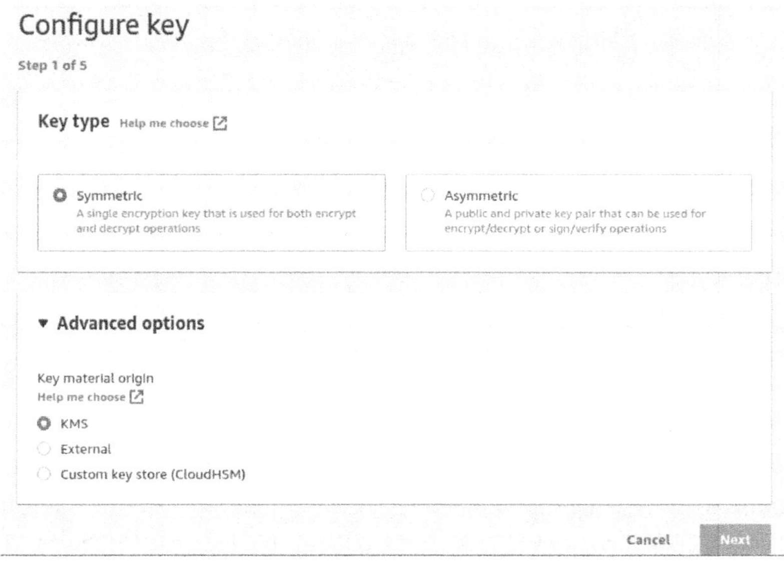

Figure 4.6: *Symmetric key material origin in KMS Console*

AWS KMS supports the imported key material for the symmetric CMKs in the AWS key stores only. Importing of the key material is not supported for the asymmetric CMKs or CMKs in the custom store.

Encryption and decryption with CMK

Now that we know how a CMK works and what a key material is, let's get into some action. We will create a symmetric CMK (with the KMS key material) from the AWS

Management Console (AWS CLI could also be used) and then use that master key through AWS CLI to encrypt and decrypt a simple text.

We will start with the assumption that two IAM users have been created and configured with a set of permissions as defined in *Table 4.1* as follows:

IAM Username	IAM Policy	Permissions	KMS Key Policy Role	AWS CLI Profile
key-manager1	AWS Key Management Service Power User	All permissions included in the AWS managed IAM policy	Key administrator	N/A
key-user1	Custom policy	kms:Encrypt, kms. Decrypt, kms: Describe Key	Key user	key-user

***Table 4.1:** CMK based encryption and decryption IAM policy permissions*

Once in the AWS KMS Console, we will click on **`Customer managed keys`** on the left pane. As part of the CMK creation process, we will complete the following steps:

1. Select **`Key type`** as Symmetric and **`Key material origin`** as *KMS* (refer to *figure 4.6*). Click on the **`Next`** button.
2. Provide a key alias name as **`bpb479`** (any other valid name could also be used) and optionally create some tags. Click on the **`Next`** button.
3. Select the key administrator and permissions. On this page, we will select the **key-manager1** user as the key administrator. We do have the option of selecting an IAM role (with proper permissions) instead of an IAM user on this page. Click on the **`Next`** button.
4. Define the key usage permissions and select the IAM user – **key-user1** (who has the permission to perform the cryptographic operations like encrypt and decrypt). Here as well, we have the option to select an IAM role. Click on the **`Next`** button.
5. View and edit the key policy. This key policy (JSON structure) is basically a resource-based policy attached to the CMK. We can edit the policy based on our needs.

Once the preceding steps have been executed, we will notice that the **`Customer managed keys`** page has our CMK with a key alias of **`bpb479`** and a unique key ID. Refer to *figure 4.7*, as follows:

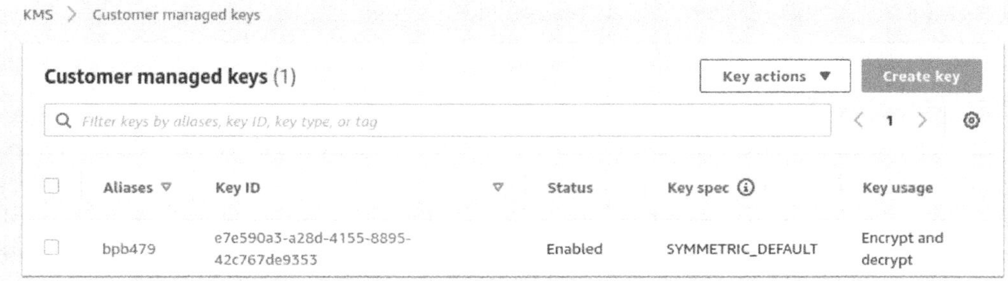

Figure 4.7: *Customer Managed Keys or CMKs*

The resource-based policy attached with the CMK should include the account root user as one of the principals. This is so because, the IAM root user cannot be deleted. Any other IAM user can be deleted, rendering the CMK unusable (if the root user is not a principal). The following is what a sample key policy statement with root as the principal looks like:

```
"Statement": [
 {
  "Sid": "Enable IAM User Permissions",
  "Effect": "Allow",
  "Principal": {
    "AWS": "arn:aws:iam::<account-id>:root"
  },
  "Action": "kms:*",
  "Resource": "*"
  }
]
```

With CMK created, we will now use AWS CLI to use this master key to perform some basic cryptographic operations.

To configure AWS CLI, we will create a profile named **key-user** and apply the AWS access key ID and the secret access key for the IAM user – **key-user1**. We must note that, if AWS CLI is used from an EC2 instance, it is best to leverage the IAM role instead of the IAM user credentials since the IAM roles work with the temporarily short-term credentials. The command to create the profile is as follows:

```
$ aws configure --profile key-user
```

Once the profile is created and configured, we can fire away the CLI commands to perform the encryption and decryption using the CMK with alias **`bpb479`**. Let's try to encrypt a sample file named **`samplefile.txt`** with the cleartext – **`This message is confidential`**. We will issue the following command:

```
$ aws kms encrypt --key-id "alias/bpb479" \
--plaintext fileb://samplefile.txt \
--profile key-user
```

Note that we have identified the CMK with its key alias and this alias is prefixed with the pattern **alias/**. The CMK could also be identified with the key ID, key ARN, or alias ARN. However, when using the CMK within a single AWS account, the best practice is to use the key alias (a friendly name) to refer to the CMKs from the applications. This actually helps with the easy rotation of CMKs.

The preceding command produces a JSON output that carries three fields – CiphertextBlob, KeyId, and EncryptionAlgorithm. The *CiphertextBlob* carries the ciphertext. To store this output to a file (named **samplefile.enc**), we can issue the following command:

```
$ aws kms encrypt --key-id "alias/bpb479" \
--plaintext fileb://samplefile.txt \
--profile key-user \
--query CiphertextBlob \
--output text | base64 -d > samplefile.enc
```

What this command does is that it queries the specific **CiphertextBlob** field, converts the output in text, performs a base64 decoding (assuming Linux operating system with base64 utility), and finally redirects the output to a file named **samplefile.enc**. At this point, our confidential text has been encrypted using the CMK that we created and is now residing in a binary file.

The next step is to perform the decryption of the binary file and get back the original cleartext. We will use the following command for that purpose:

```
$ aws kms decrypt --key-id "alias/bpb479" \
--ciphertext-blob fileb://samplefile.enc \
--profile key-user \
--query Plaintext \
--output text | base64 -d
```

Note that, in this case, we have actually queried the field *Plaintext,* which is returned by the decrypt command, converted the output to text, and finally performed a base64 decoding. The base64 decoding is important since the decrypt command returns the output in a base64 encoded format. The output of the command will be – **This message is confidential** – which is the original message contained in the **samplefile.txt** file.

Data key and data key pairs

Data keys, unlike CMKs are encryption keys used to encrypt large amounts of data and are not limited by the 4KB threshold pertaining to the size of the data being encrypted. In fact, the CMKs can be used to generate, encrypt, and decrypt the data keys. But they are not stored, managed, or tracked by AWS KMS. In essence, the data keys must be managed outside of AWS KMS.

The data key pairs are asymmetric data keys that consists of a key-pair – public key and private key. These keys are mathematically related to one another. They can be used for encryption and decryption or signing and verification outside AWS KMS. AWS KMS supports the RSA key pairs and Elliptic curve key pairs and protects the private keys in each key pair under a specified symmetric CMK. However, as with data keys, AWS KMS does not store, manage, track, or perform the cryptographic operations with the data key pairs.

Envelope encryption

Envelope encryption is a technique of having the data encrypted by the data key and encrypting the data key with a master key. So, while the data is protected by the data key, the data key itself in turn, is protected with a master key. *Figure 4.8* explains how envelope encryption works with AWS KMS, as follows:

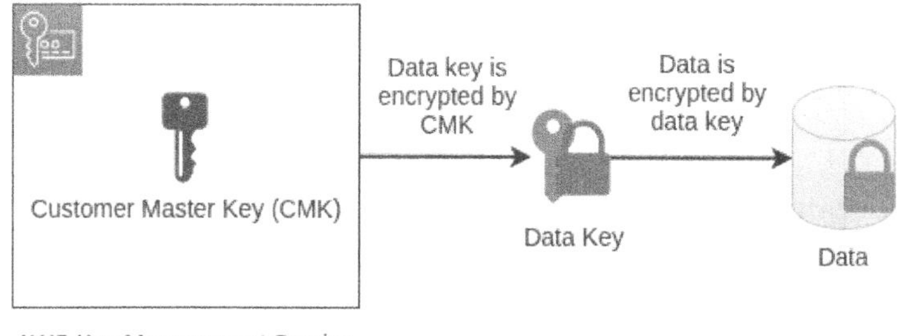

Figure 4.8: *Process of envelope encryption*

Typically, we request the AWS KMS service to generate a unique data key and specify a CMK which will be used to encrypt it. As a response, AWS KMS returns a plaintext version of the data key as well as an encrypted version. We can use the plaintext version to encrypt data and subsequently delete it (from the disk and memory). However, we can safely store the encrypted version of the data key (preferably along with the data) for decryption purposes.

During decryption, we request AWS KMS to decrypt the encrypted data key which returns the data key in plaintext. Now, the plaintext data key could be used to decrypt the data. Finally, we will erase the plaintext version of the data key from the disk as well as from the memory.

Encryption and decryption with data key

Now that we know the concepts around data keys and how they can help create envelope encryption and CMKs, let's jump into some action. We will generate a data key using AWS CLI and then use that data key to encrypt the data/file.

We will start with the assumption that there exists a CMK (with an alias **`bpb479`**) and an IAM user also exists configured with a set of permissions, as defined in *Table 4.2*. Note that, **key-user1** has the permissions to perform **`kms:GenerateDataKey`** and **`kms:Decrypt`**. Moreover, we assume that AWS CLI has been configured to use the profile of **key-user** which has been configured with the user credentials of **`key-user1`**. Refer to *Table 4.2* as follows:

Iam User Name	Iam Policy	Permissions	Kms Key Policy Role	Aws Cli Profile
key-user1	Custom policy	`kms.Decrypt,kms:DescribeKey, kms:GenerateDataKey`	Key user	key-user

Table 4.2: *Data key based IAM policy permissions*

With the configurations out of the way, we can now generate a data key using AWS KMS. To do that, we will use the following command:

```
$ aws kms generate-data-key --key-id "alias/bpb479" \
--profile key-user \
--key-spec AES_256
```

The key-spec option specifies the length of the data key to be generated. The possible values are AES_128 (128-bit key) and AES_256 (256-bit key).

The preceding command produces a JSON output that carries three fields – CiphertextBlob, Plaintext, and KeyId. *CiphertextBlob* carries the encrypted data key (encrypted with CMK identified by the key-id). *Plaintext* carries the data key in cleartext. We must remember that both these formats of the data key are in fact, base64 encoded.

Thus, to decode the ciphertext data key and plaintext data key, we can use the following commands:

```
$ echo "<CiphertextBlob value>" | base64 -d > encrypted.key
$ echo "<Plaintext value>" | base64 -d > plaintext.key
```

Once decoded, we can use the plaintext data key file (named **`plaintext.key`**) to encrypt the data (outside AWS KMS), using tools like *openssl*. Once the file/data is encrypted, we will remove the **`plaintext.key`** and keep the decoded version of the encrypted key file (named **`encrypted.key`**) to be used during decryption.

During decryption, we will use the encrypted key file to fetch the plaintext key from AWS KMS, using the following command:

```
$ aws kms decrypt --key-id "alias/bpb479" \
--profile key-user \
--ciphertext-blob fileb://encrypted.key
```

The preceding command produces a JSON output that carries three fields – KeyId, Plaintext, and **EncryptionAlgorithm**. *Plaintext* carries the data key in cleartext that is base64 encoded. Once decoded, the plaintext key could be used to decrypt the data/file with tools like *openssl*, outside AWS KMS.

More KMS features

Let's go through some more features of AWS KMS like encryption context, grants, and key rotation.

Authenticated encryption with encryption context

Authenticated encryption provides confidentiality, integrity, and authenticity on the encrypted data by using **additional authenticated data** (**AAD**). AWS KMS supports AAD by the use of encryption context option with all the cryptographic operations about symmetric CMKs. Encryption context is used to introduce additional contextual information about the data being encrypted and takes the form of comma-separated set of key-value pairs (key1=value1, key2=value2).

When the encryption context option is used during encryption, the key-value pairs get cryptographically bound with the ciphertext in such a way that the same encryption context is required for successful decryption of the data. The key-value pairs can appear in any order in the encryption context, but they are case-sensitive.

At this point, we will assume that there exists a CMK (with an alias **bpb479**). IAM user- **key-user1** has been granted **kms:Encrypt** and **kms:Decrypt** permissions (as defined in *Table 4.3*). Additionally, AWS CLI has been configured to use the profile of **key-user**, which has been configured with the user credentials of key-user1. Refer to *Table 4.3* as follows:

Iam User Name	Iam Policy	Permissions	Kms Key Policy Role	Aws Cli Profile
key-user1	Custom policy	kms.Decrypt, kms: DescribeKey, kms: Encrypt	Key user	key-user

Table 4.3: *IAM policy permissions for encryption and decryption*

The following shows how to add the encryption context with the encrypt command:

```
$ aws kms encrypt --key-id "alias/bpb479" \
--profile key-user \
--plaintext fileb://samplefile.txt \
--query CiphertextBlob --output text \
--encryption-context"country=India,state=WB" | base64 -d > samplefile.enc
```

To successfully decrypt the contents of the **samplefile.enc**, we can supply the same encryption context during decryption, as follows:

```
$ aws kms decrypt --key-id "alias/bpb479" \
--profile key-user \
--ciphertext-blob fileb://samplefile.enc \
--query Plaintext --output text \
--encryption-context"state=WB,country=India" | base64 -d
```

If the same encryption context is not supplied during decryption, AWS CLI issues the following error – **An error occurred (InvalidCiphertextException) when calling the Decrypt operation:**.

KMS grant

In addition to the key policies and optional IAM policies, KMS grants provide a very flexible access control mechanism. Normally, the KMS grants are used to provide temporary permissions to the AWS principals to use CMKs. Grants can be easily attached and detached to/from a CMK, and they control access to a single CMK. Moreover, a grant can be used to allow access to the grant operations and cannot be used to deny access.

Key rotation

The rotation of the key material in a CMK is very important to maintain *perfect forward secrecy*. Cryptographic best practices disapprove the extensive reuse of encryption keys, so that if the latest key gets compromised, it has the potential to expose only a small portion of the encrypted data, thereby making sure that the future security mistakes do not threaten the past secrets.

The rotation of CMKs can be done in the following two ways:

- We can manually rotate the keys by creating a new customer managed CMK and make the changes to the applications that refer to this CMK using the key ID or key aliases. If the key alias is used, then we can ensure minimal changes to the application by keeping the alias of the new CMK to be the same as the old one (after changing the key alias of the old CMK, of course).

However, the challenge is with the data that has been encrypted by the old CMK, which now might have to be decrypted. In this case, we need to take extra measures to ensure that the old CMKs are not deleted and are used to decrypt the old data. Manual rotation is effective in controlling the rotation schedule of the CMKs.

- We can enable the automatic key rotation for an existing customer-managed CMK. With this option, AWS KMS generates new cryptographic material for the CMK every year. Moreover, KMS does not delete any rotated key material and saves these in perpetuity (unless the CMK is deleted). This means, any data that had been encrypted with the older key material can still be decrypted. Automatic key rotation is not supported for asymmetric CMKs, CMKs in the custom key stores and CMKs with the imported key material. The only option for such CMKs is manual rotation.

AWS CloudHSM

When it comes to key management and encryption at an enterprise scale, a typical enterprise will store the encryption keys in a central key management service (like AWS KMS). A more complex enterprise with stringent regulatory and security compliance requirements may use the key hierarchy or a **hardware security module** (**HSM**). HSM is a special tamper proof hardware device that safeguards and manages the digital keys and helps perform various cryptographic functions, including encryption/decryption, message signing, **Digital Rights Management** (**DRM**), etc.

AWS CloudHSM is a managed Hardware Security Module service on the AWS cloud. The service can be used for secure key storage and high-performance cryptographic operations which meets regulatory compliance requirements for data security.

The following are some of the significant features of AWS CloudHSM that makes it an easy choice for the enterprises with complex and validated cryptographic requirements:

- AWS CloudHSM offers dedicated, single tenanted access to FIPS 140-2 Level 3 validated modules. FIPS 140-2 Level 3 is a standard that adds the requirements for physical tamper-resistance and identity-based authentication for the module, thereby making HSMs attack proof.
- AWS CloudHSM can be integrated with the applications using industry-standard APIs like PKCS#11, **Java Cryptographic Extensions** (**JCE**), and other libraries.
- AWS CloudHSM is a fully managed service with automated hardware provisioning, patching, high availability, and backups.
- AWS CloudHSM allows easy migration of the digital keys stored in AWS CloudHSM to the other commercial HSM solutions.

- AWS CloudHSM creates a CloudHSM cluster which can contain multiple HSMs spread across more than one **availability zone** (**AZ**) in a region, thereby allowing the enterprises to easily scale their HSM capacity through on-demand addition or removal of HSMs to/from the AWS CloudHSM cluster.
- AWS CloudHSM provisions HSMs within the customer's VPC for better protection and isolation.
- AWS CloudHSM has an hourly fee for each HSM that is provisioned (until the HSM is terminated). There are no upfront costs.

Amazon S3

Amazon S3 is a fully managed, serverless, planet scale object storage service that features high durability, availability, and performance. Amazon S3 supports protection of the data, both in transit and at rest. In order to protect the data in transit, secure protocols like **Secure Socket Layer** (**SSL**)/**Transport Layer Security** (**TLS**) can be used along with Amazon S3. Client-side encryption can also be employed to protect the data in flight, by encrypting the data at client side before pushing it to the wire. With client-side encryption, the customers are responsible for managing the encryption process, keys, and choice of encryption tools. To protect the objects at rest, Amazon S3 supports various server-side encryption options. Each such option essentially employs envelope encryption and stores the encrypted objects. Let's take a closer look into the server-side and client-side encryption support available with Amazon S3.

Server-side encryption

For protecting the objects at rest, Amazon S3 provides server-side encryption where the objects are encrypted before being saved to the physical disks in the Amazon data centers. When the objects are downloaded from Amazon S3, they are decrypted transparently.

For **server-side encryption** (**SSE**) of the objects, Amazon S3 provides the following three options, which can be chosen during the creation of a bucket or during copying of an individual object into S3:

- **SSE with Amazon S3 managed keys (SSE-S3)**: With SSE-S3 option, each object is encrypted with a unique AES-256 bit key, and for additional security, envelope encryption is employed, that is, the key itself is encrypted with a master key that is rotated at regular intervals. The following command can be used with AWS CLI to leverage the SSE-S3 option for an object (named **`sample.txt`**) copied into a bucket (named **`bpb-bucket`**):

  ```
  $ aws s3 cp ./sample.txt s3://bpb-bucket --sse AES256
  ```

Figure 4.9 shows how to enable the default encryption (**`Create Bucket | Default Encryption`**) with the SSE-S3 option during the creation of a new bucket from AWS Management Console. This would ensure all new objects stored in the bucket to be encrypted by default with the SSE-S3 option. Refer to *figure 4.9* as follows:

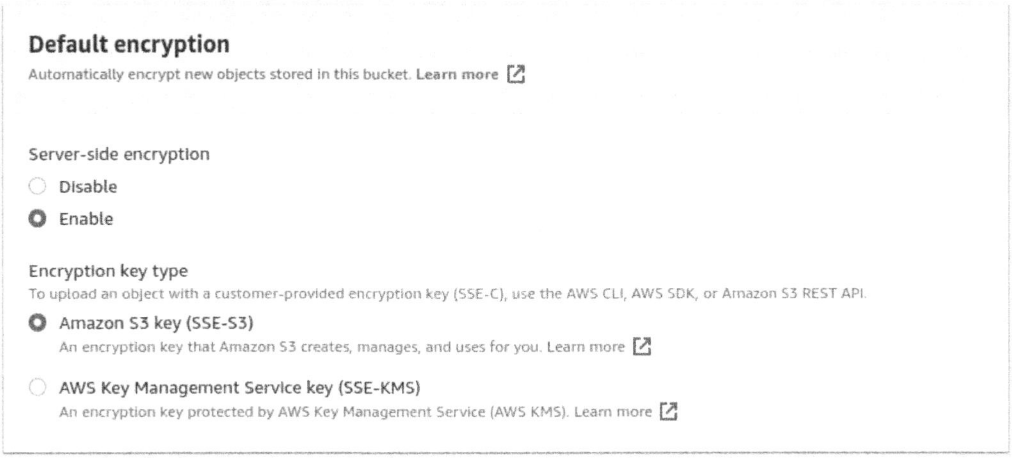

Default encryption

Automatically encrypt new objects stored in this bucket. **Learn more**

Server-side encryption

- Disable
- Enable

Encryption key type

To upload an object with a customer-provided encryption key (SSE-C), use the AWS CLI, AWS SDK, or Amazon S3 REST API.

- Amazon S3 key (SSE-S3)
  An encryption key that Amazon S3 creates, manages, and uses for you. Learn more
- AWS Key Management Service key (SSE-KMS)
  An encryption key protected by AWS Key Management Service (AWS KMS). Learn more

Figure 4.9: *Enabling default bucket encryption with SSE-S3 option*

- **SSE with CMKs stored in AWS KMS (SSE-KMS)**: With the SSE-KMS option, we (customers) can select either AWS managed CMK or customer managed CMK residing in AWS KMS. This option has some additional benefits and costs as compared to the SSE-S3 option; for example, the key usage audit trails are available with this option. With SSE-KMS, Amazon S3 Bucket Keys could be used to decrease the requested traffic from Amazon S3 to AWS KMS, thereby reducing the cost of the encryption. Basically, AWS KMS generates a bucket level key that is used to create the unique data keys for objects in the bucket. The bucket key has a time limited lifespan within Amazon S3 and is reused, thereby, reducing the number of cryptographic requests to AWS KMS. The following commands can be used with AWS CLI to leverage the SSE-KMS option for an object (named **sample.txt**) copied into a bucket (named **bpb-bucket**). The first command uses the SSE-KMS option with AWS managed CMK and the second command uses the SSE-KMS option with customer managed CMK (with a key alias – **bpb479**). Of course, instead of the key alias, we could also specify the customer managed CMK ARN to identify the **`sse-kms-key-id`**. Look at the following commands:

```
$ aws s3 cp ./sample.txt s3://bpb-bucket --sse aws:kms
$ aws s3 cp ./sample.txt s3://bpb-bucket --sse aws:kms \
--sse-kms-key-id "alias/bpb479"
```

Figure 4.10 illustrates how to enable the default encryption on a bucket with the SSE-KMS option, as follows:

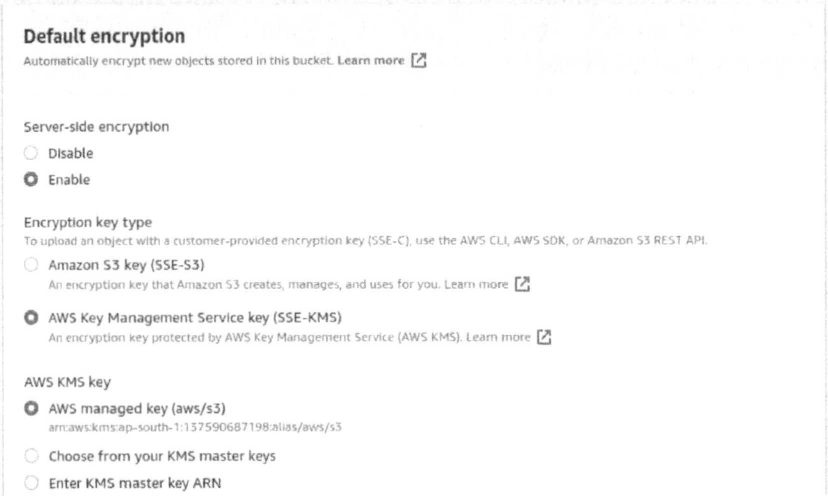

Default encryption

Automatically encrypt new objects stored in this bucket. Learn more

Server-side encryption

Disable

Enable

Encryption key type

To upload an object with a customer-provided encryption key (SSE-C), use the AWS CLI, AWS SDK, or Amazon S3 REST API.

Amazon S3 key (SSE-S3)

An encryption key that Amazon S3 creates, manages, and uses for you. Learn more

AWS Key Management Service key (SSE-KMS)

An encryption key protected by AWS Key Management Service (AWS KMS). Learn more

AWS KMS key

AWS managed key (aws/s3)

arn:aws:kms:ap-south-1:137590687198:alias/aws/s3

Choose from your KMS master keys

Enter KMS master key ARN

Figure 4.10: *Enabling default bucket encryption with SSE-KMS option*

The following permissions are required to upload/download the Amazon S3 objects encrypted with AWS KMS CMK: **`kms:Encrypt`**, **`kms:Decrypt`**, **`kms:GenerateDataKey`**, and **`kms:DescribeKey`**. *AWS Signature version 4* must be used when uploading or accessing the objects encrypted with the SSE-KMS option (AWS SDK can be used for this purpose). All GET and PUT requests for the objects secured by SSE-KMS must be made over SSL/TLS.

- **SSE with Customer provided keys (SSE-C)**: With the SSE-C option, we (or customers) are responsible for managing the lifecycle and security of the encryption keys. Amazon S3 manages the encryption of the objects using the keys provided by the customers (AES-256) before writing the objects to the disks and the decryption of the objects when they are accessed or downloaded. Amazon S3 does not store the encryption keys, and as such, the customers need to maintain the mapping of the data and the key that was used to encrypt it. All requests must be made over HTTPS when using the SSE-C option. The following is a sample command to copy an individual object to an Amazon S3 bucket with SSE-C option (Note that, both **`sse-c`** (with value AES256) and **`sse-c-key`** (non base64 encoded key) options will have to be used):

```
$ aws s3 cp <source-file> s3://<bucket-name> \
--sse-c AES256 \
--sse-c-key<generated non base64 encoded key>
```

The easiest way to enable the encryption on objects is to enable the server-side default encryption on the bucket. This ensures, all new objects placed in the bucket are encrypted by default. On the other hand, the individual objects can also be encrypted explicitly on being pushed to the bucket.

Now, let's consider a situation where we have created a bucket in Amazon S3 with the default encryption option selected as SSE-S3. However, while copying the individual objects to the bucket (using AWS CLI or otherwise), we start using a different option (like SSE-KMS). The option specified with the individual object takes precedence.

The server-side encryption option that has been used to encrypt an object could be easily verified by checking the object properties (**Properties | Server-side encryption settings**).

Client-side encryption

Client-side encryption can serve as the security of objects in transit. With this strategy, we (or customers) can encrypt the data/objects before sending the same to Amazon S3. The decryption of the objects also takes place after these have been downloaded from Amazon S3. There are essentially two options for enabling the client-side encryption, which are as follows:

- **Use a CMK stored in AWS KMS**

  In this case, while uploading an object to S3, we can make a request to AWS KMS for a symmetric data key by passing the key-id of an existing CMK. In response, we will get a plaintext version of the data key which is used to encrypt the data/object and an encrypted version of the same data key which can be uploaded to Amazon S3 as object metadata.

  During decryption, we can first download the encrypted object from Amazon S3, along with the object metadata that contains the encrypted version of the symmetric data key. Then, we can send a request to AWS KMS to decrypt the encrypted version of the data key by passing the cipher blob (from object metadata) and the CMK key-id. In response, AWS KMS will send the plaintext version of the data key, which should be used to decrypt the encrypted data/object.

- **Use a custom master key which is stored and managed outside AWS**

  Here, we provide a client-side master key (both symmetric and asymmetric keys are supported) to the Amazon S3 encryption client (supported by AWS SDK). This client uses the custom master key to encrypt the one-time used data keys that it generates locally to encrypt each object. The client then uploads the encrypted data key and its material description (to determine which client-side master key to use during decryption) as part of the object metadata. The client also uploads the encrypted data to Amazon S3 and saves the encrypted data key as object metadata (**x-amz-meta-x-amz-key**).

During decryption, the client downloads the encrypted object from Amazon S3 along with object metadata and uses the material description to determine which custom master key to use to decrypt the data key. The client uses the master key to decrypt the data key and then uses the decrypted data key to decrypt the object.

Amazon EBS

Amazon EBS provides a network attached, high performance block storage service to the Amazon EC2 instances. The service leverages the AWS KMS customer master keys (CMKs) to create encrypted boot/data volumes, snapshots, and volumes created from the encrypted snapshots. Cryptographic operations occur on the servers that host the Amazon EC2 instances so as to ensure both encryption at rest and encryption in transit (between an Amazon EC2 instance and the network attached Amazon EBS storage).

EBS volumes can be encrypted by either enabling the encryption by default (account level attribute) or by enabling the encryption during the creation of the volume. The default region specific CMK used for encryption is the AWS managed CMK (identified by key-alias: **alias/aws/ebs**). However, we can change these default settings to use a symmetric customer managed CMK of our choice. The following AWS CLI commands can be used to do each of the following:

1. Enable encryption by default with the default EBS encryption key: `$ aws ec2 enable-ebs-encryption-by-default`
2. Modify the default EBS encryption key to point to a customer managed CMK identified by key alias **alias/bpb479:**

   ```
   $ aws ec2 modify-ebs-default-kms-key-id --kms-key-id alias/bpb479
   ```

3. Reset the default EBS encryption key:

   ```
   $ aws ec2 reset-ebs-default-kms-key-id
   ```

4. Disable encryption by default:

   ```
   $ aws ec2 disable-ebs-encryption-by-default
   ```

Note that, kms-key-id could also be specified with the key ID or CMK ARN or alias ARN.

This account level attribute could also be enabled by visiting the following path – **Amazon EC2 Console** | **EC2 Dashboard** | **Account Attributes** (settings) | **EBS Encryption** | Click on **Manage**. Then, we will enable the encryption and select the default encryption key. Refer to *figure 4.11* as follows:

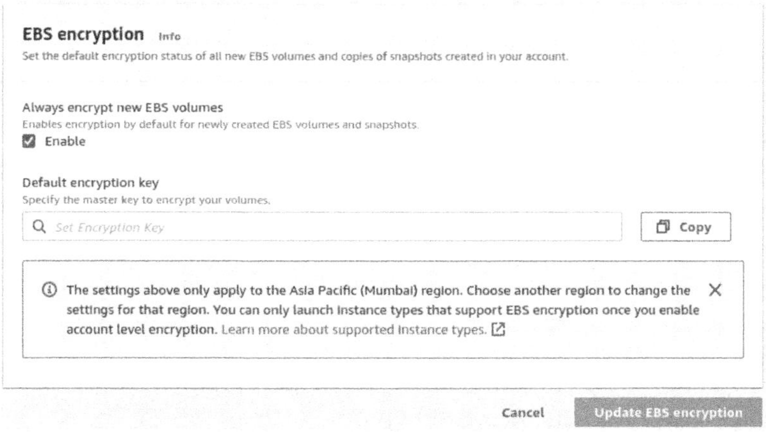

***Figure 4.11:** Enabling default encryption of EBS volumes*

For enabling the encryption during the creation of a new empty volume (in AWS Management Console), all we need to do is check the **`Encryption`** checkbox and select the **`Master Key`** (*figure 4.12*). This master key could be AWS-managed CMK or customer-managed CMK, as shown in *figure 4.12*, as follows:

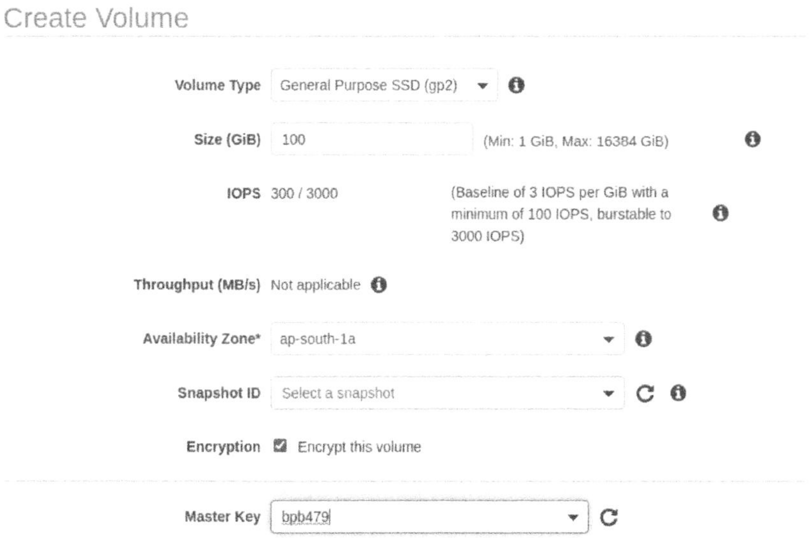

***Figure 4.12:** Selection of master key to be used for EBS encryption*

With AWS CLI, the following sample commands could be used to do the following:

1. Create an encrypted volume with the default EBS encryption key:

```
$ aws ec2 create-volume --volume-type gp2 \
--size 8 --encrypted \
--availability-zone ap-south-1a
```

2. Create an encrypted volume with the customer managed CMK identified by key ID, key alias, key alias ARN, or key ARN:

```
$ aws ec2 create-volume --volume-type gp2 \
--size 8 --encrypted \
--kms-key-id alias/bpb479 --availability-zone ap-south-1a
```

By default, if the volume is encrypted by a CMK, any snapshots that we make from that volume and the volumes that we restore from those snapshots are also encrypted by the same CMK.

There is no direct way to encrypt an existing unencrypted volume or snapshot. The easiest way to encrypt them is by creating an encrypted snapshot or restoring the unencrypted snapshot to an encrypted volume using AWS CLI or AWS SDK.

When we choose an Amazon EBS volume to be encrypted, Amazon EBS sends a **`generate data key`** (without plaintext key) request, specifying the key ID of the CMK to be used. AWS KMS generates a new data key (AES-256), encrypts it with the chosen CMK, and then returns the encrypted data key to Amazon EBS. Amazon EBS stores this key along with the volume metadata.

At some point in time, this encrypted Amazon EBS volume is attached to an Amazon EC2 instance which sends a **`decrypt`** request to AWS KMS and pass the CMK key id and the encrypted data key. Amazon EBS also sends a **`create grant`** request to AWS KMS, so that it can decrypt the data key. AWS KMS decrypts the encrypted data key and sends the decrypted data key to Amazon EC2. EC2 places the plaintext data key in memory of the hypervisor in order to encrypt disk I/O to the volume. This plaintext data key resides in the hypervisor memory as long as the volume is attached to the Amazon EC2 instance. This means, if the CMK gets deleted, the volume data can still be encrypted/decrypted using the plaintext copy of the data key from the hypervisor memory (unless it is detached).

Amazon DynamoDB

Amazon DynamoDB is a fully managed, serverless NoSQL database offering from AWS. All user data stored in an Amazon DynamoDB table is encrypted at rest, by default. In fact, just like Amazon S3 and other services, DynamoDB uses the AWS KMS service for encrypting the data stored in the tables. For protection of the data in flight, Amazon DynamoDB supports HTTPS based requests through RESTful API calls, AWS CLI, or AWS SDK. In addition, we may choose to use **client-side encryption** (**CSE**) before sending the data to the table.

Server-side encryption

Amazon DynamoDB offers three options to encrypt the data stored in the tables. These options are available during the creation of the table. On "Create DynamoDB

Table" page (AWS DynamoDB Console), we can uncheck the "Use default settings" option under "Table Settings" and select the SSE encryption option under "Encryption At Rest" section. Refer to *figure 4.13* as follows:

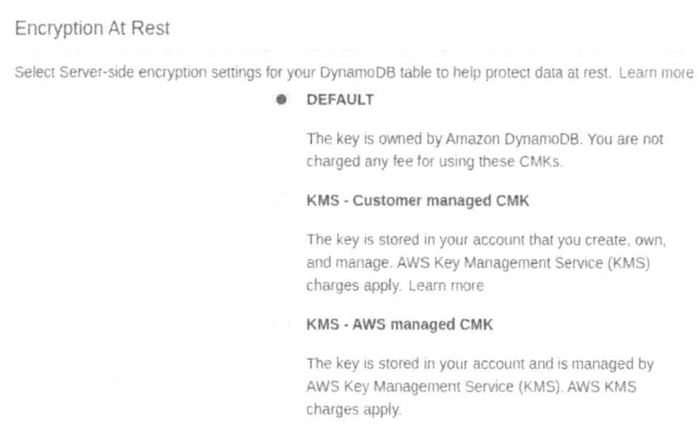

Figure 4.13: *Server-side encryption in DynamoDB*

By now, we already know what these options stand for. The default option uses AWS owned CMKs and takes effect if no option is explicitly selected. The other two options are encrypting the data with AWS managed CMK and customer managed CMK.

When the encrypted tables are accessed, Amazon DynamoDB decrypts the table data transparently. This means, all queries on the table data works seamless on the encrypted data. Moreover, we can change the SSE options for encryption at any time. Objects like DynamoDB streams, global tables, and backups that are related to an encrypted table are also encrypted.

Client-side encryption

Amazon DynamoDB supports the client-side encryption which offers end-to-end (from source to storage) protection of data. Typically, we can use DynamoDB Encryption Client, an open-sourced software library licensed under Apache 2.0 for this purpose. This library is available in Java and Python and these implementations are interoperable. DynamoDB Encryption client transparently encrypts and signs the table items (to be specific, attribute values are encrypted, and signature calculated) when we call **`PutItem`** operation and verifies and decrypts the items when we call **`GetItem`** operation on the table. Note that, the primary and sort key (if present) are not encrypted, and we should not store sensitive data in these fields.

DynamoDB Encryption Client provides several **cryptographic materials providers (CMPs)**. A CMP is the component that gathers encryption and signing keys which are used in turn, to encrypt and sign the table items. We could use Direct KMS Materials Provider which uses AWS KMS CMK to protect the table items. In fact, a

Direct KMS CMP generates unique encryption and signing keys for each item; thus, it has a tighter integration with AWS KMS for cryptographic operations.

TIP: We can use the following links to learn more about DynamoDB Encryption Client Java and Python libraries:

Java: https://github.com/aws/aws-dynamodb-encryption-java
Python: https://github.com/aws/aws-dynamodb-encryption-python

Amazon RDS

Amazon RDS is a managed relational database service characterized by support for various well known database engines and high availability, scalability, and durability. With Amazon RDS, we can secure our data stored in the RDS managed database instances. For the security of the data at rest, Amazon RDS supports strong encryption with the AES-256 keys. For the security of the data in motion, we can use SSL/TLS based connections with database instances along with client-side encryption. Additionally, native encryption features pertaining to particular database engines, like **transparent data encryption** (**TDE**) supported by Oracle databases can also be employed.

Server-side encryption

Amazon RDS supports server-side encryption (or encryption at rest) of the data for all (supported) database engines and storage types, by leveraging AWS KMS **customer master keys** (**CMKs**). We can use either AWS managed CMK (default option) or CMK, for the encryption. Enabling the encryption and choice of the master key can be made during the creation of the database instance and cannot be changed or modified later. To encrypt a database instance, we need to check **`Enable Encryption`** and select a **`Master key`** under the **`Additional Configuration`** section on the **`Create database`** page. Refer to *figure 4.14*, as follows:

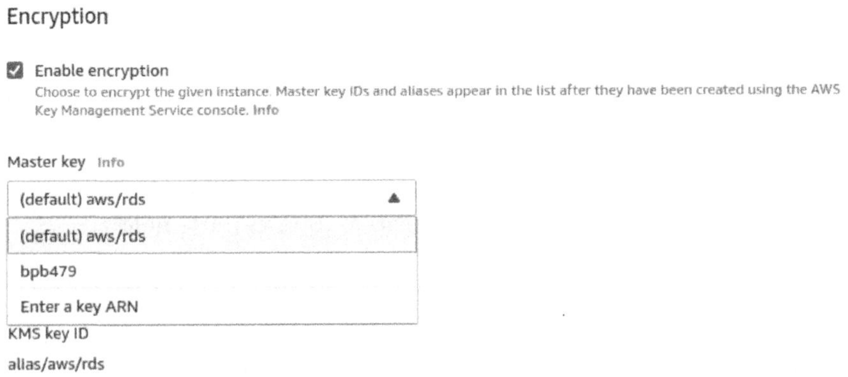

Encryption

☑ Enable encryption
Choose to encrypt the given instance. Master key IDs and aliases appear in the list after they have been created using the AWS Key Management Service console. Info

Master key Info

(default) aws/rds ▲

(default) aws/rds

bpb479

Enter a key ARN

KMS key ID

alias/aws/rds

Figure 4.14: *Server-side encryption in RDS*

Some of the limitations associated with the RDS encryption are as follows:

- RDS encryption is not supported for a few DB instance types like General purpose (M1), Memory-optimized (M2), and burst capable (T2).
- The encryption cannot be disabled for a database instance, once it is enabled.
- An encrypted database cannot be unencrypted. However, the data can be exported from an encrypted database instance and imported into an unencrypted one.
- A snapshot of an encrypted database instance must be encrypted with the same master key as the database instance.
- The encrypted read replicas in the same region as the database instance must be encrypted with the same CMK as the database instance.
- The creation of the encrypted snapshot of an unencrypted database is not possible.
- In order toTo copy an encrypted snapshot from one region to another, the CMK of the destination region must be specified.

Client-side encryption

To perform client-side encryption, we can use AWS Encryption SDK in the application code. Encryption SDK basically generates the data key (using AWS KMS) and gets a plaintext data key, as well as an encrypted version of the same key. The plaintext data key is used to encrypt the column values (and then deleted) and the encrypted data key is stored along with the encrypted column value. The final encrypted data composed of the encrypted column value and encrypted data key is stored in the database. Encryption SDK can also be used for *authenticated encryption* by performing additional integrity and authenticity checks with the use of *encryption context*.

Establishing encrypted database connection

To protect the data in motion, Amazon RDS supports the SSL/TLS encrypted secure connection for the following database engines – MySQL, MariaDB, SQL Server, Oracle, or PostgreSQL. Each database engine has its process for implementing the SSL/TLS connection. The SSL/TLS protocols can still be used if we are using Amazon RDS Proxy (a managed proxy).

Amazon Macie for data loss prevention

Amazon Macie is a fully managed, machine learning powered, sensitive data discovery, and classification service that helps to implement the **Data Loss Prevention (DLP)** solutions. Currently, Amazon Macie can detect sensitive data and leakage from the Amazon S3 buckets. It can be easily integrated with AWS Organization to provide delegated administration and visibility at the organization level. It provides a dashboard view with key controls and metrics and visibility across all accounts and buckets. *Figure 4.15* shows how a typical Amazon Macie dashboard (**`Summary`** menu on the left pane of Amazon Macie Console) looks like, as follows:

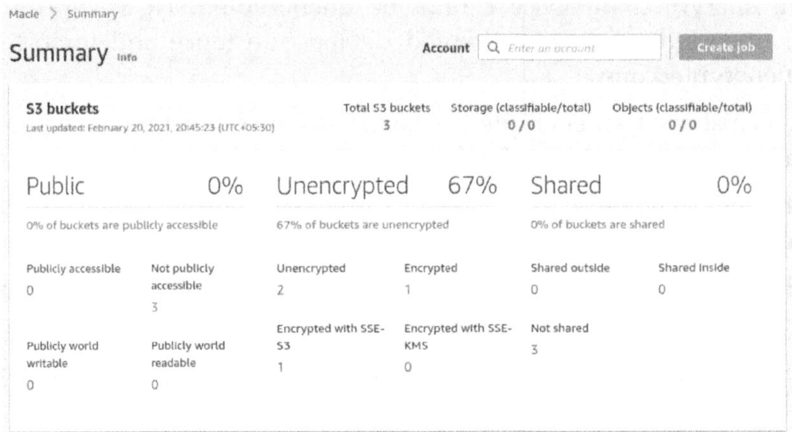

***Figure 4.15:** Amazon Macie dashboard in Amazon Macie Console*

Amazon Macie checks the following:

- Public accessibility of the buckets.
- Encryption status of the buckets.
- How the buckets and objects are shared with the other users or accounts by evaluating the buckets policies and ACLs to determine the effective permissions set.

The policy findings are published to Security Hub and CloudWatch Events. For the long term storage of the data discovery results, we can configure an S3 bucket from Amazon Macie Console.

Sensitive data discovery job

To discover sensitive data, Macie uses *managed data identifiers* that uses machine learning (ML) and pattern matching to detect the sensitive data types. These include multiple types of PII (full name, birth date, passport number, etc.) and PHI data. These data identifiers are automatically used to analyze the data.

We can create a discovery job in Amazon Macie to analyze the S3 buckets for the sensitive data and classify them. The following steps are involved in the creation of the job from the Amazon Macie Console:

1. Go to the **`Jobs`** menu (on the left pane) and click on the **`Create Job`** button.

2. On the next page, select the S3 buckets that Macie will analyze and review the selection, and click on **`Next`**.
3. Select the type of job – One time or Scheduled (daily/weekly/monthly) – and click on **`Next`**. We can choose to create the inclusion and exclusion filters that works on tags, filename extensions, etc.
4. Optionally, create and specify *custom data identifiers* (using regular expressions) and click on **`Next`**.
5. Give the job a name and description and click on **`Next`**.
6. Review the job configuration and create the job by clicking on **`Submit`**.

Once the job is created, it goes into an **`Active (running)`** state. Once completed, the job enters the **`Complete`** state. At this point, we can check the findings (the **`Findings`** menu is on the left pane of the Amazon Macie Console). These findings are categorized based on severity (low/medium/high) and we can filter the findings based on severity. Refer to *figure 4.16* as follows:

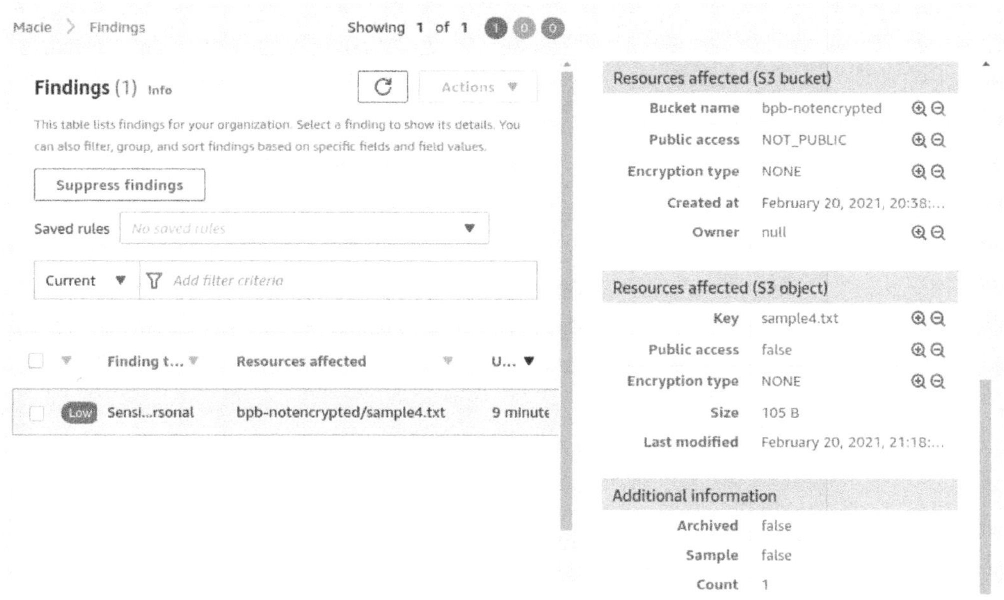

***Figure 4.16:** Amazon Macie findings*

As we can see in *figure 4.16*, each finding points to the affected resource (S3 bucket and S3 object) with details pertaining to these resources. However, these findings never reveal any sensitive information.

Conclusion

In this chapter, we learned how AWS provides an arsenal of services to ensure the protection of data at rest and in transit. The fundamental key management and storage service is AWS **Key Management Service** (**KMS**). AWS KMS, in turn, uses secured and tamper-proof **hardware security modules** (**HSMs**) to store the keys and key materials. Most of the other services like Amazon S3, Amazon EBS, Amazon RDS, Amazon DynamoDB, leverage AWS KMS for securing the data. Finally, we also introduced Amazon Macie, a managed sensitive data discovery and classification service integrated with Amazon S3.

In the next chapter, we will cover Application security and discuss AWS's significant security controls and services to minimize the application-layer vulnerabilities and protect the applications from attacks.

CHAPTER 5
Application Security

Introduction

The realm of application security deserves an entire book. There are many nuts and bolts to be tightened, doors to be locked, and keys to be hidden away from the prying eyes. The responsibility of securing custom applications on Amazon Web Services (AWS) falls primarily on the application owners. However, AWS public cloud provides several services and features that can help offload several responsibilities from the application. The application owners and developers can essentially focus more on the application features and business functionalities.

Structure

In this chapter, we will cover the following topics:

- Securing APIs
- AuthN/AuthZ with Amazon Cognito
- Securing web applications hosted on Amazon S3 and CloudFront
- Externalizing secrets and configuration parameters
- Web Application Firewall
- Securing applications with load balancer

Objectives

The objective of this chapter is to introduce the major areas of application security and how AWS can help in securing the application layer. We'll learn about the various ways in which we can protect APIs published on Amazon API Gateway. We'll also learn how Amazon Cognito can help in establishing the sound authentication and authorization scheme for the applications. Subsequently, we will attempt to grasp the details of securing the highly scalable and high-performance web applications using Amazon CloudFront and Amazon S3. We'll learn how to externalize the application secrets and configuration parameters by storing these in AWS Secrets Manager and AWS Systems Manager Parameter Store. Finally, we'll take a quick tour of AWS Web Application Firewall (WAF) and how it can help to secure the web traffic.

Securing APIs

Security of APIs is of great importance to any enterprise, primarily because APIs can help open new revenue channels, augment customer engagement, and increase collaboration with partners and other ecosystem players to expand the business. Furthermore, APIs expose resources, assets, and services to either internal or external clients. Amazon API Gateway is a highly available, managed service which can help in creating, publishing, maintaining, securing, and monitoring the APIs deployed on AWS cloud at scale. It supports REST, HTTP, and WebSocket APIs. Let's look at some of the security features available in API Gateway to protect these APIs.

API authorization

Once an API is staged or published on Amazon API Gateway, it becomes accessible with the default **execute-api** endpoint. This endpoint has the following format:

```
https://<api-id>.execute-api.<region-code>.amazonaws.
com/<stage>/<resource>
```

However, we must decide on 'who' can access this endpoint and 'which' resources or methods of the API can they access. The answer to this question is very significant as it has a direct impact on the security of the API. There are several authorization strategies that the companies incorporate. For example, a very common strategy is to have the API clients authenticate themselves against an Identity Provider (like PingIdentity, Okta, etc.), and in return, get a signed bearer token or access token. Subsequently, the API clients are required to pass this access token in the request header during an API call. The API gateway must verify this token and retrieve the authorization scopes granted with the token and provide access to the appropriate API resources based on the scope. API Gateway provides several types of authorizers (like IAM, Lambda authorizer, etc.) which, when associated with the APIs, can help implement the authorization schemes.

IAM Authorizer

The IAM policies could control the access to the API resources and methods in Amazon API Gateway. Such policies could be used to control the access to both the API management (create, deploy, manage) component and the API execution component of API Gateway. This could be a very effective strategy for private APIs that are not exposed outside the **Virtual Private Cloud** (**VPC**). This is so because controlling the access to the API resources / methods via the IAM authorizer involves the distribution of either long-term or short-term (AWS Security Token Service or STS based) credentials and warrants the use of AWS Signature Version-4 for signing the requests.

To learn more about the AWS Signature Version 4 process, visit the following link: https://docs.aws.amazon.com/general/latest/gr/signature-version-4.html

An exciting feature of IAM-based authorization is that the IAM policies could be designed to be very granular. Let's check a sample IAM policy that allows access to retrieve the details of a customer, by customer ID but denies access to the creation of a new customer in the DEV stage. Now, when this permission policy is attached to an IAM identity (like user, group, role), that identity will effectively have the following permissions:

```
{
  "Version": "2012-10-17",
  "Statement": [
    {
        "Effect": "Allow",
          "Action": "execute-api:Invoke",
          "Resource": [
"arn:aws:execute-api:<region-code>:<account-id>:<api-id>/DEV/GET/
customer/*"
          ]
      },
      {
          "Effect": "Deny",
          "Action": "execute-api:Invoke",
          "Resource": [  "arn:aws:execute-api:<region-code>:<account-
id>:<api-id>/DEV/POST/customer"
          ]
      }
   ]
```

}

At this point, we assume that this sample IAM policy is associated with an IAM user (say **api_user**) who has the programmatic access and holds the AWS access key ID and secret access key.

To associate the IAM authorizer with an API method, we just need to select the method and under the **Method Request | Settings** section, select **AWS IAM** from the **Authorization** drop-down and post the changes by clicking on the check mark button. In *figure 5.1*, AWS IAM authorization is enabled for the **GET** method of **/customer/{id}** resource, shown as follows:

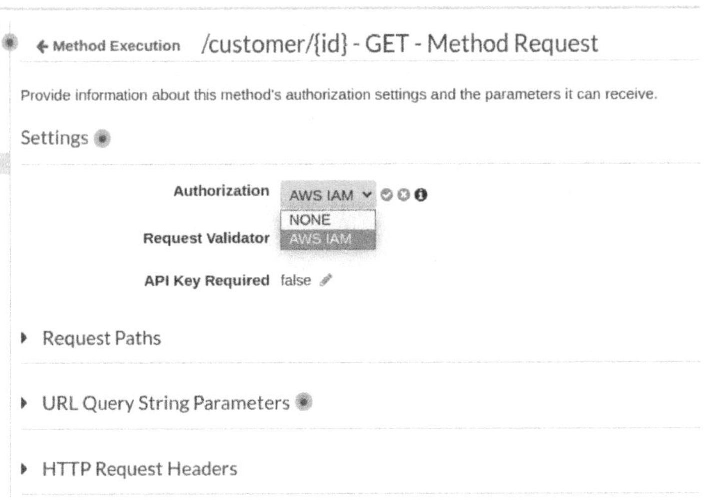

Figure 5.1: *Enabling IAM authorizer with API method*

Finally, we will use Postman to check if **api_user**, who has been assigned the IAM policy, is able to invoke the **GET** method on the **/customer/{id}** resource. In Postman, we will have to select **AWS Signature** under **Authorization Type**. The following configuration needs to be made, pertaining to the AWS Signature authorization as well (refer to *figure 5.2*):

- **AccessKey**: <AWS access key ID of api_user >
- **SecretKey**: <AWS secret access key of api_user>
- **Advanced/AWS Region**: <region-code>
- **Advanced/Service Name**: **execute-api**

Essentially, Postman uses AWS Signature Version-4 to sign the request and send it to the API endpoint. At the endpoint, the IAM policy is evaluated for the user whose credentials have been used to sign the request and the access is either granted or denied. In case of **api_user**, the access will be granted to the **GET** method of the **/customer/{id}** resource. Refer to *figure 5.2* as follows:

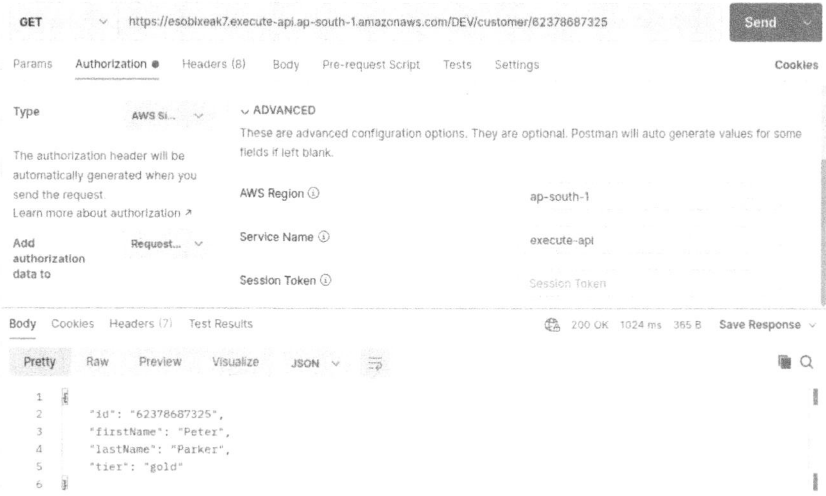

Figure 5.2: *Using Postman to call an API endpoint protected by IAM authorizer*

If we attempt to invoke the **GET** method on the **/customer/{id}** resource, without the appropriate AWS credentials, the access will be denied and API Gateway will return HTTP 403 (Forbidden), by default.

Amazon API Gateway also supports the resource based IAM policies, which could be used to securely invoke the APIs in the following scenarios:

- Cross account API access
- API access from a particular IP address range or CIDR block
- Access from specified Virtual Private Clouds (VPC) or VPC endpoints
- The resource-based policies work in tandem with identity policies to secure the API access

Lambda Authorizer

The Lambda authorizers are an Amazon API Gateway feature that can help create custom authorization schemes for the APIs using the Lambda functions. A Lambda authorizer essentially attempts to establish the identity of the caller, and then either allow or deny the access to the API resources. The Lambda authorizer could be used to implement the authorization strategies like OAuth, **Security Assertion Markup Language** (**SAML**), or any custom scheme. There are two types of Lambda Authorizers that can be used with REST APIs, which are as follows:

- A **Token authorizer** receives the caller's identity as a token that is passed by the caller in the request header (like a bearer token passed in Authorization header). This token is available under **event.authorizationToken** in the Lambda authorizer event structure. Finally, the authorizer returns an IAM policy to the API Gateway which either allows or denies the access to the requested resource.

- A **Request authorizer** receives the caller's identity as a combination of request headers, query string parameters, API Gateway context variable, or stage variables. This type of authorizer also returns an IAM policy to the API Gateway.

Figure 5.3 provides a schematic flow of how a Lambda authorizer works hand-in-hand with API Gateway to verify the identity of the caller and authorize access to the API resources. In this flow, we assume that the API user gets authenticated by an identity Provider which provides an access token, as shown in *figure 5.3* as follows:

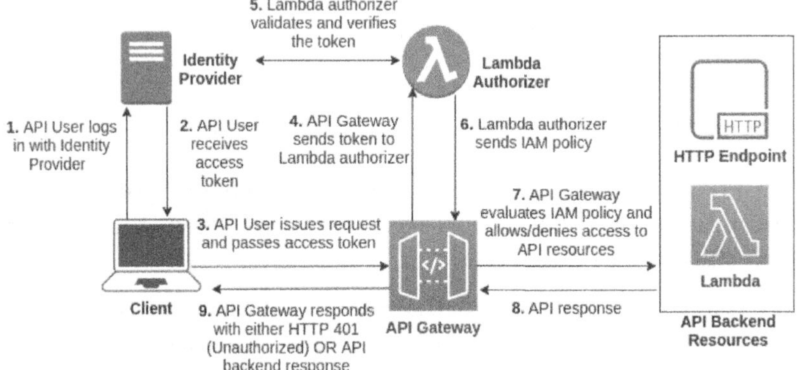

Figure 5.3: *Working of a Lambda authorizer*

The following are the basic steps involved:

- The user logs in with an identity provider by supplying credentials like user id / password / some form of **multi-factor authentication** (**MFA**), etc.
- The identity provider authenticates the user and sends back a signed access token which carries the list of scopes that the user is authorized to access. A very widely used token standard is JSON Web Token, which is used as a bearer token.

  To know more about JSON Web Token (JWT), visit the following site: https://jwt.io/introduction

- The API user now places this access token in the Authorization header of the HTTP request and sends the same to the API Gateway. The header would look somewhat like the following:

  ```
  Authorization: Bearer <token>
  ```

- API Gateway receives the request, and with the Lambda authorizer associated to the requested API, sends the token to the Lambda authorizer.

- The Lambda authorizer validates this token with the identity provider and subsequently generates an IAM policy to either allow or deny access to the requested API resource. A generated IAM policy looks somewhat like the following:

```
{
  "Version": "2012-10-17",
  "Statement": [
    {
      "Action": "execute-api:Invoke",
      "Effect": "Allow",
      "Resource": "<api-resource-arn>"
    }
  ]
}
```

- Lambda authorizer responds back to the API Gateway with this generated IAM policy.
- API Gateway evaluates the IAM policy and returns a HTTP 401 (Unauthorized) to the API user if the policy denies access, or forwards the request to the back-end API resource, if the policy allows access.
- Finally, the back-end API resource responds, and the same response is passed to the API user.

Now that we have a basic understanding of how a Lambda authorizer works, let's get our hands dirty with some code (in Node.js). We assume that the Node along with **Node Package Manage** (**NPM**) has been installed. We will start by creating a Node project and installing the **`jsonwebtoken`** module as dependency. We can use the following command for the purpose:

```
$ npm init -y && npm install --save jsonwebtoken
```

We will develop a RS256 (**Rivest-Shamir-Adleman** [**RSA**] signature with SHA-256) based JWT authorizer. Since the asymmetric cryptographic algorithm like RSA will be used, there is a private-public key pair involved. The identity provider will generate this key pair and safely store the private key (which is a confidential key). This private key will then be used to sign the JWT tokens. On the other hand, the public certificate, which has the public key embedded in it, could be used to verify the JWT token. There are various ways in which this asymmetric strategy could work. For example, a more dynamic arrangement would be to have the authorizer connect with a **JSON Web Key Set** (**JWKS**) endpoint of the identity provider and extract the public certificate based on the 'kid' (key identifier) field present in the JWT token. However, to keep things simple, we will assume that this public certificate is shared by the identity provider, and this is used by the Lambda authorizer to verify the signed JWT tokens.

To quickly generate a key pair (for testing purpose), we can use the OpenSSL commands. To generate **Privacy Enhanced Email** (**PEM**) format private keys and self-signed certificates, we can leverage the following commands in Linux; the first command creates an RSA-2048 private key, named **`private.key`** and a **certificate signing request** (**CSR**), named **`client.csr`**; the second command uses the private key and the CSR to create a self-signed public certificate, named **`public.key`**:

```
$ openssl req -newkey rsa:2048 \
   -nodes -keyout private.key \
   -out client.csr
$ openssl x509 -signkey private.key \
   -in client.csr -req -days 365 \
   -out public.key
```

With the private and public key (essentially a certificate with public key) pair generated, let's focus on the following Lambda function:

```
/*************** File: index.js **************/
/* rs256_based_token_authorizer- Sample RS256 based authorizer */
const jwt = require('jsonwebtoken');
const fs  = require('fs');
const UNAUTHORIZED = 'Unauthorized';

// Token Authorizer for JWT
exports.handler = async(event)=>{
    const BEARER = "Bearer "; // Authorization type = Bearer
    console.log("Event >> ", event);
    var token = event.authorizationToken;

    if(token && token.startsWith(BEARER)){
        console.log("Bearer token used");
        token = token.substring(BEARER.length); // extract JWT token
    }
    // Public certificate could be fetched from S3, KMS or JWKS endpoints
    var cert = fs.readFileSync('./keys/public.key');
    var response = {};
    try{
        var decoded = jwt.verify(token, cert, { algorithms: ['RS256']});
        console.log("Decoded token >> ", decoded);
```

```
        response = generate_iam_policy(
                                        decoded.uid,
                                        'Allow',
                                        event.methodArn);
        return response;
    }
    catch(err){
        console.error("Error >> ", err);
        throw UNAUTHORIZED;
    }
};

var generate_iam_policy = (principal, effect, resource)=>{
    let response = {};
    response.principalId = principal;

    let policyDocument = {};
    policyDocument.Version = '2012-10-17';
    policyDocument.Statement = [];

    let statement = {};
    statement.Action = 'execute-api:Invoke';
    statement.Effect = effect;
    statement.Resource = resource;
    policyDocument.Statement[0] = statement;

    response.policyDocument = policyDocument;
    return response;
};
```

This Lambda function (named **rs256_based_token_authorizer**) could now be deployed using either AWS Lambda console or CLI. *Figure 5.4* shows how the Lambda deployment structure would appear. Note, the public key is baked into the deployment under the **keys** folder for the sake of simplicity. This might not be the optimal solution for all the scenarios. Refer to *figure 5.4* as follows:

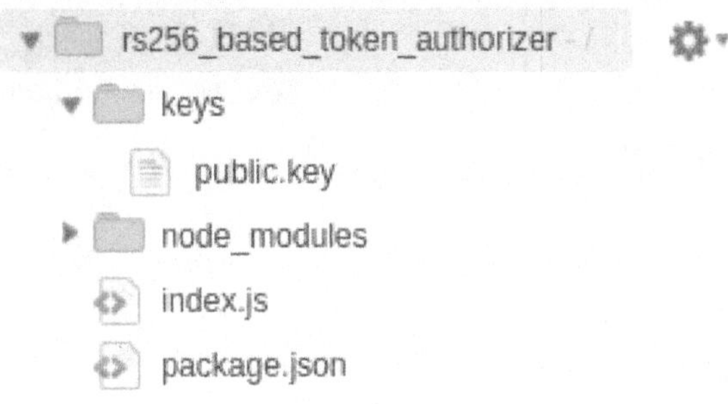

Figure 5.4: Lambda deployment folder structure

The Lambda function does the following—it extracts the bearer token from the incoming event, which appears under **event.authorizationToken**. Subsequently, it loads the public certificate file and uses the same to verify the JWT token. In addition to verifying the signature, the token is also checked for expiry (every JWT token should have an expiry timestamp assigned in the **exp** field). Once the token is successfully verified, an IAM policy is generated with the effect of **Allow** and resource equal to the **methodArn** field available in the Lambda event. Finally, this policy is returned to API Gateway for evaluation. The actual authorization process could be more complex. For example, the Lambda function might have to extract the authorized scopes assigned to the JWT token (under the **scope** field), lookup the API resources mapped to these scopes from a persistent store and then generate the IAM policy.

Once the Lambda function is successfully deployed, it can be registered as a Lambda authorizer for an API, that needs to be protected. All we need to do is select the API from the API Gateway console and click on the **Authorizers** option on the left navigation panel. On the **Authorizers** page, click on the **Create New Authorizer** button. Subsequently, on the **Create Authorizer** page (refer to *figure 5.5*), we will specify the name, type (Lambda), Lambda function ARN, Lambda event payload (Token), Token Source (Authorization header), Caching, etc., and click on the **Create** button. If **Lambda Invoke Role** was not specified on the **Create Authorizer** page explicitly, then during the creation process, we will be asked to grant permission to API Gateway to invoke the Lambda function, which should be granted. Refer to *figure 5.5* as follows:

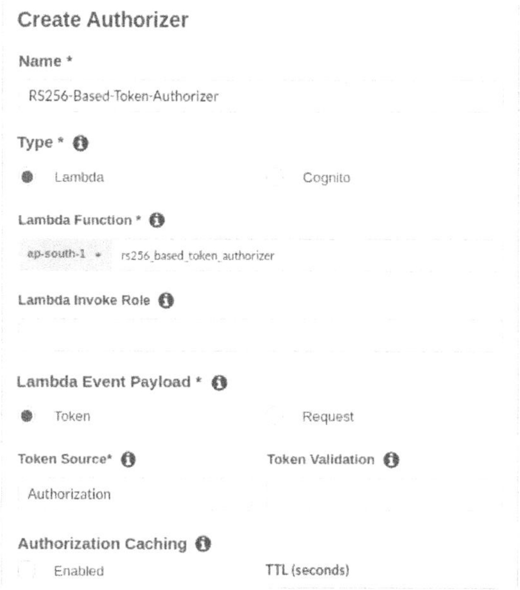

Create Authorizer
Name *
RS256-Based-Token-Authorizer
Type *
Lambda Cognito
Lambda Function *
ap-south-1 rs256_based_token_authorizer
Lambda Invoke Role
Lambda Event Payload *
Token Request
Token Source* Token Validation
Authorization
Authorization Caching
Enabled TTL (seconds)

Figure 5.5: Create an authorizer in API Gateway from AWS Management Console

Once the Lambda function has been registered as an authorizer for a selected API, we can associate the methods of this API with the authorizer. To do that, we need to select the particular API's method, and in the **`Method Request | Settings`** section, click on the **`Authorization`** drop-down and select the authorizer. Subsequently, we can deploy the API and test the authorizer, as shown in *Figure 5.6* as follows:

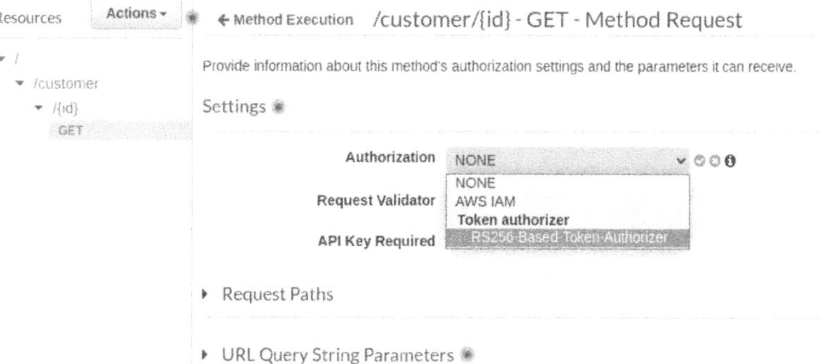

Figure 5.6: *Enabling token authorizer for an API method*

In practice, the access token (like JWT token) is generated by the identity provider. However, for the purpose of testing the authorizer, we can generate a JWT token using a simple Node.js code. We assume that a Node project has been created and the dependencies (**`jsonwebtoken`** library) installed. Additionally, the private key has been placed in the same folder as the **`index.js`** file. The following is the content of the **`index.js`** file:

```
/********** File: index.js ************/
const jwt = require('jsonwebtoken');
const fs = require('fs');
const privateKey = fs.readFileSync('./private.key');

var token = jwt.sign({
        uid: '<user-id>', // user identifier
        scope: '<list of scopes>', // like admin,guest,etc.
        exp: 1623863447  // epoch timestamp for token expiry
    }, privateKey, { algorithm: 'RS256' });

console.log(token);
```

Now, we can execute this file locally using the following command:

```
$ node index.js
```

This generated token that appears in the console could be used with the Authorization header of a request, that has been protected using the Lambda authorizer. We could use Postman for testing the API. *Figure 5.7* shows how the Authorization header looks in Postman, as follows:

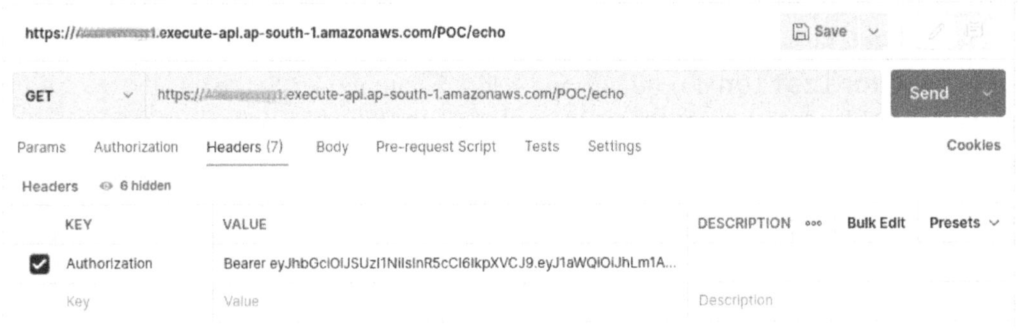

Figure 5.7: Using Postman to test an API endpoint protected by a Lambda authorizer

With the introduction of HTTP APIs in Amazon API Gateway, the Lambda authorizers support a newer version (Version 2.0) of the payload format. The authorizer payload format defines the request and response formats that are sent and received by API Gateway to and from the Lambda function. HTTP APIs do support the older version (Version 1.0) as well. However, REST APIs currently support only Version 1.0 of the payload format version, and thus, we have to use this version for compatibility with REST APIs. A notable difference is in the response format. In Version 1.0, the response from the Lambda authorizer was an IAM policy. However, in Version 2.0, the format is much simpler. The following is an example:

```
{
```

```
  "isAuthorized": true/false
}
```

Refer to the following link for relevant information around the payload formats: https://docs.aws.amazon.com/apigateway/latest/developerguide/http-api-lambda-authorizer.html

Cognito Authorizer

Amazon Cognito is a serverless offering that can act as an identity provider (IdP) as well as an identity broker. When used as an identity provider, Cognito could be used to create the user registry (known as user pool), manage authentication, authorization, and provide access to the protected resources (like APIs, databases, etc.). On the other hand, when used as an identity broker, Cognito can use federated identities to authenticate the users against the third-party identity providers through web federation or SAML federation, generate temporary access credentials, and provide access to the resources. Cognito offers out-of-the-box integration with Amazon API Gateway and supports the creation of Cognito authorizers which can authorize a user from the Cognito user pool to access the APIs. We will take a closer look at Amazon Cognito in a subsequent section.

Let us now check how to enable a Cognito Authorizer for REST API published on Amazon API Gateway. We will assume that we already have a user pool (named `bpb479-pool`) in Cognito with the following configurations made, using the Amazon Cognito management console:

- **Name/Pool Name**: `bpb479-pool`
- **Attributes**:
  - Users can use a username or verified email address to sign-up / sign-in
  - Email configured as a required attribute
- **Policies**:
  - Provide a strong password policy
  - Allow users to sign themselves
  - Temporary password set by the administrator to expire in 7 days
- **MFA and verifications**: MFA are disabled, and for everything else, accept default settings
- **Message customizations**: Accept default settings
- **Tags**: Optionally provide a tag for the user pool
- **Devices**: User device tracking disabled

- **App clients**: Add an app client (note: Cognito always authenticates a user against an application client)
    - o App client name: **`bpb479-app-client`**
    - o Accept default token expiration for Refresh, Access, and Id tokens
    - o Uncheck **`Generate client secret`**
    - o **Auth Flows Configuration**:
        - ▪ Check **`ALLOW_ADMIN_USER_PASSWORD_AUTH`**
- For everything else, accept default settings
- **Triggers**: Do not configure any workflow customization Lambda triggers

Figure 5.8 shows the **`General Settings`** page (in the Amazon Cognito Management console) of the user pool, which displays the pool ID, as follows:

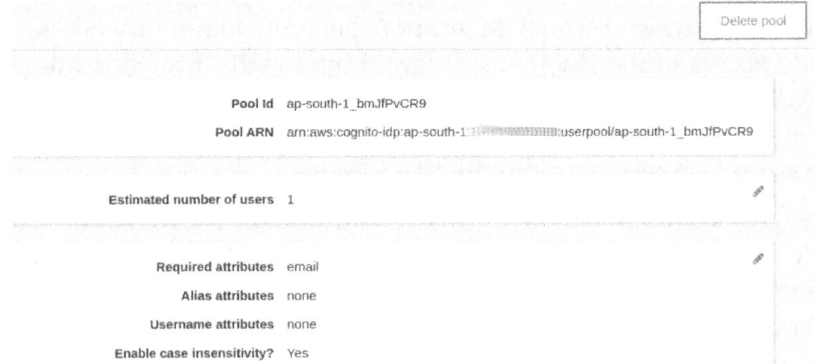

Figure 5.8: General settings of an Amazon Cognito user pool from AWS Management Console

The App client's general configuration is shown in *Figure 5.9*, as follows:

App client id

220prl5876je0nr3qcrnl3cp5f

App client secret

(no secret key)

Refresh token expiration

30 days and 0 minutes

Must be between 60 minutes and 3650 days

Access token expiration

0 days and 60 minutes

Must be between 5 minutes and 1 day. Cannot be greater than refresh token expiration

ID token expiration

0 days and 60 minutes

Must be between 5 minutes and 1 day. Cannot be greater than refresh token expiration

Figure 5.9: *Cognito User pool app-client general configuration from AWS Management Console*

`Auth Flows Configuration` setting is shown in *Figure 5.10* as follows (note that, Amazon Cognito automatically generates **`App Client Id`** for the application client):

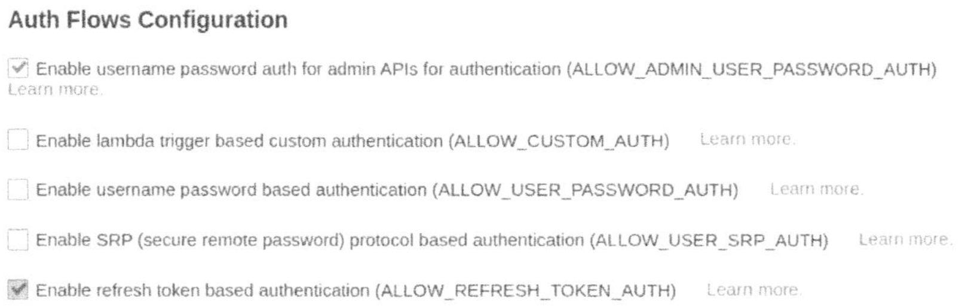

Auth Flows Configuration

- [x] Enable username password auth for admin APIs for authentication (ALLOW_ADMIN_USER_PASSWORD_AUTH) Learn more.
- [ ] Enable lambda trigger based custom authentication (ALLOW_CUSTOM_AUTH) Learn more.
- [ ] Enable username password based authentication (ALLOW_USER_PASSWORD_AUTH) Learn more.
- [ ] Enable SRP (secure remote password) protocol based authentication (ALLOW_USER_SRP_AUTH) Learn more.
- [x] Enable refresh token based authentication (ALLOW_REFRESH_TOKEN_AUTH) Learn more.

Figure 5.10: *Cognito user pool auth flow configuration from AWS Management Console*

The preceding settings for the user pool will ensure that upon sign-up, the users receive an email with a one-time temporary password set by the admin, which they will have to change during their first login.

We will also assume that a verified user (named **`user1`**) exists in this pool who has already changed the first-time login password. Now, we will go to the API Gateway Management console, select a REST API, and create a new authorizer named **`bpb479-pool-authorizer`** (refer to *Figure 5.11*) by clicking on the **`Authorizers`** option on the left navigation panel. Note that we have selected the authorizer **`Type`** as **`Cognito`** and we have also selected the existing user pool (**`bpb479-pool`**) and defined the **`Token Source`** as **`Authorization`**. This typically means that the authorizer will extract the token from the **`Authorization`** header of the request and validate against the selected Cognito user pool. Refer to *Figure 5.11* as follows:

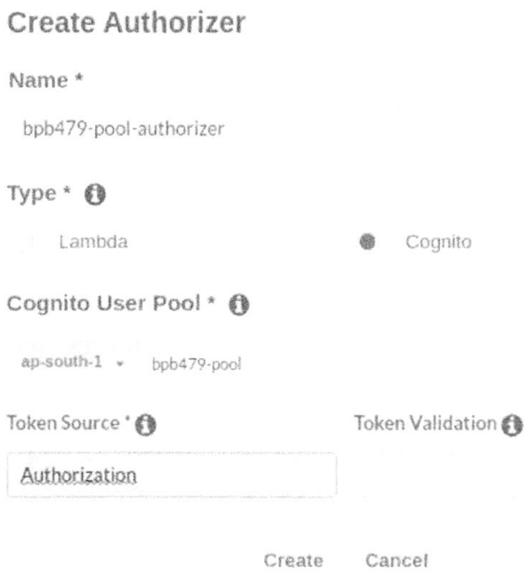

Create Authorizer

Name *

bpb479-pool-authorizer

Type *

Lambda Cognito

Cognito User Pool *

ap-south-1 bpb479-pool

Token Source * Token Validation

Authorization

Create Cancel

Figure 5.11: *Creation of a Cognito Authorizer in API Gateway*

Next, we will associate this authorizer with one of the API methods. To do that, we will select a specific method from **Resources** and in **Method Request | Settings | Authorization**, we will select the existing user pool under "**Cognito user pool authorizers** (refer to *Figure 5.12*). Once the configuration is done, we will have to deploy the API and grab the staged endpoint to test the authorizer. Refer to *figure 5.12*, as follows:

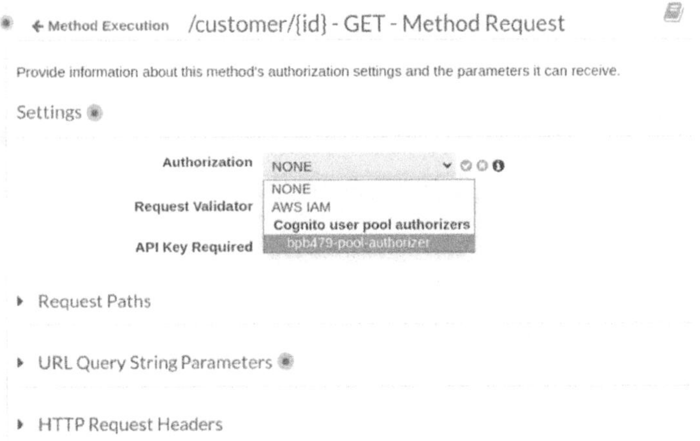

Figure 5.12: *Enabling Cognito Authorizer for an API method from AWS Management Console*

To get hold of the token that is generated by Cognito, when a user signs into the user pool, we will use the AWS CLI's Cognito-IdP admin-initiated authentication flow where a user could be signed-in by an administrator for testing purposes. This is also the reason we have enabled the **ALLOW_ADMIN_USER_PASSWORD_AUTH** flow for our app client. In practice, however, Cognito SDK will have to be used to programmatically sign-in a user to the Cognito user pool from the mobile or web applications. Additionally, the **ALLOW_ADMIN_USER_PASSWORD_AUTH** flow helps to initiate the authentication flow from the back-end applications (like Node.js or Java), also known as the server-side authentication.

The following is the CLI command to initiate a sign-in for the existing user by an administrator who has permissions pertaining to the AWS managed policy **AdministratorAccess**. Note that this is not a secured option since we are passing the password in plain text from the CLI console. We will use the following option for testing purposes only:

```
$ aws cognito-idp admin-initiate-auth \
  --user-pool-id  ap-south-1_bmJfPvCR9 \
  --client-id 220prl5876je0nr3qcrnl3cp5f \
  --auth-flow ADMIN_USER_PASSWORD_AUTH \
  --auth-parameters USERNAME=user1,PASSWORD=xxxxxxxx \
```

```
  --region ap-south-1
```

Upon success, the preceding command returns a result in the following format:

```
{
    "ChallengeParameters": {},
    "AuthenticationResult": {
        "AccessToken": "<access_token>",
        "ExpiresIn": 3600,
        "TokenType": "Bearer",
        "RefreshToken": "<refresh_token>",
        "IdToken": "<id_token>"
    }
}
```

As is evident from the result, for a verified user, this command will return three tokens – *access token, id token,* and *refresh token*. Amongst these, the id token is the one that is used to authenticate the AWS services (like API Gateway) and back-end applications. This is the token that we will include in the **`Authorization`** header and pass along with our API request using Postman. As shown in *Figure 5.13*, with the correct id token, we are able to gain access to the API and get the response, as follows:

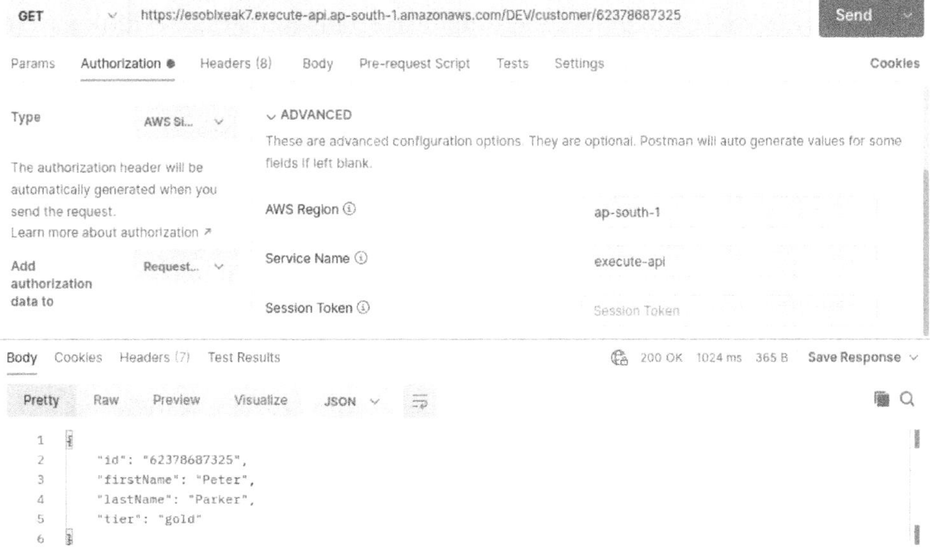

***Figure 5.13**: Using Postman to access an API endpoint protected by Cognito Authorizer*

The id token is a JWT token and could also be prefixed by the `Bearer` followed by a space.

JWT Authorizer

JWT Authorizer is a special out-of-the-box authorizer available with HTTP APIs on Amazon API Gateway. This type of authorizer could be easily used as part of **OpenID Connect** (**OIDC**) and OAuth 2.0 flows, which create JWT based access tokens. These JWT tokens could be verified and validated by JWT Authorizer, and the access could be allowed or denied to the API routes. The authorizer configuration for a HTTP API is on a per route basis.

JWT authorizer typically works with the bearer tokens and supports an `identitySource` that carries either the token itself or the token prefixed by `Bearer`. We need to specify the `Issuer URL` of the identity provider during the configuration of the authorizer. This URL is used during token verification, to fetch the public key based on the `kid` field of the token payload.

Currently, the JWT authorizer supports the RSA based algorithms only. Essentially, the authorizer fetches the token from the identity source and decodes it. It then fetches the public key from the issuer's JWKS endpoint and verifies the signature of the token along with the necessary validation of the claims (like `iss`, `exp`, `scope`, etc.). the routes in an HTTP API could be configured with scopes (`authorizationScopes`) and the JWT authorizer could be used to verify if the token has at least one of the specified scopes. If any of these validation steps fail, the access is denied.

Thus, a JWT authorizer can relieve us from the responsibility of developing a custom JWT based authorizer if we use HTTP APIs. However, while using REST APIs, we still need to create a JWT based authorizer on our own, just like we created one under the `Lambda Authorizer` section.

Controlling Cross Origin Requests

Cross Origin Resource Sharing (**CORS**) is a security feature that is used to restrict the cross-origin HTTP requests originating from the scripts running in the browser. Cross origin refers to situations where the request is made to a different domain/subdomain/protocol/port. CORS should be enabled for the API resources that receive *non-simple requests* (for example, requests with custom headers, etc.).

> **For a better understanding of simple and non-simple requests, visit the following link:**
> **https://developer.mozilla.org/en-US/docs/Web/HTTP/CORS#simple_requests**

In case of non-simple HTTP requests, the browser sends a pre-flight request to API Gateway hosting the cross-origin resource to check if the actual request will be permitted. This pre-flight request carries the **`Origin`**, **`Access-Control-Request-Method`**, and **`Access-Control-Request-Headers`** headers and uses the OPTIONS method. To support CORS, the API Gateway REST API resource implements an OPTIONS method which helps in responding to the pre-flight requests and carries the following response headers – **`Access-Control-Allow-Methods`**, **`Access-Control-Allow-Headers`**, and **`Access-Control-Allow-Origin`**.

For a non-proxy Lambda or HTTP integrations, the CORS related response headers are configured as part of the method response and integration response settings. On the other hand, for proxy integrations, the CORS response headers against the **`OPTIONS`** request will need to be configured at the back-end service, since the proxy integration does not return an integration response.

Let's check how we can enable the CORS support for one or all the methods on a REST API resource from API Gateway Console.

First, we need to select the API and select the resource (or method) under this API for which we'd want to enable the CORS support. If a resource is selected, then CORS will be enabled for all the methods and sub-resources under that resource. To enable CORS, we must select the resource, click on **`Actions`** and select **`Enable CORS`**. Refer to *figure 5.14*, as follows:

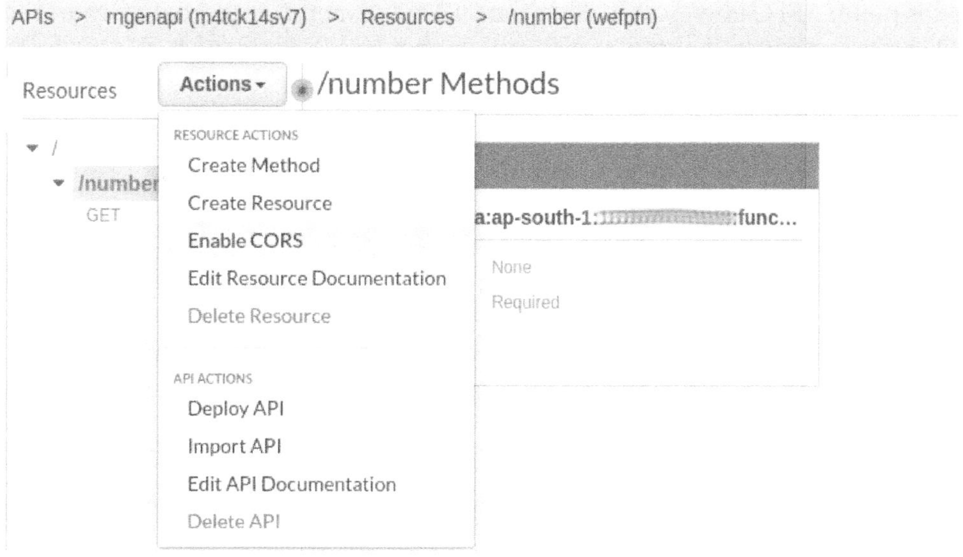

Figure 5.14: *Enabling CORS for an API resource from AWS Management Console*

On the **`Enable CORS`** page, we will specify the header values (refer to *figure 5.15*), in case we have any custom headers that needs to be specified in **`Access-Control-Allow-Headers`** and the origin needs to be updated for **`Access-Control-Allow-Origin`** (in this example, we have used **`https://portal.example.com`** as the origin). Once done, we can click on the **`Enable CORS and replace existing CORS headers`** button. Refer to *figure 5.15* as follows:

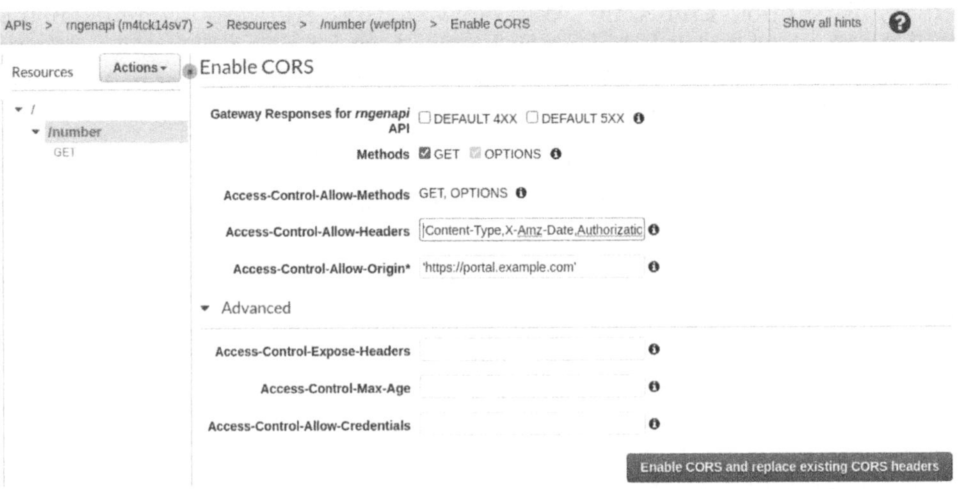

***Figure 5.15:** Specify CORS headers in AWS Management Console*

In the subsequent pop-up, we need to click on **`Yes, replace existing values`**. At this point, API Gateway will create the OPTIONS method automatically and add a MOCK integration to it along with the other changes. Refer to *figure 5.16*, as follows:

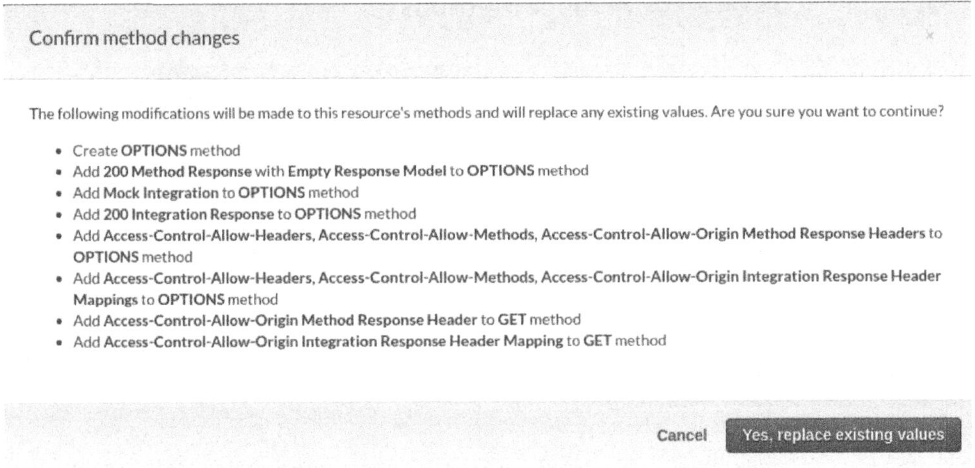

***Figure 5.16:** Automatic creation of OPTIONS method by API gateway*

To check if CORS was enabled successfully, all we need to do is go to the Integration Response page of one of the methods under the resource selected for CORS and check the response header under the **`Header Mappings`** section. It should reflect the **`Access-Control-Allow-Origin`** header along with the origin value set earlier (**https://portal.example.com**). Refer to *figure 5.17*, as follows:

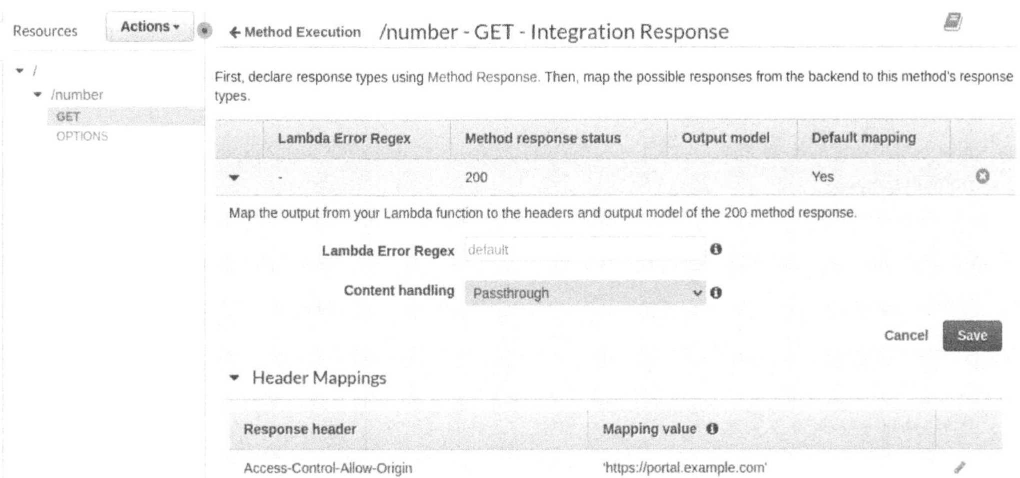

Figure 5.17: *Checking if CORS has been enabled from Integration Response in API Gateway*

Note that, we should not place the OPTIONS method under any authentication control (including the API key), since this will lead to the failure of the pre-flight requests.

Mutual TLS and client certificates

Mutual TLS and client certificates are used to improve the security posture of the API based integrations. These can be used along with the other authentication and authorization controls available in API Gateway. Mutual TLS is applied to securely authenticate the API clients with API Gateway. On the other hand, a client certificate is used to establish the API Gateway's identity to the back-end system. Let's take a quick look at these one by one.

Mutual TLS

Mutual TLS (MTLS) warrants a two-way authentication between the client and the server. Normally, with the HTTPS based communication, it is the client that challenges the server's identity. However, in a two-way authentication, both the client and the server challenge each other's identity. Typically, these identities are represented by the X.509 certificates. Mutual TLS is very common in the business-to-business (B2B) and Internet Of Things (IoT) integrations. In API Gateway, we first need to create a custom domain in order to enable the mutual TLS authentication.

The custom domain name is a powerful feature of API Gateway. It essentially supports a set of APIs deployed in various stages to be mapped and be accessible by a custom domain name, instead of the default **`execute-api`** based domain names. This also enables us to hide the staging labels for each endpoint and provide a clean and friendly URL to the API clients.

The domain can be created from the **Custom domain names** option on the left navigation panel of the API Gateway console. Refer to *figure 5.18* as follows:

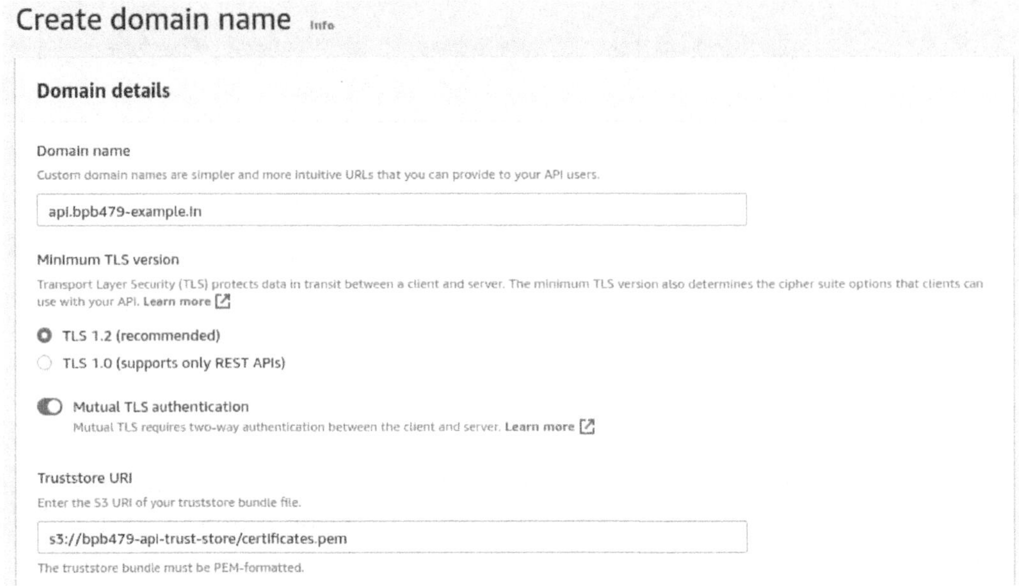

Create domain name Info

Domain details

Domain name

Custom domain names are simpler and more intuitive URLs that you can provide to your API users.

api.bpb479-example.in

Minimum TLS version

Transport Layer Security (TLS) protects data in transit between a client and server. The minimum TLS version also determines the cipher suite options that clients can use with your API. Learn more

TLS 1.2 (recommended)

TLS 1.0 (supports only REST APIs)

Mutual TLS authentication

Mutual TLS requires two-way authentication between the client and server. Learn more

Truststore URI

Enter the S3 URI of your truststore bundle file.

s3://bpb479-api-trust-store/certificates.pem

The truststore bundle must be PEM-formatted.

Figure 5.18: *Creation of "Custom Domain Name" in AWS API Gateway*

On the **Create Domain Name** page, we will provide the domain name, opt for TLS1.2 as the minimum TLS version (this is recommended) and turn on **Mutual TLS authentication**. We should also provide the URI of the trust store. The trust store is essentially an S3 bucket which carries a PEM formatted file containing all the public certificates of the API clients which are trusted by API Gateway. The following is an example of a trust store file containing two public certificates (file: *certificates.pem*):

```
----BEGIN CERTIFICATE-----
<Certificate contents>
-----END CERTIFICATE-----
-----BEGIN CERTIFICATE-----
<Certificate contents>
-----END CERTIFICATE-----
```

On the same **Create Domain Name** page, we will also have to select a publicly trusted server certificate issued by **AWS Certificate Manager** (**ACM**) which is associated with the domain name. At this point, we will assume that we own a domain and have an Amazon Route 53 hosted zone configured.

API Gateway presents this certificate to the API clients (*figure 5.19*). Note that, mutual TLS can be enabled only for the regional endpoints pertaining to the public APIs.

Mutual TLS cannot be enabled for the private APIs. Refer to *figure 5.19* as follows:

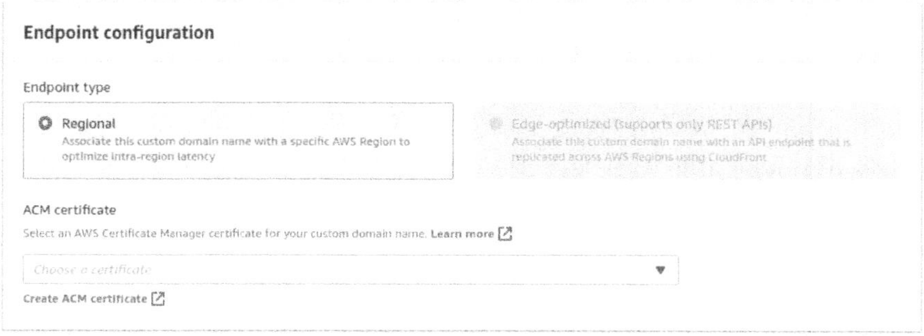

Figure 5.19: *Endpoint configuration for "Custom Domain Name" in AWS API Gateway*

Once the custom domain name is created with MTLS enabled, we will take note of the **`API Gateway domain name`** that appears under **`Custom Domain Name | Configurations`** and create an **`A`** record in the existing Route53 hosted zone. The record should have the following:

- **`Name = <Custom Domain Name>`**
- **`Value = <API Gateway Domain Name>`**

Finally, we will map the APIs and their stages, with the domain name under **`Custom Domain Name | API mappings | Configure API mappings`**. Refer to *figure 5.20* as follows:

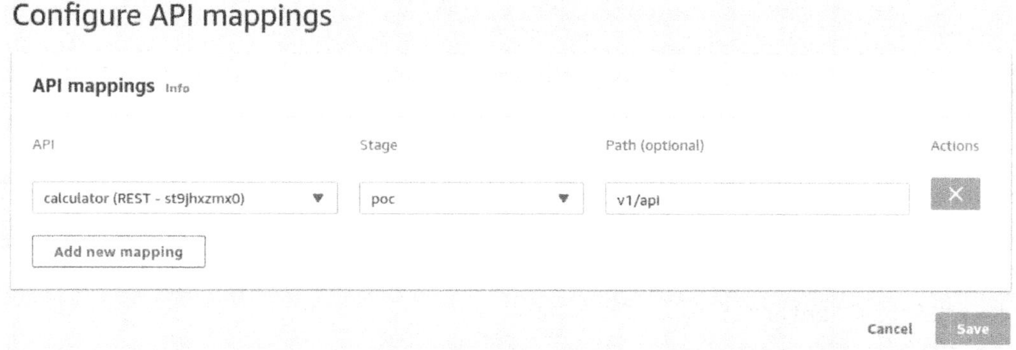

Figure 5.20: *Configure API Mapping s for "Custom Domain Name" in AWS API Gateway*

Once the custom domain name is established for accessing the APIs, the default API endpoint should be disabled, as a best practice. This is so because, these default endpoints present an additional attack surface area for the coordinated attacks like DDoS. The following AWS CLI command could be used to disable the default endpoint of a REST API and subsequently, the API needs to be re-deployed for the changes to take effect:

```
$ aws apigateway update-rest-api \
--rest-api-id <API-Id> \
--patch-operations op=replace,path=/disableExecuteApiEndpoint,value='True'
```

Once the mutual TLS is enabled, any API client that does not present a trusted certificate will not be able to access the APIs.

Client certificate

Amazon API Gateway can generate self-signed SSL certificates, which in turn could be used by the HTTP back ends (including publicly accessible back ends) to verify whether a request has originated from API Gateway. Essentially, the AWS self-signed certificate acts as a means to identify Amazon API Gateway.

The generation of a client certificate in API Gateway is very straight forward. Select an API and click on **`Client Certificates`** from the navigation panel on the left. Clicking on **`Generate Client Certificate`** generates the client certificate which has a 6-letter identifier. Refer to *figure 5.21* as follows:

To ensure HTTP requests to your back-end services are originating from API Gateway, you can use Client Certificates to verify the requester's authenticity.
+ Generate Client Certificate
f2yy4d
6/7/2021 - 6/7/2022
No description.
Copy
Edit
Configure Tags

Figure 5.21: *Generation of a Client Certificate in Amazon API Gateway*

Subsequently, we can click on **`copy`** on the certificate card and paste the content in a **`.pem`** file. The content looks somewhat like the following:

```
-----BEGIN CERTIFICATE-----
<Certificate Contents>
-----END CERTIFICATE-----
```

To use the generated client certificate with an API, we will select the certificate from the deployed stage of the API under the **`Client Certificate`** section in the **`Settings`** tab in Stage Editor and click on the **`Save Changes`** button and redeploy the API. Refer to *figure 5.22* as follows:

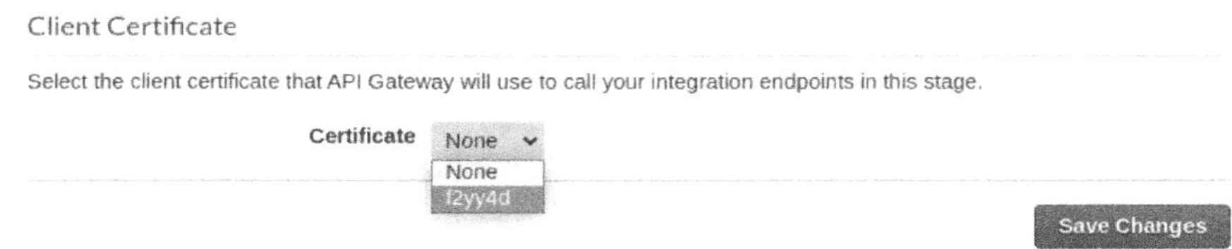

Figure 5.22: *Setting Client Certificate for a stage in Amazon API Gateway*

On the API back end, to authenticate the client (API Gateway) based on SSL certificate, we need to have access to the server-side PEM encoded private key and a certificate that is signed by a trusted **certificate authority** (**CA**). AWS does provide a list of supported authorities which includes VeriSign, GoDaddy, etc.

Refer to the following link for the entire list of supported/trusted CAs: https://docs.aws.amazon.com/apigateway/latest/developerguide/api-gateway-supported-certificate-authorities-for-http-endpoints.html

The back-end HTTPS server should configure its identity store with this private key and certificate. It should also add the PEM encoded client certificate generated by API Gateway to its trust store. It must also be configured to always request a certificate from the client and reject the request if the client certificate is not trusted or invalid. This will enable a two-way SSL between API Gateway and the back end. Thus, unless the request comes from API Gateway along with trusted client certificate, the access to the back-end server is denied, even if the back-end server's endpoint is publicly available.

Usage plan, API keys, throttling, and quota

Ideally, we should have a tight control over who calls our APIs, how many times these can be called, and at what rate. This not only helps us monitor the usage of the APIs (and thereby costs), but also to quickly find any abnormal and overwhelming usages; for instance, during the ongoing DoS/DDoS attacks. Amazon API Gateway provides various pro-active controls to moderate the usage of APIs.

The fundamental control is a *usage plan* that specifies who can access the API stages and methods, and at what rate. An *API key* is used to identify an API client and is associated with one or more usage plans and helps in implementing metering for the associated API stages. The API keys are essentially alpha-numeric values that can be distributed to the API clients. However, the API keys should not be used as the only authentication and authorization control for the APIs. They should be combined with the authorizers for better security.

A usage plan can be used to define the throttling limits and quota limits. A *throttling limit* defines the rate (requests per second) and burst that is applied to each API key associated with the usage plan. A *quota limit* is defined as the maximum number of API requests (associated with an API key), that can be submitted in a specified duration of time (like day, week, month).

Let's use the API Gateway console to create a usage plan and associate it with the API stages, and then generate an API key and link the key with the plan. At this point, we will assume that we have a set of existing APIs on which we want to apply the usage plan. We will also assume that these APIs have been deployed in one or more stages. The following are the steps:

- From the API Gateway console, select one of the APIs and subsequently select **`Usage Plans`** from the left navigation panel and click on the **`Create`** button.
- Provide an appropriate name and description to the plan and define the throttling and quota limits and click on the **`Next`** button. Note that, in this example, (*figure 5.23*), we have defined the rate equal to 3 requests per second and burst (size of bucket) equal to 50 requests under throttling limits. The quota limit has been set as 1000 requests per month (this count gets automatically reset the first day of every month). Refer to *figure 5.23* as follows:

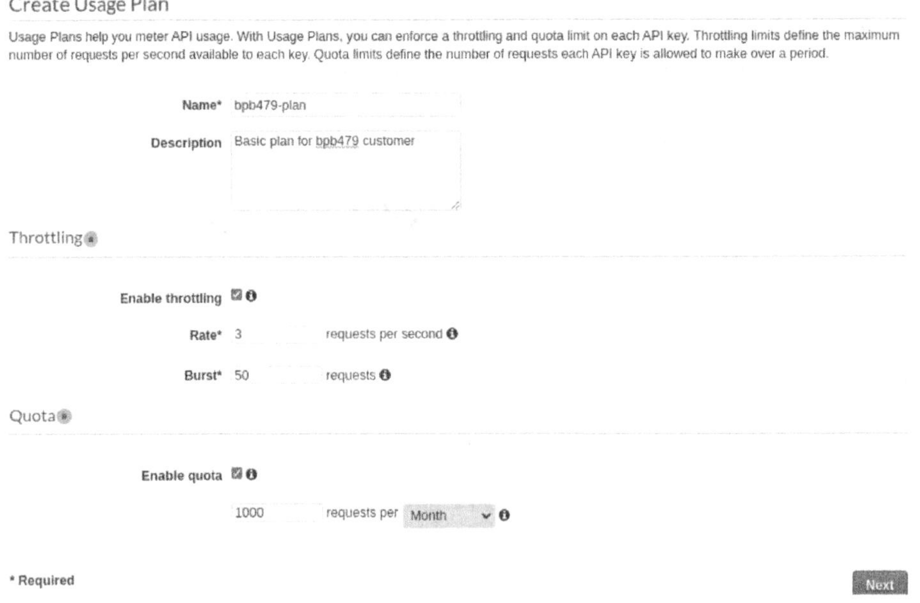
Create Usage Plan
Usage Plans help you meter API usage. With Usage Plans, you can enforce a throttling and quota limit on each API key. Throttling limits define the maximum number of requests per second available to each key. Quota limits define the number of requests each API key is allowed to make over a period.
Name* bpb479-plan
Description Basic plan for bpb479 customer
Throttling
Enable throttling
Rate* 3 requests per second
Burst* 50 requests
Quota
Enable quota
1000 requests per Month
* Required
Next

***Figure 5.23:** Creation of a Usage Plan in Amazon API Gateway*

- On the next page, associate A the PI stages with the plan by clicking on **`Add API Stage`** and selecting a specific API and stage. Note that, the throttling limits could be applied to an individual method level by clicking on **`Configure Method Throttling`**. Refer to *figure 5.24* as follows:

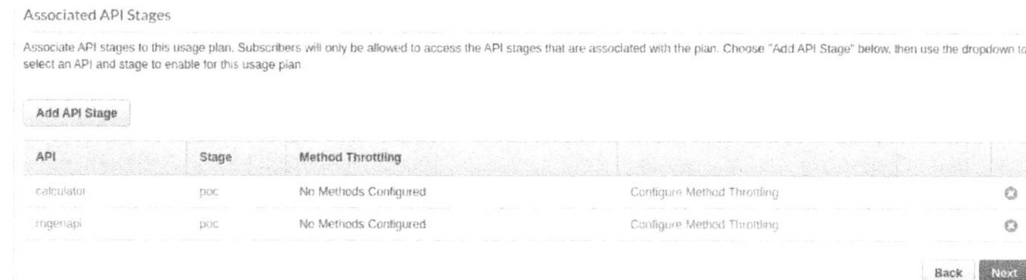

***Figure 5.24:** Associating API stages with a Usage Plan in Amazon API Gateway*

- Subsequently, on the next page, one can create an API key (or use an existing one) and associate it with the plan. However, this can be done at a later point in time as well. We will create the API key separately and associate it with the plan. Thus, at this point, we will complete the creation of the usage plan by clicking on the **`Done`** button.
- Now, to create the API key, we will select **`API Keys`** and under **`Actions`**, select **`Create API key`**.
- On the subsequent page, we will provide an appropriate name and description. At this point, we can choose whether to auto generate the key or use a custom key and then click on **`Save`**. Refer to *figure 5.25* as follows:

***Figure 5.25:** Creation of API Key in Amazon API Gateway*

- Once the API key is created, we can associate it with a plan by selecting the key and clicking on **`Add to Usage Plan`**. Refer to *figure 5.26* as follows:

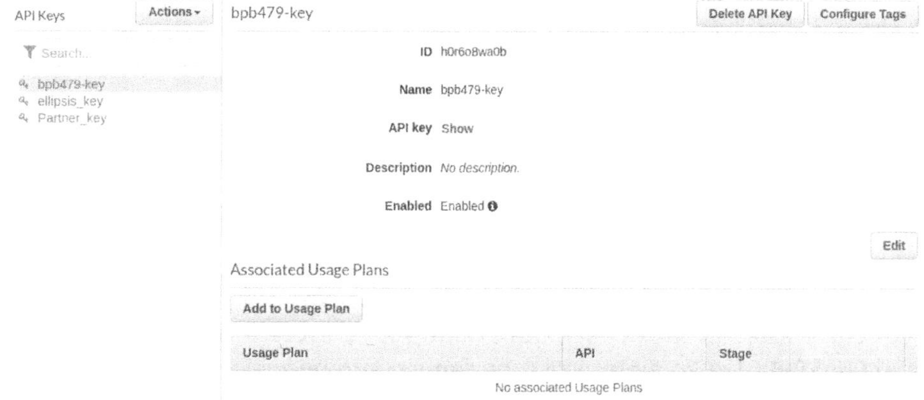

***Figure 5.26:** Adding Usage Plan to an API key in Amazon API Gateway*

- Subsequently, we will select the usage plan (named **`bpb479-plan`**) which will automatically fetch the API stages associated with the plan. Refer to *figure 5.27* as follows:

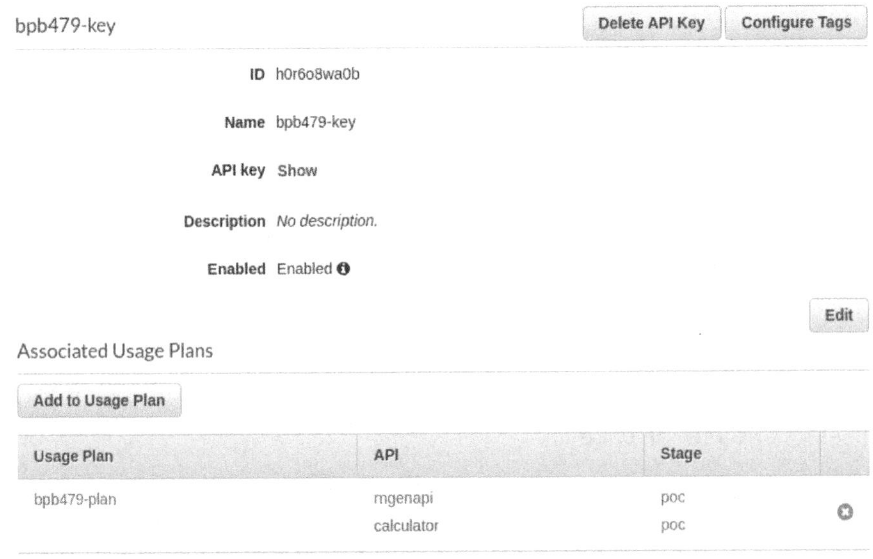

Figure 5.27: *Association of API key with Usage Plan, API, and Stage in Amazon API Gateway*

With these settings in place, the API clients will have to send the **`x-api-key`** header along with every request and pass the value of the API key. In case this header is not passed or if the incorrect API key is passed with the request, API Gateway responds with HTTP 403 (Forbidden). If the number of requests submitted by the API client exceeds the configured rate and burst or the quota is exceeded, API Gateway responds with HTTP 429 (Too Many Requests).

In essence, these pro-active measures, to check the identity of the API clients and the rate at which the requests are submitted over a short as well as long period of time, stops the APIs from getting overwhelmed with requests during a **Distributed Denial of Service** (**DDoS**) or similar attacks.

Protecting APIs with WAF

Nowadays, Web Application Firewall (WAF) has become a de-facto standard for protecting the web applications and APIs from the common layer-7 attacks like SQL injection, **cross site scripting** (**XSS**), and other vulnerabilities. API Gateway has seamless integration with AWS WAF. We will briefly discuss about AWS WAF in a subsequent section. In the event of an existing WAF **Access Control List** (**ACL**) rule (named **`OWASP-Rules`** in *figure 5.28*), the same could be selected in a particular API's stage editor, under the **`Settings`** tab. Refer to *figure 5.28* as follows:

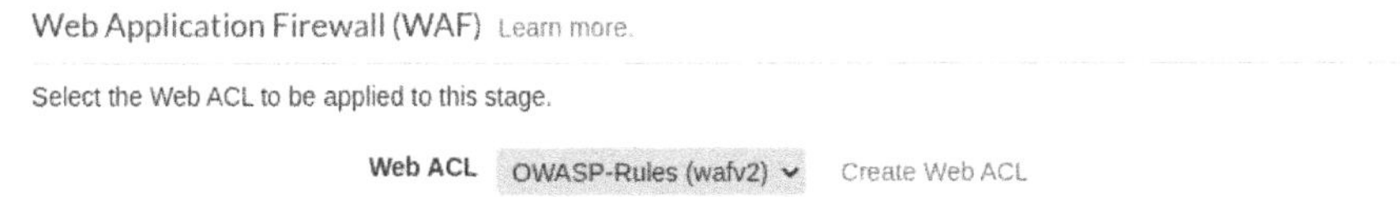

Figure 5.28: *Associating AWS WAF rules with a Stage in Amazon API Gateway*

Private APIs

Amazon API Gateway supports the private APIs, which are characterized by the fact that they are accessible from within the VPC using an interface VPC endpoint for the API Gateway **`execute-api`** component and is not exposed to the Internet interface VPC endpoint, which is powered by PrivateLink, and ensures that the traffic between VPC and the service (here API Gateway) is limited within the Amazon network and never exposed to the Internet. A single VPC endpoint could be used to access multiple private APIs.

The IAM resource policies play a vital role in granting access to the APIs from the VPCs or VPC endpoints. The following is a sample policy that allows the API execution from a particular **VPC endpoint** (**VPCE**) using the IAM policy **`condition`**:

```
{
  "Version": "2012-10-17",
  "Statement": [
    {
       "Effect": "Allow",
       "Principal": "*",
       "Action": "execute-api:Invoke",
       "Resource": [ "execute-api:/*" ]
    },
    {
       "Effect": "Deny",
       "Principal": "*",
       "Action": "execute-api:Invoke",
       "Resource": [ "execute-api:/*" ],
       "Condition" : {
           "StringNotEquals": {
```

```
                "aws:SourceVpce": "<vpce-id>"
            }
        }
    }
  ]
}
```

The resource policies could be attached to the API using the following CLI command:

```
$ aws apigateway create-rest-api \
  --name "<api-name>" \
  --policy "<jsonEscapedPolicyDocument>"
```

As a precautionary step, the endpoint policies could also be assigned to the VPC endpoint to specify the access that is being granted.

AuthN/AuthZ with Amazon Cognito

Most web applications have some kind of an authentication (AuthN) and authorization (AuthZ) scheme setup for its users. Authentication helps define "who" can access the application by virtue of knowing a secret piece of information (like a password or a token) or by virtue of possessing something (physical or virtual) like Google Authenticator App or RSA token. Authorization defines "*which*" resources can they access and "*what*" can they do with such resources. Amazon Cognito can greatly help in setting up the authentication, authorization, and user management needs of an application. It has several features including customized authentication flow, anonymous users, etc. However, we will briefly touch upon some of the basic features. Covering all the features provided by Cognito is outside the scope of this book.

Cognito essentially has the following two primary components:

- **User pool**: User pool acts as a user directory and provides a total sign-up/ sign-in solution for the mobile and web application users.
- **Identity pool**: Identity pool helps the users to access the AWS resources (like S3, DynamoDB, etc.) by obtaining the temporary AWS credentials. Identity pools also support the anonymous or guest users.

Let's look at these components in detail.

User Pool

The Cognito user pool has several features. In addition to the basic sign-up and sign-in services, the user pool also supports the federated sign-in with the Facebook, Google, OIDC, and SAML identity providers. Support for user directory and profile management and several security features like MFA, phone/email verification, etc., are also present. We have already visited the Cognito authorizers for API Gateway (refer to the *Securing APIs / API Authorization / Cognito Authorizer* section), where we used an existing Cognito user pool with some specific configurations and associated this pool to a Cognito authorizer on API Gateway and used the authorizer to allow or deny access to the API resources and methods. Users once authenticated by Cognito, receives a set of tokens including an ID token (JWT), which is passed along with an API request and used to secure and authorize an API access. Let's briefly talk about the Cognito user pool-based authentication flow.

Authentication

Figure 5.29 shows a typical client-side authentication flow based on the Cognito user pool, as follows:

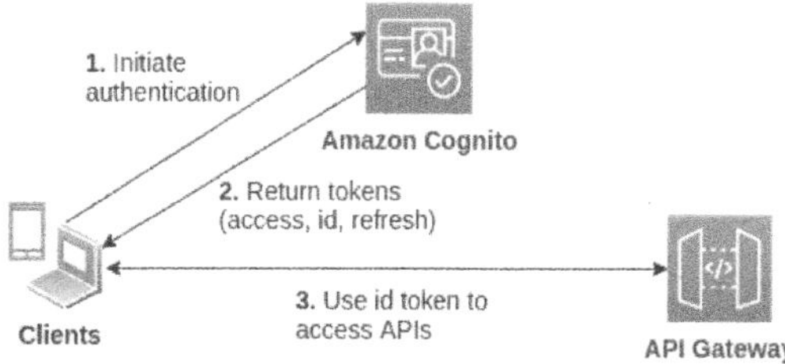

Figure 5.29: *Cognito user pool based client-side authentication flow*

- A user leverages the mobile or web application to authenticate and pass the username and password. The application initiates the authentication flow with Amazon Cognito using the API operation – **`InitiateAuth`**. This operation returns the authentication parameters. Next, the app calls **`RespondToAuthChallenge`** API operation and passes the user credentials. Optionally, Cognito can post multiple challenges (like in case of Multi-Factor Authentication or MFA) based on the user pool configuration.
- If Amazon Cognito is able to authenticate the user successfully, it returns the user's tokens (access token, id token, and refresh token) to the application.
- The application then uses the id token on the user's behalf to access the AWS resources (like API Gateway, etc.), by passing the token in the Authorization header.

This authentication flow applies not just for Amazon API Gateway. Basically, Amazon Cognito leverages the RS256 algorithm and generates two pairs of RSA keys for each user pool. The private key of each pair is used to sign the respective **id** and **access** JWT tokens. The public keys are made available by Cognito at a well-known JSON Web Key Sets or JWKS endpoint in the following format:

https://cognito-idp.<region-code>.amazonaws.com/<user-pool-id>/.well-known/jwks.json

If we have a custom web application that leverages the Cognito user pool for authenticating its users, then once the **id** token is received, the application can verify the token by using the **kid** (or public key identifier) present in the header of the JWT token and look it up in the JWKS endpoint, and subsequently, extract the corresponding public key (using popular libraries) and verify the signature used to sign the token.

In case, the application wants to perform server-side authentication from a backend application (like Node.js or Java), it needs to initiate the authentication process using the **AdminInitiateAuth** API operation which requires the AWS administrator credentials. Like **InitiateAuth**, this call returns the authentication parameters. Once the application receives the authentication parameters, it calls the **AdminRespondToAuthChallenge** API operation. However, to use the server-side authentication flow, the user pool should be configured accordingly. **ADMIN_USER_PASSWORD_AUTH** must be enabled in **auth flow configuration** of the user pool. This was done in the *Cognito Authorizer* section which helped us to sign-in an existing user by leveraging the administrator-initiated authentication process.

Authorization

Fine grained authorization could be implemented with the Cognito user pool by leveraging *'groups'*. Groups in Cognito are associated with the IAM roles. These roles, in turn, are associated with the policies that carry the necessary permissions for accessing the AWS resources. The users can be added to one or more groups. Once a user pool is created, the groups can be managed from the **General Settings | Users and groups** option on the left navigation panel of the Amazon Cognito Management console. *Figure 5.30* shows the **Create group** page. Note that each group can be assigned a **Precedence** value. If a user is associated with multiple IAM roles by virtue of being part of multiple groups, then the role pertaining to the group with the lowest **Precedence** value is selected, and it becomes the preferred role. Refer to *figure 5.30* as follows:

Figure 5.30: *Creation of group in Cognito*

Once the user is authenticated against the user pool, the **id** token generated by Cognito will carry the group and role information. These, in turn, could be used to provide the necessary authorization to the users. The following is an example of a decoded **id** token issued by Cognito that carries the user, group, and role information in the payload as claims:

```
{
  "sub": "26787590-xxxx-xxxx-xxxx-xxxxxxxxxx",
  "cognito:username": "user1",
  "cognito:groups": [
    "AppUser"
  ],
  "cognito:roles": [
    "arn:aws:iam::<account-id>:role/service-role/CustomRole"
  ],
  "cognito:preferred_role":"arn:aws:iam::<account-id>:role/service-role/
CustomRole",
  "email_verified": true,
      "iss":    "https://cognito-idp.ap-south-1.amazonaws.com/ap-south-1_
Zjus6dAmg",
  "aud": "45f4d8tph14jlve5v5c1ttul3s",
  "token_use": "id",
  ...
}
```

Identity Pool

An identity pool, as the name suggests, is a pool of unique identities with assigned permissions. Identity pools can include the users in the Cognito user pool, users who authenticate against the external identity providers (Google, Facebook, Twitter, or SAML based), or the users authenticated by the custom authentication process or unauthenticated users. Cognito issues unique identifiers for each such user and acts as an OpenID token provider that is trusted by Amazon **Simple Token Service (STS)** to access temporary, short-lived AWS credentials. Let's visit the identity pool (federated identity) authentication flow to understand this better.

Authentication

Essentially, with the identity pools, there are two associated authentication flows – *basic* and *enhanced*. The enhanced flow is a simplified version, and hence is used more often. Let's have a look at how the enhanced flow works with an external identity provider. Refer to *figure 5.31* as follows:

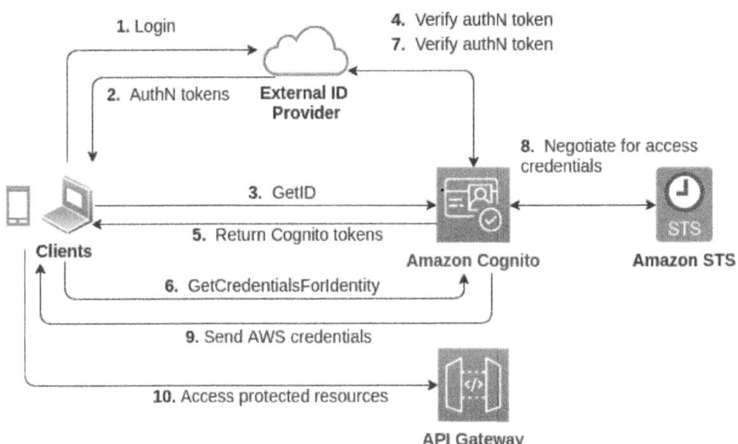

Figure 5.31: *Cognito Identity Pool based enhanced authentication flow*

The following are the steps:

- The user authenticates with the external identity provider or IdP (like Google, Facebook, etc.) via the application.
- The IdP issues the authentication tokens for the user.
- The application calls the **`GetID`** API operation to establish a new identity in Amazon Cognito and passes the authentication token from the external IdP.
- Upon receiving the authentication token, Cognito validates this token with the external IdP.
- Once validated, Cognito issues its own tokens to the user.

- Next, the application calls the **`GetCredentialsForIdentity`** API operation and passes the Cognito tokens received in the previous step.
- Amazon Cognito validates the token yet again with the external IdP.
- Amazon Cognito internally negotiates with Amazon STS and receives the AWS credentials. Note that, these steps involve assuming a role with the web identity on behalf of the user, and therefore, the identity pool must have appropriate IAM roles associated with it.
- Amazon Cognito responds back to the application and passes the AWS credentials.
- With the AWS credentials, the application can now call the protected AWS resources (like API Gateway, DynamoDB, etc.) based on the permissions associated with the credentials.

The basic flow is slightly different from the enhanced flow, in that, the application negotiates directly with Amazon STS to get the AWS credentials via a **`AssumeRoleWithWebIdentity`** API call. In the enhanced flow, Amazon Cognito does this automatically when the application calls the **`GetCredentialsForIdentity`** API operation. In fact, this operation internally does two things – retrieves the OpenID token (**`GetOpenIdToken`**), and then assumes a role to fetch the AWS credentials from Amazon STS (**`AssumeRoleWithWebIdentity`**).

In most scenarios, it is recommended to use the enhanced flow as it leads to fewer network calls and the IAM role ARNs need not be embedded into the application.

An important thing to note here is that, with the Cognito identity pool, it's always a temporary AWS credential (AWS access key ID and secret access key combination) that is used to access the protected resources. This means, if we want to protect the APIs (published on Amazon API Gateway with an identity pool), we will have to use an IAM authorizer (refer to the *Securing APIs / API Authorization / IAM Authorizer* section).

Authorization

With an identity pool, the authorization is governed by the IAM roles defined during the creation of the pool for the authenticated and unauthenticated users. On the **`Create new identity pool`** page in the Amazon Cognito Management console, we need to supply a unique pool name, decide whether the unauthenticated users will be allowed to get authenticated against the identity pool, select the basic authentication flow (if required), and select one or more authentication providers (like Facebook, Google+, Twitter, etc.). On the next page, the IAM roles need to be configured. These roles should, in general, follow the principal of least privilege. Refer to *figure 5.32* as follows:

▾ Hide Details

Role Summary

Role Description Your authenticated identities would like access to Cognito.

IAM Role Create a new IAM Role

Role Name Cognito_bpb479_idpoolAuth_Role

▸ View Policy Document

Role Summary

Role Description Your unauthenticated identities would like access to Cognito.

IAM Role Create a new IAM Role

Role Name Cognito_bpb479_idpoolUnauth_Role

Figure 5.32: *IAM role configuration for authenticated and unauthenticated users in Cognito Identity Pool*

These roles and the associated permissions could define the authorization scheme for the users authenticated against a third-party identity provider.

Granular authorization with user pool and identity pool

We can leverage both the user pool and the identity pool to create a fine-grained authorization scheme based on the user pool groups, where each group is mapped with an IAM role. The following is how the solution would look, as shown in *figure 5.33*:

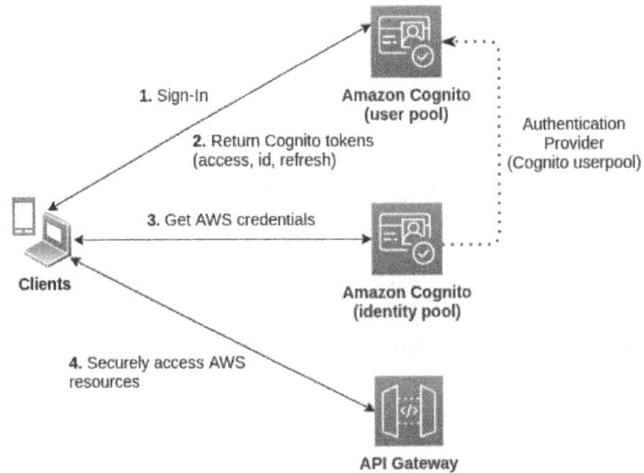

Figure 5.33: *Authorization with User Pool and Identity Pool*

The following are the steps pertaining to the solution:

1. The Mobile or Web client authenticates the user against the Cognito user pool. This pool is configured with the users assigned to the groups and each group is associated with an IAM role.
2. The user pool responds with the Cognito tokens (id, access, and refresh tokens). The "id" token carries the JWT claims pertaining to the groups and IAM roles associated with the user.
3. The **`id`** token is passed to the Cognito identity pool and the preferred IAM role is chosen from the JWT claims. The identity pool negotiates with Amazon STS to generate the AWS scoped credentials with permissions based on the chosen IAM role. The AWS credentials are sent back to the client.
4. The client can use the AWS credentials to access the AWS resources based on the privileges defined in the IAM role, based on which the credentials were generated.

The important thing to note here is that the identity pool needs to inspect the JWT claims and decipher the IAM role to be used to generate the AWS credentials which will be returned to the client. The identity pool needs to be configured to perform this action. Here's how the identity pool needs to be configured.

Firstly, the **`Authentication provider`** for the identity pool needs to be the Cognito user pool identified by the pool ID and the application client ID during the creation of the identity pool. Refer to *figure 5.34* as follows:

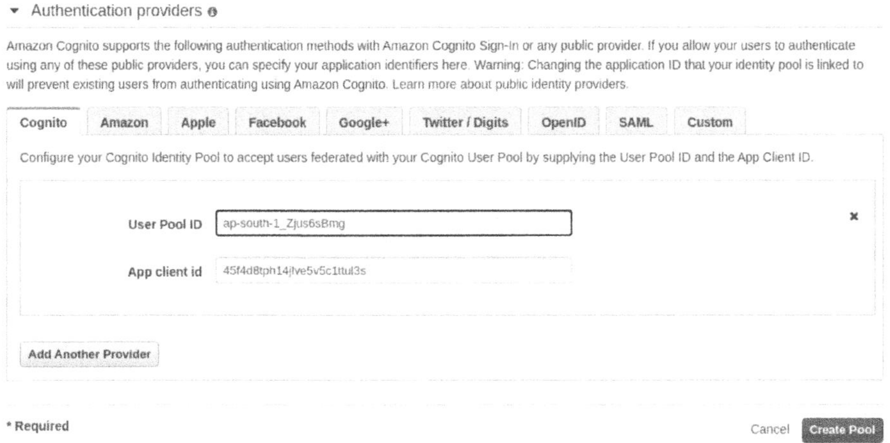

Figure 5.34: *Configuration of Cognito User Pool as authentication provider in Identity Pool*

Secondly, the identity pool needs to be edited, and under the "Authentication providers" section, in the "Cognito" tab, where the user pool has been selected, we need to select the Authentication role as "Choose role from token", and if no roles are specified in the token, then the request needs to be denied. This role setting will essentially override the default IAM role for the authenticated users. Refer to *figure 5.35* as follows:

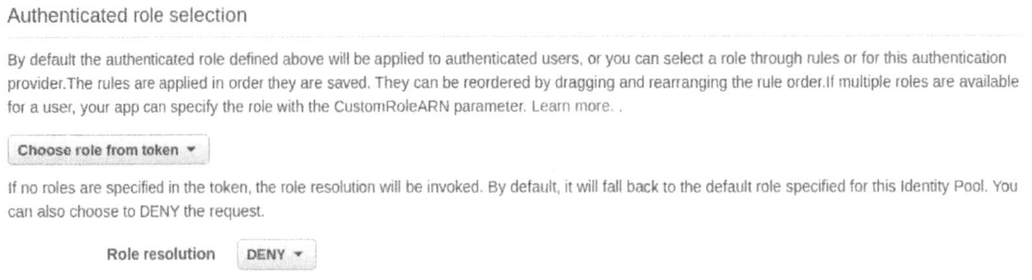

Authenticated role selection

By default the authenticated role defined above will be applied to authenticated users, or you can select a role through rules or for this authentication provider.The rules are applied in order they are saved. They can be reordered by dragging and rearranging the rule order.If multiple roles are available for a user, your app can specify the role with the CustomRoleARN parameter. Learn more. .

Choose role from token ▾

If no roles are specified in the token, the role resolution will be invoked. By default, it will fall back to the default role specified for this Identity Pool. You can also choose to DENY the request.

Role resolution DENY ▾

Figure 5.35: *Configuring Cognito Identity Pool to retrieve role from authentication token*

A quick introduction to AWS Amplify

AWS Amplify is a framework that comprises of a set of tools and services which can help the mobile and front-end web developers to build scalable applications powered by AWS quickly. Amplify supports JavaScript, React, Angular, Vue, Next.js, Android, iOS, React Native, Flutter, and other popular web and mobile frameworks. Amplify includes an array of services, which includes Authentication, DataStore, PubSub, Storage, Push Notification, and others.

> **The following link provides details on how to install Amplify CLI which is used to add services to the application and deploy them: https://docs.amplify.aws/cli/start/install**

Amazon Cognito is used as the primary authentication provider by the AWS Amplify framework and AWS recommends using Amplify to integrate the mobile and front-end web applications with Cognito. Essentially, Amplify makes it easy to integrate with Cognito. Once the authentication service has been added to the project and deployed using Amplify CLI, a configuration file named **`aws-exports.js`** gets created in the source (**`src`**) folder with the Cognito resource information (like region code, identity pool ID, user pool ID, etc.). The application can now start to use Amplify by loading this configuration file in the app's entry point (say **`index.js`**), as follows:

```
import Amplify from 'aws-amplify';
import awsconfig from './aws-exports';

Amplify.configure(awsconfig)
```

Subsequently, we may choose either to use the pre-built Amplify UI components or call the authentication APIs manually to enable the sign-up/sing-in and sign-out flows.

The following is a sample JavaScript code that shows the functions for sign-up, sign-in, and sign-out. The code attempts to introduce how the AWS Amplify authentication APIs could be easily used with the front-end applications. Note that, this is not a full-fledged application. Refer to the following code:

```
// SignUp, SignIn and SignOut utility functions
import { Auth } from 'aws-amplify';
async function userSignUp(username, password, email) {
  try {
    const { user } = await Auth.signUp({ username, password,
                      attributes: { email }});
    console.log("User details: ", user);
  }
  catch (err) {
    console.log('Unable to sign-up user:', err);
  }
}
async function userSignIn(username, password) {
  try {
    const user = await Auth.signIn(username, password);
    console.log("User signed in successfully: ", user);
  }
  catch (err) {
    console.log('Unable to sign-in user', err);
  }
}
async function userSignOut() {
  try {
    await Auth.signOut();
  }
  catch (err) {
    console.log('Unable to sign-out user: ', err);
  }
}
```

The process of integrating Amplify with the front-end web application is explained in the following link: https://docs.amplify.aws/lib/auth/getting-started/q/platform/js

Securing web applications hosted on Amazon S3 and CloudFront

Amazon S3 and Amazon CloudFront could be used together to host the secured web applications. Amazon S3 supports the hosting of static web applications in the form of static websites. A static website is characterized by static contents in the individual web pages along with the client-side scripts. We can also deploy a highly scalable and maintainable **single page application** (**SPA**) that is characterized by the client-side rendering and can dynamically fetch the data from the back ends (like Node.js, Java, .Net, etc.), using a combination of Amazon S3 and Amazon CloudFront (**Content Distribution Network** (**CDN**)). This combination of services can help deploy a web application with the required level of protection from common attacks and vulnerabilities.

Using AWS CLI to create/manage the CloudFront distributions is relatively more challenging when compared with working via the AWS Management console. Hence, we will use the AWS Management console specifically for the CloudFront related activities in this section. For any other operations, we will use AWS CLI and assume that the associated credentials have permissions of an Administrator (`AdministratorAccess` IAM policy).

Securing S3 access with Origin Access Identity

Let's assume we want to create a web application and host the static contents (HTML pages, CSS files, JavaScript files, and other static files) in Amazon S3. Moreover, we assume that the custom domain name for our website is `app.example.com` and that we own the `example.com` domain and it has been configured in Amazon Route 53. Finally, using HTTPS, we can securely verify the identity of the website and encrypt the HTTP traffic between the client browser and the website. For this, we assume that we already have an **Amazon Certificate Manager** (**ACM**) certificate with the domain name `app.example.com` or a wildcard certificate `*.example.com` in the North Virginia (`us-east-1`) region. The region selection is important since CloudFront can work with the certificates in the `us-east-1` region only.

At this point, we can start by simply creating a bucket with a same name as the custom domain name and put all the relevant files in it (along with the directory structure), using the following AWS CLI commands:

```
$ aws s3api create-bucket --bucket app.example.com \
```

```
  --region ap-south-1 --acl public-read\
  --create-bucket-configuration LocationConstraint=ap-south-1

$ aws s3 cp . s3://app.example.com/ --recursive \
  --acl public-read --region ap-south-1
```

Now, we can create a CloudFront web distribution from the AWS management console with the following configurations under **Origin Settings**:

- **Origin Domain Name**: We can select the S3 bucket just created.

  The domain name of the bucket will have the following form: **app.example.com.s3.amazonaws.com**.

- **Restrict Bucket Access**: Select **Yes**.

  This setting will ensure that only CloudFront Origin Access Identity (OAI) will be able to access the S3 bucket.

- **Origin Access Identity**: Select **Create a New Identity**.

  With this setting, CloudFront will create an identity which will have the permission to access the S3 bucket. The public contents in S3 will thus be accessible only through the CloudFront distribution, which will utilize the Amazon S3 REST endpoints to access S3 contents.

- **Grant Read Permissions on Bucket**: Select **Yes, Update Bucket Policy**.

  This setting will automatically create a bucket policy and associate it with the S3 bucket. The policy will define OAI as the **Principal**. The following is a sample bucket policy:

```
{
    "Version": "2008-10-17",
    "Id": "PolicyForCloudFrontPrivateContent",
    "Statement": [
        {
            "Sid": "1",
            "Effect": "Allow",
            "Principal": {
                  "AWS": "arn:aws:iam::cloudfront:user/CloudFront
Origin Access Identity E1PLG6IRNVYY7R"
            },
           "Action": "s3:GetObject",
```

```
                "Resource": "arn:aws:s3:::app.example.com/*"
            }
        ]
    }
```

Refer to *figure 5.36* which shows these configurations in AWS Management console, as follows:

Create Distribution

Origin Settings

Origin Domain Name: app.[redacted].s3.amazonaws.com

Origin Path:

Enable Origin Shield: Yes / No (selected)

Origin ID: S3-app.[redacted]

Restrict Bucket Access: Yes (selected) / No

Origin Access Identity: Create a New Identity (selected) / Use an Existing Identity

Comment: access-identity-

Grant Read Permissions on Bucket: Yes, Update Bucket Policy (selected) / No, I Will Update Permissions

Origin Connection Attempts: 3

Origin Connection Timeout: 10

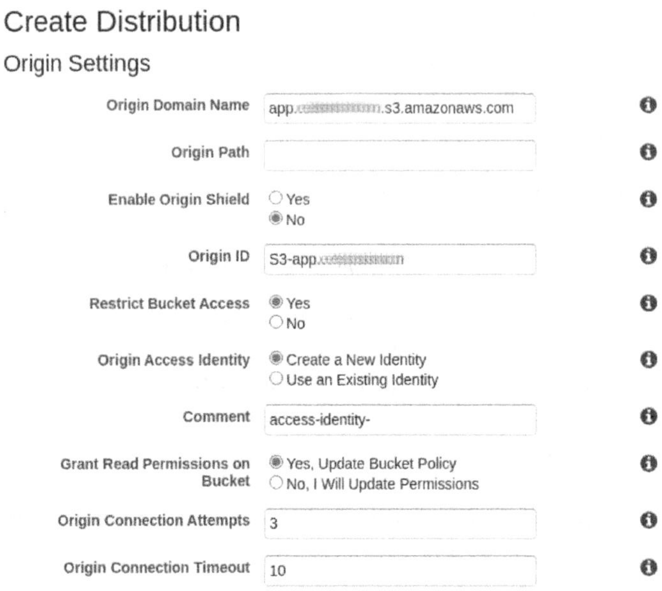

***Figure 5.36:** Configuration of "Origin Settings" in CloudFront Web distribution*

Under **`Default Cache Behaviour Settings`** of the **`Create Distribution`** page, we can make the following changes:

- **Viewer Protocol Policy**: Select **`Redirect HTTP to HTTPS`**.
- **Allowed HTTP Methods**: Select **`GET, HEAD`**

It is recommended to use HTTPS for the websites. Under **`Distribution Settings`** of the **`Create Distribution`** page, we can make the following configuration:

- **Alternate Domain Names (CNAMEs)**: **`app.example.com`**
- **SSL Certificate**: Select **`Custom SSL Certificate`** and select the ACM certificate from the **us-east-1** region. The default **`*.cloudfront.net`** certificate could also be used. However, we will stick with the custom certificate.

Refer to *figure 5.37* which shows these configurations in the AWS Management console, as follows:

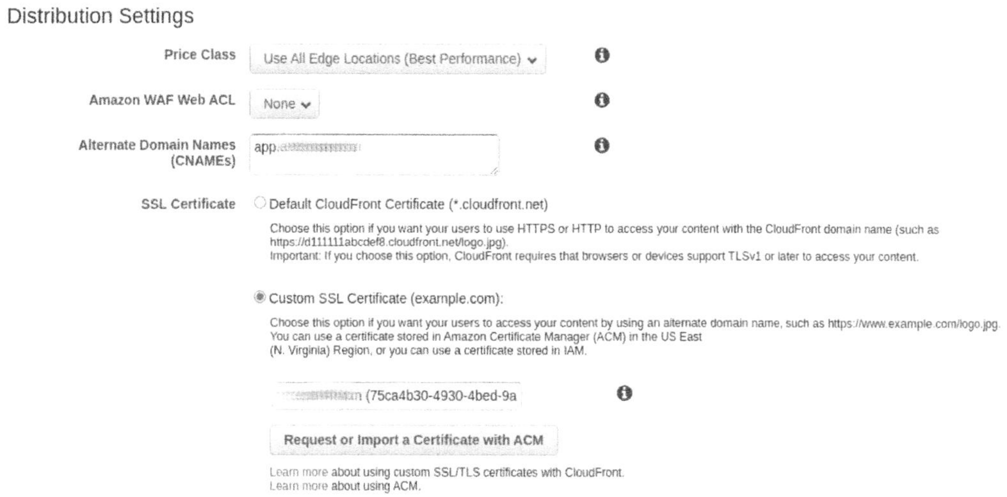

Distribution Settings

Price Class: Use All Edge Locations (Best Performance)

Amazon WAF Web ACL: None

Alternate Domain Names (CNAMEs): app.

SSL Certificate: Default CloudFront Certificate (*.cloudfront.net)

Choose this option if you want your users to use HTTPS or HTTP to access your content with the CloudFront domain name (such as https://d111111abcdef8.cloudfront.net/logo.jpg).
Important: If you choose this option, CloudFront requires that browsers or devices support TLSv1 or later to access your content.

Custom SSL Certificate (example.com):

Choose this option if you want your users to access your content by using an alternate domain name, such as https://www.example.com/logo.jpg.
You can use a certificate stored in Amazon Certificate Manager (ACM) in the US East (N. Virginia) Region, or you can use a certificate stored in IAM.

(75ca4b30-4930-4bed-9a

Request or Import a Certificate with ACM

Learn more about using custom SSL/TLS certificates with CloudFront.
Learn more about using ACM.

Figure 5.37: *Configuring the web distribution to use HTTPS*

At this point, we can create the distribution.

Finally, with the web distribution created, we can create an alias record in Route 53 with the alias target as the CloudFront domain name which appears as **Domain Name** under the **General** tab of **Distribution Settings** of the web distribution, and it looks like **d213h8n9k35vft.cloudfront.net**. We can create this record with the AWS CLI commands.

First, we have to create a JSON file with Route53 record set contents (filename: **cloudfront-alias-record.json**) as follows:

```
{
  "Comment": "CREATE/DELETE/UPSERT a record ",
    "Changes": [{
      "Action": "UPSERT",
      "ResourceRecordSet": {
         "Name": "app.example.com",
         "Type": "A",
         "AliasTarget": {
            "HostedZoneId": "Z2FDTNDATAQYW2",
            "DNSName": "d213h8n9k35vft.cloudfront.net",
            "EvaluateTargetHealth": false
         }
      }
    }]
}
```

In the preceding file, we are simply attempting to "upsert" a Route53 record with name "app.example.com" and change it's target to the alias of the CloudFront domain name.

We must note that the hosted zone ID for CloudFront distribution has been specified as **Z2FDTNDATAQYW2**. This is always the hosted zone ID when we create an alias record that routes the traffic to a CloudFront distribution.

Subsequently, we will have to apply the change to our own Route 53 hosted zone, with the following CLI command:

```
$ aws route53 change-resource-record-sets \
 --hosted-zone-id <R53-hosted-zone-id> \
 --change-batch file://cloudfront-alias-record.json
```

At this point, we can easily test that the web application is accessible via the following URL: **https://app.example.com/index.html**

Securing S3 Website access with Referrer Header

In the previous section, we saw how to secure a website by restricting access to the S3 REST endpoint using OAI. Another way is to first create an S3 based website (enable static website hosting) on the bucket and put the contents in it. Then, use the S3 website endpoint (**app.example.com.s3-website-region.amazonaws.com**) as the **Origin Domain Name** while creating a CloudFront web distribution. In this case, we will not get the option of restricting the bucket access with OAI. Instead, we can supply a header under **Origin Custom Headers** with the header name as **Referrer** and a secret string as the header value. This custom header is forwarded to the origin (S3 bucket). This secret string is only shared and known by the web distribution and the S3 bucket, thereby restricting access. It is also recommended to rotate this secret periodically.

Configure additional Security Headers

We can add the security headers to each response served by Amazon CloudFront. For this purpose, we can leverage **Lambda@Edge**. Essentially, a Lambda function could be configured with the CloudFront **Origin Response** trigger (after CloudFront receives the response from the origin) to add the security headers to the response. The most common security headers are the following – HTTP Strict Transport Security (HSTS), Content-Security-Policy, X-Content-Type-Options, X-Frame-Options, X-XSS-Protection, Referrer-Policy, etc. These security headers actually tell the browser how to behave when handling the site's content.

For more information on individual security headers, refer to the following link: https://owasp.org/www-project-secure-headers/

Let's consider the example of the HSTS policy. Communication over plain HTTP connection is not secure since the traffic is not encrypted and could be subject to network level eavesdropping. The **Strict-Transport-Security** response header informs the browser to always use HTTPS to load the site (for a specified duration), shown as follows.

```
Strict-Transport-Security: max-age=31536000
```

The value passed as max-age is basically the number of seconds for which the browser will access the domain via HTTPS without any redirects. A sample Lambda function (in Node.js) that sets the HSTS security header is shown as follows:

```
exports.handler = (event, context, callback)=>{
    const response = event.Records[0].cf.response;
    const headers = response.headers;
    // Add security headers
    headers["strict-transport-policy"] =
        [
          {
            key: "Strict-Transport-Security",
               value: "max-age=63072000" // Duration= 1 year
}
          ];
    // Add more headers here

    callback(null, response);
}
```

This Lambda function will have to be deployed in the **us-east-1** region, in order to configure CloudFront as the trigger and deploy it as **Lambda@Edge**. We will use the AWS Lambda Management console for this purpose. The following are the steps:

1. Deploy the Lambda function in **us-east-1** (using Management console or AWS CLI or any other preferred means).
2. Select the deployed function from the AWS Lambda Management console.
3. From the **Function Overview** section, we will select the **Add trigger**" button, which will open up the **Add trigger** page.

4. Next, from the **`Trigger Configuration`** drop-down, we will select CloudFront, which will provide us with an option to deploy this function as **`Lambda@Edge`**. Refer to *figure 5.38* as follows:

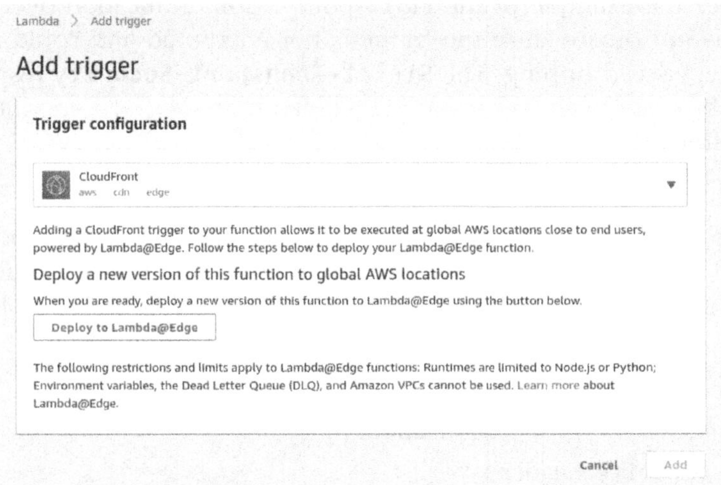

Figure 5.38: *Configuring Amazon CloudFront as a trigger for Lambda@Edge deployment*

Next, we will click on the **`Deploy to Lambda@Edge`** button which opens another page where we will select the CloudFront distribution and CloudFront event (Origin Response), and finally, check on **`Confirm deploy to Lambda@Edge`**. Refer to *figure 5.39* as follows:

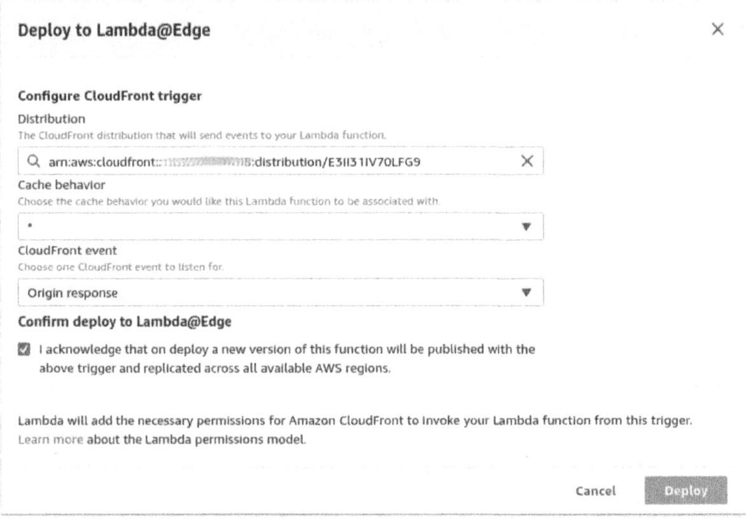

Figure 5.39: *Deploying a Lambda function to Lambda@Edge*

One can easily test if this Lambda works as expected by checking the response headers of a request placed to the CloudFront distribution.

Configure Geo Restrictions

We can leverage the Amazon CloudFront distribution features, if the web application needs to be geo restricted. This means, the web traffic will be served by the distribution only if they are triggered from the whitelisted countries, otherwise, any web traffic arising from any of the blacklisted countries will be dropped by the distribution.

To enforce the geo-restriction rules, we need to select the web distribution from the CloudFront console, go to the **`Restrictions`** tab, and edit the **`Geo Restriction`** rule. Refer to *figure 5.40* as follows:

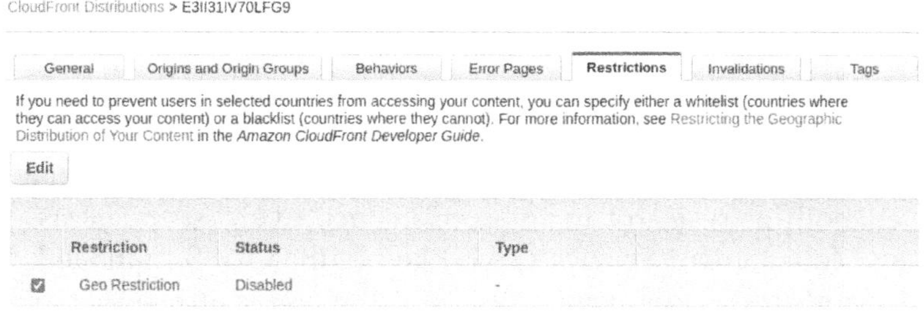

Figure 5.40: *Configuring Geo Restriction for CloudFront distribution*

On the **`Edit Geo-Restrictions`** page, we can **`Enable Geo-Restriction`**, select the restriction type to be either **`Whitelist`** or **`Blacklist`**, select the countries accordingly, and save the changes. Refer to *figure 5.41* as follows:

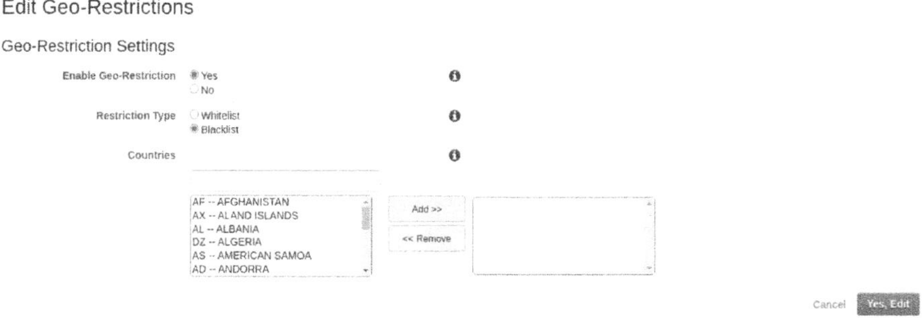

Figure 5.41: *Specifying the countries to be whitelisted or blacklisted for "Geo Restriction"*

Externalizing the secrets and configuration parameters

Applications use secrets like database passwords, API keys, and other tokens to integrate with the various components and systems to function properly. However, it's considered an antipattern and a major security risk to hardcode sensitive information, either in the application configuration files or embed them in the application code.

These practices might lead to a security incident. In fact, modern applications externalize these sensitive configuration parameters to some secure secret storage service, and subsequently, either look them up at runtime programmatically for use or inject them as environment variables during deployment time.

AWS provides us the choice of using two services for this purpose – AWS Secrets Manager and AWS Systems Manager Parameter Store. In this section, we will first take a quick look at these services and then compare them to understand when to use them.

AWS Secrets Manager

AWS Secrets Manager is a regional, managed service that helps protect the secrets and centrally manage the lifecycle of these secrets, including their rotation. The service has built-in integrations with some of the widely used database services in the AWS ecosystem, like Amazon RDS, Amazon DynamoDB, and Amazon Redshift. AWS Secrets Manager leverages IAM to control the access to the secrets. The secrets are protected both at rest and in motion. In fact, every secret is associated with an AWS Key Management Service (KMS) key (either AWS managed or Customer Master Key), and this key is used to encrypt the secret at rest. HTTPS is used for securing the secrets in motion.

Anatomy of a Secret

A secret essentially comprises of an encrypted secret text (like credentials, connection details, etc.) and some metadata elements that describes the secret and tells the Secrets Manager how to handle it. *Figure 5.42* shows the logical structure of a secret in Secrets Manager, as follows:

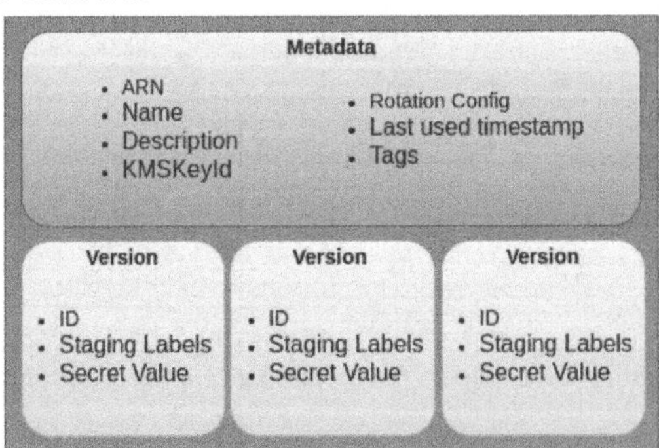

Figure 5.42: *Logical structure of a secret in SecretsManager*

The structure comprises of metadata and a set of versions, which are described as follows:

- **Metadata:** Metadata carries the basic details of a secret like its Amazon Resource Name (ARN), name, description, KMS key identifier, frequency of rotation along with Lambda function details, and tags (essentially custom key-value pairs used for logical grouping, cost allocation, etc.).

- **Version**: It is possible for a single secret to have multiple versions. This is specifically true for secrets that are rotated. Each version holds a version identifier, an encrypted secret value, and one or more staging labels used to identify the stage of the secret rotation cycle.

Creation and Retrieval of Secrets

Creation of a secret in Amazon Secrets Manager is straightforward, if we use AWS Management Console. The wizard supports multiple types of secrets based on built-in integrations with database services. It also supports custom secrets. *Figure 5.43* shows the partial first screen of the **`Store a new secret`** wizard with all the types of secrets that can be created, as follows:

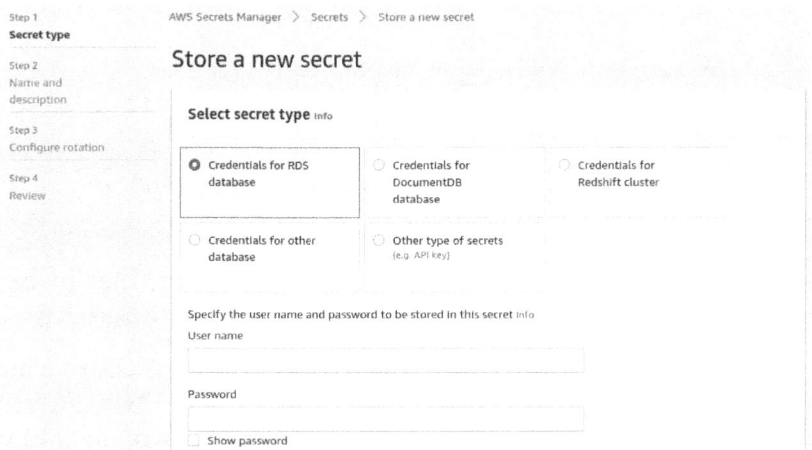

Figure 5.43: *Creation of a new secret in SecretsManager from AWS Management Console*

After specifying the username and password, we need to select the AWS KMS key which will be used to encrypt the secret at rest, followed by the selection of the database in case of RDS, Redshift, DynamoDB, or any other database. In the subsequent pages, we will specify the name, description, tags (optional), and any resource-based policy (optional) for the secret. On the **`Configure rotation`** page, we can enable automatic rotation and select the interval and Lambda function that will be used to rotate the secret. Finally, on the **`Review`** page, we can review the configuration that we specified and then store the secret in Secrets Manager.

Let us now get into the details of how to create and retrieve the secrets with the help of AWS CLI v2. At this point, we will assume that AWS CLI is already installed and configured in the host from which the CLI will be invoked. The permissions required are **`secretsmanager:CreateSecret`** and **`secretsmanager:GetSecretValue`** and these permissions are granted for the profile user named **`secuser`**.

The following command will create a secret (named **`bpb479-secret`**) in AWS Secrets Manager. Note that the command uses the **`--secret-string`** option, which means that the secret text is a string (and not binary). Moreover, the **--secret-string** option can take a secret value directly as a string or we can refer to a file. AWS recommends using secrets in the JSON format. However, we can also place a text directly as a secret value. If Customer Master Key (CMK) is not explicitly specified, the default AWS managed CMK is used to encrypt this secret. Refer to the following command:

```
$ aws secretsmanager create-secret --name bpb479-secret \
  --description "a sample secret" \
  --secret-string file://secret.json --profile secuser
```

The preceding command creates a version of a secret and returns a response similar to the following:

```
{
    "ARN": "arn:aws:secretsmanager:ap-south-1:<account-
id>:secret:bpb479-secret-WadAS7",
    "Name": "bpb479-secret",
    "VersionId": "c60629bb-934a-480d-846a-4c028a94ee6d"
}
```

It is a good practice to encode the secret value with Base64 and then place the secret in Secrets Manager. While retrieving the value, we will need to decode it.

Secrets could also be created using a custom defined AWS KMS CMK, which is used to encrypt the value of the secret. The key is identified by the CMK ARN, key ID, or key alias. The option used for this purpose along with the **create-secret** command is **--kms-key-id**. The required permissions for this operation to be successful are **kms:GenerateDataKey** and **kms:Decrypt**.

The retrieval of the secret from Secrets Manager is straightforward. We can use the following command:

```
$ aws secretsmanager get-secret-value --secret-id bpb479-secret \
  --profile secuser
```

The output of the command is a JSON that looks somewhat like the following:

```
{
    "ARN": "arn:aws:secretsmanager:ap-south-1:<account-
id>:secret:bpb479-secret-WAdAS7",
    "Name": "bpb479-secret",
    "VersionId": "c60629bb-934a-480d-846a-4c028a94ee6d",
    "SecretString": "{\n   \"username\": \"guest\"\n   \"password\":
\"P@$$w0rd\"\n}\n",
    "VersionStages": [
```

```
        "AWSCURRENT"
    ],
    "CreatedDate": "2021-05-30T00:06:20.870000+05:30"
}
```

To directly fetch the secret value, we will use the **--query** option and fetch the output as text using the **--output** option. This time, we will get the secret value as response in text shown as follows:

```
$ aws secretsmanager get-secret-value --secret-id bpb479-secret \
  --query 'SecretString' --output text --profile secuser
```

The creation and retrieval of the binary secrets are very similar to what we have seen so far. However, note that the binary secrets cannot be created from AWS Management Console. In this case, we will need to use the **--secret-binary** option. The following are the corresponding CLI commands to create a binary secret and fetch the value:

```
$ aws secretsmanager create-secret --name "bpb479-binary-secret" \
  --description "Private key file" --secret-binary fileb://./private.key \
  --profile secuser
```

A binary secret is automatically Base64 encoded while being stored in Secrets Manager, and thus needs to be decoded in the retrieval cycle, as follows:

```
$ aws secretsmanager get-secret-value \
--secret-id "bpb479-binary-secret" \
--query "SecretBinary" --output text \
--profile secuser | base64 --decode
```

In the previous command, we have used the *base64* Linux utility to decode the secret. The **get-secret-value** command supports the use of the options **--version-id** and **--version-stage**, to further identify the secret. In fact, version-id is the unique version identifier and version-stage refers to the staging label attached to the version. If these options are not used, then the command returns the value of the current version, identified by the **AWSCURRENT** staging label. Yet another valid staging label is **AWSPREVIOUS**. We will learn more about these labels under *Rotation of Secrets*.

Now, let's use AWS SDK (for JavaScript) to fetch a secret from Secrets Manager. Most often, applications will fetch secrets at runtime and the following example will help to understand how it is done. The example shows a simple function that accepts a secret identifier and attempts to fetch the secret value (**string**) from Secrets Manager using AWS SDK. The function can be called from the code to fetch the value of the supplied secret. Note that, this code will work only if it has the required permission of **secretsmanager:GetSecretValue**, through the IAM role or AWS credentials. Moreover, AWS Secrets Manager is a regional service, which means, we need to specify the region code before calling the service. Refer to the following code:

```
/* Fetch a secret from AWS Secrets Manager using AWS SDK */
const AWS = require('aws-sdk');
const REGION_CODE = process.env.REGION_CODE || "ap-south-1";

async function fetchSecret(secretId){
  const SECRET_STRING = "SecretString";
  if( !secretId || secretId.trim() == ""){
    throw Error("Invalid secret");
  }

  try{
    AWS.config.update({region: REGION_CODE});

    let request = new AWS.SecretsManager()
                     .getSecretValue({SecretId: secretId});
    let secretValue=null;
    await request.promise()
        .then(function(data){
             if(SECRET_STRING in data){
              secretValue = data.SecretString;
              console.log("Secret value = ", secretValue);
            }
            else{
             console.error("Expecting secret string..not found");
             throw Error("Invalid secret");
            }
        })
        .catch(function(err){
             throw err;
        });
    return secretValue;
  }
  catch(err){
      console.error("Error > ", err);
    throw Error("Unable to fetch secret from SecretsManager");
  }
}
```

To invoke this function, we can use the following construct (or any other function calling construct):

```
(async()=>{
  let secret = await fetchSecret("bpb479-secret");
  console.log("Secret = ", secret);
})();
```

Rotation of Secrets

AWS Secrets Manager can automatically rotate the secrets. In fact, this is the driving factor for selecting Secrets Manager under scenarios where automated secret rotation is required. Secrets Manager natively supports the secret rotation for databases like Amazon RDS, Amazon Redshift cluster, and Amazon DynamoDB. Essentially, Secrets Manager leverages pre-defined Lambda functions for each database for facilitating the rotation. Secrets Manager can also rotate secrets pertaining to the other databases (which are not natively supported), and the other types of secrets. We are required to customize the Lambda function to implement specific details of rotating a secret.

There are four distinct steps that need to be implemented in the Lambda function for rotating a secret. The Lambda function is then invoked with a JSON event that has the following structure for each of the steps:

```
{
    "Step" : "createSecret OR setSecret OR testSecret OR finishSecret",
    "SecretId" : "<ID or ARN of the secret to rotate>",
    "ClientRequestToken" : "<UUID for idempotency>"
}
```

The steps involved and sent as "**request.type**" along with the JSON event, to trigger the Lambda function are described as follows:

1. **CreateSecret**: In this step, the Lambda function generates a new version of the secret. This can be as simple as generating a new API key or password or some arbitrarily complex set of steps. This new version is assigned the staging label **AWSPENDING**, which marks it as in-process version of the secret. Applications still access the version labeled as **AWSCURRENT.**
2. **SetSecret**: In this step, the rotation function retrieves the version of the secret marked as **AWSPENDING** and then invokes the database or identity service to change or create the password or key. The Lambda function would thus require permissions to perform this task. Applications are still associated with the **AWSCURRENT** version of the secret.
3. **TestSecret**: This step enables the Lambda function to verify the **AWSPENDING** version of the secret by using it to access the protected resource in the same

way that the application would. Even in this step, the applications are still using the **AWSCURRENT** version.

4. **FinishSecret**: In this step, the Lambda function performs any leftover resource specific activities on the **AWSPENDING** version of the secret. Subsequently, as the final step, the **AWSCURRENT** label is associated with the new version of the secret. The old version is labeled as **AWSPREVIOUS** and used (if required) for recovery as the last known good version of the secret. At this point, the applications could start to use the new version of the secret as the **AWSCURRENT** version.

The implementation of the Lambda function for rotating a secret is outside the scope of this book. However, AWS has a set of pre-defined Lambda functions for the natively supported databases which can be studied as the starting point to create a custom Lambda for a specific secret type and identity service. Moreover, AWS provides several templates that can be used to create a custom Lambda rotation function.

The latest rotation templates are available at the following link: https://docs.aws.amazon.com/secretsmanager/latest/userguide/reference_available-rotation-templates.html

Access Control for Secrets

The IAM policies represent the fundamental building blocks for providing access to the secrets that reside in AWS Secrets Manager. Secrets Manager supports two types of policies – *identity based* and *resource based*. The identity-based policies are attached directly to identities like IAM user, group, or role, and the resource-based policies are attached to the secrets. The resource-based policies are particularly helpful when allowing access to the secrets from the other AWS accounts.

Let's consider an example of the identity-based policy. When this policy is associated to an identity, like the IAM user, the user becomes the principal implicitly. The user will be allowed to call the **GetSecretValue** operation on any secret in a defined AWS account in the **ap-south-1** region which has a name starting with **bpb479-secret**. In addition, this secret should also have a resource tag named **env** with the value **dev**, associated with it. The following is how the policy will look like:

```
{
    "Version": "2012-10-17",
  "Statement": [
     {
        "Sid": "BPB479",
        "Effect": "Allow",
```

```
            "Action": "secretsmanager:GetSecretValue",
            "Resource": "arn:aws:secretsmanager:ap-south-1:<account-
id>:secret:bpb479-secret*",
            "Condition": {
                "StringEqualsIgnoreCase": {
                    "secretsmanager:ResourceTag/env": "dev"
                }
            }
        }
    ]
}
```

Now, let's consider an example of the resource-based policy. In a resource-based policy, we will have to explicitly define the principal. The secret to which this policy is attached implicitly becomes the resource. Each secret can have one resource-based policy attached to it and can be used for the cross-account access of the secrets. In the following example, we are simply allowing another account to invoke the **`GetSecretValue`** operation on the secret with ARN **`arn:aws:secretsmanager:ap-south-1:<account-id>:secret:bpb479-secret-WAdAS7`** and a condition that the staging label associated with the request will have to be **`AWSCURRENT`**; this means, only the requests for accessing the current version of the secret are allowed:

```
{
    "Version" : "2012-10-17",
    "Statement" : [
        {
            "Effect": "Allow",
            "Principal": {"AWS": "arn:aws:iam::<another-acct-id>:root"
},
            "Action": "secretsmanager:GetSecretValue",
            "Resource": "arn:aws:secretsmanager:ap-south-1:<account-
id>:secret:bpb479-secret-WAdAS7",
            "Condition": {
                "ForAnyValue:StringEquals": {
                    "secretsmanager:VersionStage" : "AWSCURRENT"
                }
            }
        }
    ]
}
```

Once the resource-based policy is defined, we can use the AWS CLI command to apply this policy to a secret. At this point, we assume that we have placed the preceding policy content in a file named **resource-policy.json**. The following CLI command will associate the resource-based policy to the secret named **bpb479-secret**:

```
$ aws secretsmanager put-resource-policy --secret-id bpb479-secret \
  --resource-policy file://resource_policy.json
```

AWS Systems Manager Parameter Store

AWS SSM Parameter Store is a capability of the AWS Systems Manager service that provides secure and hierarchical storage for secrets and other configuration data. The service enables strict separation of configuration from the code, which is in line with the *Twelve Factor App* methodology and improves the security posture. The configuration data could be pushed into SSM Parameter Store, thereby ensuring that the same could be changed/updated very easily across deployments without making any changes to the code. The configuration data could be injected as environment variables for the code to use.

The parameters stored in SSM Parameter Store could be classified as either *standard* or *advanced*. This classification takes place during the creation of the parameter. Subsequently, a standard parameter could be changed to advanced parameter but not the other way round, due to the risk of data loss. This is so because, an advanced parameter supports a value of size 8KB, whereas a standard parameter supports 4KB value size. While the standard parameters do not incur any additional costs, additional charges do apply to the advanced parameters. Additionally, the number of standard parameters supported per AWS account per AWS region is 10000, whereas the limit is 100000 for the advanced parameters.

Creation and retrieval of parameters

SSM Parameter Store supports three types of parameters – **String**, **StringList** (comma separated list of values), and **SecureString** (encrypted parameter value). We will delve into the nitty-gritty of how to create each type of parameter and then learn how to retrieve the parameter value and other details.

We will use the AWS CLI v2 commands to create and retrieve the parameters. At this point, we assume that the required permissions have been given to the user **param_user** and the user's programmatic credentials have been configured in AWS CLI and associated with a new profile named **param_user**.

The following is the CLI command to create a parameter named **/dev/app1/integration/requestTimeout** in SSM Parameter Store of type **String** (specified with the option **type**). Also, by default, the **Standard** tier is assumed. If required, the tier could be changed using the **tier** option that can have three possible values – **Standard**, **Advanced**, and **Intelligent-Tiering**. Refer to the following command:

```
$ aws ssm put-parameter --name /dev/app1/integration/requestTimeout \
  --value "20" --type String --tier Standard
```

The command, if successful, returns the version number and tier of the new parameter. Also notice that we have used a hierarchical name. This parameter naming convention can help to fetch multiple parameters nested in a common directory structure with a single retrieval command, as follows:

```
{
    "Version": 1,
    "Tier": "Standard"
}
```

In case we want to change the value of an existing parameter, we can still use the **put-parameter** operation along with the **overwrite** flag, as shown in the following command. Note that, this following command will create a new version of the existing parameter:

```
$ aws ssm put-parameter --name /dev/app1/integration/requestTimeout \
  --value "30" --type String --overwrite
```

The command returns the new version number (version 2) in the following response format:

```
{
    "Version": 2,
    "Tier": "Standard"
}
```

The other types of parameters (**StringList** and **SecureString**) could also be created as follows:

```
$ aws ssm put-parameter --name /dev/app1/supportedCountries \
  --value "IN,US,GB,ES,FR,JP" --type StringList

$ aws ssm put-parameter --name /dev/app1/apiKey \
  --value file://apikey.txt --type SecureString
```

For creating a parameter of type **SecureString**, it's best practice to use a file (**apikey.txt** in the preceding example) and delete the file, once done. We must note here that **SecureString** can be encrypted with a KMS CMK, and for that purpose, we can use the **kms-id** option along with the **put-parameter** option and pass the CMK identifier. If **kms-id** is not specified, the default KMS key is assumed.

Now, to retrieve the parameters created, we can use three commands – **get-parameter**, **get-parameters**, and **get-parameters-by-path**. Let's go through each one of them. The following command(s) could be used to retrieve the details of a single parameter by its name:

```
$ aws ssm get-parameter --name /dev/app1/integration/requestTimeout
```

The output of the preceding command is as follows:

```
{
    "Parameter": {
        "Name": "/dev/app1/integration/requestTimeout",
        "Type": "String",
        "Value": "30",
        "Version": 2,
        "LastModifiedDate": "2021-05-31T19:15:47.594000+05:30",
         "ARN": "arn:aws:ssm:ap-south-1:<account-id>:parameter/dev/app1/
integration/requestTimeout",
        "DataType": "text"
    }
}
```

In case the parameter is of type **Secure String** the value is returned in the encrypted format. However, if we want to view the decrypted value, we should use the following **with-decryption** option:

```
$ aws ssm get-parameter --name /dev/app1/apiKey --with-decryption
```

The following is the output of the command (note that, the "Value" field contains a decrypted value):

```
{
    "Parameter": {
        "Name": "/dev/app1/apiKey",
        "Type": "SecureString",
        "Value": "Hdfs6878gshTy_tt567",
        "Version": 1,
        "LastModifiedDate": "2021-05-31T23:53:10.213000+05:30",
         "ARN": "arn:aws:ssm:ap-south-1:<account-id>:parameter/dev/app1/
apiKey",
        "DataType": "text"
    }
}
```

To retrieve the details of more than one parameter by their respective names, we could use the following command:

```
$ aws ssm get-parameters --names \
  "/dev/app1/integration/requestTimeout" "/dev/app1/supportedCountries"
```

Finally, if we want to retrieve the parameter details based on a specific hierarchy, then the following command can do just that for us:

```
$ aws ssm get-parameters-by-path --path /dev/app1
```

Note that, the **path** option in the preceding command doesn't specify any particular parameter name, rather it specifies a hierarchical path. In case, we want to recursively view all the parameters in the hierarchy, we can use the **recursive** flag along with the **get-parameters-by-path** operation, as follows:

```
$ aws ssm get-parameters-by-path --path /dev/app1 --recursive
```

The **get-parameters-by-path** is a powerful command, since it can be used to fetch all the parameter details in a single call, say for a particular application (here **app1**).

Comparison: AWS Secrets Manager v/s AWS SSM Parameter Store

Now that we know about the relevant features from both AWS Secrets Manager and AWS SSM Parameter Store services, it's time to understand when to leverage them. Both have similar features, and a comparison is summarized in *Table 5.1*, as follows:

Dimensions	Aws Ssm Parameter Store	Aws Secrets Manager
Support for KMS based encryption	Yes	Yes
Support for 4KB values	Yes	Yes
Built-in password generator	No	Yes
Automated secret rotation	No	Yes
Costs	No additional charges for standard tier	$0.40 per secret per month $0.05 per 10000 API calls

Table 5.1: *Comparison between AWS SecretsManager and AWS SSM Parameter Store*

In short, both SSM Parameter Store and Secrets Manager supports KMS based encryption of the secrets/parameters, and as such, they could be used to store the secrets securely. However, SSM Parameter Store is a less costly option as compared to Secrets Manager. But if we are looking for complex scenarios like rotation of secrets, automated secret generation, etc., then Secrets Manager is a better choice.

Web Application Firewall

A **Web Application Firewall (WAF)** is an application layer (layer-7) firewall that is used to protect the web applications against threats and vulnerabilities like SQL injection (SQLi), **cross site scripting (XSS)**, malware infections, impersonation, DDoS, and other zero-day exploits. A typical WAF analyzes the HTTP requests and applies a set of rules to find if the request has any malicious content.

AWS WAF is a managed Web Application Firewall service that could be used to monitor the HTTP/S based application traffic from Amazon CloudFront, Amazon API Gateway, Application Load Balancer, or AWS AppSync GraphQL API. Any traffic that is found to be malicious based on the configured WAF rules, is blocked with a HTTP 403 (Forbidden) response.

Typically, we can create *web* **ACLs (Access Control List)** to protect the AWS resources. A web ACL is associated with a set of *rules*, which define the protection strategy or inspection criteria along with an *action* (allow or deny). If a web request meets the criteria, it can be allowed or blocked based on the corresponding defined action. The rules could be logically grouped into reusable *rule groups*. We could use both managed rule groups (by AWS or AWS marketplace vendors) or create our own rules and rule groups. Once a web ACL is defined, it is associated with one or more supported AWS resources.

Web ACL Capacity Unit (WCU) is used to calculate and control the resources that are required to run the rules, rules groups, and web ACLs. WCUs are enforced on the rule groups and web ACLs. The costs pertaining to each rule is directly linked with WCU. Simple rules use fewer WCUs and are less costly compared to the complex rules which consume more WCUs and are expensive.

To start creating a web ACL, we will visit the WAF and Shield Console and click on the **`Web ACLs`** option from the left navigation panel. On the create web ACL page, we will select the appropriate region and click on the **`Create web ACL`** button to open a wizard. As the first step, we will specify the name, description, and the resource type (CloudFront distributions or regional resources) to which this web ACL will be associated. Refer to *figure 5.44* as follows:

Web ACL details
Name
bpb479-waf-acl
The name must have 1-128 characters. Valid characters: A-Z, a-z, 0-9, - (hyphen), and _ (underscore).
Description - optional
Sample web ACL
The description can have 1-256 characters.
CloudWatch metric name
bpb479-waf-acl
The name must have 1-128 characters. Valid characters: A-Z, a-z, 0-9, - (hyphen), and _ (underscore).
Resource type
Choose the type of resource to associate with this web ACL.
CloudFront distributions
Regional resources (Application Load Balancer, API Gateway, AWS AppSync)
Region
Choose the AWS region to create this web ACL in.
Asia Pacific (Mumbai)

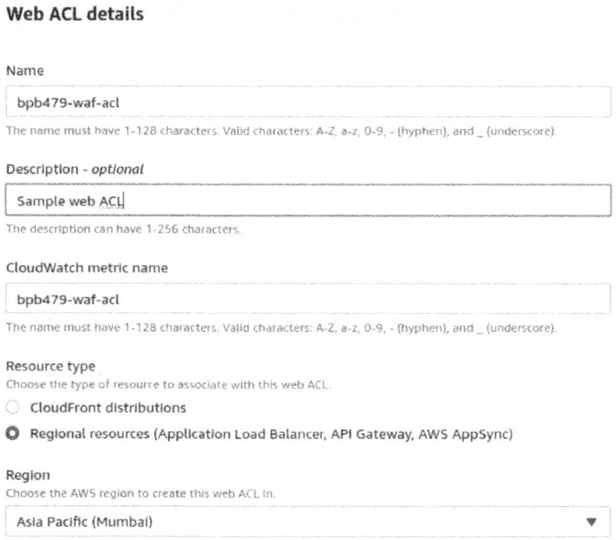

Figure 5.44: *Creation of a Web ACL from AWS Management Console*

On the same page, under the **`Associate AWS resources`** section, we could optionally add the AWS resources by clicking on the **`Add AWS resources`** button which opens a popup where the resources could be selected and added to the web ACL. *Figure 5.45* shows the AWS resource options available for the regional resource type selection. Once the resources are selected, clicking on the **`Next`** button takes us back to the original wizard page. Refer to *figure 5.45* as follows:

Add AWS resources
Resource type
Select the resource type and then select the resource you want to associate with this web ACL.
Amazon API Gateway
Application Load Balancer
AWS AppSync
Select the resources you want to associate with the web ACL.
Find AWS resources to associate
1
Name
product - DEV
customer - DEV
Cancel
Add

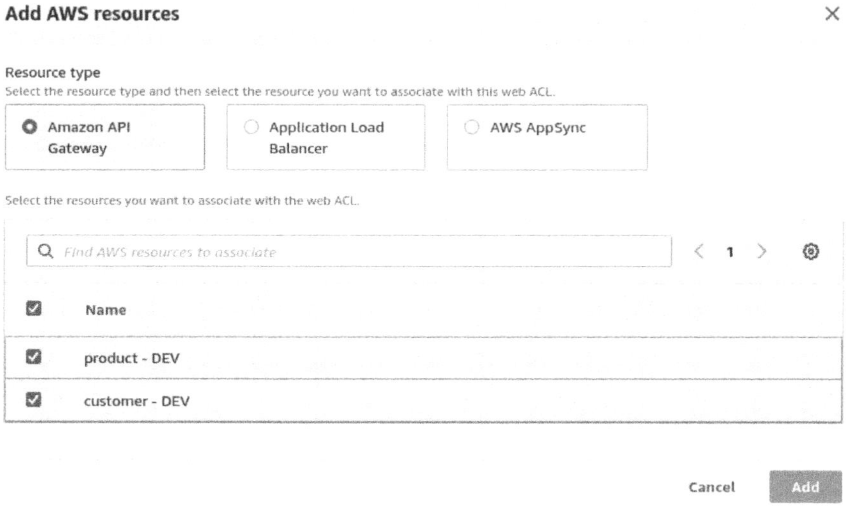

Figure 5.45: *Associating supported AWS resources with a Web ACL*

In the next step, we will add the rules and rule groups to the web ACL. We could choose to add the managed rule groups or the custom rules / rule groups (*figure 5.46*). There are quite a few options for the managed rule groups from AWS and from the other marketplace vendors like Fortinet, GeoGuard, Imperva, ThreatSTOP, etc. Refer to *figure 5.46* as follows:

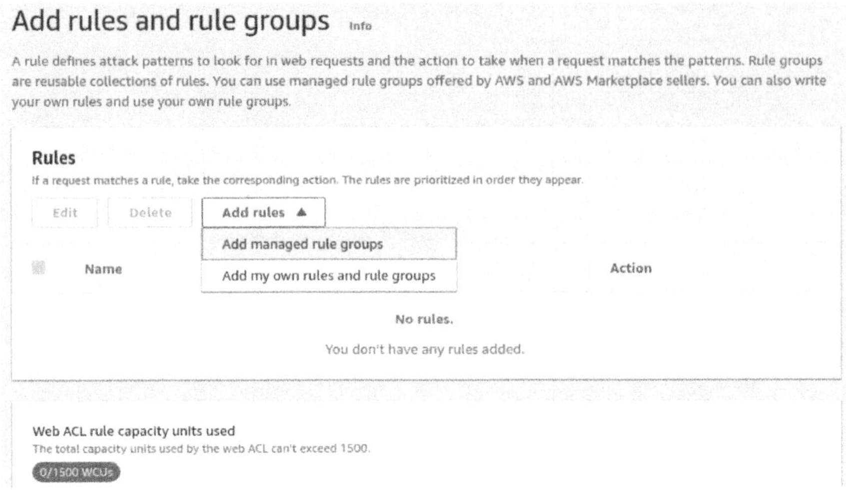

Add rules and rule groups Info

A rule defines attack patterns to look for in web requests and the action to take when a request matches the patterns. Rule groups are reusable collections of rules. You can use managed rule groups offered by AWS and AWS Marketplace sellers. You can also write your own rules and use your own rule groups.

Rules

If a request matches a rule, take the corresponding action. The rules are prioritized in order they appear.

Edit | Delete | Add rules ▲

Add managed rule groups

Add my own rules and rule groups

Name | Action

No rules.

You don't have any rules added.

Web ACL rule capacity units used

The total capacity units used by the web ACL can't exceed 1500.

0/1500 WCUs

***Figure 5.46**: Adding rules to a Web ACL from AWS Management Console*

On the **`Add managed rule groups`** page, we can select one or more rule groups. There is a selection of both paid and free rule groups. *Figure 5.47* shows how a free rule group named **`Core rule set`** which includes general rules to protect the web applications including the OWASP vulnerabilities, is added to the web ACL by selecting **`Add to web ACL`** under the **`Action`** column, as follows:

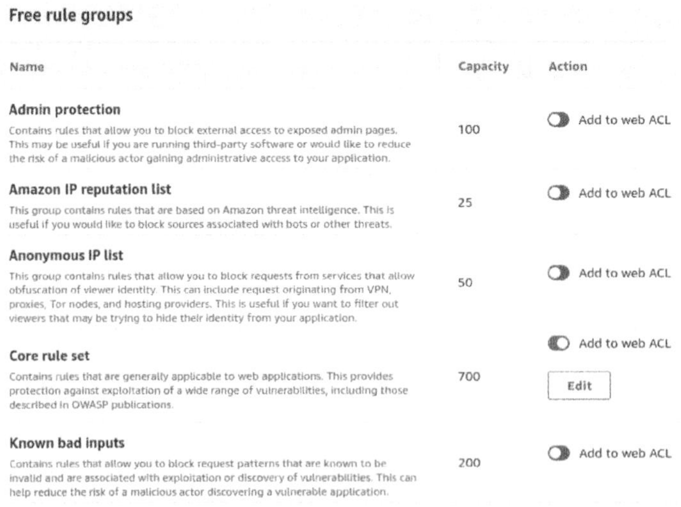

Free rule groups

Name	Capacity	Action
Admin protection Contains rules that allow you to block external access to exposed admin pages. This may be useful if you are running third-party software or would like to reduce the risk of a malicious actor gaining administrative access to your application.	100	Add to web ACL
Amazon IP reputation list This group contains rules that are based on Amazon threat intelligence. This is useful if you would like to block sources associated with bots or other threats.	25	Add to web ACL
Anonymous IP list This group contains rules that allow you to block requests from services that allow obfuscation of viewer identity. This can include request originating from VPN, proxies, Tor nodes, and hosting providers. This is useful if you want to filter out viewers that may be trying to hide their identity from your application.	50	Add to web ACL
Core rule set Contains rules that are generally applicable to web applications. This provides protection against exploitation of a wide range of vulnerabilities, including those described in OWASP publications.	700	Add to web ACL Edit
Known bad inputs Contains rules that allow you to block request patterns that are known to be invalid and are associated with exploitation or discovery of vulnerabilities. This can help reduce the risk of a malicious actor discovering a vulnerable application.	200	Add to web ACL

***Figure 5.47:** Selection of a managed rule group to associate with Web ACL*

Once the selection is done, we must click on the **Add rules** button at the bottom of the page. At this point, we need to keep a watch on the WCU consumed due to the addition of the rule set and select the **Default web ACL action for requests that don't match any rules** (by default, it's **Allow**) and then click on the **Next** button.

On the next page, if multiple rule groups are selected, we could set the **Rule priority** and click on **Next**. We could also configure the **Amazon CloudWatch metrics** and **Request sampling** options on the next page, and then finally, review the configurations made to the web ACL before clicking on the **Create web ACL** button.

When using the WAF appliances (like Barracuda, etc.), there are several clouds native WAF patterns that are used by the organizations on the AWS cloud; a couple of interesting ones are as follows:

- **WAF sandwich**: In a WAF sandwich pattern, the WAF layer is sandwiched between two ELBs. Essentially, the incoming traffic is converged into the WAF layer which must be scalable and then the traffic is directed to the backend application layer.
- **WAF based VPC**: WAF based VPC directs the incoming traffic through an ELB into the WAF layer which is placed in a separate VPC. This WAF VPC has a VPC peering with the application VPC.

For the web applications exposed to the Internet, AWS WAF is an effective tool in the security arsenal that helps protect such applications deployed on AWS cloud from several layer-7 attacks.

Securing applications with load balancer

Elastic Load balancers or ELBs are used to distribute traffic across multiple targets residing in multiple **Availability Zones** (**AZs**). This strategy essentially increases the availability of an application. There are four types of load balancers currently supported by AWS – **Application Load Balancer** (**ALB**), **Network Load Balancer (NLB)**, Gateway Load Balancer, and Classic Load Balancer (legacy). ELBs play a significant role as they often act as the entry point for the applications. In case of Internet facing ELBs, external traffic first hits the ELB and are then subsequently distributed across targets. ELB is a managed service when it comes to maintenance and security of the load balancer nodes. However, we can still take some steps to ensure better protection of our applications when the traffic passes through a load balancer.

WAF rules for Application Load Balancer

ALBs can be integrated with AWS WAF. Once a web ACL is created with rules to safeguard the applications from the layer-7 attacks, we can associate the regional resource like an ALB with the web ACL. *Figure 5.48* shows how to add an ALB named **`bpb479-alb`** to the web ACL from WAF & Shield Console, as follows:

Add AWS resources
Resource type
Select the resource type and then select the resource you want to associate with this web ACL.
Amazon API Gateway
Application Load Balancer
AWS AppSync
Select the resources you want to associate with the web ACL.
Find AWS resources to associate
Name
bpb479-alb
Cancel
Add

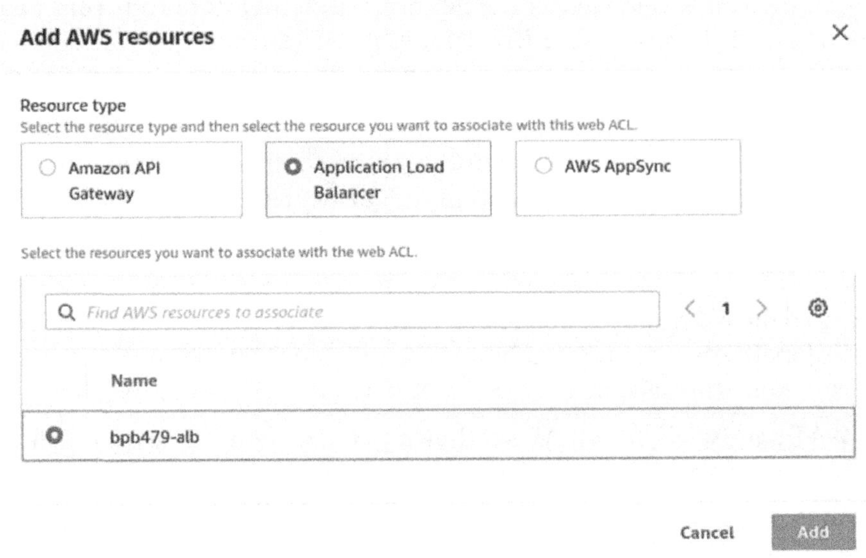

Figure 5.48: *Add an ALB to AWS WAF web ACL*

Once this association is done, we can validate this from the ELB Console, by selecting the ALB (named **`bpb479-alb`**) and checking the **`Integrated services`** tab. The particular ALB will be shown as WAF enabled and the corresponding web ACL will also be displayed. *Figure 5.49* shows the status of an WAF enabled ALB, as follows:

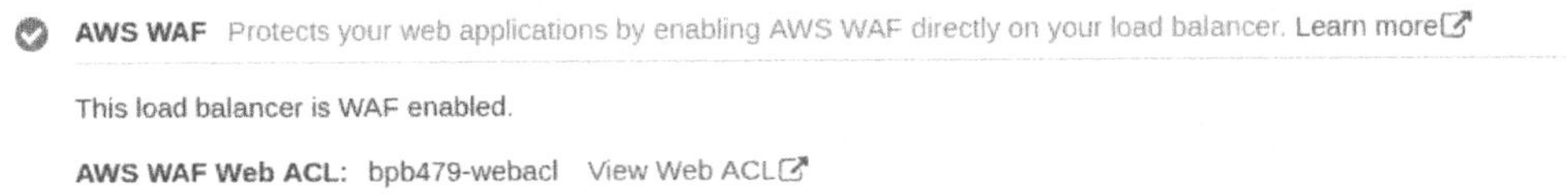
AWS WAF Protects your web applications by enabling AWS WAF directly on your load balancer. Learn more
This load balancer is WAF enabled.
AWS WAF Web ACL: bpb479-webacl View Web ACL

Figure 5.49: *AWS WAF enabled Application Load Balancer*

Elastic Load Balancing and TLS

Applications can leverage ELB to offload the TLS/SSL handling. We will primarily focus on **Application Load Balancer** (**ALB**) and **Network Load Balancer** (**NLB**) and check the process of enabling **Transport Layer Security** (**TLS**) on them. This entails the use of a (TLS/SSL) secured protocol and deploying a server-side certificate. The load balancers have two components – the *listeners* which listen to specific protocol/port combination for incoming connections and *targets* across which the traffic is distributed. The targets are registered and grouped into *target groups* and *health checks* can be configured on them. *Figure 5.50* shows the schematics of a load balancer, as follows:

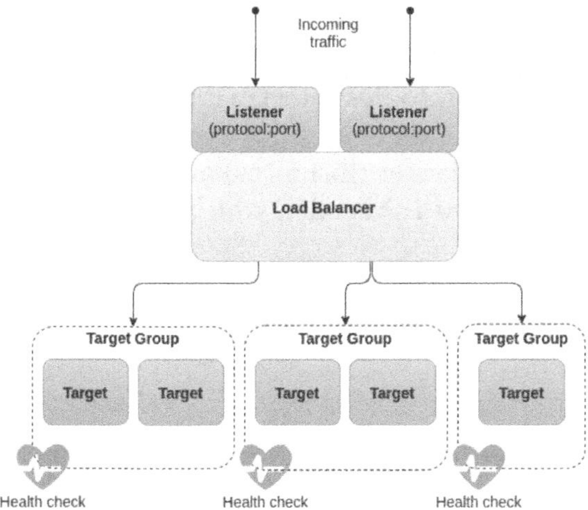

***Figure 5.50:** Components of a load balancer*

Application Load Balancer (**ALB**), as the name suggests, is a layer-7 (application layer) load balancer, which means an ALB is application context aware. ALB supports HTTP/HTTPS listeners only and can intelligently route traffic based on the HTTP headers, HTTP methods, source IP addresses, query parameters, path parameters, URI, etc. In case of an ALB, the targets can be based on EC2 instance IDs, IP addresses, or Lambda functions.

Network Load Balancer (**NLB**) operates at layer-4 (transport layer). NLB is unaware of the application context and distributes the traffic solely by matching protocol and port to the targets. In case of an NLB, the supported target types are EC2 instance IDs and IP addresses.

TLS termination

TLS termination or SSL offloading is a technique where encryption and decryption of an SSL secured connection (like HTTPS) is offloaded to the load balancer, instead of the backend application having to carry out this heavy lifting. This also makes the management of the TLS certificates easier as we don't have to distribute the server certificates to a fleet of backend targets or servers.

Application Load Balancer

Application Load Balancers support TLS termination, thus enabling traffic encryption between the clients that initiate a TLS or SSL session and the load balancer. In ALBs, when we create an HTTPS listener, we must deploy a TLS/SSL server certificate on the load balancer. This certificate can be stored in **AWS Certificate Manager** (**ACM**) or IAM, and it helps to terminate the front-end connection and decrypts the request to route them to the appropriate targets based on the listener rules. Thus, the connection between the ALB and the targets (backend application) is over simple un-encrypted HTTP. *Figure 5.51* shows how the incoming requests are over HTTPS and ALB terminates the connection by use of a certificate (that resides in Certificate Manager) and then routes the HTTP traffic to the targets (here shown as EC2 instances). Note that, in case of an ALB, the source IP address presented to the targets is that of the load balancer (instances) and not the actual source IP. In fact, ALBs support the *X-Forwarded-For* header, which carries the client IP address. Refer to *figure 5.51* as follows:

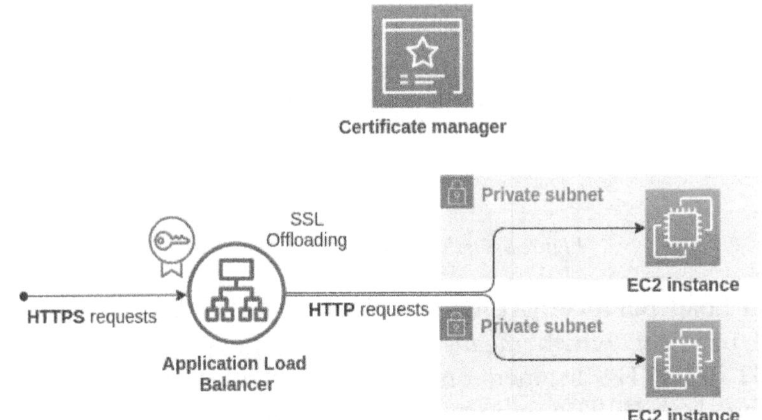

Figure 5.51: *SSL offloading implementation*

To enable TLS termination on an ALB, all we need to do is configure an HTTPS listener. *Figure 5.52* shows the HTTPS listener configuration for an ALB. In the EC2 Console, we must click on the **Load Balancing | Load Balancers** link from the left navigation panel, then click on the **Create Load Balancer** button on the load balancer's details page, followed by the selection of **Application Load Balancer** on the **Select load balancer type** page. Once we have provided the basic configuration, network mapping, and security groups related information, we must configure the **Listeners and routing** section. As part of the listener configuration, we must select the HTTPS protocol on port **443** and associate a default target group that accepts the HTTP traffic. We also need to specify the SSL certificate that will be used as the server identity by the ALB. This certificate could be created in ACM or IAM or could be imported and stored in these two services. This listener configuration will automatically terminate the TLS/SSL connection at the ALB.

Note that, at the time of writing, the default ALB security policy is **ELBSecurityPolicy-2016-08**. ELB security policies are used to negotiate the SSL connections between the client and the ALB. A security policy is essentially a collection of protocols and ciphers, which determines the algorithms to be used to encrypt and decrypt the traffic. Refer to *figure 5.52* as follows:

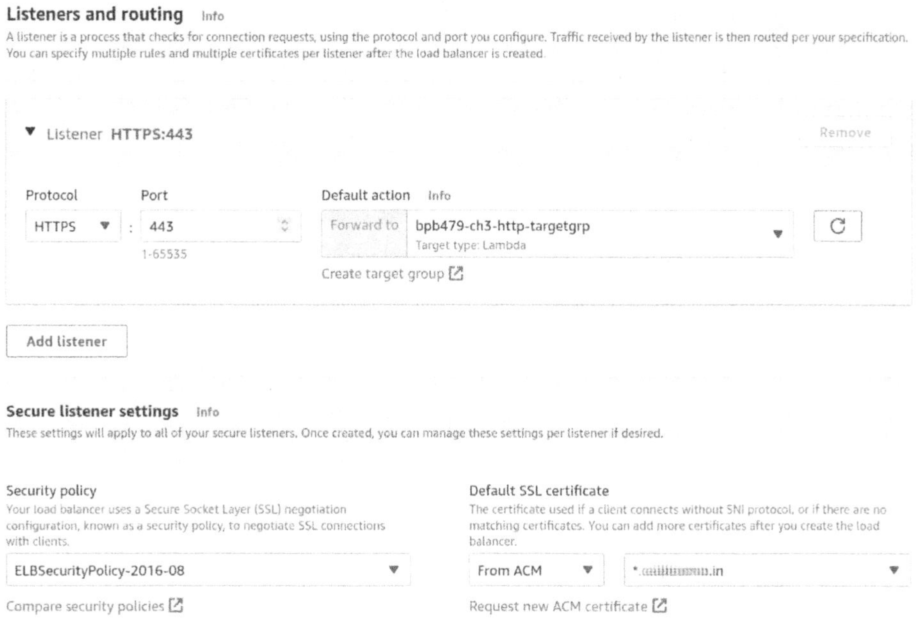

Listeners and routing Info

A listener is a process that checks for connection requests, using the protocol and port you configure. Traffic received by the listener is then routed per your specification. You can specify multiple rules and multiple certificates per listener after the load balancer is created.

▼ Listener **HTTPS:443** Remove

Protocol: HTTPS | Port: 443 (1-65535) | Default action Info: Forward to bpb479-ch3-http-targetgrp (Target type: Lambda)

Create target group

Add listener

Secure listener settings Info

These settings will apply to all of your secure listeners. Once created, you can manage these settings per listener if desired.

Security policy

Your load balancer uses a Secure Socket Layer (SSL) negotiation configuration, known as a security policy, to negotiate SSL connections with clients.

ELBSecurityPolicy-2016-08

Compare security policies

Default SSL certificate

The certificate used if a client connects without SNI protocol, or if there are no matching certificates. You can add more certificates after you create the load balancer.

From ACM | *.[illegible].in

Request new ACM certificate

Figure 5.52: *Configuration of HTTPS listener in an ALB from EC2 Console*

Network Load Balancer

NLBs also support the TLS termination and can free the backend applications from the compute intensive heavy lifting activity of encryption and decryption. NLBs can also preserve the source IP and present the same to the backend application. The fundamentals of terminating TLS on NLB are similar to ALB, except the fact that NLB does not recognize the HTTPS protocol (since NLB does not understand layer-7 protocol like HTTPS). Thus, in case of NLB, the associated target group must be configured with TCP and the listener protocol must be TLS. This configuration will automatically enable the TLS termination at NLB. *Figure 5.53* shows the listener configuration on the **`Create Network Load Balancer`** page in the EC2 console, as follows:

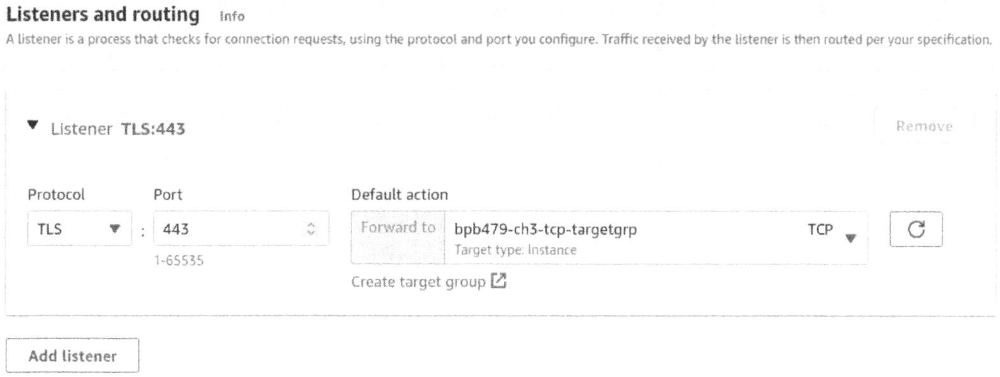

Listeners and routing Info

A listener is a process that checks for connection requests, using the protocol and port you configure. Traffic received by the listener is then routed per your specification.

▼ Listener **TLS:443** Remove

Protocol: TLS | Port: 443 (1-65535) | Default action: Forward to bpb479-ch3-tcp-targetgrp TCP (Target type: Instance)

Create target group

Add listener

Figure 5.53: *Configuration of TLS listener in a NLB from EC2 Console*

End-to-end TLS

In most cases, the TLS termination at the load balancer suffices the requirements of an encrypted channel. However, strict security regulations might warrant a more stringent use of the TLS encrypted traffic, also known as the end-to-end TLS encryption. In this case, the load balancer receives an encrypted request and then passes the request to the targets over a secured channel. This typically means that the backend certificates need to be distributed across the targets.

Application Load Balancer

With ALBs, we can create an HTTPS listener and associate an ACM certificate with the listener. Then, we can associate the HTTPS based target groups, so that the requests are re-encrypted with the application back-end's certificate. This could be a self-signed certificate as well. *Figure 5.54* shows two types of certificates – one that is deployed on the load balancer and encrypts the traffic between the client and the ALB, and the second type that is installed on each target (here EC2 instances). In case of a containerized application, end-to-end TLS could be achieved by using a sidecar proxy (like Envoy) along with the application containers that can terminate the TLS connection and send the unencrypted traffic to the application containers. Refer to *figure 5.54* as follows:

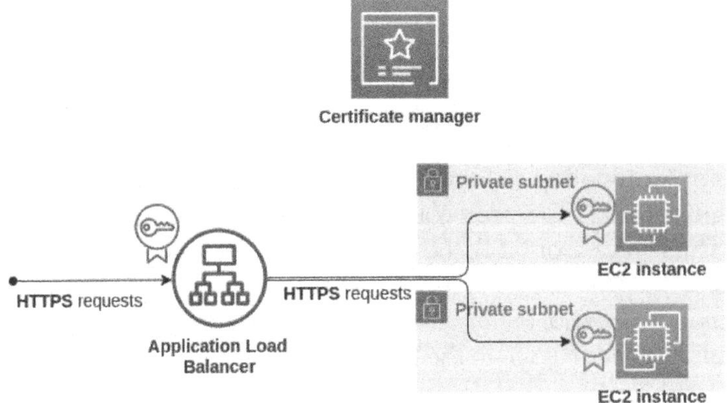

Figure 5.54: *End-to-End TLS implementation*

- To enable end-to-end TLS on an ALB, we must ensure to create a target group that will forward the traffic over the HTTPS protocol (on a given port like **`443`**). *Figure 5.55* shows how to configure this from the EC2 Console. We will click on **`Load Balancing | Target Groups`** from the left navigation panel in the EC2 Console. Then, on target group's details page, we will click on the **`Create target group`** button, and on the following **`Specify group details`** page, under the **`Basic configuration`** section, we will select the target type (Instances or IP addresses), specify the target group name along with the protocol as HTTPS and port. Refer to *figure 5.55* as follows:

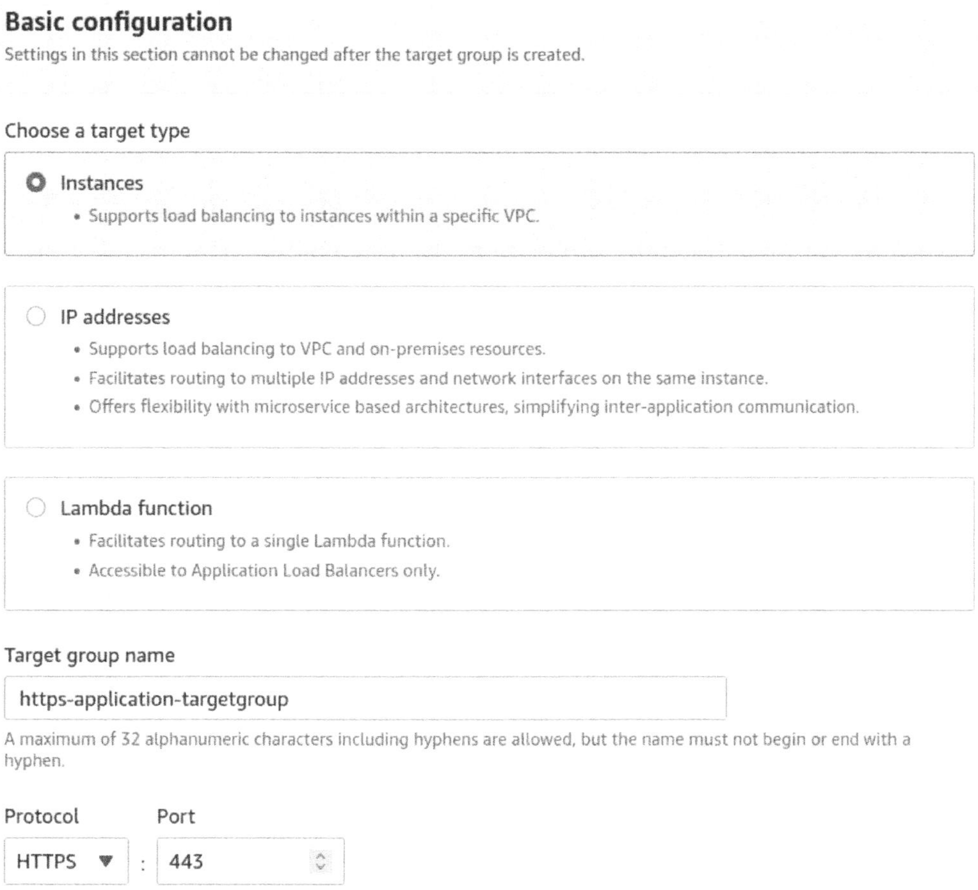

Basic configuration

Settings in this section cannot be changed after the target group is created.

Choose a target type

- Instances
  - Supports load balancing to instances within a specific VPC.

- IP addresses
  - Supports load balancing to VPC and on-premises resources.
  - Facilitates routing to multiple IP addresses and network interfaces on the same instance.
  - Offers flexibility with microservice based architectures, simplifying inter-application communication.

- Lambda function
  - Facilitates routing to a single Lambda function.
  - Accessible to Application Load Balancers only.

Target group name

https-application-targetgroup

A maximum of 32 alphanumeric characters including hyphens are allowed, but the name must not begin or end with a hyphen.

Protocol: HTTPS

Port: 443

Figure 5.55: *Target group configuration for end-to-end TLS in ALB from EC2 Console*

Once the target group is created and assuming that the application back-end is configured with a certificate, the next step is to create the ALB with the HTTPS listener configuration (as shown in *figure 5.52*) and associate this target group with it. With this configuration, the ALB establishes the TLS connections with the application back-ends using certificates deployed in the application. These TLS connections use the **`ELBSecurityPolicy-2016-08`** security policy for the SSL negotiations. Moreover, the ALB does not validate these certificates, and hence they could be self-signed as well.

Network Load Balancer

To enable end-to-end TLS in NLB, we need to configure the target group as well as the listener with the TLS protocol.

Conclusion

This chapter acts as an introduction to some of the significant AWS services that can help build secure applications. However, there are several other tools and processes that can enhance application security. DevSecOps is all about continuous integrated security with the right tools being baked into the application build and deployment process. Application security testing methodologies like **static application security testing** (**SAST**) and **dynamic application security testing** (**DAST**) are common practices to perform white box and black box security testing, respectively. They have different set of benefits and are effective in different phases of the software development lifecycle. Application layer penetration testing, or pen test could also prove very helpful to find specific application vulnerabilities that could be exploited.

Pursuing security best practices and leveraging AWS *security* services to create applications are not enough. We must continuously log, monitor, and audit the application health, look for unsolicited access patterns, fix security defects, and look for application vulnerabilities that can impact the application ecosystem and business.

In the next chapter, we will visit logging, monitoring, and auditing on AWS cloud.

Chapter 6
Logging, Monitoring, and Auditing

Introduction

Appropriate monitoring and logging strategies and analytics can help an organization with audits, aimed at meeting the various compliance requirements and equip the organization to harvest security insights and respond quickly and effectively to security incidents. Services like Amazon CloudWatch, AWS CloudTrail, and other services are fundamental to logging and monitoring, and helps with governance and auditing in the AWS public cloud.

Structure

In this chapter, we will cover the following topics:

- Amazon CloudWatch
- AWS CloudTrail
- Necessary logs managed by AWS
- AWS Config
- Amazon GuardDuty
- AWS Security Hub
- Amazon Detective

- AWS Artifact
- AWS Service Catalog

Objectives

In this chapter, we will learn about the integral monitoring, logging, and auditing services available in the AWS public cloud, and how and when to use them. We will also learn about the Amazon CloudWatch and AWS CloudTrail services, including the features and integration capabilities that they support. We will browse through the essential logs managed by AWS and establish methods to store and process these log files. In this chapter, we will also explore AWS Config and scratch the surface of services like Amazon GuardDuty, AWS Security Hub, AWS Artifact, and AWS Service Catalog, which play a vital role in governance and auditing to meet the compliance requirements.

Amazon CloudWatch

Amazon CloudWatch is a fundamental logging and monitoring service in the AWS service landscape. It can monitor both the AWS resources and the custom applications that run on the AWS cloud in real-time. CloudWatch can collect and track metrics. When a defined threshold is breached, it can also create alarms that watch these metrics and send notifications or make the automated changes to the monitored resources. Thus, in short, CloudWatch can help with visibility into resource utilization, application performance, and operational health.

We will primarily focus on Amazon CloudWatch Logs and touch upon the other significant components of the Amazon CloudWatch service.

CloudWatch Logs

Amazon CloudWatch Logs is a fully managed and highly scalable service that could monitor, store, and access the log files generated by Amazon EC2, Amazon ECS, Route 53, and the other sources, including custom sources. CloudWatch Logs is used to collect, ship, aggregate, and centralize the logs from a multitude of systems, applications, and other services in a single repository. Amazon CloudWatch Logs also provide easy visualization of these logs along with searching/filtering capabilities.

CloudWatch Logs are categorized into log group and log stream, which are defined as follows:

- **Log stream**: A log stream is a sequence of log events that has a common source. Hence, each separate source of the log can make up a separate log stream.

- **Log group**: A log group is a group of log streams that share the same monitoring, acc ess control, and retention settings. A single log group can have multiple log streams associated with it.

Some important services that publish logs to CloudWatch Logs are Amazon API Gateway, AWS CloudTrail, Amazon ECS, Amazon EKS, AWS Lambda, Amazon Route53, Amazon SNS, Amazon VPC, etc.

TIP: For the complete list of such services, refer to the following link: https://docs.aws.amazon.com/AmazonCloudWatch/latest/logs/aws-services-sending-logs.html

While publishing logs into CloudWatch Logs, AWS services also follow the same grouping and organization as explained earlier. For example, to access the logs produced by a Lambda function, we need to first identify the log group identified by the name **`/aws/lambda/<lambda-function-name>`** from the CloudWatch console and then drill into the specific log streams which carry the log events. With this knowledge of how logs are organized by CloudWatch Logs, let's explore how the logs could be collected and shipped to CloudWatch Logs.

Unified CloudWatch agent

A recommended way to collect logs and metrics (we will discuss CloudWatch metrics in a subsequent section) is to use the unified CloudWatch agent. The agent supports multiple operating systems and is highly performant. It also supports the collection of custom metrics using *Statsd* or *collectd*. The agent is available as a package with the Amazon Linux 2 operating system, which makes it very easy to install. The following shell command will install the unified agent:

```
$ sudo yum install amazon-cloudwatch-agent
```

For the other operating systems, relevant RPM, DEB, MSI (for Windows) packages are also available. Needless to say, if we run the unified agent from the EC2 instances, an appropriate IAM role must be assigned to those instances. The following Amazon-managed policies could be associated with the IAM role based on the scenario:

- **`CloudWatchAgentServerPolicy`**
- **`CloudWatchAgentAdminPolicy`**

Figure 6.1 shows the IAM policies page with the AWS-managed IAM policies that could be used with unified CloudWatch agent, as follows:

Figure 6.1: *AWS-managed IAM policies required for unified agent*

The unified agent is configured with the help of an agent configuration file. The agent configuration file specifies the metrics (including custom metrics) and logs that need to be collected. While the agent configuration file is written manually, the unified agent ships with an *agent configuration wizard* program, which can help generate this configuration file. To run the wizard (in Amazon Linux 2), the following command can be used:

```
$ sudo /opt/aws/amazon-cloudwatch-agent/bin/amazon-cloudwatch-agent-config-wizard
```

The wizard asks a set of questions to customize the configuration file, such as, whether the agent is being installed on an Amazon EC2 instance or an on-premise server, whether the server is Linux or Windows, whether we want to collect custom metrics using **Statsd** or **collectd**, etc. The wizard generates a configuration file named **config.json** which carries the customizations. The configuration file has the following three sections:

- **Agent**: The **agent** section represents the overall configuration of the unified agent. The wizard, however, does not generate this particular section.
- **Metrics**: The **metrics** section specifies the custom metrics for collection by the unified agent and subsequent publishing of these to Amazon CloudWatch. However, if we intend to use the agent solely for log collection, then this section could be omitted.
- **Logs**: The **logs** section specifies the logs that gets published to Amazon CloudWatch. The following is a snippet of the **logs** section that captures all the logs under the **/var/log** directory:

```
"logs": {
  "logs_collected": {
      "files": {
        "collect_list": [
          {
            "file_path":"/var/log/**",
            "log_group_name": "var.logs",
            "log_stream_name": "var_log_stream_1"
          }
        ]
      }
  }
}
```

The wizard is configured with a predefined set of metrics that are collected by the unified agent. *Table 6.1* lists all the predefined metrics available in the Linux systems categorized by three detail levels, as follows:

Detail Level	Metric Category	Metric Name
Basic	Memory	mem_used_percent
	Disk	disk_used_percent
Standard	CPU	cpu_usage_idle, cpu_usage_iowait, cpu_usage_user, cpu_usage_system
	Memory	mem_used_percent
	Disk	disk_used_percent, disk_inodes_free
	Diskio	diskio_io_time
	Swap	swap_used_percent
Advanced	CPU	cpu_usage_idle, cpu_usage_iowait, cpu_usage_user, cpu_usage_system
	Memory	mem_used_percent
	Disk	disk_used_percent, disk_inodes_free
	Diskio	diskio_io_time, diskio_write_bytes, diskio_read_bytes, diskio_writes, diskio_reads
	Swap	swap_used_percent
	Netstat	netstat_tcp_established, netstat_tcp_time_wait

Table 6.1: *List of predefined metrics in Linux*

Finally, once the unified agent is configured, we can use the following command to start it:

```
$ sudo /opt/aws/amazon-cloudwatch-agent/bin/amazon-cloudwatch-agent-ctl
-a fetch-config -m ec2 -s -c file:<config file path>
```

The **`-a fetch-config`** option loads the latest version of the agent configuration file and the **`-s`** option starts the agent. At this point, we should note that the installation, configuration, and starting/stopping of the unified agent can be carried out by using AWS Systems Manager, that we have discussed in *Chapter 3 "Infrastructure Security"*.

Logs Insights

Logs Insights is essentially an extension of Amazon CloudWatch Logs and provides interactive query interface for the log data. It has log analytics capabilities, and some visualization features as well. The service is available in the AWS CloudWatch console, as shown in *figure 6.2* as follows:

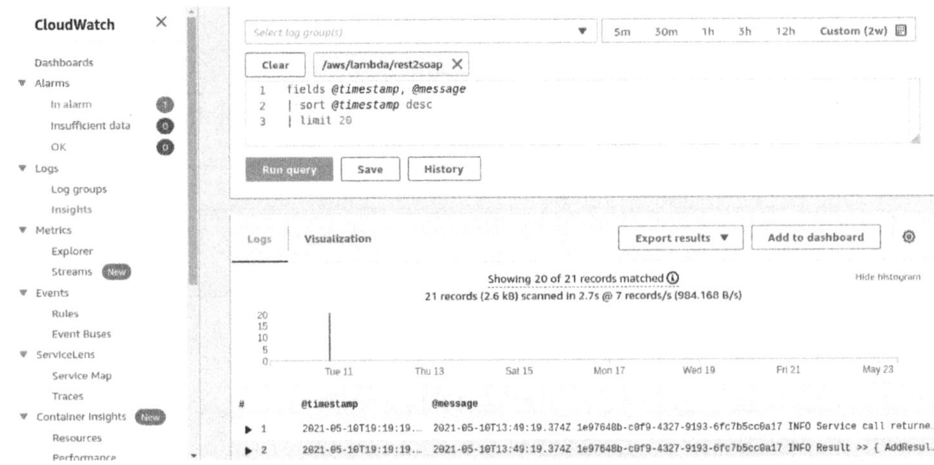

***Figure 6.2:** Logs Insights query interface*

Figure 6.2 shows the Logs Insights query interface, which is accessible under the **CloudWatch console | Logs | Insights** navigation pane. We need to select the log groups, based on which, we want to run the query, then write the query, and subsequently run it. The relevant log events are fetched and presented along with some basic charts.

Let's have a look at some examples leveraging the query language to search and filter the log events. The following is a simple query that fetches all the relevant log events from the selected log group and displays, the automatically generated system fields @ **timestamp** and **@message**, sorted by **@timestamp** and is limited to the first 10 records:

```
fields @timestamp, @messsage
| sort @timestamp desc
| limit 10
```

> **The following link provides a deeper understanding of the query syntax used with Logs Insights:**
> **https://docs.aws.amazon.com/AmazonCloudWatch/latest/logs/CWL_QuerySyntax.html**

Note that, each log event in CloudWatch Logs supports five system fields, which can be used in the query, as follows:

- **@message**: Contains unparsed and raw log event.
- **@timestamp**: Contains the event timestamp.
- **@ingestionTime**: Contains the time when CloudWatch Logs received the log event.

- **`@logStream`**: Contains the name of the log stream, where the log event was added.
- **`@log`**: Carries the log-group identifier.

In addition to the system fields, CloudWatch Logs can automatically discover several other log fields contained in the logs, for the specific log types. For example, in case of Lambda logs, the following Lambda specific fields can be used in the Logs Insights query – **`@requestId`**, **`@duration`**, **`@billedDuration`**, **`@type`**, **`@maxMemoryUsed`**, **`@memorySize`**.

> **TIP: The following link provides details on the supported log types and automatically discovered fields:**
> **https://docs.aws.amazon.com/AmazonCloudWatch/latest/logs/CWL_AnalyzeLogData-discoverable-fields.html**

The following query can be used to filter the **`message`** objects with **`ERROR`**; the query language supports regular expressions as well:

```
fields @timestamp, @messsage
| filter @message like 'ERROR'
| sort @timestamp desc
```

JSON logs can also be easily queried with Logs Insights. For example, if we have a JSON log event instance with the structure **`{ "code": '500', "severity": 'CRITICAL', "error": "Internal Server Error"}`**, the event can be easily queried with the following:

```
fields @timestamp, @message
| filter code = '500' and severity = 'CRITICAL'
| display error
| sort @timestamp desc
```

Logs Insights also support aggregation for analysis purposes, which can then be visualized using Line, Stacked Area, Bar, or Pie chart. The following example can be used with any Lambda log group to visualize the billed duration of all the invocations grouped into 10-minute buckets:

```
fields @timestamp, @message
| stats sum(@billedDuration) by bin(10m)
```

Finally, we will exemplify a very useful query. This query will help us extract all the log events (limited by 5000 in this example) pertaining to a log stream in a log group, by the log stream identifier. In the following example, the log stream identifier is equal to **`2f2e33ec53aa4414b8dc2e6e4464f7ca`**:

```
fields @timestamp, @message, @LogStream
| filter @logStream like /2f2e33ec53aa4414b8dc2e6e4464f7ca/
```

```
| sort @timestamp desc
| limit 5000
```

Logs Insights is thus a very powerful tool for near real-time analysis and visualization of CloudWatch logs.

Along with Logs Insights, there are other similar features available from CloudWatch Console under "Insights" on the left navigation panel, like "Containers Insights", "Lambda Insights", and "Application Insights", which can prove to be very useful in monitoring the containerized workloads, Lambda functions, and resources with the SSM agents installed respectively.

Subscriptions for real-time processing of logged data

Subscriptions are a way to get access to real time, base64 encoded and compressed (**gzip** format) log events feed from CloudWatch Logs and get the same delivered to services like Elasticsearch, Kinesis stream, Kinesis Firehose stream, or Lambda for further processing, analysis, and loading the log event feed to the other systems.

Let's take a quick tour of the steps involved to create a subscription filter that sends the log data to an AWS Lambda function, as follows:

1. First, we will create a Lambda execution role along with a trust policy, which will enable the AWS Lambda service to assume the role.

   The following is how the trust policy looks like, let's name this file **trustpolicy.json**:

   ```
   {
     "Version":  "2012-10-17",
     "Statement": [
        {
          "Effect": "Allow",
          "Principal": {
            "Service": "lambda.amazonaws.com"
          },
          "Action": "sts:AssumeRole"
        }
     ]
   }
   ```

   Next, we will create the **policy.json** file, which defines all the actions taken by the trusted entity that is allowed to assume the role (in this case, that's the AWS Lambda service). For the sake of simplicity, we will simply provide CloudWatch Logs the access to the Lambda function. However, we must understand that any set of relevant actions could be taken by the Lambda function, such as pushing the log events to a different system, etc. The following is how the **policy.json** file looks like:

```
{
  "Version": "2012-10-17",
  "Statement": [
     {
       "Effect": "Allow",
       "Action": [
          "logs:CreateLogStream",
          "logs:CreateLogGroup",
          "logs:PutLogEvents"
       ],
       "Resource": [
         "arn:aws:logs:*:<account-id>:log-group:/aws/lambda/
CWLogsSubscriptionLambda:log-stream:*",
               "arn:aws:logs:*:<account-id>:log-group:/aws/
lambda/CWLogsSubscriptionLambda"
       ]
     }
   ]
}
```

After creating the trust policy and the policy documents, it's time to actually create the IAM policy and the Lambda execution role (IAM role) and attach the policy to the role. While these operations could have been carried out in the AWS management console, we will look at the AWS CLI option. Let's assume that we have the appropriate AWS credentials to carry out these activities and that AWS CLI v2 has been configured on the host where the CLI will be used. Now, fire away the CLI commands to create the IAM policy, then create the IAM role, and finally, associate the policy to the role, as follows:

```
$ aws iam create-policy \
--policy-name CWLogsSubscriptionLambdaPolicy \
--policy-document file://./policy.json

$ aws iam create-role --role-name CWLogsSubscriptionLambdaRole \
--assume-role-policy-document file://./trustpolicy.json
$ aws iam attach-role-policy \
--role-name CWLogsSubscriptionLambdaRole \
--policy-arn arn:aws:iam::<account-id>:policy/
CWLogsSubscriptionLambdaPolicy
```

2. The next step is to create the Lambda function (we'll use Node.js for this example) and deploy the same. We start with the implementation of the Lambda function. Basically, we want this function to zip (**gunzip**) the log event data sent by the sub-scription, parse the JSON structure, and then simply use console logging to publish the event to CloudWatch Logs. So, we start by creating a Node.js package and in-stalling the required NPM dependencies (specifically **node-gzip** package will be used for gunzipping

the logged data). We must recall here that the subscriptions al-ways send base64 encoded and **gzip** compressed log events. Here are the com-mands to create the project and install dependencies, as follows:

```
$npm init -y  # create the package.json
$npm install --save node-gzip  # creates node_modules folder with node-gzip package installed
```

The following is how the function implementation might look like (file: **index.js**):

```
// File: index.js
const {ungzip} = require('node-gzip');
const ENCODING_BASE64 = "base64";
const ENCODING_ASCII = "ascii";
exports.handler = async function(event, context) {
    var payload = Buffer.from(event.awslogs.data, ENCODING_BASE64);
    try{
      const decompressed = await ungzip(payload);
      let result = JSON.parse(decompressed.toString(ENCODING_ASCII));
      // Process the log data and persist
      console.log("Log Event > ", JSON.stringify(result, null, 2));
        context.succeed();
    }
    catch(e){
      context.fail(e);
    }
};
```

Now, let's use AWS CLI to deploy this function. We need to zip the **package.json**, index.js and **node_modules** folder into a **ZIP** file named **subscription_lambda.zip** and use the following command:

```
$ aws lambda create-function \
--function-name CWLogsSubscriptionLambda \
--runtime nodejs14.x \
--zip-file fileb://subscription_lambda.zip \
--handler index.handler \
--role arn:aws:iam::<account-id>:role/CWLogsSubscriptionLambdaRole
```

3. Next, we need to create a resource-based policy to allow CloudWatch Logs to invoke the Lambda function. The following is the relevant CLI command:

```
$ aws lambda add-permission \
  --function-name CWLogsSubscriptionLambda \
  --principal logs.ap-south-1.amazonaws.com \
  --statement-id cwlogsinvoke --action "lambda:InvokeFunction" \
  --source-arn "arn:aws:logs:ap-south-1:<account-id>:log-group:TestCWLogsSubscriptionLambda:*"
```

4. Finally, we need to create a subscription filter with the following CLI command:

```
$ aws logs put-subscription-filter \
--log-group-name TestCWLogsSubscriptionLambda \
--filter-name sampleFilter \
--filter-pattern "" \
--destination-arn "arn:aws:lambda:ap-south-1:<account-id>:functio
n:CWLogsSubscriptionLambda"
```

In the preceding command, the filter-pattern is used for subscribing to a filtered stream of CloudWatch log events.

In order to test everything that we have done so far, we will put some sample log events to an already existing **`LogGroup`** and **`LogStream`** (one can create a Log Group and Log Stream quite easily from the AWS Management console or use the **`aws logs create-log-group`** and **`aws logs create-log-stream`** CLI commands). We can use the following CLI command to put the log events to an existing log group named **`TestCWLogsSubscriptionLambda`** and log stream named **`stream1`**:

```
$ aws logs put-log-events \
--log-group-name TestCWLogsSubscriptionLambda \
--log-stream-name stream1 \
--log-events "[{\"timestamp\":1621097629000 , \"message\": \"Sample
CloudWatch Logs Subscription test with Lambda destination\"}]"
```

If everything works out, we should see the sample log event that was put to stream1 of **`LogGroup TestCWLogsSubscriptionLambda`**, ending up in the **`LogGroup /aws/lambda/CWLogsSubscriptionLambda`** that the Lambda writes to (as per the Lambda execution role). *Figure 6.3* shows how the subscription log event looks in AWS Management Console, as follows:

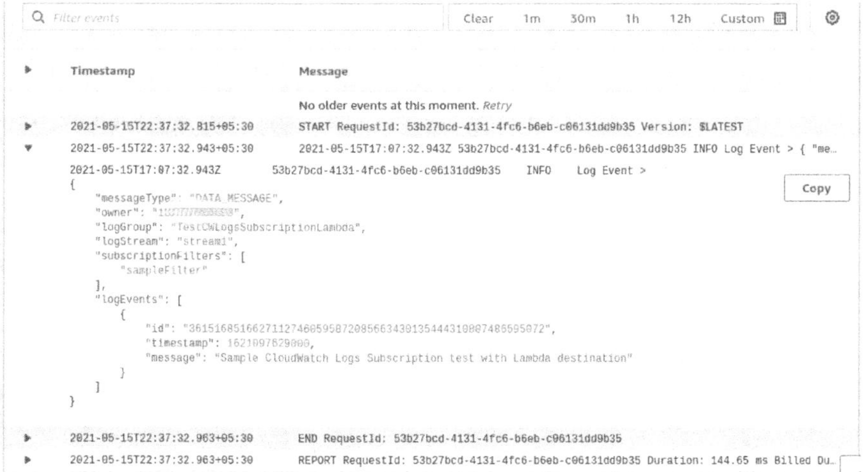

***Figure 6.3:** The subscription log event in AWS Management Console*

Export logs to Amazon S3

While Logs Insights and subscriptions could be used for near real-time or real-time analysis and processing of CloudWatch Logs, we can create an export task to export all the logged data from a CloudWatch Logs log group to an Amazon S3 bucket, in the form of gzipped files. Log data can take up to 12 hours to become available for export. This can greatly help in custom analysis and processing of the logged data and optionally load this data to the other systems. Log data cannot be exported to an S3 bucket that is encrypted with SSE-KMS. However, we still can export to an S3 bucket that is encrypted using AES-256.

Let's go through the steps to create an export task and export the CloudWatch log data to an S3 bucket. We will use AWS CLI for the purpose. At this point, we assume that we have installed AWS CLI v2 in the host from where we will fire the commands and the appropriate AWS credentials are configured with AWS CLI. The relevant steps are as follows:

1. The first step is to ensure that the IAM credentials configured with AWS CLI, allows full access to Amazon S3 and CloudWatch Logs and read-only access to IAM. In fact, the read-only access to IAM is required to issue the **`list-attached-user-policies`** command (as shown in the following code). We could actually issue this command using a different profile which has the IAM read-only permission. But to keep things simple, we will assign all the required permissions to the profile user. The following is the CLI command:

   ```
   $ aws iam list-attached-user-policies --user-name exporter \
     --profile exporter
   ```

   In the preceding command, we have used the AWS CLI profile of **`exporter`**, which corresponds to a user with the same name, who has the required permissions. The command should give the following result:

   ```
   {
       "AttachedPolicies": [
           {
               "PolicyName": "AmazonS3FullAccess",
            "PolicyArn": "arn:aws:iam::aws:policy/AmazonS3FullAccess"
           },
           {
               "PolicyName": "CloudWatchFullAccess",
          "PolicyArn": "arn:aws:iam::aws:policy/CloudWatchFullAccess"
           },
           {
               "PolicyName": "IAMReadOnlyAccess",
             "PolicyArn": "arn:aws:iam::aws:policy/IAMReadOnlyAccess"
           }
       ]
   }
   ```

2. Next, we will create an S3 bucket named **bpb479-exported-logs** in the ap-south-1 region. Needless to say, an existing bucket could also be used. However, its best to create a separate bucket for the exported logs. Issue the following command to create the bucket:

```
$ aws s3api create-bucket --bucket bpb479-exported-logs \
  --create-bucket-configuration LocationConstraint=ap-south-1 \
  --profile exporter
```

3. Now, we will create a bucket policy which will allow CloudWatch Logs to export the log data to the S3 bucket and apply the policy to the **bpb479-exported-logs** bucket.

   The following is how the policy file (**bucketpolicy.json**) might look like:

```
{
    "Version": "2012-10-17",
    "Statement": [
        {
            "Action": "s3:GetBucketAcl",
            "Effect": "Allow",
            "Resource": "arn:aws:s3:::bpb479-exported-logs",
            "Principal": {
              "Service": "logs.ap-south-1.amazonaws.com"
}
        },
        {
            "Action": "s3:PutObject" ,
            "Effect": "Allow",
            "Resource": "arn:aws:s3:::bpb479-exported-logs/*",
                "Condition": { "StringEquals": { "s3:x-amz-acl":
"bucket-owner-full-control" } },
            "Principal": { "Service": "logs.ap-south-1.amazonaws.
com" }
        }
    ]
}
```

   Once the policy file is ready, we can use the following command to apply this policy to the S3 bucket:

```
$ aws s3api put-bucket-policy --bucket bpb479-exported-logs \
  --policy file://bucketpolicy.json --profile exporter
```

4. Finally, we must create the export task that will essentially export the log data from a CloudWatch Logs log group to the S3 bucket. This export process can typically take anywhere between few seconds to few hours, depending on the export volume. We will export the log data from an existing log group named **SampleLogGroup**. The following CLI command could be used to create the export task:

```
$ aws logs create-export-task --profile exporter \
  --task-name "sample-export-task-bpb479" \
  --log-group-name "SampleLogGroup" \
  --from 1620654532000 --to 1620654559000 \
  --destination "bpb479-exported-logs" \
  --destination-prefix "bpb479-export-task"
```

   We note that the volume of log data exported depends on the "from" and "to" parameters which represent the start time and the end time, respectively, of the range of the request (expressed as number of milliseconds after Jan 1, 1970 00:00:00 UTC). The files are delivered as gzip files, and the export task organizes the files under the **destination-prefix** folder. The S3 URI of a delivered file might look like the following:

```
s3://bpb479-exported-logs/bpb479-export-task/b865250c-5737-44b5-
b38b-011520ef759b/2021-05-10-[$LATEST]2f2e33ec53aa4414b8dc2e6e446
4f7ca/000000.gz
```

   In the S3 bucket, these files can be processed by Lambda or persisted in some other system for further analysis.

CloudWatch metrics and alarms

CloudWatch is often described as a repository of metrics. The AWS services are designed to place the metrics in this repository and extract the statistics based on these metrics. We can also put custom metrics (that we define) into this repository and fetch the statistics based on them. The calculated statistics could subsequently be represented graphically for visualization and combined in the CloudWatch dashboards. We could also configure the CloudWatch alarms based on these metrics, which can perform some actions like sending out the email notification (using Amazon SNS) or scaling in/scaling out a set of auto scaled EC2 instances based on some criteria. In short, the CloudWatch metrics and alarms play an important role in monitoring the applications deployed on the AWS cloud and the cloud infrastructure that they use.

CloudWatch metrics are essentially the data about the performance of systems, services, components, etc. There are several AWS services that publish free metrics to CloudWatch. Among them, Amazon API gateway, Amazon CloudFront, Amazon

CloudWatch Logs, Amazon DynamoDB, Amazon EC2, and Amazon S3 are significant. Detailed monitoring could be enabled for some of these resources (e.g., Amazon EC2 instances). CloudWatch stores the metric data for 15 months. To view the available metrics and search them, we can select **`Metrics`** from the navigation pane in the AWS Management Console (as shown in *figure 6.4*). The metrics shown on this page depend on the services that are being actively used in the AWS account. Refer to *figure 6.4* as follows:

***Figure 6.4:** CloudWatch Metrics in AWS Management Console*

The data associated with a metric could be used to generate the graphs for efficient visualization of the metric activity on the services.

Let's focus on the alarms now, which essentially leverage the metrics. CloudWatch supports the following two kinds of alarms:

- **Metric alarm**: This type of alarm watches a single metric or result of a math expression based on the CloudWatch metrics. The alarm can perform one or more actions like sending notification, auto scaling action, etc.
- **Composite alarm**: A composite alarm includes a rule expression that is created based on the alarm states of the other alarms. This type of alarm goes into the ALARM state only if all the conditions of the rule are satisfied. While a composite alarm can send a notification, it cannot perform EC2 or auto scaling actions.

Metric alarms can have the following three possible states:

- **OK**: The metric or expression is within the defined threshold.
- **ALARM**: The metric or expression is outside the defined threshold.
- **INSUFFICIENT_DATA**: The alarm has just started, and the metric is either not available or enough data is not available to determine the state of the alarm.

Let's get into action and try to create a metric alarm based on a specific CloudWatch metric that is generated by Amazon S3. For this, we will use AWS Management Console. In this example, we will make necessary configurations to trigger an alarm if the **`NumberOfObjects`** of an S3 bucket is more than two (we are just selecting an arbitrary small number for simplicity). **`NumberOfObjects`** happens to be a *daily* *storage metrics* for the buckets that are monitored by Amazon S3. The alarm will be configured to trigger an Amazon SNS email notification. Assume that we have already created an Amazon S3 bucket and an SNS topic along with an active **`EMAIL`** subscription. The following are the steps:

1. In the CloudWatch management console, we will proceed with the creation of an alarm by selecting **`Alarms`** on the navigation pane. On the **`Specify metric and conditions`** page, we will click on the **`Select Metric`** button, as shown in *figure 6.5* as follows:

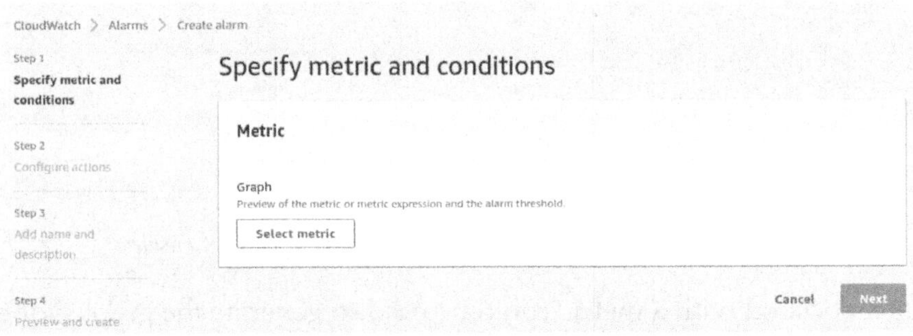

Figure 6.5: *Specify Metric and Conditions*

2. On the next page, we will select **`S3 | Storage Metrics`** under the **`Metrics`** section. We must select the actual metric named **`NumberOfObjects`** for the existing S3 bucket named **`bpb479-exported-logs`** and click on the **`Select metric`** button, as shown in *figure 6.6* as follows:

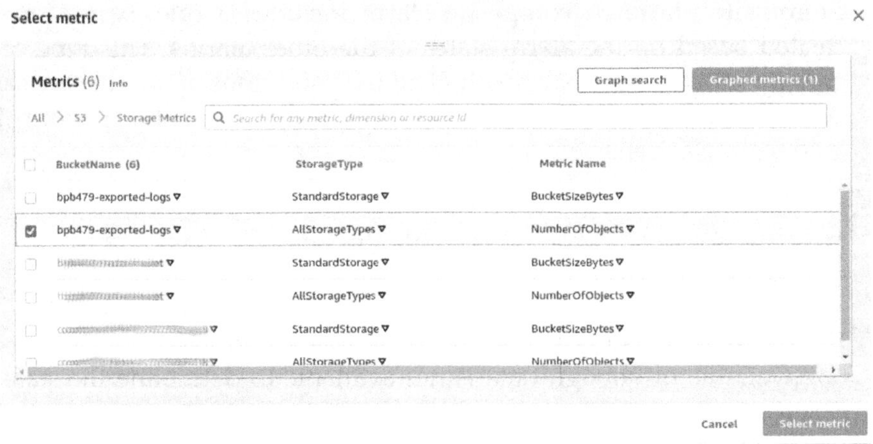

Figure 6.6: *Select metric*

3. On the next page, we provide the **`Statistic`** as average and an evaluation **`Period`** of one day. This means, the metric will calculate the average number of objects in a period of five minutes, as shown in *figure 6.7* as follows:

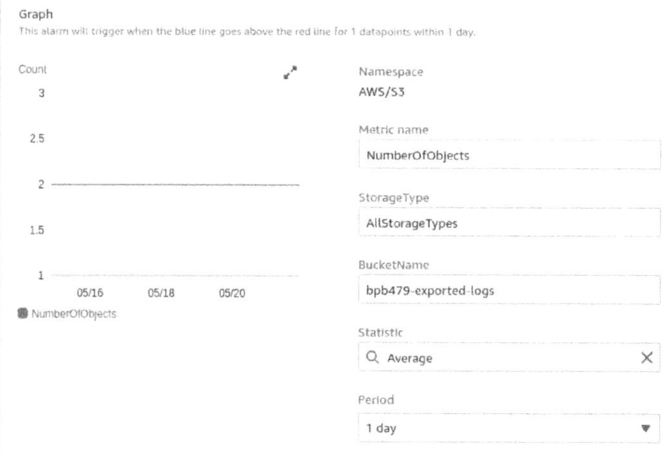

Figure 6.7: Configure aggregation statistic and period

Also, under the **`Condition`** section, we select the **`Threshold type`** as Static (which means, a threshold value will be explicitly defined as a number) and create a rule that defines the alarm condition as **`Whenever NumberOfObjects is greater than or equal to 2`**, as shown in *figure 6.8* as follows:

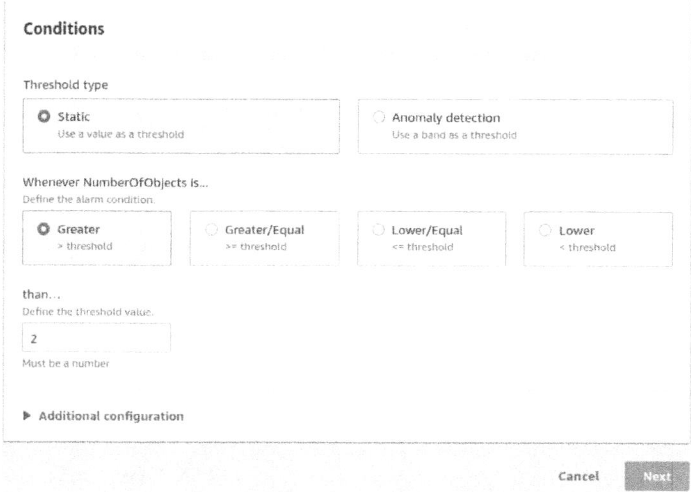

Figure 6.8: Specify threshold value

Under **`Additional configuration`**, we will define the number of data points within the evaluation period that must be breached to trigger the alarm. In this example, we will define **`1 out of 1`** data point and **`treat missing data as missing`**, as shown in *figure 6.9* as follows:

▼ Additional configuration

Datapoints to alarm
Define the number of datapoints within the evaluation period that must be breaching to cause the alarm to go to ALARM state.
1 out of 1

Missing data treatment
How to treat missing data when evaluating the alarm.
Treat missing data as missing ▼

***Figure 6.9:** Alarm datapoints*

4. On the next page of **`Configure actions`**, we will define the Alarm state that will trigger the Notification action (as shown in *figure 6.10*) and select the SNS topic as **`bpb479-alarm-topic`** and then click on the **`Next`** button. The other actions that could have been selected based on the scenario are auto scaling action, EC2 action, and Systems Manager OpsCenter action. Refer to *figure 6.10* as follows:

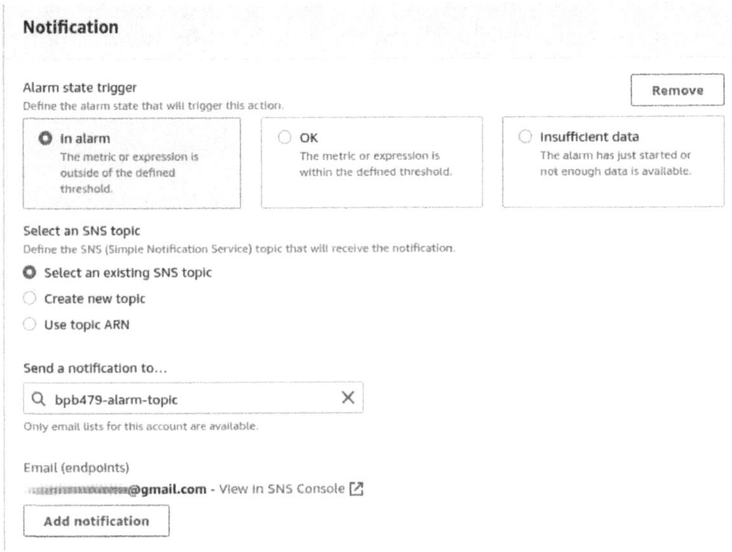

***Figure 6.10:** Configure alarm state trigger and SNS notification*

5. On the next page, we will give the alarm a name (**`bpb479-s3-numberofobjects-alarm`**) and a description and click on the **`Next`** button. Finally, we can preview the configuration and create the alarm.

Initially, the alarm would be in the **`INSUFFICIENT_DATA`** state. If, within a period of one day, more than or equal to two objects are placed in the S3 bucket named **`bpb479-exported-logs`**, then this alarm will go to the **`ALARM`** state and the SNS notification will get triggered, as shown in *figure 6.11* as follows:

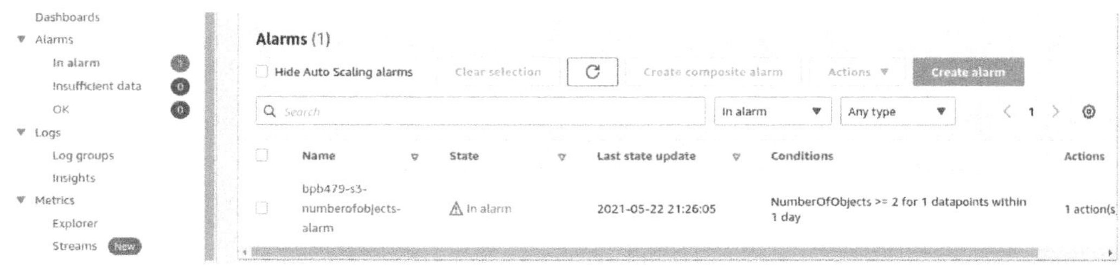

Figure 6.11: The alarm goes to the "ALARM" state

Figure 6.12 shows how the alarm notification email sent via Amazon SNS service looks like, as follows:

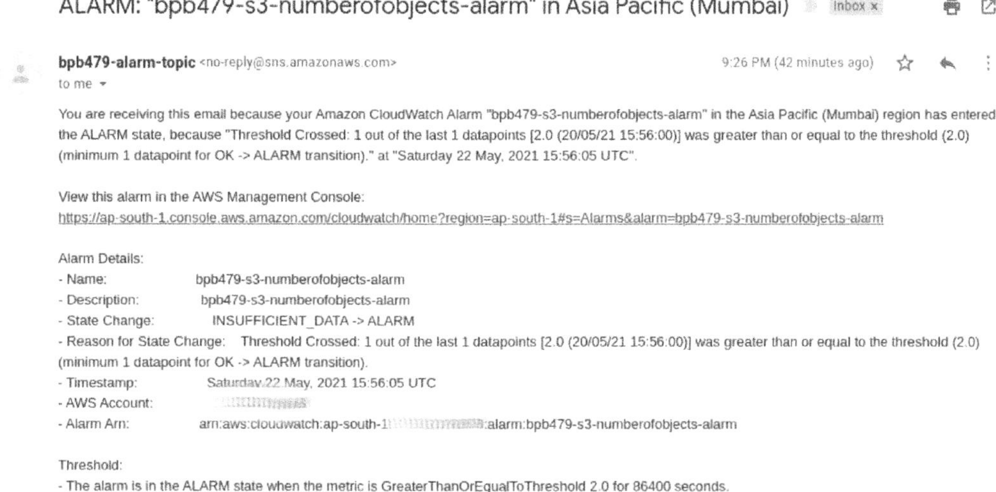

ALARM: "bpb479-s3-numberofobjects-alarm" in Asia Pacific (Mumbai) Inbox x

bpb479-alarm-topic <no-reply@sns.amazonaws.com> 9:26 PM (42 minutes ago)
to me

You are receiving this email because your Amazon CloudWatch Alarm "bpb479-s3-numberofobjects-alarm" in the Asia Pacific (Mumbai) region has entered the ALARM state, because "Threshold Crossed: 1 out of the last 1 datapoints [2.0 (20/05/21 15:56:00)] was greater than or equal to the threshold (2.0) (minimum 1 datapoint for OK -> ALARM transition)." at "Saturday 22 May, 2021 15:56:05 UTC".

View this alarm in the AWS Management Console:
https://ap-south-1.console.aws.amazon.com/cloudwatch/home?region=ap-south-1#s=Alarms&alarm=bpb479-s3-numberofobjects-alarm

Alarm Details:
- Name: bpb479-s3-numberofobjects-alarm
- Description: bpb479-s3-numberofobjects-alarm
- State Change: INSUFFICIENT_DATA -> ALARM
- Reason for State Change: Threshold Crossed: 1 out of the last 1 datapoints [2.0 (20/05/21 15:56:00)] was greater than or equal to the threshold (2.0) (minimum 1 datapoint for OK -> ALARM transition).
- Timestamp: Saturday 22 May, 2021 15:56:05 UTC
- AWS Account:
- Alarm Arn: arn:aws:cloudwatch:ap-south-1:alarm:bpb479-s3-numberofobjects-alarm

Threshold:
- The alarm is in the ALARM state when the metric is GreaterThanOrEqualToThreshold 2.0 for 86400 seconds.

***Figure 6.12**: Sample alarm notification email*

CloudWatch events

The Amazon CloudWatch Events delivers the stream of system events describing the changes to the AWS resources/environment in real-time. We can create simple rules that match the event source to targets. An event source is an AWS resource that undergoes a change and generates a CloudWatch Event. A rule essentially matches the incoming events and routes them to one or more targets for further processing. Finally, the targets process the events. CloudWatch Events support several targets, like Kinesis Stream, Lambda function, SNS topic, SQS queue, Step Functions state machine, SSM Run command, etc.

Let's create a simple yet useful rule to automate the notifications of any AWS health event (e.g., issue with the EC2 service in a certain availability zone or region). The following are the steps:

1. As the first step, we choose **`Events | Rules`** from the navigation pane in AWS Management Console for CloudWatch and click on the **`Create Rule`** button.

2. On the next page, we can select the **`Event Source`** which can either be an **`Event Pattern`** or a **`Schedule`** (defined by fixed rate or cron expression). For this example, we will select **`Event Pattern`** and build the event pattern to match the events by service – the service name being **`Health`** and the event type being **`All Events`**. The event pattern JSON format can be previewed as well. The event pattern in the JSON format looks like the following:

```
{
  "source": [
    "aws.health"
  ]
}
```

3. On the same page, we can define one or more targets. For this example, we can use an existing Amazon SNS Topic named **`bpb479-cw-events-targets`** with an active **`EMAIL`** subscription. *Figure 6.13* shows the source and target configuration for tracking and notifying the AWS health events. We must note that, multiple targets could be configured with the same event source by clicking on the **`Add target`** button in the **`Targets`** section. Once the source and target(s) have been configured, we can click on the **`Configure details`** button, as shown in *figure 6.13* as follows:

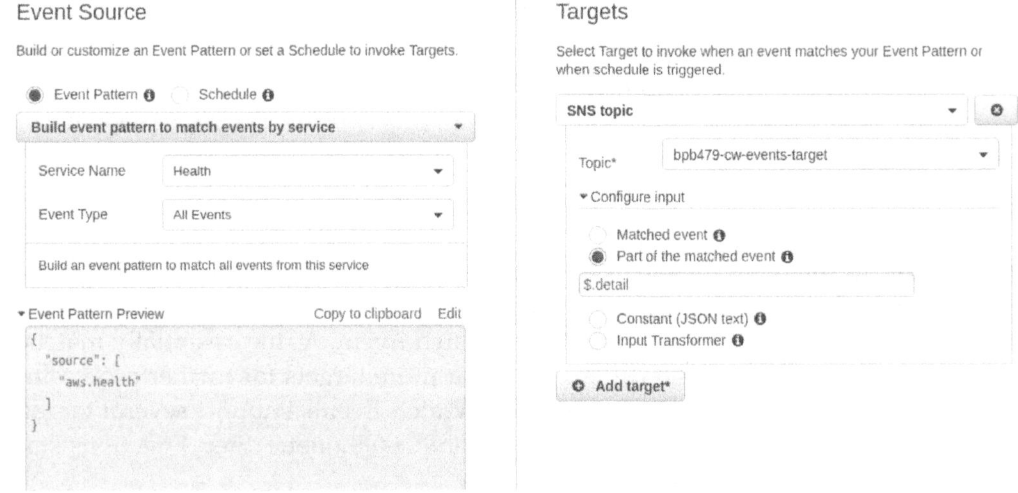

Figure 6.13: Configure event source and target

4. On the next page, we can supply a **`Name`** (**`HealthNotificationRule`**) and **`Description`** to the rule and mark the **`State`** as enabled and then click on

the **Create rule** button. The required permissions to add the events to the target(s) is taken care of automatically. Refer to *figure 6.14* as follows:

Step 2: Configure rule details

Rule definition

Name* HealthNotificationRule

Description Track AWS health events

State Enabled

CloudWatch Events will add necessary permissions for target(s) so they can be invoked when this rule is triggered.

* Required

Cancel Back Create rule

Figure 6.14: *Provide the name and description of the rule*

Amazon EventBridge

Amazon EventBridge is a serverless, highly available, and scalable event bus service. It was formerly called Amazon CloudWatch Events and uses the same CloudWatch Events API. The default event bus and any rules that we create in CloudWatch Events are also displayed in the EventBridge console. All the existing CloudWatch Events features are present in EventBridge. However, we must note that, as new features are added to EventBridge, they will not get added to CloudWatch Events. Hence, it is recommended to use EventBridge to manage the events instead of CloudWatch Events. The most interesting feature of EventBridge is that it supports the creation of custom event bus, apart from the default one, which can help in building the event-driven applications. *Figure 6.15* shows the **Event buses** page of Amazon EventBridge in the AWS Management Console as follows:

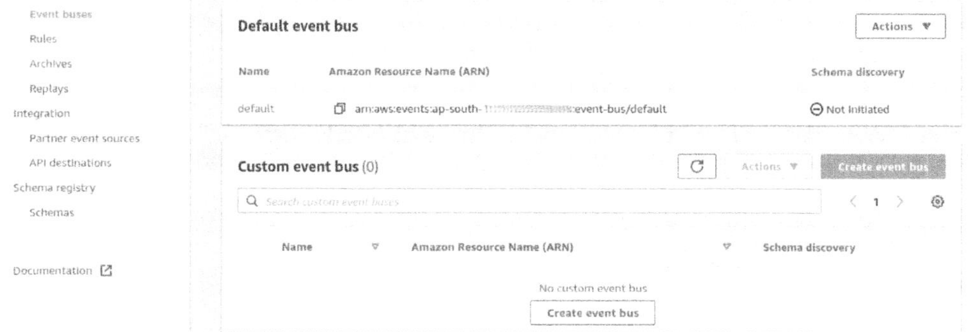

Figure 6.15: *"Event buses" page of Amazon EventBridge in AWS Management Console*

AWS CloudTrail

AWS CloudTrail essentially records all the actions taken by a user, role, or an AWS service. These actions could be generated through AWS Management Console, AWS

CLI, AWS SDK, or API calls made by the other services. Thus, AWS CloudTrail service holds a special place in the monitoring, governance, and auditing arsenal when working with the AWS public cloud. The service is automatically enabled when an AWS account gets created and records any activity in a CloudTrail event. The most recent events captured can be viewed, searched, and downloaded from **`Event history`** in the CloudTrail Management Console. *Figure 6.16* shows how a typical **`Event history`** page looks like. By default, only the **`create`**, **`modify`**, and **`delete`** events appear in the AWS CloudTrail Management Console, and we can view the events from the last 90 days. Each event can provide the details on what action was performed, who or what performed the action, when it occurred, and which AWS resources were involved. Refer to *figure 6.16* as follows:

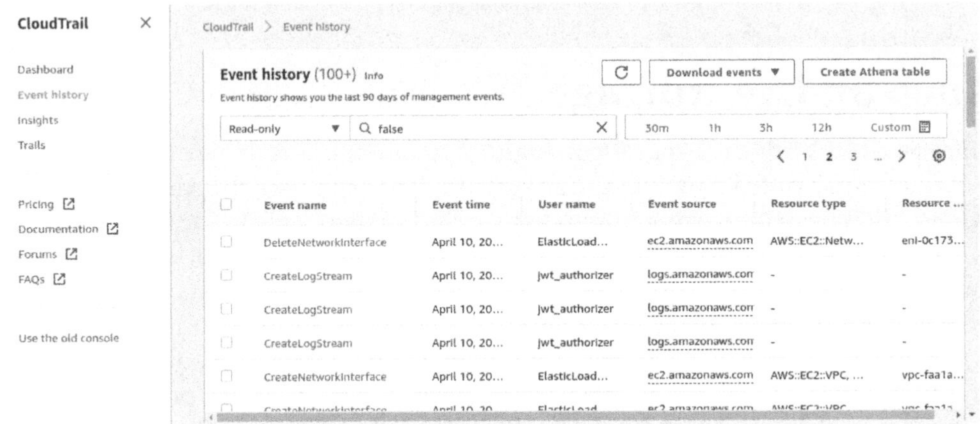

Figure 6.16: CloudTrail "Event history" page

While **`Event history`** can be a good start, it might not be able to serve the security compliance and auditing requirements of an organization. A better option is to create one or more trails to generate a continuous and ongoing record of events and store the same in the Amazon S3 buckets, send the log file delivery notifications to the S3 buckets in Amazon **Simple Notification Service** (**SNS**) topic, or stream the events to Amazon CloudWatch Logs for monitoring and further storage and analysis.

AWS CloudTrail Events

An AWS CloudTrail event represents a record of an activity in an AWS account. There are the following three types of events that can be logged, and all these types use the same JSON log format:

- **Management Events**: These type of events captures *control plane operations* or management operations like ConsoleLogin event, setting up CloudTrail logging, creation of VPC and subnets, etc.
- **Data Events**: Data events provide information on *data plane operations*. These are not logged by default as these are high-volume activities like AWS

Lambda execution activity, Amazon DynamoDB object level activities on a table, Amazon S3 object level API activity, etc.

- **Insights Events**: This identifies unusual or abnormal activities, user behaviors, or errors in the AWS account.

Creation of a Trail

A trail is a configuration that we can create to deliver the events in the form of log files to an Amazon S3 bucket. The Amazon S3 lifecycle policies could be used to archive the log files in Amazon Glacier to satisfy the compliance requirements. Moreover, the S3 events could be used to further process these files with the help of AWS Lambda, Amazon SQS, or Amazon SNS.

There are primarily two distinct types of trails – one that applies to all the regions and the other that applies to a single region. The recommended practice is to create a trail that applies to all the regions, which enables us to capture all the events across all the regions in an AWS account. This is also the default option while creating a trail from the AWS CloudTrail console.

There is a special type of trail, apart from the two that we have already introduced – an *organization trail*. An organization trail can help capture all the logs pertaining to all the member accounts in an organization defined in AWS Organization, which in turn can help define a uniform CloudTrail event logging strategy for the entire organization.

The following is the simplest form of AWS CLI command to create a single region trail named **bpb479-sample-trail**:

```
$ aws cloudtrail create-trail --name bpb479-sample-trail \
  --s3-bucket-name bpb479-trails-bucket \
  --profile cloudtrailcreator
```

If invoked successfully, the command should return a JSON response similar to what is shown in the following response snippet:

```
{
    "Name": "bpb479-sample-trail",
    "S3BucketName": "bpb479-trails-bucket",
    "IncludeGlobalServiceEvents": true,
    "IsMultiRegionTrail": false,
    "TrailARN": "arn:aws:cloudtrail:ap-south-1:137XXXXXXXXX:trail/
bpb479-sample-trail",
    "LogFileValidationEnabled": false,
    "IsOrganizationTrail": false
```

```
}
```

The next step is to start the logging process with the following CLI command:

```
$ aws cloudtrail start-logging --name bpb479-sample-trail \
  --profile cloudtrailcreator
```

We will assume that an AWS CLI profile named **cloudtrailcreator** has already been created with the required permissions to create the trail. In addition, we will also assume that an Amazon S3 bucket named **bpb479-trails-bucket** is already created and configured with the appropriate bucket policy. A sample bucket policy is shown as follows:

```
{
    "Version": "2012-10-17",
    "Statement": [
        {
            "Effect": "Allow",
            "Principal": {
                "Service": "cloudtrail.amazonaws.com"
            },
            "Action": "s3:GetBucketAcl",
            "Resource": "arn:aws:s3:::bpb479-trails-bucket",
            "Condition": {}
        },
        {
            "Effect": "Allow",
            "Principal": {
                "Service": "cloudtrail.amazonaws.com"
            },
            "Action": "s3:PutObject",
            "Resource": "arn:aws:s3:::bpb479-trails-bucket/*",
            "Condition": {}
        }
    ]
}
```

The bucket policy essentially allows the CloudTrail service to call the **GetBucketAcl** and **PutObject** action on the selected S3 bucket.

The following is the AWS CLI command to create a multi-region trail named **bpb479-sample-mr-trail**:

```
$ aws cloudtrail create-trail --name bpb479-sample-mr-trail \
    --s3-bucket-name bpb479-trails-bucket \
    --is-multi-region-trail \
    --profile cloudtrailcreator
```

To create an organization trail, either of the following Boolean flag could be used either during the creation of the trail or trail update:

- **`is-organization-trail`**
- **`no-is-organization-trail`**

The JSON log files delivered to the Amazon S3 buckets are in the gzip format (**`.gz`** extension) and CloudTrail ensures to store these files region wise and date wise. A typical hierarchy of folders within the S3 bucket looks like the following:

```
bpb479-trails-bucket/AWSLogs/<account-id>/CloudTrail/<region-code>/yyyy/
mm/dd/
```

Trail configuration

In the following sub-sections, we will introduce some of the important features that can be used to configure a trail. These features could be set during the creation of the trail, or the trail could be modified later to enable these features.

Encryption support for log files

When the log files are delivered by AWS CloudTrail to an Amazon S3 bucket, they are encrypted using SSE-S3 (described in *Chapter 4: Data Security*) by default. To add more control and manageability of the encryption keys, we can choose to use the SSE-KMS option (described in *Chapter 4: Data Security*). With this option, we need to create a new CMK or select an existing CMK to encrypt the log files. *Figure 6.17* shows how we can select an existing AWS KMS CMK during the creation of a trail from the AWS CloudTrail console. We should note that, when creating a trail from the AWS Management Console, the SSE-KMS encryption option is automatically selected. Refer to *figure 6.17* as follows:

Log file SSE-KMS encryption Info

Enabled

AWS KMS customer managed CMK

New

Existing

AWS KMS alias

bpb479

bpb479

Figure 6.17: *Selection of an existing CMK for the trail*

The following CLI command could be used to specify the CMK key-id to an existing trail:

```
$ aws cloudtrail update-trail --name bpb479-sample-trail \
  --kms-key-id <key-id OR key alias with 'alias/' prefix OR full alias
ARN OR full key ARN>
```

The CMK should have an appropriate key policy to allow the CloudTrail service to use the key.

Log file integrity

This feature helps determine if the log files were modified or deleted after CloudTrail delivered them to the Amazon S3 bucket. CloudTrail creates a hash using the SHA256 algorithm for every log file that is delivered to Amazon S3. CloudTrail also delivers an hourly *digest file* (to a separate folder within the same bucket) that references the log files delivered in the last hour and the corresponding hashes. Each digest file is signed by the RSA private key of a key pair. The public key can then be used to validate the digest file. *Figure 6.18* shows the **`Log file validation`** option available (under **`Additional Settings`**) to enable the log file integrity check from the CloudTrail console, as follows:

▼ Additional settings

Log file validation Info

☑ Enabled

Figure 6.18: *Enable the log file integrity validation*

An existing trail could be updated with a Boolean flag – **`enable-log-file-validation`** or **`no-enable-log-file-validation`** – using the following AWS CLI command:

```
$ aws cloudtrail update-trail --name bpb479-sample-trail
  --enable-log-file-validation
```

To validate the CloudTrail logs for a given period, we can use the **`validate-logs`** command. This command uses the digest files delivered to the S3 bucket for validation. The **`start-time`** option specifies that the log files delivered on or after the specified UTC value should be validated. There is also an optional **`end-time`** option to bracket the time, as follows:

```
$ aws cloudtrail validate-logs \
  --trail-arn 'arn:aws:cloudtrail:ap-south-1:137XXXXXXXXX:trail/bpb479-
sample-trail' \
  --start-time 20210419T19:00:00Z
```

Notification for log file delivery

Every time a log is delivered to the selected Amazon S3 bucket by AWS CloudTrail, we can choose to receive the SNS notification for every such delivery. This can help process the files for further analysis automatically. For example, we can create a new SNS topic or use an existing one with subscriptions to AWS Lambda. AWS Lambda can then pick up the log file from the S3 location and further process it. *Figure 6.19* shows the option to associate an SNS topic to send the notifications on the log file delivery from the AWS CloudTrail console. This option is available under **`Additional Settings`** on the create trail page, as shown in *figure 6.19* as follows:

Figure 6.19: *Configure log file delivery notification*

The following AWS CLI command could be used to integrate an existing SNS topic with an existing trail:

```
$ aws cloudtrail update-trail --name bpb479-sample-trail \
  --sns-topic-name <topic-name>
```

The SNS topic still needs to have the appropriate access policy to allow CloudTrail to place the delivery event in the topic.

Event selectors and advanced event selectors

Event selectors can be used to specify the event settings for a trail. By default, if an event selector is not used, a trail is configured to log all the read and write management events only. However, when used, CloudTrail evaluates the event selector for all the trails when any activity occurs in the AWS account. Suppose the event is found to match an event selector, the trail processes and logs that event. The basic event selectors can be used to log the management events, data events, and insights events. Currently, we can log the data events on the following three resources:

- Amazon S3 API activities at the object level (for example, **`GetObject`**, **`PutObject`**, etc.)
- AWS Lambda function invocation activities
- Amazon DynamoDB data activities

The advanced event selectors are used to create the fine-grained selectors that essentially help control the costs by logging only the selective data events, based on **`eventSource`**, **`eventName`**, **`eventCategory`**, and several properties of an event. We must remember that both **EventSelector** and **AdvancedEventSelector** cannot be applied to a single trail.

The following is the AWS CLI command to configure the standard event selectors for a trail:

```
$ aws cloudtrail put-event-selectors \
        --trail-name bpb479-sample-trail \
        --event-selectors '<json-value>'
```

The default standard event selector JSON format looks like the following:

```
[
        {
            "ReadWriteType": "All",
            "IncludeManagementEvents": true,
            "DataResources": [],
            "ExcludeManagementEventSources": []
        }
]
```

The advanced event selectors could be configured for a trail with the following CLI command:

```
$ aws cloudtrail put-event-selectors \
        --trail-name bpb479-sample-trail \
        --advanced-event-selectors '<json-value>'
```

The advanced event selector JSON structure looks a little different from the standard selectors. The following is an example:

```
[
  { "Name": "Log PutObject events for a specifc S3 bucket",
    "FieldSelectors": [
        { "Field": "readOnly", "Equals": ["false"] },
        { "Field": "eventCategory", "Equals": ["Data"] },
        { "Field": "resources.type", "Equals": ["AWS::S3::Object"] },
        { "Field": "eventName", "Equals": ["PutObject"] },
        { "Field": "resources.ARN", "Equals": ["arn:aws:s3:::bpb479-
bucket/"] }
    ]
  }
]
```

For a comprehensive JSON structure pertaining to the standard and advanced event selectors, please refer to the following AWS CLI reference link: https://docs.aws.amazon.com/cli/latest/reference/cloudtrail/put-event-selectors.html

Monitoring a trail

A trail could be optionally configured to send the events to CloudWatch Logs. Subsequently, CloudWatch Logs could be used to monitor specific API calls and events in the AWS account. Furthermore, the CloudWatch Logs metric filters could be defined and assigned to the CloudWatch metrics and the CloudWatch alarms could be configured to send out the notifications (using Amazon SNS) when any specific event of interest occurs in the account. *Figure 6.20* shows the configuration required to send the trail events to Amazon CloudWatch during the creation of a trail, as follows:

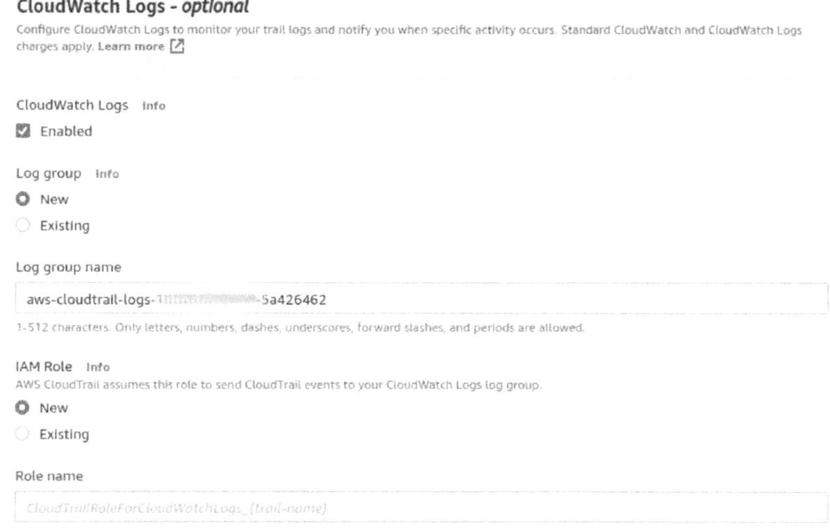

Figure 6.20: *Configuration to send a trail to CloudWatch Logs*

To configure an existing trail to stream the events into CloudWatch Logs using AWS CLI, we can use the following command:

```
$ aws cloudtrail update-trail --name bpb479-sample-trail \
  --cloud-watch-logs-log-group-arn <CloudWatch Log Group ARN> \
  --cloud-watch-logs-role-arn <Role ARN>
```

CloudWatch Log Group ARN represents the log group to which the CloudTrail logs will get delivered and role ARN specifies the IAM role that the CloudTrail service will assume to write the log streams and put the log events to the log group.

Important logs managed by AWS

While the applications can create their own logs and then ship them to Amazon CloudWatch Logs for further analysis, there are some special logs that are created and managed by AWS and these logs are shipped to Amazon S3 and/or Amazon CloudWatch Logs. Here's the list of some noteworthy AWS managed logs:

- **CloudTrail Logs**: AWS CloudTrail Logs can be pushed into the Amazon S3 buckets and could also be streamed to CloudWatch Logs. We have dedicated an entire section on AWS CloudTrail and associated logging in this chapter.
- **VPC Flow Logs**: VPC Flow Logs help to capture the details on the kind of traffic accepted or rejected at the network interface level. VPC Flow Logs can be created at the VPC level, subnet level, or the individual network interface level. Flow logs can be streamed into CloudWatch Logs. Amazon S3 can also act as another delivery destination for VPC Flow Logs. One can use AWS CLI to deliver these logs directly to S3.

  The following is the format for the VPC Flow log event:

  ```
  <version> <account-id> <interface-id> <src-addr> <dest-addr>
  <src-port> <dest-port> <protocol-number> <packets> <bytes>
  <start-time> <end-time> <action> <log status>
  ```

  Sample event: 2 1xxxxxxxxxxx eni-xxxxxxxx 172.31.10.32 172.31.10.74 443 8080 6 3 164 1618393937 1618393988 ACCEPT OK
- **Route 53 Query Logs**: Amazon Route 53 could be configured to log the public DNS queries received by Route 53. These logs are sent to Amazon CloudWatch Logs.

  The following is the format for the DNS Query log event:

  ```
  <log-format-version> <query-timestamp> <hosted-zone-id> <query-
  name> <query-type> <response-code> <layer-4 protocol> <edge-
  location> <resolver-ip> <EDNS-client-subnet>
  ```

  Sample event: 1.0 2021-02-14T08:15:50.235Z Z123456789101 example.com AAAA NOERROR TCP IAD12 192.168.3.1 192.168.222.0/24
- **CloudFront Access Logs and Real-time Logs**: Amazon CloudFront can be configured to create detailed log events when CloudFront receives a request. These standard or *access logs* are saved in an Amazon S3 bucket. These log files contain detailed information on every user request received by CloudFront. As usual, SSE-KMS could be enabled on the S3 bucket for a better control on the CMK. Log files are delivered to S3 in a gzip format (`.gz` extension). CloudFront can stream the real-time logs as well. These log streams could be configured to be delivered to Amazon Kinesis Data Streams.
- **Load Balancer Access Logs**: Access logging is disabled by default on **Elastic Load Balancer (ELB)**. However, when enabled, they capture

detailed information on the requests that are sent to ELB. ELB stores the logs as compressed files in a specified Amazon S3 bucket. Each access log is encrypted with SSE-S3 automatically before being stored in the S3 bucket.

- **Amazon S3 Server Logs**: While we can leverage the Amazon S3 server logs to capture all the actions taken by the users, roles, or other AWS services on Amazon S3 resources, AWS recommends using AWS CloudTrail for the same. It is easier to record the bucket and object level actions with CloudTrail. As discussed in the section dedicated to AWS CloudTrail, using CloudTrail has several advantages, like forward logs to other systems, cross account log delivery, integrity validation, etc. However, the Amazon S3 server logs carry no additional cost (other than the charges pertaining to their storage) and are delivered within a few hours as well as space separated and newline character-delimited files.

AWS config

AWS Config is a regional service that helps track the configuration changes made to the AWS resources and relationships between these resources, over time. This can greatly help in compliance audits, security analysis, and troubleshooting configuration changes. The following significant AWS resource types are supported by AWS Config: Amazon CloudFront, Amazon API Gateway, Amazon EBS, Amazon EC2, Amazon ECS, Amazon EKS, Amazon ECR, Amazon RDS, Amazon S3, Amazon VPC, etc.

TIP: For an exhaustive and comprehensive list of supported resources, refer to the following link: https://docs.aws.amazon.com/config/latest/developerguide/resource-config-reference.html

AWS Config can monitor the global resources, such as IAM, and ensure that the IAM users, groups, roles, and policies comply with the defined baselines. We must note that while setting up AWS Config, we must explicitly check the `Include global resources` checkbox in the AWS Config console to enable this behavior.

Figure 6.21 shows a snapshot of how AWS Config is setup in AWS Management Console with options to record all the supported resources or specific resource types, the choice to include global resources and creation/selection of the IAM role for AWS Config to retrieve the necessary details from each AWS resource, as follows:

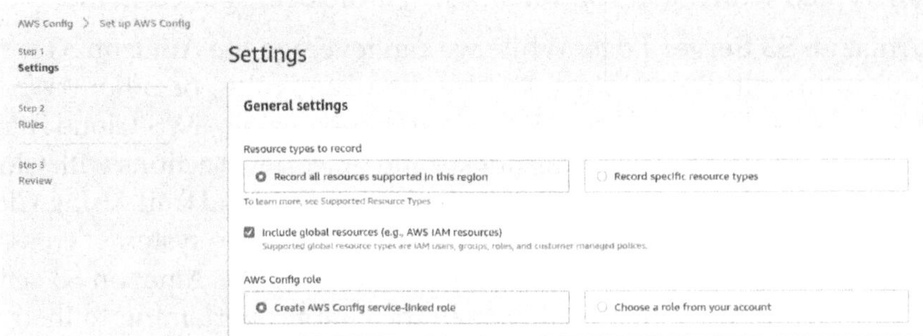

Figure 6.21: AWS Config setup in AWS Management Console

Once AWS Config has been set up, the dashboard will provide the inventory of resources, compliance status, non-compliant rules, etc. *Figure 6.22* shows how a typical dashboard might look like, as follows:

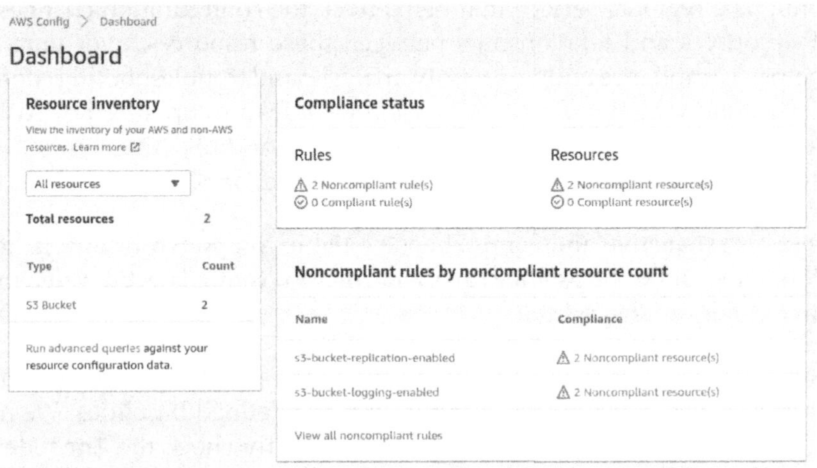

Figure 6.22: AWS Config dashboard

Delivery of configuration items

AWS Config can deliver the configuration items through the following channels:

- **Amazon S3 Bucket**: We can choose an Amazon S3 bucket where the configuration history and configuration snapshot files can be delivered. The bucket could be selected either from the same AWS account or from a different AWS account. An appropriate bucket policy should be applied to the S3 bucket.
- **Amazon SNS Topic**: The SNS topic could be configured to stream all the configuration changes and notifications. The topic could be from the same

AWS account or another account. The access policy needs to be appropriately configured for the SNS topic.

Figure 6.23 shows the various delivery methods that can be selected during the AWS Config setup in the AWS Management Console, for the delivery of the configuration history, changes, or snapshots, as follows:

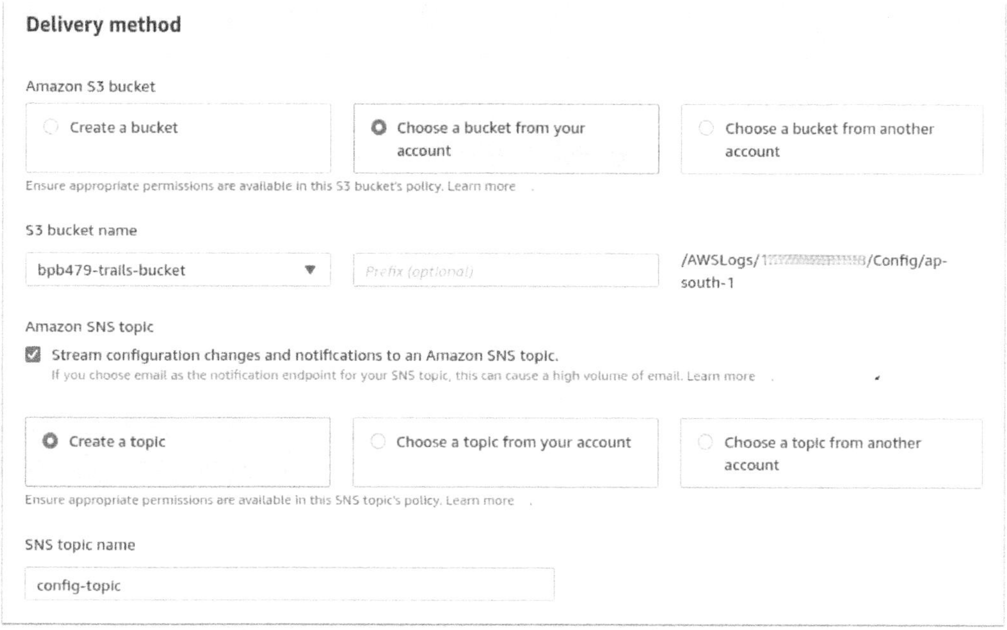

Delivery method

Amazon S3 bucket

Create a bucket | Choose a bucket from your account | Choose a bucket from another account

Ensure appropriate permissions are available in this S3 bucket's policy. Learn more

S3 bucket name

bpb479-trails-bucket | Prefix (optional) | /AWSLogs/[illegible]/Config/ap-south-1

Amazon SNS topic

Stream configuration changes and notifications to an Amazon SNS topic.

If you choose email as the notification endpoint for your SNS topic, this can cause a high volume of email. Learn more

Create a topic | Choose a topic from your account | Choose a topic from another account

Ensure appropriate permissions are available in this SNS topic's policy. Learn more

SNS topic name

config-topic

***Figure 6.23:** AWS Config delivery method selection*

Config rules

To evaluate the configuration settings of the AWS resources, AWS Config leverages the AWS Config rules. The Config rules represent the desired or ideal state of configuration settings for these resources. AWS Config continuously tracks the changes made to the AWS resources and checks whether these changes violate the conditions specified in the config rules. If a resource violates the rule, it is flagged (along with the rule) as **`NON_COMPLIANT`**. There are two types of rules supported by AWS Config, which are as follows:

- **AWS-managed rules**: The AWS-managed rules are predefined rules by AWS Config to assess and evaluate a set of AWS resources. These rules can be customized to fit specific needs. There are 130+ managed rules at the time of writing this book. Some interesting managed rules that can be selected as part of the AWS Config setup are defined as follows:
    - **`cloudtrail-enabled`**: This rule checks if AWS CloudTrail has been enabled in the AWS account. Similar related rules are **`cloud-trail-`**

log-file-validation-enabled, **cloud-trail-encryption-enabled**, **cloud-trail-cloud-watch-logs-enabled**, etc.

- **restricted-ssh:** This rule checks if the unrestricted SSH access is allowed in any security group.
- **ec2-instance-no-public-ip**: This rule checks if any EC2 instance is associated with a public IP address, and if so, the rule is **NON_COMPLIANT**.
- **encrypted-volumes**: This rule checks if the EBS volumes attached to the EC2 instances are encrypted.
- **iam-password-policy**: This rule checks if the account password policy for the IAM users meets the specified requirements.
- **iam-root-access-key-check**: This rule checks whether the root user access key exists. If so, the rule is **NON_COMPLIANT**.
- **iam-user-mfa-enabled**: This rule checks if the AWS IAM users have MFA enabled.

There is a unique sub-type of managed config rule known as *service linked AWS Config rule*. These are owned by the AWS service teams and we cannot edit these rules. Such rules support the other services to create the AWS Config rules in the AWS account.

- **Custom rules**: Custom rules, on the other hand, are essentially the AWS Lambda functions that contain the logic to assess the compliance of the AWS resources and send the evaluation results to AWS Config. The Lambda function needs to be associated with the rule. The rule, in turn, can invoke the function in response to the configuration changes or periodically.

Aggregator

An aggregator is a special AWS Config resource type that can help collect the AWS Config configuration and compliance data in situations where there are multiple AWS regions or several AWS accounts or an AWS Organization (with AWS Config enabled) involved. Essentially, all the recorded data are aggregated from multiple sources (for example, regions, accounts, etc.) and presented in an aggregated dashboard view. The aggregator is typically defined in the aggregator account, and then the source accounts or the organization along with the regions are selected to create the aggregator. The recorded data from the source accounts gets replicated to the aggregator account. The aggregator, in turn, could be used to create a single pane of glass for all the configuration and compliance data.

Amazon GuardDuty

Amazon GuardDuty is a regional intrusion detection system or intelligent threat detection service that continuously monitors three AWS-managed log files to detect malicious behavior and report findings. GuardDuty monitors the following logs:

- CloudTrail Event Logs (management event logs and S3 data event logs)
- VPC Flow Logs
- Route 53 (DNS) Logs

GuardDuty analyses these logs based on the configured rules and attempts to detect threats like Bitcoin mining, DNS exfiltration, Trojans, SSH brute-force, unauthorized and unusual data access, etc. The service categorizes the alerts as findings and gives each finding a severity (high, medium, low).

GuardDuty leverages the threat intelligence feeds (malicious IP lists and domains) and machine learning to identify malicious activities in the AWS environment.

AWS Security Hub

AWS Security Hub provides a centralized, comprehensive view of the state of security in an AWS account or AWS Organization. It acts as a single pane of glass across multiple security and compliance tools and helps ensure that our infrastructure meets the compliance requirements and security alerts gets prioritized. AWS Security Hub is integrated with several AWS security services (as shown in *figure 6.24*) as well as the third-party security solutions (like AlertLogic, Twistlock, Qualys, Symantec, Barracuda, etc.). Once enabled, these services can push the security findings automatically to AWS Security Hub in a standardized format known as **AWS Security Finding Format (ASFF)**. Refer to *figure 6.24* as follows:

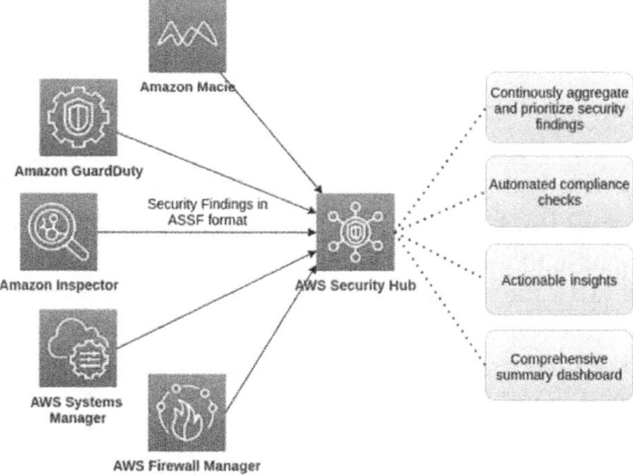

Figure 6.24: *AWS Security Hub integrations and features*

AWS Security Hub starts to receive the security and compliance findings which follow a normalized severity scoring system, from various integrated security tools and services. The security findings are aggregated and prioritized. AWS Security Hub also performs automated compliance checks (like CIS AWS Foundations Benchmark, etc.). The compliance checks have a dependency on AWS Config, and as such, AWS Security Hub requires AWS Config to be enabled (*figure 6.25*). AWS Security Hub also recommends enabling AWS Organizations, which helps centralize the findings from all the member accounts and automatic detection of new accounts when they join the organization. Refer to *figure 6.25* as follows:

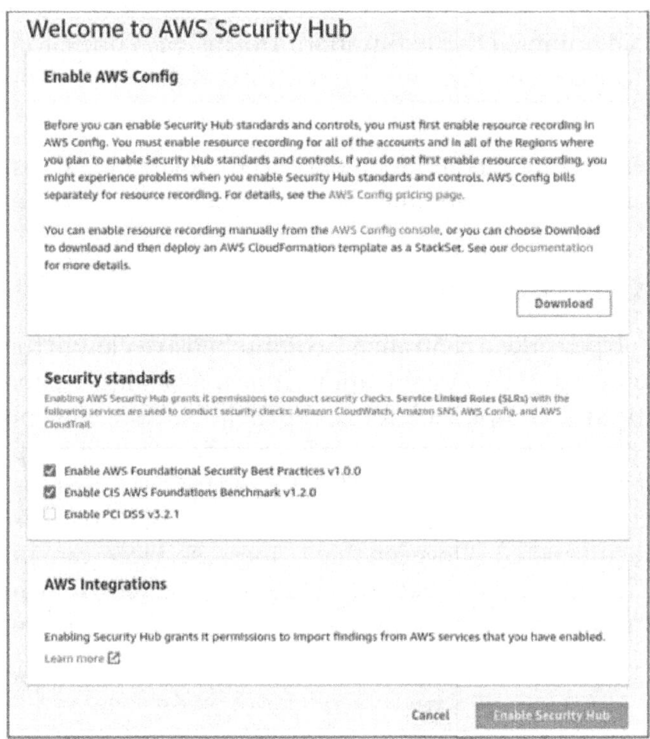

Figure 6.25: *Enabling Security Hub from AWS Security Hub Console*

AWS Security Hub is integrated with Amazon EventBridge and it sends all the new findings or updates to the existing ones as events to Amazon EventBridge. We can also select the findings of interest and take *custom actions*. The custom actions are created with a friendly name and custom action ID that must be unique for each AWS account. The custom actions are emitted as events and delivered to Amazon EventBridge with a custom action ID. This custom action ID is used to match against an EventBridge rule. These rules, in turn, can define targets like Lambda, Step Functions, SNS topic, SQS queue, etc. These services can further process the data and then send the data to the ultimate destinations like Slack, PagerDuty, SIEM solutions, incident response and management tool, etc.

Amazon Detective

Amazon Detective is an advanced, regional security analytics service that can help investigate and identify the root cause of the security issues. Once enabled, Amazon Detective automatically collects the log data from various resources like VPC Flow Logs, CloudTrail Logs, Amazon GuardDuty findings, etc., and subsequently runs machine learning, statistical analysis, and graph theory to generate insightful visualizations that can help with faster and efficient security investigations. Amazon Detective can maintain the aggregated analytical data up to a year. While Amazon Detective can be used directly from Detective Console, it is also integrated with the security investigation services like Amazon GuardDuty and Amazon Security Hub and can be easily invoked from these services as well.

When Amazon Detective is enabled for a master account, it creates a security *behavior graph* from the various Amazon Detective data sources. This graph model helps provide a unified interactive view of users, resources, and interactions between them over time. In a multi account scenario, when the member accounts accept the invitation of the master, the VPC flow logs, CloudTrail management events, and GuardDuty findings from these member accounts flow into the same behavior graph of the master. Refer to *figure 6.26* as follows:

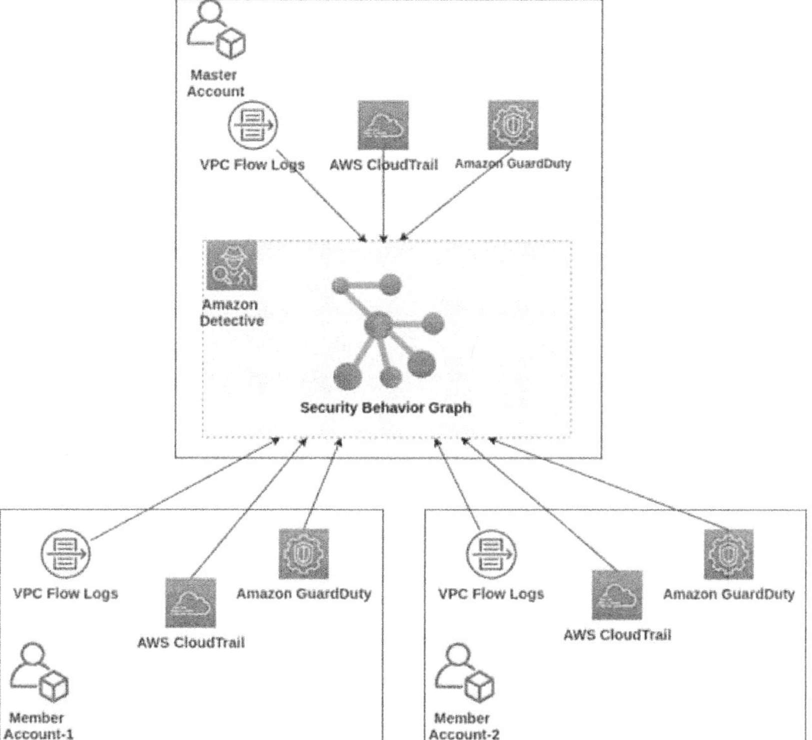

Figure 6.26: *Enabling Security Hub from AWS Security Hub Console*

AWS Artifact

AWS Artifact is a central repository for all the AWS security and compliance reports, or in short, *audit artifacts*. AWS Artifact has two primary Use cases – reports and agreements. The AWS Artifact reports provide on-demand download facility for documents like AWS ISO certifications, **Service Organization Control** (**SOC**), and **Payment Card Industry** (**PCI**) reports. These AWS reports are generated from the third-party auditors who have reviewed and verified the security standards and regulations followed in the AWS cloud. These reports could be handed over to the auditors as guidelines to evaluate our own cloud infrastructure on the AWS cloud. They can also be used to assess the effectiveness of the applied controls.

The AWS Artifact agreements could be used to review, accept/terminate agreements about the AWS account or AWS Organization as a whole, where an agreement could be accepted on behalf of all the accounts present in the organization.

It is customary and considered a best practice to provide access to AWS Artifact to an IAM group meant for the auditors or a specific group that requires access to download reports and/or manage agreements.

Figure 6.27 shows how to select and download an AWS Artifact report from the AWS console, as follows:

Figure 6.27: *Selection of AWS Artifact report and option to download*

AWS Service Catalog

AWS Service Catalog is a regional service that can help organizations to create and manage approved catalogs of IT services, which the end users can then access through a personalized portal. The service thus promotes centralized management, standardization, fine-grained access control, and self-service. An IT service is referred to as a *product*, that is deployed on AWS. A product can comprise of one or more Amazon EC2 instances, Amazon EBS volumes, databases, networking components, packaged applications (from AWS marketplace), etc. Essentially, a product can range from a single virtual machine to a full-fledged multi-tier web application and is created by importing the AWS CloudFormation templates. Products are versionable.

A *portfolio* is defined as a collection of products along with the configuration information and it helps manage who can access specific products and how they can access these products through *permissions* and *constraints*.

AWS Service Catalog supports two types of users – administrators and end users. The administrators create and manage the catalog of products, organize them into portfolios, and grant the required permissions to the end users. The administrators are responsible for the creation of the CloudFormation templates as well, along with the necessary constraints and IAM roles.

The end users or users, on the other hand, launch specific products from the AWS management console, using credentials supplied to them. The permissions are granted to the users based on the operational requirements.

Conclusion

In this chapter, we learned that AWS provides a compelling collection of services that could be used for logging, monitoring, and auditing. While Amazon CloudWatch and AWS CloudFront are the essential services that could be leveraged, services like AWS Config, Amazon GuardDuty, AWS Security Hub, Amazon Detective, AWS Artifact, AWS Service Catalog, etc., deserve special mention.

In the next chapter, we will focus on the security best practices. These best practices will help us create a reliable and secure AWS cloud environment for the applications and workloads.

CHAPTER 7
Security Best Practices

Introduction

The security posture of an enterprise lies in the spectrum. If the posture is too loose, there can be security breaches and loss of customer confidence and trust. Whereas, if it is too strict or tight, it might lead to loss of agility and security teams being treated as blockers to progress and innovation. The ideal goal should be to reach the *Goldilocks* zone based on the security context. In Astrophysics, the *Goldilocks* zone refers to the habitable zone around a star where the conditions are favorable for life. In security, it is used to refer to the security posture that is effective and strikes the right balance. The security philosophy is pivoted around the centralized administration and delegation of the authority, governed by the separation of duties and principle of least privilege. This chapter will discuss some of the recommended security best practices on the AWS cloud, which helps in achieving the harmony of security controls and processes.

Structure

In this chapter, we will cover the following topics:

- Shared responsibility model (revisited)
- IAM best practices

- Infrastructure security best practice
- Data security best practices
- Application security best practices
- Logging and monitoring best practices

Objectives

In this chapter, we will learn about the best practices related to AWS security. With these best practices, we will be able to build secure infrastructure, environments, and applications from the ground up on the AWS cloud. We will start by recounting the tenet of shared security model, and then visit each important layer starting with IAM and infrastructure, and then covering data and application security on the way. Finally, we will take a quick look at the best practices related to monitoring and logging in AWS.

Shared responsibility model

While we have provided an in-depth coverage of shared responsibility model in *Chapter 1: Introduction to security in AWS*, the topic deserves a revisit in this chapter on security best practices. The model essentially requires both AWS and its customers to collaborate and work together towards meeting the security objectives. AWS is responsible for the 'security of the cloud', while customers are responsible for the 'security in the cloud'.

AWS is responsible for the security of its global infrastructure that includes regions, availability zones, and endpoints. But, when it comes to the AWS services, things are not so straightforward. AWS offers a wide variety of infrastructure and platform services which can be broadly categorized into the following two service types:

- **Infrastructure Services:** For these types of services, which primarily include compute services (like Amazon EC2) and the other related services (like Amazon EBS, Amazon VPC, etc.), we, the customers, control the operating system and anything installed or configured on top of it, which includes the access control and applications hosted on the computer. AWS controls the hypervisor layer along with the physical hardware, and the related infra controls the hypervisor layer along with the physical hardware and related infra.
- **Abstract Services:** Services like Amazon S3, Amazon DynamoDB, Amazon SQS, etc. fall in this category. The customers generally access the service endpoints via APIs and are responsible for classifying and managing the data and leveraging the IAM tools provided by the services. AWS is responsible for the underlying infrastructure, operating system, service components, integration with AWS IAM, etc.

In addition, one may also hear about 'Container Services' as a service type in the shared security model parlance. However, the delineation between the container services and abstract services is not quite simple. The container services are just less abstract than their 'abstract' counterparts. The abstract services also include Amazon RDS and Amazon EMR, where AWS manages the operating system (including patching) and the application platform. The security of the data, firewalls, and other IAM features are the responsibility of the customer.

IAM best practices

AWS **Identity and Access Management** (**IAM**) provides the building blocks for creating a highly reliable and secure AWS based application ecosystem. This section will discuss some of the crucial best practices that can help us leverage the most out of AWS IAM.

Safeguarding the account root user

One of the foremost things to take care of, right after the creation of an AWS account, is to take appropriate measures to protect the *AWS account root user*. The root has enormous power (full access to all the resources within the AWS account), and hence we should make sure that this kind of power does not land into the wrong hands. The following are some of the steps to protect the root:

- Delete the root account's access keys (access key ID and secret access key) and never create any programmatic access key for the root. To delete any existing access key, we can log in to the AWS management console with the root credentials and access the `My Security Credentials` page from the drop-down menu that appears when the username is clicked on the top panel, as shown in *figure 7.1* as follows:

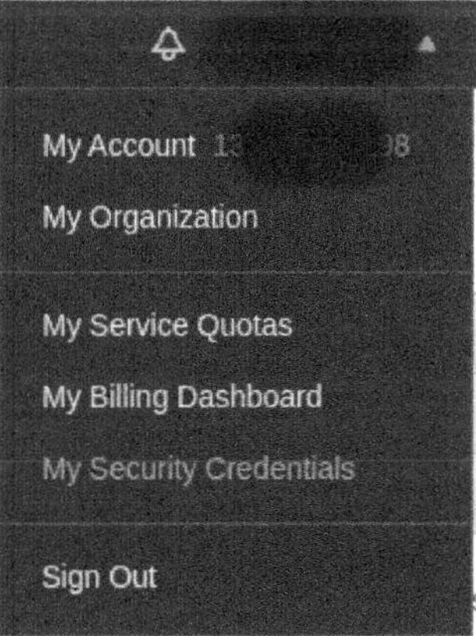

***Figure 7.1**: Access "My Security Credentials" page*

Once on the **`My Security Credentials`** page, browse the **`Access keys`** section and check if any access key exists. If so, delete the same. Refer to *figure 7.2* as follows:

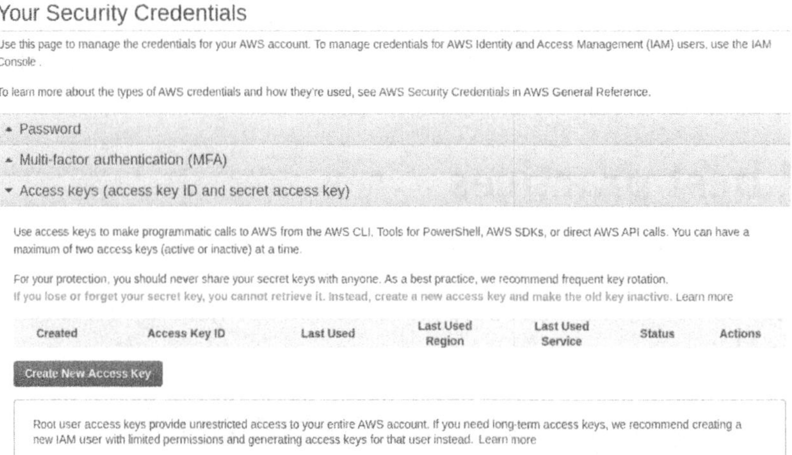

***Figure 7.2**: Remove any access keys from "Your Security Credentials" page*

- Create a strong password policy to help protect the account level access from the AWS management console. The default password policy should suffice for most purposes. However, if some further stringent policy is required, the default password policy could be tweaked or a new policy could be created on the **`Account Settings`** page from the IAM console. Refer to *figure 7.3* as follows.

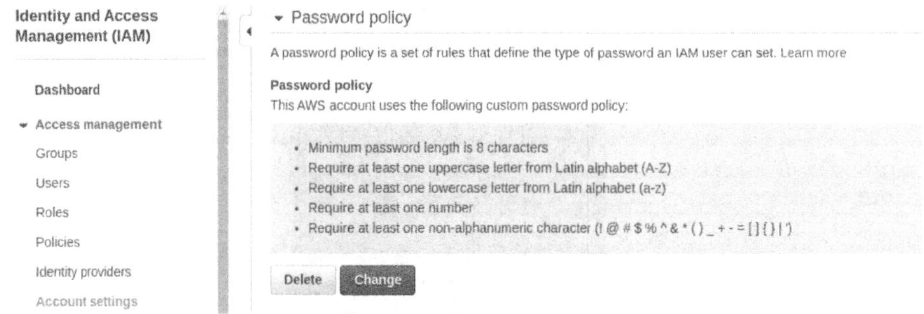

***Figure 7.3**: Apply a strong password policy*

- Lock the AWS account root user password and never use it for the day-to-day activities.

- Enable multi-factor authentication (MFA) on the AWS root user account. This provides an additional layer of security on top of the password. *Figure 7.4* shows how the MFA section might look like, once an MFA device is configured, as follows:

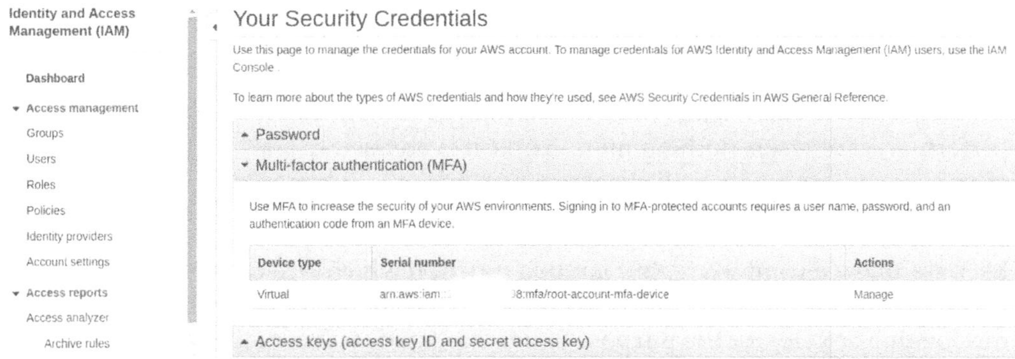

***Figure 7.4**: Configure multi factor authentication for root user*

Creating and managing IAM users/groups

To perform the day-to-day activities in the AWS account, we should create the IAM users and give them unique credentials (credentials should never be shared) to log into the AWS management console. These credentials could follow a strict password policy and should be required to change right after the first login by the user. Additionally, **multi-factor authentication** (**MFA**) could be set up for each user.

As for the permissions, it's always a good idea to logically group multiple IAM users in a single group and then assign the permissions to the group instead of directly assigning them to the individual users. All the users in a group inherit the permissions assigned to the group. This essentially makes permission management much easier.

The groups and users can be created and assigned permissions from the IAM console. *Figure 7.5* shows the IAM console with two groups – one group (named **`administrators`**) has two users in it, shown as follows:

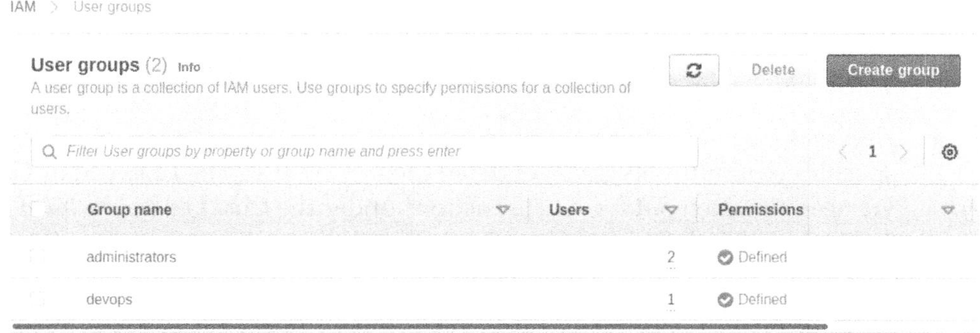

***Figure 7.5**: IAM groups*

Following the principle of least privilege

While creating the IAM policies, we should follow the standard security practice of *least privilege*. This means that we should grant only the permissions required to perform a set of tasks, nothing more. Thus, it is advised to start with a minimum set of permissions and add additional permissions only when required. The following is an example to understand this better.

Let's assume we want to create a lambda function which will carry out some specific set of activities. CloudWatch logging is one such activity and we will concentrate on this logging activity for the purpose of our explanation. Normally, to write to CloudWatch logs, three permissions are required – **logs:CreateLogGroup**, **logs:CreateLogStream**, and **logs:PutLogEvents**. If we follow the principle of least privilege, there is no need to provide a lambda function with the permission to create a new log group. A log-group with the name **/aws/lambda/<lambda-name>** could be created separately. The lambda then could be given the permissions to create the log streams in that particular log group and put the log events in the respective log streams. The following is how the IAM policy statement snippet may look like (the region and account ID need to be replaced by actual values):

```
{
  "Effect": "Allow",
      "Action": [
    "logs:CreateLogStream",
        "logs:PutLogEvents" ],
  "Resource": [
    "arn:aws:logs:<region>:<acct-id>:log-group:/aws/lambda/<lambda
name>:log-stream:*" ]
}
```

It is important to follow the practice of regular review of each IAM policy to ensure that they grant the least privilege that is required to perform only the necessary actions. The IAM console provides some useful tools for the purpose of review, which are as follows:

- **Access Level:** The **Permissions** tab on the policy summary page has a specific column for access level detail (*figure 7.6*). It can be **Limited** or **Full**. We need to watch out for specific actions under the **Limited** access level and **Full** access level. Refer to *figure 7.6* as follows:

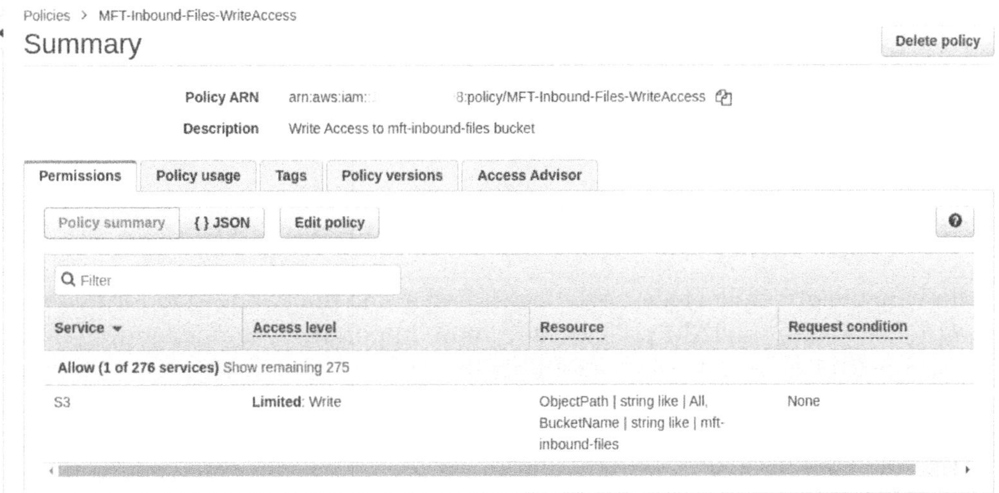

Figure 7.6: Access level

- **Access Advisor:** The **`Access Advisor`** appears as a tab on the IAM policy summary page (*figure 7.7*) and helps set the permission guardrails. It provides details like which entities accessed the policy or role and when it was last accessed. This information provides insights into whether the policy or role is currently being used or not, and by whom. Refer to *figure 7.7* as follows:

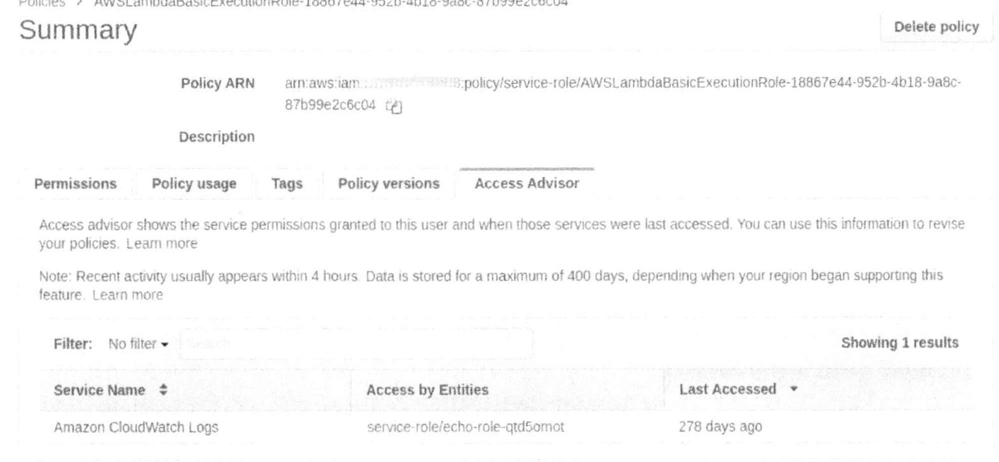

Figure 7.7: Access advisor

- **Access Analyzer:** The AWS IAM Access Analyzer can help us identify the resources in AWS Organization and the related accounts that are shared with the external parties or entities (another AWS account, an IAM user/role, federated user, an AWS service, etc.). The Access Analyzer generates a finding against each instance of a resource that is shared with an external entity (like cross-account roles, publicly accessible S3 buckets, etc.) and thus helps identify the unintended access to the AWS resources and data. The Access Analyzer is easily accessible from the IAM management console. Once enabled, the analyzer provides findings for the entire AWS Organization or account.

Using AWS managed and custom policies

Following the principle of least privilege is easier said than done. It requires detailed comprehension of the IAM policies, and more importantly, understanding of what the user or group needs to perform within the AWS account. Moreover, such policies need to be tested as well. However, to kick-start our IAM journey, AWS provides us with the AWS managed policies. These are the IAM policies curated, managed, and maintained by AWS and they work for most of the common use-cases. *Figure 7.8* shows the available AWS managed policies, when filtered by **S3**. We must note here that these AWS managed policies range from **FullAccess** to **ReadOnlyAccess**. The orange colored *'box'* icon alongside the policy name signifies that the policy is managed by AWS. Refer to *figure 7.8* as follows:

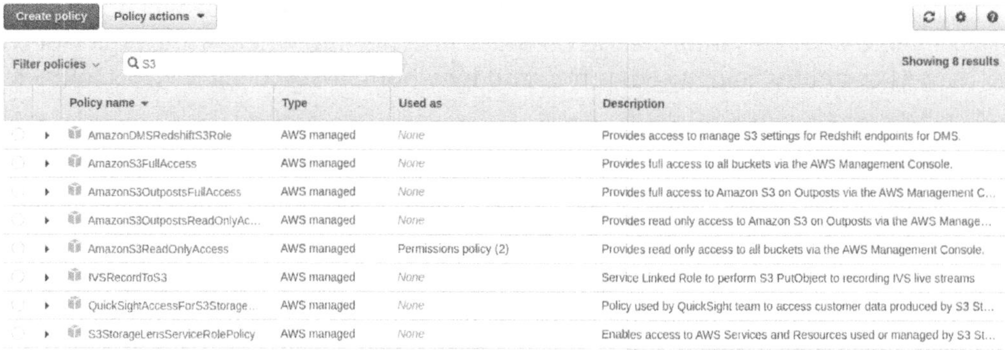

***Figure 7.8**: AWS managed policies*

When the AWS managed policies are not enough, we can also use the customer managed policies. These are custom policies that we can define and fine tune to suit our needs. An easy way to start with the creation of custom policies is to use the Visual Editor available during the **Create policy** operation from the IAM management console, as shown in *figure 7.9* as follows:

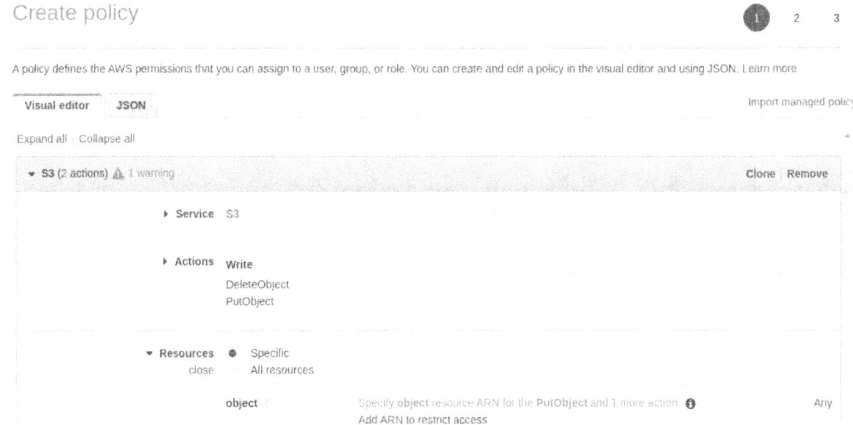

Figure 7.9: Visual policy editor

The custom policies are undoubtedly better than the inline policies associated with a single IAM identity (user, group, or role). The challenge with the inline policies is that they cannot be reused, and thus are difficult to maintain, and result in duplication.

Using temporary credentials

It's always better to use short-term or temporary credentials rather than the long-term credentials (like the IAM user password or programmatic access with the long-term access key ID and secret access key).

The IAM Roles are first class citizens of the AWS IAM world which use temporary credentials powered by AWS **Security Token Service (STS)** and are commonly used for the service-to-service integration. These temporary credentials are automatically rotated. The temporary credentials can prove beneficial in the following scenarios:

- **Access AWS Resources from EC2:** If an application hosted in the EC2 instance needs to access the AWS resources like Amazon S3 buckets, it's best to use the IAM roles with appropriate permissions along with EC2, instead of using the hard-coded long term access keys which is a security risk.
- **Cross Account Access:** The IAM roles enable us to share the access to the resources in one AWS account (trusting account) with the IAM users in another account (trusted account). The trusting account simply creates an IAM policy that grants the trusted account the access to specific resources. This policy is then associated with a cross account IAM role that defines the trust relation. The trusted account can then delegate this access to its own IAM users, who can in turn, assume the cross-account role to access specific resources allowed by the trusting account.
- **Identity Federation:** For the federated identities (identities defined outside AWS) who still need to access the AWS resources, the identity broker

authenticates and authorizes them against the identity provider. The identity broker has permissions to access AWS STS and requests for temporary credentials. The federated identities can then use these temporary credentials to log into the AWS account through a temporary sign-in URL.

Some more IAM best practices

The following are a few more points which can help boost the security of the IAM users and roles:

- **Delegation of Permission:** Instead of sharing the security credentials between multiple accounts, it's always a safer option to delegate the permissions using the cross-account roles. The IAM users in the other account can then assume the role to perform the actions.
- **Usage of External ID:** While defining the cross-account roles, the best practice is to specify `ExternalId` as a policy condition. This ensures that anyone who wants to assume the role should provide this external identifier, without which the access is not granted. `ExternalId` is used to address the *confused deputy problem* (introduced in *Chapter 2: Identity and Access Management*).
- **Rotation of Credentials:** The rotation of passwords and access keys can be a good option to limit the usage of compromised credentials. The custom password policies could be used to warrant the password rotation.
- **Removal of Unnecessary Credentials:** The passwords and access keys that have not been used recently are good candidates for deletion. Keeping the unused credentials is a security risk.
- **Break glass access:** As an extension of the principle of least privilege, companies often follow the "*Break Glass*" pattern. A break-glass account or emergency account is created to provide emergency access to the secure systems and/or sensitive operations. This is sufficed by a break glass role. This role not only protects the sensitive operations, but it also results in the notification being sent to the security teams whenever it gets used. The usage of this role is often restricted within a region for better safety. In times of emergency, the admins can assume this role temporarily to perform sensitive operations. In short, this process works like a break-glass fire alarm system.

Infrastructure security best practices

In this section, we will cover the security best practices pertaining to networking and working with the compute resources in AWS cloud, which are as follows:

- **Utilize VPC based network isolation:** AWS VPC allows us to create a chunk of private cloud within the AWS public cloud. AWS VPC can be assigned CIDR blocks from the RFC-1918 private address space. The idea is to limit the usage of the public IPs (Internet accessible), thereby reducing the surface area of any internet-based attacks. AWS VPC also supports site-to-site VPN connectivity with the IPSec-based tunneling. In fact, in scenarios where hybrid connectivity is required, AWS VPN could be leveraged to encrypt the traffic over the internet. This is true even when AWS Direct Connect is used to establish high bandwidth connectivity between AWS and the on-premise data center.

- **Use network segmentation:** Network segmentation and security zoning with similar security controls can help diminish the blast radius of an attack by isolating one network from another. We can leverage Amazon VPC, subnets, route tables, etc., to create such segmentation. Following the access control features can be used to create isolated network segments, like security groups, NACLs, host-based firewalls, threat protection layer, etc.
- **Bake security elements into IaC process:** It is a good practice to create custom AMIs and container images, harden the operating system, install the necessary security softwares/agents (like agent-based *Intrusion Prevention System* or *Intrusion Detection System*), and incorporate the necessary configurations. These golden AMIs or container images can then be used in the AWS account and referenced from the **Infrastructure as Code (IaC)** pipelines, thereby creating repeatable secure infrastructure. The use of untrusted AMIs, container images, and softwares are a strict no-no.
- **Patch VMs/instances regularly:** The AWS SSM Patch Manager can automate the patching process for the managed instances. The AWS SSM Patch Manager's Patch Baseline service could be helpful in creating the baselines for approved patches (including security patches) and can scan the managed instances for the missing patches.
- **Use SSM Session Manager for SSH access:** Unmanaged and/or misplaced SSH keys are a big security concern. To mitigate this risk, we can leverage the AWS SSM Session Manager to start a session on any managed EC2 instance that has the SSM agent installed and get the access to the instance from a browser-based shell. The commands executed by the user in the session could be streamed to the Amazon CloudWatch logs or stored in the Amazon S3 buckets for analysis purposes. The best part is that all this can be done without opening any inbound ports (like port **22**) on the managed instances. Moreover, there is no need to use VPN to connect to the instances that reside in the private subnets.
- **Plan to safeguard the resources from the DoS/DDoS attacks:** The Denial of Service (DoS) and **Distributed Denial of Service (DDoS)** attacks are quite common and such threats need to be taken very seriously. The AWS Shield can help safeguard our workloads from layer-3 and layer-4 DDoS attacks. The AWS Shield comes in two flavors – Standard (free of cost) and

Advanced (additional charges apply). The standard version can provide a basic protection against the most common network and transport layer DDoS attacks. The advanced version, being a paid service, opens a 24x7 access to AWS **DDoS Response Team** (**DRT**) and cost protection during an attack. The AWS WAF rules can help minimize the layer-7 DDoS attacks. In addition to using AWS Shield and AWS WAF, the following steps could be taken to mitigate such an attack:

  - Scale to absorb the attack that comes in the form of traffic surges (use AWS ELB, Auto-scaling, etc.).
  - Minimize the attack surface area (use private subnets, AWS ELBs, Route53, etc.).
  - Create the knowledge around normal traffic patterns.
  - And finally create a plan of attack to respond better during a DoS/DDoS onslaught.

- **Perform vulnerability scanning of networks and hosts:** Vulnerability scanning can provi de insights into the security loop holes in our networks and hosts. AWS Inspector is a security assessment tool, similar to a vulnerability scanner. AWS Inspector is agent based and can perform two types of assessments – host based and network based. It is a scheduled tool that can be triggered based on the Amazon CloudWatch events, or manually, on-demand. AWS Inspector has pre-defined templates like CIS benchmarks, which can go a long way to help us in hardening our EC2 instances.

- **Manage firewall rules centrally:** The firewall rules can easily get very complex and messy, thereby opening the chances of misconfiguration and associated security vulnerabilities. As the best practice, AWS Firewall Manager could be used to manage the firewall rules centrally across all the accounts in an AWS Organization to enforce the standard security rules. Additionally, AWS Firewall Manager can roll out the AWS WAF rules across the AWS ALB, AWS API Gateway, and Amazon CloudFront distributions.

Data security best practices

The security of data is very crucial for any enterprise. The following are some of the best practices that can help secure sensitive data on AWS cloud:

- **Encrypt always:** Encryption is fundamental to the security of the data. We have covered encryption in *Chapter 4: Data Security in AWS*. The data encrypted with strong cryptographic algorithms are more likely to be better protected. The AWS **Key Management Service** (**KMS**) is central to the AWS cloud's key management and encryption/decryption. The AWS KMS **Customer Master Key** (**CMK**) supports both the symmetric and the asymmetric encryption, and thus should be leveraged for encrypting or signing the messages and/or requests wherever required.

- **Use additional authenticated data: Additional Authenticated Data (AAD)** is a way to achieve authenticated encryption. Encryption context (explained in *Chapter 4: Data Security in AWS*) should be used while performing the KMS encryption/decryption actions.
- **Rotate keys regularly:** Regular rotation of the encryption keys helps maintain *perfect forward secrecy*. Both the manual and the automated rotation (for symmetric keys) is supported. It is best to refer to **Customer Master Keys (CMKs)** within the application code with the key aliases (instead of key IDs). This helps in easy key rotation as the alias can remain the same, even when the key material is rotated internally.
- **Classify data:** It is important to discover and classify the sensitive data. This helps us create adequate security controls around such data. Amazon Macie can help classify the data that is stored in Amazon S3.
- **Secure data at rest and in transit:** Data stored in Amazon S3, Amazon EBS, Amazon RDS, Amazon DynamoDB, etc., needs to be protected at rest. For this purpose, these services provide the various **Server-Side Encryption (SSE)** options which typically use the AWS managed CMKs or customer-managed CMKs. The best practice is to leverage the SSE options while storing the data. To secure the data in flight, all the AWS service APIs must be called over HTTPS, including the data retrieval ones.
- **Take regular data backups:** Backups and snapshots can save the day when there is some failure or disaster pertaining to any storage services (like Amazon EBS, Amazon RDS, etc.), or an AWS region, and the data needs to be restored quickly. Often, more elaborate disaster recovery strategies (like multi-site, warm-standby, etc.) are designed to protect the data as well as comply with the business continuity guidelines based on **Recovery Time Objective (RTO)** and **Recovery Point Objective (RPO)**. Thus, regular testing of the backup and disaster recovery processes is crucial.

Application security best practices

Application Security or AppSec involves various tools and processes to find, fix, and prevent the security vulnerabilities in the applications. The following are some best practices around application security:

- **Application AuthN and AuthZ:** Each application should have strong authentication and authorization schemes. Modern applications generally use federated identities. As such, the applications do not manage the identities on their own. They just establish a trust relationship with the web identity providers like Google, Facebook, etc., or the enterprise identity providers like Microsoft AD or LDAP servers. The federation can help in creating temporary credentials for all the application users. The Amazon Cognito identity pools can help federate the identities with the SAML or OpenID based identity providers. The AWS Directory Services could be leveraged for the managed Microsoft Active Directory services or Samba 4 based Simple AD service, or the AD Connector proxy service to integrate the cloud-based applications with the existing on-premise AD.

- **Store application secrets securely:** The application secrets (like database credentials, API keys, and the other application credentials) must not be a part of the code or configuration files. Ideally, these sensitive parameters should be stored either in AWS Secrets Manager or AWS SSM Parameter Store, and looked up and retrieved securely at runtime. There can be other scenarios where these secrets are pushed into the runtime environment during deployment using the CI/CD pipelines.
- **Leverage AWS Web Application Firewall (WAF):** Web Application Firewall or WAF is a layer-7 firewall that provides security to the HTTP based applications against the common application layer attacks like XSS, SQL injection, etc., and provides protection against the layer-7 DDoS attacks as well. While there are several WAF products from the third parties (like Barracuda, Cisco, etc.), AWS WAF seamlessly integrates with Amazon CloudFront, AWS Application Load Balancer, and AWS API Gateway.
- **Communicate over secure protocols:** The applications should communicate over secured protocols (like HTTPS, SFTP, etc.) only. There are situations where regulatory compliance dictates the end-to-end security where TLS/SSL traffic is terminated at the applications. On other occasions, TLS could be terminated at the AWS **Application Load Balancer** (**ALB**) layer. All AWS APIs are serviced over HTTPS and use the *AWS Signature Version 4* signing process.
- **Static and Dynamic Application Security Testing:** SAST (white-box security testing) and DAST (black-box security testing) are important and help find the security flaws before these get baked into the final application release. The AWS Marketplace has several SAST/DAST offerings by different vendors and AWS partners.
- **Penetration testing:** For applications that operate with sensitive data or have strict security requirements, it is often considered the best practice to perform penetration testing to unearth any application vulnerabilities that could be exploited. Xploits are run against the application to compromise. Presently, AWS allows penetration testing against its infrastructure without any prior approval for eight services, including Amazon EC2, AWS ELB, Amazon RDS, Amazon Aurora, Amazon CloudFront, and AWS API Gateway.

Logging and monitoring best practices

AWS provides the following best-in-class logging and monitoring services. The best practice would be to log and monitor everything. Some enterprises also deploy full-fledged **Security Information and Event Management** (**SIEM**) solutions on AWS that provide real-time analytics of the security events and help gather actionable security insights. Refer to the following best practices:

- **Tag AWS Resources:** Appropriate tagging strategy helps organize and logically group the AWS resources and monitor their usage and behavior.
- **Capture all Logs:** Logs can provide deep insights into the health and behavior of the networks, servers, applications, databases, etc. Logs are crucial in detecting failures, errors, and security events, and provide the basis for metrics and alerts.

  The following is a non-exhaustive list of logs that might have to be configured / captured in AWS – VPC flow logs, AWS CloudTrail logs, Amazon Route53 DNS query logs, OS logs, application logs, database logs, Amazon S3 access logs, AWS ALB access logs, etc.
- **Keep track of infrastructure changes:** Keeping track of the changes made to the infrastructure is vital for obvious reasons and AWS Config can help with that for all the supported AWS resources (like AWS CloudTrail, Amazon EC2, Amazon RDS, Amazon Redshift, Amazon S3, etc.). AWS Config can also help monitor the IAM resources and ensure they comply with the defined baselines. It is considered the best practice to use an AWS Config aggregator to aggregate the configuration and compliance data from multiple accounts and multiple regions or all accounts in an AWS Organization. The aggregator then presents the aggregated data in a single dashboard. The pre-defined config rules generally serve most of the everyday situations. However, if required, the custom rules could be written using AWS lambda.
- **Monitor usage of AWS KMS keys:** Monitoring the state and usage of CMKs is significant to understand if these are being used in some unintended ways. Ideally, we need to establish a baseline for the normal CMK usage for our environment over time. The *Data plane* operations (Encrypt, Decrypt, GenerateDataKey, etc.) and *control plane* operations (EnableKey, DisableKey, ScheduleKeyDeletion, etc.) need to be monitored for establishing standard patterns. AWS KMS is integrated with AWS CloudTrail that captures all the API calls to AWS KMS as events. The trails could be configured to send the events to the CloudWatch Logs for further analysis. Moreover, CMKs can be monitored using Amazon CloudWatch which collects and processes the raw AWS KMS data into near real-time, pre-defined metrics.
- **Leverage AWS Guard Duty:** AWS Guard Duty is a regional threat detection service. The service monitors the AWS CloudTrail events, AWS VPC Flow

Logs, and Amazon Route53 (DNS) logs for malicious activities and detects threats like trojans, SSH brute force, BitCoin mining, etc.

- **Leverage AWS Security Hub:** AWS Security Hub provides a comprehensive regional view of the high-priority security alerts and compliance status across multiple AWS accounts. AWS Security Hub can present aggregated findings from AWS GuardDuty, AWS Inspector, AWS Macie, and AWS Firewall Manager. AWS Security Hub can be integrated with multiple third-party security solution providers like Twistlock, AlertLogic, Symantec, Barracuda, etc.
- **Consolidate AWS CloudTrail logs for AWS Organization:** We can configure AWS CloudTrail to deliver the log files from multiple AWS accounts into a single Amazon S3 bucket (belonging to a separate, highly secured AWS account). If we operate as an AWS Organization, we can create an organization trail that will log all the events for all the accounts in that organization.
- **Create custom Amazon CloudWatch metrics and alarms:** Amazon CloudWatch provides a wide range of useful pre-defined metrics. For example, the pre-defined metrics for Amazon EC2 generally fall into the three basic types – CPU, Network, and Disk I/O. However, there are times when the pre-defined metrics are not enough, and we will need to create the custom metrics and alarms to serve our fine-grained purposes.

Conclusion

A chain is only as strong as its weakest link. Each layer and component in AWS must be independently secured. Weakness in one layer or one application can wreak havoc to the entire AWS account. AWS provides services and security controls for each such layer.

In this chapter, we traversed through all the major layers and discussed some of the best practices and the AWS services that could be leveraged to make security more effective. In the end, the enterprises should develop a security culture and drive it top-down. Every member in an organization should take responsibility for securing the assets and services of the organization and play their respective parts.

Index

J

K

L

U